essential**law**

MARINE INSURANCE LEGISLATION

Arbitration Act 1996
by Robert Merkin
(2000)

Marine Insurance Legislation
by Robert Merkin
(2000)

MARINE INSURANCE LEGISLATION

BY

ROBERT MERKIN, LLB, LLM

Lloyd's Law Reports
Professor of Commercial Law
Cardiff Law School

Consultant
DENTON WILDE SAPTE

Solicitors

LONDON   HONG KONG
2000

LLP Professional Publishing
(a trading division of Informa Publishing Group Ltd)
69–77 Paul Street
London EC2A 4LQ
Great Britain

EAST ASIA
LLP Asia
Sixth Floor, Hollywood Centre
233 Hollywood Road
Hong Kong

First published as *Annotated Marine Insurance Legislation* 1997
This edition 2000

British Library Cataloguing in Publication Data
A catalogue record
for this book is available
from the British Library

ISBN 1–85978–532–8

Typeset in 10/12 Plantin by
Interactive Sciences Ltd, Gloucester
Printed in Great Britain by
Headway Press,
Reading, Berkshire

Preface

This, second, edition of *Marine Insurance Legislation* takes account of the numerous legal and market developments which have taken place since the publication of the first edition. Of the many cases decided in the last three years which have been added to the annotations, the most important include: *Kusel* v. *Atkin*, "*The Catariba*" (measurement of loss and successive losses); *Chapman* v. *Kadirga* (premiums); *Wunsche* v. *Tai Ping* (duration of marine policy); *Arab Bank* v. *Zurich Insurance* (policy placed by broker); *Norwich Union* v. *Qureshi* (insurer's duty of disclosure); *FNCB* v. *Barnet Devanney* (composite policy); *Eide* v. *Lowndes Lambert*, "*The Sun Tender*" (broker's lien for premium); *Zeus Tradition* v. *Bell* (inspection condition); *Kirkaldy* v. *Walker* (inspection condition); *AIG* v. *Ethniki* (breach of warranty). As far as the market developments are concerned, the most recent versions of the Institute Clauses are included, as is the new policy form issued by the International Underwriting Association of London.

The annotations are based on materials available to the author as at the end of October 1999. Thanks are due to LLP for their assistance at every stage, and to my family for their tolerance of the usual problems raised by living with an author.

Sidmouth, November 1999   ROB MERKIN

Preface

Contents

Marine Insurance (Gambling Policies) Act 1909

Marine and Aviation Insurance (War Risks) Act 1952

PUBLIC ORDER ACT 1986

APPENDICES—INSTITUTE CLAUSES

CONTENTS

Table of Cases

Introduction

History of Marine Insurance Legislation

Marine insurance is probably as old as the activity of international trade, and in its origins appears to have taken a mutual form. Here, a group of shipowners would come together and pay sums into a fund, that fund being used to meet losses incurred by any one of them. The principle of mutuality remains important to this day in the marine insurance context, and is the primary form of insurance for maritime liabilities. There are reports of marine insurance cases coming before the English courts in the sixteenth and seventeenth centuries, and it is clear from the early cases that the courts were prepared to enforce marine policies according to their terms. The first statutory intervention in marine insurance law was the Marine Insurance Act 1745, which sought to put an end to the practice of wagering disguised by marine policies whereby persons without interest in a vessel or its cargo would insure using a marine policy form. The 1745 Act required those procuring marine policies to be interested in the subject matter. The 1745 Act similarly prohibited the practice of insuring on the basis of "policy proof of interest", which had become the standard method of gambling by means of insurance and which rendered enforceable insurances without interest at common law. The 1745 Act remained in force until its incorporation into the Marine Insurance Act 1906. Later legislation did little substantive. The Marine Insurance Act 1788 required the names of all parties interested in a marine policy to be inserted into the policy, thereby bringing marine insurance law into line with the position established for life insurance by the Life Assurance Act 1774. The Marine Insurance Act 1788 was largely ineffective, as its provisions were satisfied as long as the assured's agent was named in the policy, and it was repealed by the Marine Insurance Act 1906 in so far as it applied to marine insurance: it still operates as regards non-marine policies on goods. Finally, the Policies of Marine Insurance Act 1868 facilitated the assignment of marine policies in the face of the common law's refusal to accept the assignment of insurance contracts and other choses in action: that Act has been reproduced in ss 50–51 of the Marine Insurance Act 1906.

The Marine Insurance Act 1906

The early marine insurance legislation, in so far as it was concerned with substantive issues, affected only insurable interest, and it was left to the market and the courts to develop the principles of marine insurance law. Those principles were ultimately codified in the Marine Insurance Act 1906. This Act was drafted by Sir Mackenzie Chalmers, and was the last of his famous pieces of codifying legislation. The 1906 Act did not seek to change the law, but rather was a codification of some 200 years of judicial decisions. There was, and remains, no equivalent non-marine codification, although at various points the 1906 Act reflects both marine and non-marine law. The Act is still in force, but has to be viewed with some degree of caution, for three reasons.

First, much of the Act is concerned with laying down presumptions which operate only in the absence of any contrary agreement between the parties: in practice marine insurance contracts written in England are governed by the various sets of standard marine clauses published by the International Underwriting Association of London, and these frequently oust many of the Act's presumptions. Secondly, the 1906 Act must be viewed as a snapshot of the law relating to marine insurance practice as it existed in 1906. However, since that date there have been significant changes in practice, and certain of the Act's concepts relate to superseded forms of dealing. There are also a number of important post-Act decisions refining the meaning of the Act's wording. Thirdly, the Act is not fully exhaustive, although most of the important principles of marine insurance law have been enshrined in it.

The Marine Insurance Market Practice

The London market rapidly developed standard wordings, and in 1779 Lloyd's formally adopted its Ship and Goods (SG) Policy, which remained the governing contract for over a century and faint echoes of which still exist in modern day wording despite trenchant judicial criticism as to the complex nature of the wording dating back almost to its inception. The SG Policy is indeed included in the Schedule to the Marine Insurance Act 1906, and much of the codification contained in the Act concerns cases decided on its wording. However, by 1906 the SG Policy had commenced its decline. The Institute of London Underwriters, formed in 1884 and consisting of non-Lloyd's marine insurers, took on the responsibility of drafting clauses to deal with aspects of the SG Policy thought to be unsatisfactory, and these were appended to policies. During the twentieth century the Institute Clauses became more extensive, and ultimately standard form clauses for all aspects of marine insurance were adopted as annexes to the SG Policy. New clauses issued in 1982 and 1983 finally broke the link with the SG Policy: the old SG wording was scrapped and replaced with a simplified form of wording (one version for Lloyd's and another version for companies) to be used as a cover sheet for the relevant Institute Clauses. The Institute Clauses were revised in 1995, and it is those versions which are reproduced in this book. Policies issued in London by Lloyd's and corporate insurers are generally in Institute Clauses form, although frequently modified to meet the needs of particular assureds. The Institute of London Underwriters merged with the London Insurance and Reinsurance Market Association (LIRMA) in 1998, to form the International Underwriting Association of London (IUA). New policy forms and schedules were issued following the merger, but the marine insurance clauses were not affected. The clauses continue to be referred to as the "Institute Clauses" in this work.

It will be appreciated that a number of different forms of insurance will be required to provide full cover for a marine adventure and these are nearly all available under Institute Clause wording. There are three main heads of cover: cargo, hulls and freight. As far as cargo is concerned there are basic standard cargo wordings for marine risks (the Institute Cargo A clauses covering all risks while the B and C clauses cover specified risks) and for cargo in containers. In addition, there are different standard wordings for particular types of cargo, including seeds and fats, commodities, oil, coal, rubber, timber, jute and frozen food and frozen meat. Hull and machinery insurance, primarily for trading vessels but also for fishing vessels, speedboats and yachts, is available on a time or voyage basis, either on a full risks or restricted risks basis, in respect of all losses or total loss only and including port risks if so required. Disbursements are separately insurable. Hull building risks insurance is also obtainable under standard wordings. Freight is insurable on a time or voyage basis, generally on more or less the same terms as hull insurance. These three categories of marine insurance exclude war and strikes risks, although such risks are separately insurable under wordings which are identical to marine cover but which exclude marine risks and replace them with war and strikes risks.

Other forms of cover are also available, eg, mortgagees' interest insurance and liability insurance, although collision liability is included in standard hulls wording and other forms of liability insurance have traditionally been obtained on a mutual basis through P & I Clubs. The Institute Clauses also provide standard form extensions for matters such as malicious damage, increased value, and additional marine perils. The most important provisions of the Institute Clauses are noted at relevant points in the annotations to the legislation. There is reference only to the general Institute Cargo Clauses, as the cargo clauses relating to specific forms of cargo follow their pattern and vary only as regards the nature of the risk insured. A complete set of Institute Clauses is reproduced at the end of this work.

In the case of a large risk, insurance may be arranged on a co-insurance basis (a number of insurers accept a proportion of the risk—this is the method of doing business at Lloyd's) or in layers, with successive insurers providing excess of loss cover (as to which, see *Hong Kong Borneo Services Ltd* v. *Pilcher* [1992] 2 Lloyd's Rep 593—obligation of excess of loss insurers to follow settlements of first layer insurer).

Marine Insurance Act 1906

(6 Edw 7 c 41)

GENERAL NOTES

The Marine Insurance Act 1906 was drafted by Sir Mackenzie Chalmers, and was the last of his famous pieces of codifying legislation. The Act does not seek to change the law, but rather is a codification of some 200 years of judicial decisions. There is no equivalent non-marine codification, although at various points the 1906 Act reflects both marine and non-marine law. The Act has to be viewed with some degree of caution, for three reasons. First, much of the Act is concerned with laying down presumptions which operate only in the absence of any contrary agreement between the parties: in practice marine insurance contracts written in England are governed by the various sets of standard marine clauses published by the Institute of London Underwriters, and these frequently oust many of the Act's presumptions. There are separate clauses for, *inter alia*, cargo policies (marine risks—the A clauses are all risks, whereas the B and C clauses cover specified risks), cargo policies (war risks and strike risks), hulls time policies, hulls voyage policies, freight time policies, freight voyage policies, and war and strikes clauses for each type of hull and freight time and voyage policy. The most important provisions of the cargo and hulls clauses are noted in the relevant places in the following annotations (the freight clauses are not noted separately, and for the most part follow the hulls clauses). Secondly, the 1906 Act must be viewed as a snapshot of the law relating to marine insurance practice as it existed in 1906, but there have been significant changes in practice since that date and certain of the Act's concepts relate to superseded forms of dealing. There are also a number of important post-Act decisions refining the meaning of the Act's wording. Thirdly, the Act is not exhaustive, although most of the important principles of marine insurance law have been enshrined in it.

A number of different forms of insurance may be required to provide full cover for a marine adventure. These may include:

(a) a standard marine policy on hulls and machinery;

(b) cargo insurance;

(c) insurance of the freight to be earned by the carrier;

(d) increased value insurance, to deal with the possibility of the subject-matter's increase in value during the currency of the policy;

(e) mortgagee's interest insurance, covering the mortgagee of the vessel in the event that the insurer under the marine policy does not accept liability for a loss;

(f) strikes and war risks insurance;

(g) liability insurance, for collisions (covered by the hull and machinery policy) and for other forms of liability (generally insured on a mutual basis by P & I clubs).

In the case of a large risk, insurance may be arranged on a co-insurance basis (a number of insurers accept a proportion of the risk—this is the method of doing business at Lloyd's) or in layers, with successive insurers providing excess of loss cover (as to which, see *Hong Kong*

Borneo Services Ltd v. *Pilcher* [1992] 2 Lloyd's Rep 593—obligation of excess of loss insurers to follow settlements of first layer insurer).

The annotations cite many of the early cases upon which the 1906 Act was based, and should be regarded as illustrations of the operation of the Act.

Marine Insurance

Marine insurance defined

1. A contract of marine insurance is a contract whereby the insurer undertakes to indemnify the assured, in manner and to the extent thereby agreed, against marine losses, that is to say, the losses incident to marine adventure.

NOTES

The distinction between marine and non-marine insurance is significant for two general reasons:

    (a) separate authorisation is required under the Insurance Companies Act 1982;

    (b) there are a number of distinctions between marine and non-marine insurance law.

The following is a non-exhaustive list:

    (1) in determining the assured's loss, marine policies value the assured's interest at the date of the policy rather than at the date of the loss (s 16);

    (2) a marine contract is enforceable only if embodied in a policy (s 22);

    (3) marine warranties may be express or implied by operation of law (ss 36–41) whereas non-marine warranties must be expressly created;

    (4) marine voyage policies terminate automatically where the voyage is changed or there is deviation from the accepted route (ss 42–49), whereas an increase of risk does not affect a non-marine policy unless the policy otherwise provides;

    (5) marine policies, unlike non-marine policies, are freely assignable (ss 50–51);

    (6) under a marine policy the broker is responsible to the insurer for the premium (s 53);

    (7) non-marine law recognises only total and partial losses, whereas marine insurance recognises an intermediate form of loss, constructive total loss (s 60);

    (8) it is the obligation of the assured under a marine policy to take steps to avoid or mitigate the loss, and the insurer has the concurrent duty to indemnify the assured for the costs of "suing and labouring" of this type (s 78);

    (9) marine insurance law permits return of premium to the assured in a greater number of situations than exist in non-marine law (s 84).

A policy in marine form is not necessarily a marine policy, as the substance has to be maritime in nature (*Re London County Commercial Reinsurance Office Ltd* [1922] 2 Ch 67 (peace policy); *Re Argonaut Marine Insurance Co Ltd* [1932] 2 Ch 34 (fire policy).

Mixed sea and land risks

2.—(1) A contract of marine insurance may, by its express terms, or by usage of trade, be extended so as to protect the assured against losses on inland waters or on any land risk which may be incidental to any sea voyage.

(2) Where a ship in course of building, or the launch of a ship, or any adventure analogous to a marine adventure, is covered by a policy in the form of a marine

policy, the provisions of this Act, in so far as applicable, shall apply thereto; but, except as by this section provided, nothing in this Act shall alter or affect any rule of law applicable to any contract of insurance other than a contract of marine insurance as by this Act defined.

NOTES

Subs (1) It has long been the practice for policies on cargo to cover risks other than pure maritime risks, and the standard cargo cover written in the London market—the Institute Cargo Clauses, cl 8—is on a "warehouse to warehouse" basis. This replaces earlier policy terms, which previously covered cargo until "safely landed" (as to which see the Marine Insurance Act 1906, Sched, r 5, page 97), "safely delivered" (*Deutsch-Australische Dampfschiffsgesellschaft* v. *Sturge* (1913) 109 LT 905) or "discharged" (*G H Renton & Co Ltd* v. *Black Sea and Baltic General Insurance Co Ltd* [1941] 1 KB 206). Wider forms of cover, stated to be from specified origin to specified destination, are also marine policies as long as the marine voyage constitutes the most significant part of the cover. Of the many illustrations of the point, see: *Rodocanachi* v. *Elliott* (1874) LR 9 CP 518; *Ide and Christie* v. *Chalmers and White* (1900) 5 Com Cas 212; *Allagar Rubber Estates Ltd* v. *National Benefit Assurance Co* (1922) 10 Ll LR 564; *Leon* v. *Casey* [1932] 2 KB 576; *Cousins & Co* v. *D & C Carriers Ltd* [1971] 2 QB 230; *Fuerst Day Lawson Ltd* v. *Orion Insurance Co Ltd* [1980] 1 Lloyd's Rep 656; *Simon, Israel & Co* v. *Sedgwick* [1893] 1 QB 303; *Wunsche International* v. *Tai Ping Insurance Co* [1998] 2 Lloyd's Rep 8; *Hibernia Foods plc* v. *McAuslin, The Joint Frost* [1998] 1 Lloyd's Rep 310. A non-marine policy may itself cover marine risks which are incidental to the main cover (*Moore* v. *Evans* [1918] AC 185).

Equally, the fact that the policy covers "all risks", including some risks which may occur only on land, does not mean that it ceases to be a marine policy (*Hyderabad (Deccan) Co* v. *Willoughby* [1899] 2 QB 530; *Schloss Brothers* v. *Stevens* [1906] 2 KB 665; *British and Foreign Marine Insurance Co* v. *Gaunt* [1921] 2 AC 41).

Subs (2) There are many illustrations in the case of marine policies on building risks, eg: *Jackson* v. *Mumford* (1904) 9 Com Cas 114; *Youell* v. *Bland Welch (No 1)* [1992] Lloyd's Rep 127; *National Oilwell (UK) Ltd* v. *Davy Offshore Ltd* [1993] 2 Lloyd's Rep 582.

Marine adventure and maritime perils defined

3.—(1) Subject to the provisions of this Act, every lawful marine adventure may be the subject of a contract of marine insurance.

(2) In particular there is a marine adventure where—

(a) Any ship goods or other moveables are exposed to maritime perils. Such property is in this Act referred to as "insurable property";

(b) The earning or acquisition of any freight, passage money, commission, profit, or other pecuniary benefit, or the security for any advances, loan, or disbursements, is endangered by the exposure of insurable property to maritime perils;

(c) Any liability to a third party may be incurred by the owner of, or other person interested in or responsible for, insurable property, by reason of maritime perils.

"Maritime perils" means the perils consequent on, or incidental to, the navigation of the sea, that is to say, perils of the seas, fire, war perils, pirates, rovers, thieves, captures, seisures, restraints, and detainments of princes and peoples, jettisons, barratry, and any other perils, either of the like kind or which may be designated by the policy.

3

NOTES

Subs (1) A marine policy is stated to insure a marine "adventure". This concept has no modern significance, and modern policies insure particular risks forming part of the overall adventure. There is an inclusive definition of "marine adventure" in subs (2).

The adventure must be lawful, eg not prohibited by statute or contrary to the public interest, for the policy to be valid. If the voyage is not lawful from the outset, the assured is in breach of the warranty of legality under s 41 of the 1906 Act, and the risk will not attach (see page 40). If the adventure is lawful at its inception, s 3(1) is satisfied, although the assured may be in breach of the continuing warranty in s 41 in so far as any unlawful conduct taking place during the currency of the adventure is within his control.

Subs (2) This subsection lists the most important forms of cover available under a marine policy: property damage in respect of the vessel and its cargo, loss of freight, and liability incurred to third parties. Cargo policies are commonly written on an "all risks" basis (Institute Cargo Clauses A). The B and C clauses are against specific risks, including fire, explosion, stranding and jettison.

As to *fire*, see: *Gordon* v. *Rimmington* (1807) 1 Camp 123 (fire to prevent vessel falling into enemy hands covered by policy); *Busk* v. *Royal Exchange* (1818) 2 B & Ald 73 (fire caused by negligence covered by policy); *Symington & Co* v. *Union Insurance Society of Canton* (1928) 31 Ll LR 179 (water damage as consequence of fire proximately caused by fire, and cf *The Knight of St Michael* [1898] P 30); *Watson & Son Ltd* v. *Firemen's Fund Insurance Co of San Francisco* [1922] 2 KB 355 (steam damage not covered, and cf *Thames and Mersey Marine Insurance Co Ltd* v. *Hamilton Fraser & Co* (1887) 12 App Cas 484). The older forms of policy excluded partial loss unless the vessel was "burnt", as to which see *The Glenlivet* [1894] P 48.

As to stranding, see the note to the Marine Insurance Act 1906, Sched, r 14.

As to explosion, see *Commonwealth Smelting Ltd* v. *Guardian Royal Exchange Assurance Ltd* [1984] 2 Lloyd's Rep 608 (physical or chemical reaction required, and not merely equipment failure resulting in outward pressure and propulsion).

As to jettison, there is some ambiguity, for jettison of cargo is frequently encountered in the context of an attempt to preserve a vessel in distress or the remaining cargo, in which case jettison constitutes a general average sacrifice and attracts general average contributions from its beneficiaries (see s 66 and the note thereto, page 70). Some cases treat the act of throwing cargo overboard as jettison in its own right despite the fact that some other peril was the cause of the jettison (*Butler* v. *Wildman* (1820) 3 B & Ald 398; *Symington & Co* v. *Union Insurance Society of Canton Ltd* (1928) 34 Com Cas 23) whereas others have held that it is not possible to convert an uninsured peril into an insured peril by jettison (*Taylor* v. *Dunbar* (1869) LR 4 CP 206).

Under an all risks policy the insurer is liable for all risks, including accidental damage (*Jacob* v. *Gaviller* (1902) 7 Com Cas 116; *Schloss Brothers* v. *Stevens* [1906] 2 KB 665) other than excepted risks (as to which, see the Institute Cargo Clauses, cl 4), and also that the assured' burden of proof in the event of a loss is satisfied if he proves that the loss has occurred—the burden of proof then shifts to the insurer to show that the loss was proximately caused by an excluded peril, although the assured may be required to rebut any evidence of the operation of an excluded peril brought forward by the insurer (*Re National Benefit Assurance Co Ltd* (1933) 45 Ll LR 147; *Theodorou* v. *Chester* [1951] 1 Lloyd's Rep 204; *British and Foreign Marine Insurance Co* v. *Gaunt* [1921] 2 AC 41; *Fuerst Day Lawson Ltd* v. *Orion Insurance Co Ltd* [1980] 1 Lloyd's Rep 656). For the scope of hulls cover, see Institute Time Clauses Hulls, cll 6–7, and Institute Voyage Clauses Hulls, cll 4–5 (sea perils including fire and explosion, mechanical breakdown, and pollution hazards).

Subs (2)(a) The Term "movables" is defined in s 90 (see page 93), the term "ship" is defined in the Schedule, r 15 (see page 103) and the term "goods" is defined in the Schedule, r 17 (see page 103). Policies on ships and goods do not cover consequential losses, including loss of profits, unless specifically covered (*Lucena* v. *Craufurd* (1806) 2 Bos & PNR 269; *Royal Exchange Assurance* v. *M'Swiney* (1850) 14 QB 646; *Halhead* v. *Young* (1856) 6 E & B 312; *Mackenzie* v. *Whitworth* (1875) 1 Ex D 36; *Anderson* v. *Morice* (1875) LR 10 CP 609; *Inglis* v. *Stock* (1885) 10 App Cas 263; *Yangtse Insurance Association* v. *Lukmanjee* [1918] AC 585). Thus if the assured has no insurable interest in the subject-matter, he cannot make any claim at all under a policy which does not cover loss of profits (see *Stockdale* v. *Dunlop* (1840) 6 M & W 224 and the note to s 6, page 8). It is a matter of construction whether a policy is on goods or against loss of profits, with the presumption being in favour of the former (*Agra Trading Ltd* v. *McAuslin, The Frio Chile* [1995] 1 Lloyd's Rep 182, distinguished in *Hibernia Foods plc* v. *McAuslin, The Joint Frost* [1998] 1 Lloyd's Rep 310 in which both cargo and profits were insured under the same clause).

Subs (2)(b) the term "freight" is defined in s 90 (see page 93). The other terms used here are not defined by the 1906 Act. For insurance against loss of profits see: *Barclay* v. *Cousins* (1802) 2 East 544; *Wilson* v. *Jones* (1867) LR 2 Exch 139, *Asfar* v. *Blundell* [1896] 1 QB 123; for insurance on disbursements see *Buchanan & Co* v. *Faber* (1899) 4 Com Cas 223, *Lawther* v. *Black* (1901) 6 Com Cas 196; *New Zealand Shipping Co Ltd* v. *Duke* [1914] 2 KB 682; and for insurance against loss of commission on freight see *Ward & Co* v. *Weir & Co* (1899) 4 Com Cas 216. The Hulls clauses (Institute Time Clauses Hulls, cl 22; Institute Voyage Clauses Hulls, cl 20) contain a disbursements warranty, introduced following the decision in *Thames and Mersey Marine Insurance Co* v. *Gunford Ship Co, "The Gunford"* [1911] AC 529. It was there held that a disbursement policy simply duplicated the cover conferred by a freight policy, and constituted double insurance. The disbursements warranty permits additional insurance for freight, return of premium, etc, only to the extent of 25% of the stated value and requires the assured to warrant that there is no insurance in excess of that amount.

Subs (2)(c) See the Institute Time Clauses Hulls, cl 8, and the Institute Voyage Clauses Hulls, cl 6, for collision liability. The collision clause covers the assured in respect of three-fourths of damages payable for loss or damage caused to any other vessel or property on any other vessel by reason of collision. As to another "vessel", see: *M'Cowan* v. *Baine & Johnson, "The Niobe"* [1891] AC 401; *Re Margetts & Ocean Accident & Guarantee Corporation* [1901] 2 KB 792 (tug is vessel); *Bennet SS Co* v. *Hull Mutual SS Protecting Society* [1914] 3 KB 57 (fishing nets not vessel); *Merchants' Marine Insurance Co Ltd* v. *North of England Protecting and Indemnity Association* (1926) 26 Ll LR 201 (crane not a vessel); *Polpen Shipping Co Ltd* v. *Commercial Union Assurance Co Ltd* [1943] KB 161 (flying boat not a vessel). Where a submerged vessel is involved, there is a collision only where the owner of the submerged vessel has a reasonable hope of successfully continuing salvage operations (*Pelton SS Co Ltd* v. *North of England Protecting and Indemnity Association, The Zelo* (1925) 22 Ll LR 510, disapproving the navigability test laid down in *Chandler* v. *Blogg* [1898] 1 QB 32). It is possible to extend the definition to encompass fixed objects such as piers. (*Union Marine Insurance Co* v. *Borwick* [1895] 2 QB 279). Liability for a collision between the insured vessel and vessel A, which causes vessel A to collide with vessel B, is within the collision clause (*France, Fenwick & Co Ltd* v. *Merchants' Marine Insurance Co Ltd* [1915] 3 KB 290).

If both vessels are to blame, the indemnity is determined by means of cross-liabilities. At common law the principle of single liability was recognised (*Stoomvaart Maatschappij Nederland* v. *P & O Steam Navigation Co* (1882) 7 App Cas 795; *London Steamship Owners Insurance Co* v. *Grampian Steamship Co* (1890) 2 QB 663). Under the single liability basis of calculation, the liability of each vessel is determined and a set off of the liabilities is applied, so that the vessel which is liable for the greater sum simply pays the balance to the other. That principle is ousted by the Institute Time Clauses Hulls, cl 8, and the Institute Voyage Clauses Hulls, cl 6 in favour of cross-liabilities. Under the cross-liabilities approach, the respective liability of each vessel to the other is assessed and 3/4ths of the liability of one vessel to the other is paid by the underwriters, with the other 1/4 being borne by the assured. The collision clause appears to apply only to tort liabilities, and not to those which arise in contract (*Furness Withy & Co Ltd* v. *Duder* [1936] 2 KB 461) or under statute (*Hall Brothers SS Co Ltd* v. *Young, "The Trident"* [1939] 1 KB 748). The collision clause does not extend to liability for personal injury or for consequential losses (*Taylor* v. *Dewar* (1864) 5 B & S 58; *Xenos* v. *Fox* (1869) LR 4 CP 665) or the removal of obstructions (*"The North Britain"* [1894] P 77; *Tatham, Bromage & Co* v. *Burr, "The Engineer"* [1898] AC 382).

There is a distinction between insuring property against liability, in which case the measure of the assured's interest is potential liability, and insuring property on a first party basis, in which case the measure of the assured's interest is the value of the property (*Hill* v. *Scott* [1895] 2 QB 713). For the property insurable interest of a person in possession of goods, see s 5, page 7.

"Maritime perils": Various of the terms used in this provision are partly defined in the Schedule to the Marine Insurance Act 1906: perils of the sea (Sched, r 7); pirates (Sched, r 8); thieves (Sched, r 9); arrests, etc (Sched, r 10); barratry (Sched, r 11). The definition of "maritime perils" is not exhaustive (as evidenced by the words "that is to say"), and may include ancillary forms of loss, such as mortgagee's interest insurance or mechanical failure (*Continental Illinois National Bank & Trust Co of Chicago* v. *Bathurst, "The Captain Panagos"* [1985] 1 Lloyd's Rep 625). It is not possible, despite the concluding words of the definition, to convert a non-marine risk into a marine risk merely by designation (*"The Captain Panagos"* [1985] 1 Lloyd's Rep 625).

Insurable Interest

Avoidance of wagering or gaming contracts

4.—(1) Every contract of marine insurance by way of gaming or wagering is void.

(2) A contract of marine insurance is deemed to be a gaming or wagering contract—

    (a) Where the assured has not an insurable interest as defined by this Act, and the contract is entered into with no expectation of acquiring such an interest; or

    (b) Where the policy is made "interest or no interest," or "without further proof of interest than the policy itself," or "without benefit of salvage to the insurer," or subject to any other like term:

Provided that, where there is no possibility of salvage, a policy may be effected without benefit of salvage to the insurer.

NOTES

Wagers were lawful contracts at common law but a wager on a marine risk ran the risk of being rendered unenforceable where the court construed the contract as one requiring proof of loss by the assured (*Whittingham* v. *Thornburgh* (1690) 2 Vern 206; *Martin* v. *Sitwell* (1691) 1 Show 156; *Goddard* v. *Garrett* (1692) 2 Vern 269; *Le Pypre* v. *Farr* (1716) 2 Vern 516; *Fitzgerald* v. *Pole* (1754) 4 Bro Parl Cas 439). For this reason, the practice developed of specifically stating in the policy that no proof of interest was required: such policies became known as "ppi" (policy proof of interest) contracts, although the term "ppi" encompasses other forms of wording to the same effect. Wagering policies and ppi policies were outlawed by the Marine Insurance Act 1745, and wagers in general were rendered void by s 18 of the Gaming Act 1845. Section 4 of the 1906 Act replicates the effect of these two earlier provisions.

Assuming that the assured possesses an insurable interest, the nature of that interest is not a material fact for the purposes of disclosure under s 18 of the 1906 Act (*Carruthers* v. *Sheddon* (1815) 6 Taunt 14; *Irving* v. *Richardson* (1831) 2 B & Ad 193; *Crowley* v. *Cohen* (1832) 3 B & Ad 478; *Mackenzie* v. *Whitworth* (1875) LR 1 Ex D 36).

Subs (1) For a contract to contravene this provision, there must be some intention on the part of the assured to wager rather than to insure a possible future interest (*Kent* v. *Bird* (1777) 2 Cowp 583; *Gedge* v. *Royal Exchange Assurance Corporation* [1900] 2 QB 214; *Coker* v. *Bolton* [1912] 3 KB 315, and cf *Newbury International Ltd* v. *Reliance National Insurance Co (UK) Ltd* [1994] 1 Lloyd's Rep 83). Subs (2) sets out two specific situations in which a policy is deemed to be by way of gaming or wagering, but it would seem that subs (1) is not confined to these situations.

Subs (2) The two limbs of subs (2) are alternative grounds on which a contract may fall within s 4.

Subs (2) (a) The contract is valid if the assured either possesses an insurable interest at the outset, or has an expectation of acquiring an interest during the currency of the policy. The test for expectation is both subjective and objective, in that the assured must believe that an interest will be acquired and there must be a reasonable basis for this belief (*Hodgson* v. *Glover* (1805) 6 East 316; *Knox* v. *Wood* (1808) 1 Camp 543; *Eyre* v. *Glover* (1812) 16 East 218; *Anderson* v. *Morice* (1876) 1 App Cas 713; *Buchanan & Co* v. *Faber* (1899) 4 Com Cas 223; *Moran, Galloway & Co* v. *Uzielli* [1905] 2 KB 555). Where the assured possesses some insurable interest, overinsurance is not wagering within s 4(2)(a) (*Glafki Shipping Co SA* v. *Pinios Shipping Co, "The Maria"* [1984] 1 Lloyd's Rep 660), although the assured may be required to disclose substantial overinsurance under s 18, page 16.

Subs (2) (b) Where a policy is made in this or equivalent form, the policy is void even though it is made on good interest (*Cheshire & Co* v. *Vaughan Bros & Co* [1920] 3 KB 240; *Edwards & Co* v. *Motor Union Insurance Co* [1922] 2 KB 249; *Re Overseas Marine Insurance Co Ltd* (1930) 36 Ll LR 183), although the premium may be recoverable in such a case (*Re London County Commercial Reinsurance Office Ltd* [1922] 2 Ch 67, putting a gloss on s 84(3)(c) of the Marine Insurance Act 1906, page 88). It is immaterial that the ppi clause is detachable (*Re London County Commercial Reinsurance Office Ltd* [1922] 2 Ch 67).

Insurable interest defined

5.—(1) Subject to the provisions of this Act, every person has an insurable interest who is interested in a marine adventure.

(2) In particular a person is interested in a marine adventure where he stands in any legal or equitable relation to the adventure or to any insurable property at risk therein, in consequence of which he may benefit by the safety or due arrival of insurable property, or may be prejudiced by its loss, or damage thereto, or by the detention thereof, or may incur liability in respect thereof.

NOTES

Subs (1) For the definition of "marine adventure", see s 3(2), page 3.

Subs (2) The definition of insurable interest is derived from the judgment of Lawrence J in *Lucena* v. *Craufurd* (1806) 2 Bos & PNR 269. The definition is not exhaustive, and was extended by Colman J in *National Oilwell (UK) Ltd* v. *Davy Offshore Ltd* [1993] 2 Lloyd's Rep 582 to cover cases in which the assured is not the owner or possessor of property but his relation to it is such that he may incur liability in respect of it should it be damaged. See also

State of Netherlands v. *Youell* [1997] 2 Lloyd's Rep 440, confirming the concept of the "pervasive insurable interest", and *Deepak Fertilisers & Petrochemical Corporation* v. *Davy McKee* [1999] 1 Lloyd's Rep 387 in which the Court of Appeal held that a sub-contractor may have an insurable interest in the entirety of the insured subject-matter on the basis that its loss or destruction will deprive the sub-contractor of the opportunity to carry out its contract (the insurable interest by definition coming to an end when the sub-contractor's tasks have been performed in full).

There are specific illustrations of insurable interest given in ss 7 to 14, but there are also many decided cases dealing with other forms of interest. What follows is a list of authorities on the insurable interest required to obtain a valid policy.

Insurance on ship or cargo: A person may insure a ship or its cargo:

    (a) which he owns (*Herbert* v. *Carter* (1787) 1 TR 745), even if it is mortgaged (insurance being possible under s 14(1) of the Marine Insurance Act 1906, page 12 up to the full value of the property) or chartered (*Hobbs* v. *Hannam* (1811) 3 Camp 93).

    (b) which is in his custody, in which case he may insure for the full insurable value and not merely in respect of his own liability (*North British Insurance Co* v. *Moffatt* (1871) LR 7 CP 25, and see the note to s 14(2), page 12);

    (c) which he has agreed to buy (whether or not property has passed to him) or which is at his risk (*Stephens* v. *Australasian Insurance Co* (1872) LR 8 CP 18; *Allison* v. *Bristol Marine Insurance Co* (1876) 1 App Cas 209; *Wunsche International* v. *Tai Ping Insurance Co* [1998] 2 Lloyd's Rep 8);

    (d) which he has agreed to sell (*Re National Benefit Assurance Co Ltd* (1933) 45 Ll LR 147); or

    (e) over which he has a security (*Wolff* v. *Horncastle* (1798) 1 Bos & P 316—right to lien; *Briggs* v. *Merchant Traders Association* (1849) 13 QB 167—lien; *Sutherland* v. *Pratt* (1843) 11 M & W 296—pledge). For mortgages, see s 14, page 12.

A shareholder or other unsecured creditor of a company cannot insure its assets (*Manfield* v. *Maitland* (1821) 4 B & A 582; *Moran, Galloway & Co* v. *Uzielli* [1905] 2 KB 555; *Sharp* v. *Sphere Drake Insurance Co, "The Moonacre"* [1992] 2 Lloyd's Rep 501, but see *Wilson* v. *Jones* (1867) LR 2 Exch 139—shareholder has right to insure adventure undertaken by company), and a person in possession of property but without any right to use or enjoy it has no insurable interest in it (*Sharp* v. *Sphere Drake Insurance Co Ltd, "The Moonacre"* [1992] 2 Lloyd's Rep 501). A person who stands to benefit from the arrival of a vessel or cargo has no right to insure it, as his interest is a mere expectation not recognised by the law (*Price* v. *Maritime Insurance Co* [1901] 2 KB 412, and see, on expectations: *Devaux* v. *Steele* (1840) 6 Bing NC 358; *Buchanan & Co* v. *Faber* (1899) 4 Com Cas 223).

Freight: Freight may be insured when it is at the assured's risk: in the usual case in which the carrier of goods earns freight only when the goods arrive safely he has insurable interest from the commencement of the voyage (*Miller* v. *Warre* (1824) 1 C & P 237; *Flint* v. *Flemyng* (1830) 1 B & Ad 45; *Dakin* v. *Oxley* (1864) 15 CBNS 646; *Barber* v. *Fleming* (1869) LR 5 QB 59). For advance freight, see s 12, page 11.

Liability: A person may insure his potential liability, whether contractual or tortious, to third parties.

When interest must attach

    6.—(1) The assured must be interested in the subject-matter insured at the time of the loss though he need not be interested when the insurance is effected:

Provided that where the subject-matter is insured "lost or not lost," the assured may recover although he may not have acquired his interest until after the loss, unless at the time of effecting the contract of insurance the assured was aware of the loss, and the insurer was not.

(2) Where the assured has no interest at the time of the loss, he cannot acquire interest by any act or election after he is aware of the loss.

NOTES

Subs (1) This subsection reflects s 4(2)(a), requiring actual or potential interest at the date of the policy. Its effect is reproduced in cl 11.1 of the Institute Cargo Clauses. If the assured fails to acquire an insurable interest, or loses that interest, during the currency of the policy, the principle of indemnity—embodied in s 6(1)—prevents recovery by him. In the case of the sale of a vessel or cargo, it will be important to know whether the assured has either the property or risk in the subject-matter at the date of the loss, as either will support an insurable interest (*Powles* v. *Innes* (1843) 11 M & W 10, *Joyce* v. *Swann* (1864) 13 CBNS 84; *Seagrave* v. *Union Marine Insurance Co* (1866) LR 1 CP 305; *North of England Oil Cake Co* v. *Archangel Insurance Co* (1875) LR 10 QB 249; *Anderson* v. *Morice* (1876) 1 App Cas 713; *Colonial Insurance Co of New Zealand* v. *Adelaide Marine Insurance Co* (1886) 12 App Cas 128; *Piper* v. *Royal Exchange Assurance* (1932) 44 Ll LR 103; *Re National Benefit Assurance Co Ltd* (1933) 45 Ll LR 147).

In the case of insurance against loss of earnings in respect of a vessel, there is insurable interest only when the vessel is not off-hire, so that the question of insurable interest must be looked at on a day-to-day basis: *Cepheus Shipping Corporation* v. *Guardian Royal Exchange Assurance plc* [1995] 1 Lloyd's Rep 622.

An agent of the assured has no insurable interest in the insured subject-matter, and cannot recover in the event of its loss (*Wolff* v. *Horncastle* (1798) 1 Bos & P 316; *Seagrave* v. *Union Marine Insurance Co* (1866) LR 1 CP 305), although by way of exception the assured's broker is permitted to sue on the policy (*Provincial Insurance Co of Canada* v. *Leduc* (1874) LR 6 PC 224; *Transcontinental Underwriting Agency* v. *Grand Union Insurance Co Ltd* [1987] 2 Lloyd's Rep 409; *Pan Atlantic Insurance Co Ltd* v. *Pine Top Insurance Co Ltd* [1994] 3 All ER 581).

If the assured has a mere expectation of obtaining an insurable interest, he has no actual insurable interest in the subject-matter which can support a claim, and his only loss will be of profit which is not covered unless the policy expressly so provides (*Stockdale* v. *Dunlop* (1840) 6 M & W 224; *Halhead* v. *Young* (1856) 6 E & B 312, and see the authorities cited in the note to s 3(2)(a), page 5). On the same principle, if the unpaid vendor of goods exercises his right of stoppage in transit, under s 44 of the Sale of Goods Act 1979, the purchaser has no insurable interest and cannot sustain a claim under the policy (*Clay* v. *Harrison* (1829) 10 B & C 99), and if goods are insured and are not delivered, the assured's loss would seem to be not the goods themselves but loss of profits (*Anderson* v. *Morice* (1876) 1 App Cas 713; *Fuerst Day Lawson Ltd* v. *Orion Insurance Co Ltd* [1980] 1 Lloyd's Rep 656).

Proviso: The proviso deals with the situation in which property is insured on the assumption that it is undamaged at the date of the policy, eg, cargo which is thought to be in course of transit. As long as the assured is unaware of any loss, the policy is valid and the insurer must pay even though the loss has occurred prior to the insurance becoming effective. Equally, the insurer may bring an action for the premium (*Bradford* v. *Symondson* (1881) 7 QBD 456). The proviso is echoed by the Schedule, r 1, and is based on, *inter alia*; *Mead* v. *Davison* (1835) 3 Ad & El 303; *Sutherland* v. *Pratt* (1843) 11 M & W 296; *Gibson* v. *Small*

(1853) 4 HL Cas 353; *Gledstanes* v. *Royal Exchange Assurance Corporation* (1864) 34 LJQB 30. The proviso is repeated in art 11.2 of the Institute Cargo Clauses.

Subs (2) This is based on *Anderson* v. *Morice* (1876) 1 App Cas 713.

Defeasible or contingent interest

7.—(1) A defeasible interest is insurable, as also is a contingent interest.

(2) In particular, where the buyer of goods has insured them, he has an insurable interest, notwithstanding that he might, at his election, have rejected the goods, or have treated them as at the seller's risk, by reason of the latter's delay in making delivery or otherwise.

NOTES

Subs (1) A defeasible interest is one which is liable to be defeated by subsequent events. The principle is based on: *Lucena* v. *Craufurd* (1806) 2 B & PNR 269; *Stirling* v. *Vaughan* (1809) 11 East 619; *Colonial Insurance Co of New Zealand* v. *Adelaide Marine Insurance Co* (1886) 12 App Cas 128.

Subs (2) For common law illustrations, see: *Sparkes* v. *Marshall* (1836) 2 Bing NC 761; *Anderson* v. *Morice* (1876) 1 App Cas 713.

Partial interest

8. A partial interest of any nature is insurable.

NOTES

A partial interest will include the interest of a joint owner of property (*Page* v. *Fry* (1800) 2 B & P 240; *Robertson* v. *Hamilton* (1811) 14 East 522; *Griffiths* v. *Bramley-Moore* (1878) 4 QBD 70) and the case in which the risk in an undivided bulk cargo has passed to the purchaser (*Inglis* v. *Stock* (1885) 10 App Cas 263). Under the Sale of Goods Act 1979, s 20A (inserted by the Sale of Goods (Amendment) Act 1995), property in part of an undivided bulk will pass to a buyer who has paid for that part.

Re-insurance

9.—(1) The insurer under a contract of marine insurance has an insurable interest in his risk, and may re-insure in respect of it.

(2) Unless the policy otherwise provides, the original assured has no right or interest in respect of such re-insurance.

NOTES

Subs (1) It is well established that the reinsured's insurable interest for the purpose of a reinsurance agreement is his liability to the assured. Reinsurance is not a separate contract by the reinsured on the original subject-matter. For a general discussion of reinsurance, see, Butler and Merkin, *Reinsurance Law*, Kluwer Publishing 1986, looseleaf.

Subs (2) This provision merely reflects the doctrine of privity of contract: the contract of insurance and the contract of reinsurance are separate arrangements, so that the assured cannot sue on the reinsurance. It is doubtful, contrary to the assumption in subs (2), whether any reinsurance term permitting the assured to sue the reinsurer directly (eg, a cut-through clause operating where the reinsured becomes insolvent) is enforceable by the assured, due to the operation of the privity doctrine.

Bottomry

10. The lender of money on bottomry or respondentia has an insurable interest in respect of the loan.

NOTES

These forms of security are now obsolete. Under each, the master of the vessel was permitted, in time of emergency to raise money on security of the vessel and freight (bottomry bond) or cargo (respondentia) to enable the voyage to be completed. For a fuller definition, see *"The James W Elwell"* [1921] P 351. Cf also: *Simonds* v. *Hodgson* (1832) 3 B & Ad 50; *Stainbank* v. *Fenning* (1851) 11 CB 59; *Stainbank* v. *Shepard* (1853) 13 CB 418.

Master's and seamen's wages

11. The master or any member of the crew of a ship has an insurable interest in respect of his wages.

NOTES

At common law the wages of seamen could not be insured, on the basis that wages were payable only if freight was earned by the vessel. The link between freight and wages was severed by the Merchant Shipping Act 1854, s 183 (now s 38 of the Merchant Shipping Act 1995), thereby removing any objection to the crew insuring their wages.

Advance freight

12. In the case of advance freight, the person advancing the freight has an insurable interest, in so far as such freight is not repayable in case of loss.

NOTES

This section is a specific illustration of the general rule that the person who bears the risk of the loss of freight may insure it (see the note to s 5(2) of the Marine Insurance Act 1906, page 8). If advance freight is not repayable in the event of loss of cargo, the cargo owner may insure the sum at risk. Conversely, if advance freight is repayable in the event of loss of cargo, the carrier may insure the sum at risk. The principles are discussed in *Allison* v. *Bristol Marine Insurance Co* (1876) 1 App Cas 209.

A distinction has to be drawn between advance freight, which is generally not repayable unless the contract provides to the contrary, and some other form of repayable advance to the carrier (*Manfield* v. *Maitland* (1821) 4 B & Ald 582; *Droege* v. *Stuart*, *"The Varnak"* (1869) LR 2 PC 505; *Wilson* v. *Martin* (1856) 11 Exch 684; *Hicks* v. *Shield* (1857) 26 LJQB 205; *Allison* v. *Bristol Marine Insurance* (1876) 1 App Cas 209).

Charges of insurance

13. The assured has an insurable interest in the charges of any insurance which he may effect.

NOTES

This section is based on *Usher* v. *Noble* (1810) 12 East 639. Charges include the premium and the broker's commission, assuming (contrary to the usual practice) that it is not incorporated in the gross premium (*United States Shipping Co* v. *Empress Assurance Co* [1907] 1 KB 259).

Quantum of interest

14.—(1) Where the subject-matter insured is mortgaged, the mortgagor has an insurable interest in the full value thereof, and the mortgagee has an insurable interest in respect of any sum due or to become due under the mortgage.

(2) A mortgagee, consignee, or other person having an interest in the subject-matter insured may insure on behalf and for the benefit of other persons interested as well as for his own benefit.

(3) The owner of insurable property has an insurable interest in respect of the full value thereof, notwithstanding that some third person may have agreed, or be liable, to indemnify him in case of loss.

NOTES

The interests of a mortgagor and mortgagee are distinct, even if insured under the same policy. The fact that the insurer has a defence against one of the parties will not, therefore, mean that the other is denied a claim (*Small* v. *United Kingdom Marine Mutual Insurance Association* [1897] 2 QB 311), although if the mortgagor has been guilty of scuttling the vessel, the loss is not by perils of the sea and the mortgagee will be defeated by want of insured peril (*Samuel & Co Ltd* v. *Dumas* [1924] AC 431).

Subs (1) This provision reflects the common law principle of indemnity. See, eg: *Alston* v. *Campbell* (1779) 4 Bro Parl Cas 476; *Irving* v. *Richardson* (1831) 2 B & Ad 193; *Hutchinson* v. *Wright* (1858) 25 Beav 444; *Ward* v. *Beck* (1863) 13 CBNS 668. An assured with an equitable right to a mortgage (eg where the mortgage has yet to be executed) has an insurable interest under the general provisions of s 5 of the 1906 Act, page 7 (*Samuel & Co Ltd* v. *Dumas* [1924] AC 431).

Subs (2) It is now generally accepted that a person interested in subject-matter can insure his interest as well as those of other interested parties under a single composite policy. If other interests have not been insured, the assured can recover only the amount of his own interest (*Irving* v. *Richardson* (1831) 2 B & Ad 193; *Labroke* v. *Lee* (1850) 4 De G & Sm 106; *Scott* v. *Globe Marine Insurance Co Ltd* (1896) 1 Com Cas 370), although it is established that a warehouseman or other person in possession of property can insure and recover its full value and must account to other interests for any sums in excess of his own interest (*Crowley* v. *Cohen* (1832) 3 B & Ad 478; *Joyce* v. *Kennard* (1871) LR 7 QB 78; *Stephens* v. *Australasian Insurance Co* (1872) LR 8 CP 18; *Williams* v. *Atlantic Assurance Co Ltd* [1933] 1 KB 81; *Hepburn* v. *Tomlinson (Hauliers)* [1966] AC 451; *Re Dibbens* [1990] BCLC 677—the last-mentioned case demonstrating that if there is a contractual duty to insure, the surplus proceeds are held on trust). Cf also: *Robertson* v. *Hamilton* (1811) 14 East 522; *Irving* v. *Richardson* (1831) 2 B & Ad 193; *Ebsworth* v. *Alliance Marine Co* (1873) LR 8 CP 596). Where the mortgage has been paid off, the mortgagee will in the ordinary course of events not suffer any loss in the event of the occurrence of an insured peril (*Levy & Co* v. *Merchants' Marine Insurance Co* (1885) Cab & Ell 474, where there was recovery on other grounds; *Chartered Trust & Executor Co* v. *London Scottish Assurance Corporation Ltd* (1923) 39 TLR 608).

Subs (3) For common law authority on this point, see: *Hobbs* v. *Hannam* (1811) 3 Camp 93; *Provincial Insurance Co of Canada* v. *Leduc* (1874) LR 6 PC 224. If the third party has paid the assured, the assured has suffered no loss and cannot make any claim against his insurers. By contrast, if the third party has yet to pay the insurers, the insurers will, having themselves paid, be subrogated to the assured's rights against the third party to the extent of their payment: see the Marine Insurance Act 1906, s 79, page 82.

Assignment of interest

15. Where the assured assigns or otherwise parts with his interest in the subject-matter insured, he does not thereby transfer to the assignee his rights under the contract of insurance, unless there be an express or implied agreement with the assignee to that effect.

But the provisions of this section do not affect a transmission of interest by operation of law.

NOTES

The rule in this section is based on: *Powles* v. *Innes* (1843) 11 M & W 10; *North of England Pure Oil Cake Co* v. *Archangel Maritime Insurance Co* (1875) LR 10 QB 249. The effect of an assignment of the subject-matter without the policy is to bring the policy to an end (Marine Insurance Act 1906, s 51, page 49). Equally, an assignment of the policy without a contemporaneous assignment of the subject-matter terminates the policy.

For the form and consequences of assignment, see Marine Insurance Act 1906, s 50, page 48.

Insurable Value

Measure of insurable value

16. Subject to any express provision or valuation in the policy, the insurable value of the subject-matter insured must be ascertained as follows—
   (1) In insurance on ship, the insurable value is the value, at the commencement of the risk, of the ship, including her outfit, provisions and stores for the officers and crew, money advanced for seamen's wages, and other disbursements (if any) incurred to make the ship fit for the voyage or adventure contemplated by the policy, plus the charges of insurance upon the whole:
   The insurable value, in the case of a steamship, includes also the machinery, boilers, and coals and engine stores if owned by the assured, and, in the case of a ship engaged in a special trade, the ordinary fittings requisite for that trade:
   (2) In insurance on freight, whether paid in advance or otherwise, the insurable value is the gross amount of the freight at the risk of the assured, plus the charges of insurance:
   (3) In insurance on goods or merchandise, the insurable value is the prime cost of the property insured, plus the expenses of and incidental to shipping and the charges of insurance upon the whole:
   (4) In insurance on any other subject-matter, the insurable value is the amount at the risk of the assured when the policy attaches, plus the charges of insurance.

NOTES

The definition of insurable value is significant where the policy is unvalued. Under a valued policy the measure of the assured's indemnity is based on the agreed value, whereas under an unvalued policy "insurable value" determines the amount recoverable in most cases (see ss 67–70, pages 71 *et seq*). The insurable value takes the value of the subject-matter when the risk attaches and not—as in the case of non-marine insurance—immediately before the occurrence of the event causing the loss, although the presumption that this is the appropriate date is rebuttable where the evidence demonstrates that the assured's loss is properly felt at the time and place of the casualty ("*The Captain Panagos*" [1985] 1 Lloyd's Rep 625, a mortgagee's interest policy).

Subs (1) For the common law basis of valuation at the date of the commencement of the risk, see *Herring* v. *Janson* (1895) 1 Com Cas 177. The definition of "ship" in r 15 of the Schedule to the Marine Insurance Act, page 103, is somewhat narrower, a discrepancy which may be of significance where the policy itself does not define the limits of the cover, as indeed is the case with the Institute Hulls Clauses which refer merely to the "vessel". For "stores and provisions" see *Brough* v. *Whitmore* (1791) 4 TR 206, *Hill* v. *Patten* (1807) 8 East 373 and *Forbes* v. *Aspinall* (1811) 13 East 323, and for "ordinary fittings" see *Hogarth* v. *Walker* [1900] 2 KB 283. Early cases held that fishing equipment was not covered by a hulls policy (*Hoskins* v. *Pickersgill* (1783) 3 Dougl 222; *Gale* v. *Laurie* (1826) 5 B & C 156), but the concluding words of the definition appear to reverse this position. At common law a hull and machinery policy on a steamship did not cover coal or provisions (*Roddick* v. *Indemnity Mutual Marine Insurance Co* [1895] 2 QB 380), the position under the statute being reversed.

Subs (2) For the common law basis, see: *Palmer* v. *Blackburn* (1822) 1 Bing 61; *United States Shipping Co* v. *Empress Assurance Corporation* [1908] 1 KB 115.

Subs (3) For the common law basis, see: *Usher* v. *Noble* (1810) 12 East 639. *Prima facie* evidence of the prime cost of goods is the invoice price paid by the assured, but if the value has altered before the policy incepts, the value at the latter date is the relevant value (*Williams* v. *Atlantic Assurance Co Ltd* [1933] 1 KB 81; *Berger and Light Diffusers Pty Ltd* v. *Pollock* [1973] 2 Lloyd's Rep 442).

Disclosure and Representations

Insurance is uberrimae fidei

17. A contract of marine insurance is a contract based upon the utmost good faith, and, if the utmost good faith be not observed by either party, the contract may be avoided by the other party.

NOTES

Section 17 states the general principle of utmost good faith which has been applicable to insurance contracts since the decision of Lord Mansfield in *Carter* v. *Boehm* (1766) 3 Burr 1905.

The duty of utmost good faith is stated to be of a general nature (*Container Transport International* v. *Oceanus Mutual* [1984] 1 Lloyd's Rep 476; *Marc Rich & Co AG* v. *Portman* [1996] 1 Lloyd's Rep 430), but two specific illustrations of it as applied to the assured are provided by s 18 (duty to disclose material facts before the contract is made) and s 20 (duty to avoid pre-contractual misrepresentation).

Utmost good faith may, however, be post-contractual, although to date the situations in which the assured owes a post-contractual duty of utmost good faith are confined to a number of clear categories, and in particular there is no general obligation on the assured to disclose facts material to the risk after the risk has incepted (*Ionides* v. *Pacific Fire and Marine Insurance Co Ltd* (1871) LR 6 QB 674; *Cory* v. *Patton* (1872) LR 7 QB 304; *Lishman* v. *Northern Maritime Insurance Co* (1875) LR 10 CP 179; *Niger Co Ltd* v. *Guardian Assurance Co* (1922) 12 Ll LR 175; *Willmott* v. *General Accident Fire and Life Assurance Corporation* (1935) 53 Ll LR 156; *Kausar* v. *Eagle Star Insurance Co Ltd* (1996) *The Times*, 15 July; *Sirius International Insurance Corporation* v. *Oriental Assurance Corporation* [1999] Lloyd's Rep IR 343). This is one consequence of the rule in s 21 of the Marine Insurance Act 1906, page

25, that the contract is completed when the slip is signed. The special situations are as follows.

(a) In the case of insurance at Lloyd's, a duty of utmost good faith is owed to each successive subscribing underwriter, on the basis that a separate contract is made with each underwriter. A false statement made to the leading underwriter is not, however, deemed to have been made to each underwriter in the following market (*Bell* v. *Carstairs* (1810) 2 Camp 543; *Forrester* v. *Pigou* (1813) 1 M & S 9; *General Accident Fire and Life Assurance Corporation* v. *Tanter, "The Zephyr"* [1984] 1 Lloyd's Rep 58; *Bank Leumi Le Israel BM* v. *British National Insurance Co Ltd* [1988] 1 Lloyd's Rep 71). Earlier authority to the contrary is probably unsafe (*Barber* v. *Fletcher* (1779) 1 Doug KB 305; *Pawson* v. *Watson* (1778) 2 Cowp 785; *Brine* v. *Featherstone* (1813) 4 Taunt 869). However, it was held in *Aneco Reinsurance Underwriting Ltd* v. *Johnson & Higgins* [1998] 1 Lloyd's Rep 565 that if a false statement is made to the leading underwriter but not repeated to the following market, the following market can avoid on the basis that the broker has failed to disclose that a false statement was made to the leading underwriter.

(b) When a marine policy is renewed, a fresh contract is made and further disclosure is required. Similarly, where the assured seeks to benefit from a "held covered" clause in a marine policy, under which cover is extended following breach of warranty or expiry of the cover, material facts must be disclosed to the insurer (*Overseas Commodities* v. *Style* [1958] 1 Lloyd's Rep 546; *Liberian Insurance Agency* v. *Mosse* [1977] 2 Lloyd's Rep 560).

(c) The assured is under a duty of utmost good faith when submitting details of a loss in order to make a claim, although the cases require the assured only to avoid fraud in this regard (*Black King Shipping Co* v. *Massie, "The Litsion Pride"* [1985] 1 Lloyd's Rep 437; *"The Captain Panagos"* [1986] 2 Lloyd's Rep 470; *Parker & Heard Ltd* v. *Generali Assicurazioni SpA* 1988, unrep; *Bucks Printing Press Ltd* v. *Prudential Assurance Co* 1991, unreported; *Orakpo* v. *Barclays Insurance Services Ltd* [1995] LRLR 443; *Transthene Packaging* v. *Royal Insurance (UK) Ltd* [1996] LRLR 32; *Galloway* v. *Guardian Royal Exchange (UK) Ltd* [1999] Lloyd's Rep IR 209). In any event, the duty comes to an end once the assured has issued proceedings against the insurer (*Manifest Shipping Co Ltd* v. *Uni-Polaris Insurance Co Ltd, "The Star Sea"* [1995] 1 Lloyd's Rep 651, affirmed [1997] 1 Lloyd's Rep 360, rejecting the trial judge's view that the duty comes to an end as soon as the insurer has rejected the assured's claim). The assured may also be ordered to produce the ships' papers to the insurer when a claim is made. The power to make such an order was set out in RSC, Ord 72, r 10, superseded by the Civil Procedure Rules 1998, Part 31. As to the exercise of the discretion, see: *North British Rubber Co* v. *Cheetham* (1938) 61 Ll LR 337; *Keevil and Keevil Ltd* v. *Boag* (1940) 67 Ll LR 263; *Probatina Shipping Co Ltd* v. *Sun Insurance Office Ltd, "The Sageorge"* [1974] QB 635. The power was available under any marine policy, including one which involved some land transit (*Leon* v. *Casey* [1932] 2 KB 576), and could have been exercised against a mortgagee (*Graham Joint Stock Shipping Co Ltd* v. *Motor Union Insurance Co* [1922] 2 KB 563) and in reinsurance cases (*China Traders Insurance Co* v. *Royal Exchange Assurance* [1898] 2 QB 187) as well as against the assured himself. RSC, Ord 72, r 10 replaced an earlier right of the insurer to obtain an order for the ship's papers on demand.

(d) *"The Litsion Pride"* [1985] 1 Lloyd's Rep 437 is authority for a wider proposition, namely, that there is a duty of disclosure owed by the assured to the insurer during the currency of the policy in any situation in which the assured is required to give information to the insurer under the terms of the policy, eg, where there is an increase of risk. In *New Hampshire Insurance Co* v. *MGN Ltd* [1997] LRLR 24, the Court of Appeal held that the mere fact that a policy is cancellable by the giving of notice at the option of the insurer is not enough to put the assured under a general duty of disclosure, rejecting the views expressed on "*The Litsion Pride*" on this very point, and the Court of Appeal reserved its opinion on the general correctness of "*The Litsion Pride*". Subsequently, in *Hussain* v. *Brown (No 2)* 1996, unreported, the High Court was prepared to accept the correctness of "*The Litsion Pride*", and held that there could be a continuing duty of utmost good faith, and that proof of fraud on the part of the assured was unnecessary, but that the operation of the continuing duty depended upon the wording of the clause under which the assured was required to provide information: it was held that a clause requiring the assured to give notice to the insurer of any increase of risk was exhaustive, and operated to exclude by implication any further duty on the assured's part.

(e) Under a non-obligatory open cover, where the insurer has the right to refuse to accept declarations made to him, a duty of disclosure attaches to each declaration (*Berger* v. *Pollock* [1973] 2 Lloyd's Rep 442, and for floating policies see s 29 of the 1906 Act, page 129).

Section 17 further provides that the duty of utmost good faith is bilateral. This is based upon dicta of Lord Mansfield in *Carter* v. *Boehm* (1766) 3 Burr 1905, confirmed in principle by the House of Lords in *La Banque Financière de la Cité* v. *Westgate Insurance Co* [1990] 2 All ER 947. This case also decides that there is no independent duty of care in tort owed by an insurer to the assured, a point applied in *Searle* v. *A R Hales & Co Ltd* [1996] LRLR 68. *La Banque Financière* decided that whatever the content of the insurer's duty of utmost good faith, the only available remedy was avoidance by the assured; of necessity this is of little use where the assured has suffered a loss and seeks to recover under the policy rather than merely to recover his premiums. The principle was applied in *Norwich Union Life Insurance Society* v. *Qureshi* [1999] Lloyd's Rep IR 263, in which Rix J ruled that an insurer did not owe a duty to the assured to disclose that the risk to which the policy related was a serious one, but that in any event the assured's only remedy was avoidance of the policy. This ruling was upheld on appeal, 1999, unreported.

Disclosure by assured

18.—(1) Subject to the provisions of this section, the assured must disclose to the insurer, before the contract is concluded, every material circumstance which is known to the assured, and the assured is deemed to know every circumstance which, in the ordinary course of business, ought to be known by him. If the assured fails to make such disclosure, the insurer may avoid the contract.

(2) Every circumstance is material which would influence the judgment of a prudent insurer in fixing the premium, or determining whether he will take the risk.

(3) In the absence of inquiry the following circumstances need not be disclosed namely:—

(a) Any circumstance which diminishes the risk;

(b) Any circumstance which is known or presumed to be known to the insurer. The insurer is presumed to know matters of common notoriety or knowledge, and matters which an insurer in the ordinary course of his business, as such, ought to know;

(c) Any circumstance as to which information is waived by the insurer;

(d) Any circumstance which it is superfluous to disclose by reason of any express or implied warranty.

(4) Whether any particular circumstance, which is not disclosed, be material or not is, in each case, a question of fact.

(5) The term "circumstance" includes any communication made to, or information received by, the assured.

NOTES

The drafting of s 18 is based to a large extent on the judgment of Lord Mansfield in *Carter v. Boehm* (1766) 3 Burr 1905.

Subs (1) The contract is concluded when offer and acceptance coincide (cf s 21 of the Marine Insurance Act 1906, page 25): the date of the issue of the policy and the inception of the risk are irrelevant. A fact must be disclosed if the assured ought to have been aware of it in the usual course of business (*London General Insurance Co* v. *General Marine Underwriters Association* [1921] 1 KB 104). This does not mean that the assured is required to investigate matters outside his knowledge, as these are for the insurer alone to uncover in reaching an underwriting decision (*Simner* v. *New India Insurance Co* [1995] LRLR 240; *Economides* v. *Commercial Union* [1997] 3 All ER 636). The assured is generally not required to disclose facts which are known to his agent. The rule here is that the facts known to an agent who is authorised to insure on behalf of the assured in respect of the risk in question must be disclosed by the agent (*Fitzherbert* v. *Mather* (1785) 1 TR 12; *Gladstone* v. *King* (1813) 1 M & S 35; *Proudfoot* v. *Montefiore* (1867) LR 2 QB 511; *Blackburn Low & Co* v. *Vigors* (1887) 12 App Cas 531; *Berger* v. *Pollock* [1973] 2 Lloyd's Rep 442), but information in the possession of a general agent or employee is not deemed to be known by the assured (*Stribley v. Imperial Marine Insurance Co* (1876) 1 QBD 507; *Wilson* v. *Salamandra Assurance Co of St Petersburg* (1903) 88 LT 96; *Blackburn Low & Co* v. *Haslam* (1881) 21 QBD 144; *Australia and New Zealand Bank Ltd* v. *Colonial and Eagle Wharves Ltd* [1960] 2 Lloyd's Rep 241; *Simner* v. *New India Insurance Co* [1995] LRLR 240; *SAIL* v. *Farex Gie* [1995] LRLR 116; *PCW Syndicates* v. *PCW Insurers* [1996] 1 Lloyd's Rep 241; *Group Josi Re* v. *Walbrook Insurance Ltd* [1996] 1 Lloyd's Rep 345; *Kingscroft* v. *Nissan Fire and Marine Insurance Co Ltd* [1999] Lloyd's Rep IR 371; *Arab Bank* v. *Zurich Insurance Co* [1999] 1 Lloyd's Rep 262. The common law rules on disclosure by an agent to insure are codified in s 19 of the 1906 Act; see page 22).

The insurer's right is to avoid the contract *ab initio* on an all or nothing basis, although if the policy is composite in that there are two or more assureds with different interests, the position of each assured is to be considered separately: *New Hampshire Insurance* v. *MGN Ltd* [1997] LRLR 24; *Arab Bank* v. *Zurich Insurance Ltd* [1999] 1 Lloyd's Rep 262; *FNCB Ltd* v. *Barnet Devanney (Harrow) Ltd* [1999] Lloyd's Rep IR 459. The assured cannot require the insurer to reinstate the contract by proffering an additional premium, as proportionality does not form part of English law (*Pan Atlantic Insurance Co Ltd* v. *Pine Top Insurance Co Ltd* [1994] 3 All ER 581). The right may be lost by waiver or affirmation where the insurer, in full knowledge of the assured's breach of duty, acts in a fashion which induces the assured to believe that the right will not be exercised (*Imperio* v. *Iron Trades Mutual* 1989, unreported; *Svenska Handelsbanken* v. *Sun Alliance & London Insurance plc* [1996] 1 Lloyd's Rep 519; *Insurance Corporation of the Channel Islands* v. *Royal Hotel* [1998] Lloyd's Rep IR 151; *Cape plc* v. *Iron Trades Employers Insurance Association Ltd* 1999, unreported). At Lloyd's, the issue of a policy is not regarded as waiver, as this act is merely ministerial and does no more than to allow the assured to contest the insurer's avoidance in civil proceedings (*Universal Marine Insurance Co* v. *Morrison* (1873) LR 8 Exch 197). See also *Nicholson* v.

Power (1869) 20 LT 580, where the policy was issued subject to a reservation of rights. Before there can be waiver in this form, it must be shown that the insurer was actually aware of the assured's breach of duty, and this may mean that information disclosed to the insurer for other reasons may be treated as not having been received for waiver purposes (*Malhi* v. *Abbey Life Assurance Co Ltd* [1996] LRLR 237). If the policy provides that it is not to be voidable or cancellable, the insurer may not rely on an innocent breach of the duty of utmost good faith, although the right to avoid for a negligent breach is unaffected unless the clause clearly so provides: *Toomey* v. *Eagle Star Insurance Co (No 2)* [1995] 2 Lloyd's Rep 88. *Toomey* also decides that an action for damages for non-innocent misrepresentation, under s 2(1) of the Misrepresentation Act 1967, is not precluded by a clause referring only to avoidance or cancellation.

Subs (2) The test of materiality was considered by the Court of Appeal in *Container Transport International Ltd* v. *Oceanus Mutual Underwriting Association (Bermuda) Ltd* [1984] 1 Lloyd's Rep 476, where it was held that the test is purely objective and does not involve consideration of the question whether the assured appreciated the materiality of the fact or whether the insurer in question was actually influenced by it: the only relevant point is whether a prudent insurer would have been interested in the information. The test was given detailed consideration by the House of Lords in *Pan Atlantic Insurance Co Ltd* v. *Pine Top Insurance Co Ltd* [1994] 3 All ER 581 and much of the Court of Appeal's reasoning in *CTI* was overturned. In *Pan Atlantic* the House of Lords held that there is a two-limb test for materiality:

(i) Would a prudent insurer have been influenced by the information? In determining whether this is the case, the question is not whether the information would have had a decisive influence on a prudent underwriter, nor whether a prudent underwriter would have refused the risk or charged a higher premium, but rather whether the information would have had an effect on the insurer's thought processes. Cf also the *St Paul Fire* case (see (ii) below). It is necessary for market evidence to be adduced to prove whether or not a prudent underwriter would have been influenced by the information. The admissibility of the evidence of other underwriters was originally denied as pure hearsay (*Carter* v. *Boehm* (1766) 3 Burr 1905; *Campbell* v. *Rickards* (1833) 5 B & Ad 840), but its admissibility was established in other cases (*Berthon* v. *Loughman* (1817) 2 Stark 258; *Richards* v. *Murdoch* (1830) 10 B & C 527).

(ii) Was the actual insurer influenced by the assured's failure to disclose the information in question? The insurer must thus show that there was an inducement upon which he relied. Although there is no mention of this requirement in the Act itself, their Lordships held that it should be implied in order to bring insurance law into line with the general law. Where materiality has been demonstrated, the insurer can rely on a presumption that he has been induced to enter the contract: *St Paul Fire and Marine Insurance Co (UK) Ltd* v. *McConnell Dowell Constructors Ltd* [1995] 2 Lloyd's Rep 116. Evidence of the underwriter's imprudence in relation to the risk itself may rebut the presumption of inducement, but it remains open to the insurer to prove actual inducement: *Marc Rich & Co AG* v. *Portman* [1996] 1 Lloyd's Rep 430, which also decides that an insurer cannot rely upon the presumption by deliberately refraining from giving evidence. See also *Sirius International Insurance Corporation* v. *Oriental Assurance Corporation* [1999] Lloyd's Rep IR 343. Even where evidence of actual inducement is presented, it is open to the court to take the view that the insurer could not have been influenced by the fact in question (*Kausar* v. *Eagle Star Insurance Co Ltd* (1996) *The Times*, 15 July. A broker sued for breach of duty may rely upon the presumption to establish that a risk was uninsurable *Gunns* v. *Par Insurance Brokers* [1997] 1 Lloyd's Rep 173.

The views of the assured himself or those of a prudent assured are irrelevant to the test of materiality (*Pan Atlantic Insurance Co Ltd* v. *Pine Top Insurance Co Ltd* [1994] 3 All ER 581).

Materiality has to be assessed at the date of the making of the contract, and not in the light of subsequent events (*Seaman* v. *Fonnereau* (1743) 2 Str 1183; *Lynch* v. *Hamilton* (1810) 3 Taunt 37; *"The Dora"* [1989] 1 Lloyd's Rep 69). These cases also demonstrate that there is no need for any connection between the information withheld and the loss, as breach of the duty of utmost good faith rests upon the insurer having been given a false impression (*Pan Atlantic Insurance Co Ltd* v. *Pine Top Insurance Co Ltd* [1994] 3 All ER 581).

Material facts: There are numerous reported cases in which the materiality of facts, for the purposes of both non-disclosure and misrepresentation (see s 20(2) of the Marine Insurance Act 1906), has been discussed by the courts. The following list is illustrative of the position.

(1) Any fact which affects directly the risk insured ("physical hazard") is material.

(a) Any physical attributes of the insured subject-matter which render it a greater risk than would normally be assumed must be disclosed (*Da Costa* v. *Scandret* (1723) 2 P Wms 170; *Seaman* v. *Fonnereau* (1743) 2 Str 1183; *Lynch* v. *Hamilton* (1810) 3 Taunt 37; *Lynch* v. *Dunsford* (1811) 14 East 494; *Kirby* v. *Smith* (1818) 1 B & Ald 672; *Westbury* v. *Aberdein* (1837) 2 M & W 267; *Russell* v. *Thornton* (1860) 6 H & N 140; *Bates* v. *Hewitt* (1867) LR 2 QB 595; *Ionides* v. *Pacific Fire and Marine Insurance Co* (1872) LR 7 QB 517; *Bird's Cigarette Manufacturing Co Ltd* v. *Rouse* (1924) 19 Ll LR 301; *Neue Fischmehl Vertriebs-Gesellschaft Haselhorst mbH* v. *Yorkshire Insurance Co Ltd* (1934) 50 Ll LR 151; *Berger and Light Diffusers Pty Ltd* v. *Pollock* [1973] 2 Lloyd's Rep 442; *Liberian Insurance Agency* v. *Mosse* [1977] 2 Lloyd's Rep 560; *Inversiones Manria SA* v. *Sphere Drake Insurance Co Ltd, "The Dora"* [1989] 1 Lloyd's Rep 69).

(b) Previous losses and claims may constitute material facts. It is the circumstances of a loss rather than its amount which is the relevant fact (*Sharp* v. *Sphere Drake Insurance Co Ltd, "The Moonacre"* [1992] 2 Lloyd's Rep 501).

(c) Any particular hazards of the voyage constitute material facts if the insurer could not have discovered those facts or if they have been misstated (*Middlewood* v. *Blakes* (1797) 7 TR 162; *Edwards* v. *Footner* (1808) 1 Camp 530; *Feise* v. *Parkinson* (1812) 4 Taunt 640; *Sawtell* v. *Loudon* (1814) 5 Taunt 359; *Westbury* v. *Aberdein* (1837) 2 M & W 267; *Anderson* v. *Thornton* (1853) 8 Exch 425; *Harrower* v. *Hutchinson* (1870) LR 5 QB 584; *Leigh* v. *Adams* (1871) 25 LT 566; *Ionides* v. *Pacific Fire and Marine Insurance Co* (1871) LR 6 QB 674; *Laing* v. *Union Marine Insurance Co Ltd* (1895) 1 Com Cas 11). This would include the manner in which insured cargo is being carried or has been treated prior to the voyage (*Blackett* v. *Royal Exchange Assurance Co* (1832) 2 Cr & J 244; *Hood* v. *West End Motor Car Packing Co* [1917] 2 KB 38; *Alluvials Mining Machinery Co* v. *Stowe* (1922) 10 Ll LR 96; *Greenhill* v. *Federal Insurance Co* [1927] 1 KB 65), the time at which the vessel sailed or was due to sail, provided that the time of sailing affected the risk (*Fillis* v. *Bruton* (1782) 1 Park's Marine Insurances 414; *Macdowall* v. *Fraser* (1779) 1 Doug KB 260; *M'Andrew* v. *Bell* (1795) 1 Esp 373; *Fort* v. *Lee* (1811) 3 Taunt 381; *Foley* v. *Moline* (1814) 5 Taunt 430; *Bridges* v. *Hunter* (1813) 1 M & S 15; *Stribley* v. *Imperial Marine Insurance* (1876) 1 QBD 507; *Scottish Shire Line Ltd* v. *London and Provincial Marine and General Insurance Co* [1912] 3 KB 51; *Harper & Co Ltd* v. *Mackechnie & Co* (1925)

22 Ll LR 514); port risks (*Kingston* v. *Knibbs* (1808) 1 Camp 508n; *Stewart* v. *Bell* (1821) 5 B & Ald 238; *Marc Rich & Co AG* v. *Portman* [1996] 1 Lloyd's Rep 430; *Fraser Shipping Ltd* v. *Colton* [1997] 1 Lloyd's Rep 586 and war risks dangers which were not of common knowledge (*Beckwaite* v. *Nalgrove* (1810) 3 Taunt 41n). The disclosure must be made even if the policy is written on an all risks or all losses basis (*Cheshire & Co* v. *Thompson* (1919) 24 Com Cas 198).

(d) The assured must disclose that he has entered into a contract with a third party, not found in the ordinary course of commerce, which potentially increases the insurer's liability or diminishes its right of subrogation in the event of a loss (*Mercantile Steamship Co* v. *Tyser* (1881) 7 QBD 73; *Tate* v. *Hyslop* (1885) 15 QBD 368; *"The Bedouin"* [1894] P 1; *Scottish Shire Line* v. *London and Provincial Marine Insurance Co* [1912] 3 KB 51; *Marc Rich & Co AG* v. *Portman* [1996] 1 Lloyd's Rep 430).

(2) Any fact which goes to the "moral hazard" is material.

(a) If the assured has overinsured to an excessive amount, the overinsurance must be disclosed, although this is less significant in an unvalued policy as the assured is unable to recover more than his actual loss (*Ionides* v. *Pender* (1874) LR 9 QB 531; *Herring* v. *Janson* (1895) 1 Com Cas 177; *Thames & Mersey Marine Insurance Co Ltd* v. *Gunford Ship Co* [1911] AC 529; *Pickersgill* v. *London and Provincial Marine Insurance Co* [1912] 3 KB 614; *Gooding* v. *White* (1913) 29 TLR 312; *Visscherij Maatschappij Nieuw Onderneming* v. *Scottish Metropolitan Assurance Co Ltd* (1922) 27 Com Cas 198; *Piper* v. *Royal Exchange Assurance* (1932) 44 Ll LR 103; *Williams* v. *Atlantic Assurance Co Ltd* [1933] 1 KB 81; *Slattery* v. *Mance* [1962] 1 Lloyd's Rep 60; *Berger* v. *Pollock* [1973] 2 Lloyd's Rep 442).

(b) Information as to other policies on the same risk is material if it converts the risk from genuine to speculative (*Sibbald* v. *Hill* (1814) 2 Dow 263; *Thames & Mersey Marine Insurance Co Ltd* v. *Gunford Ship Co* [1911] AC 529; *Mathie* v. *Argonaut Insurance Ltd* (1925) 21 Ll LR 145), as is information as to previous losses or claims under other policies (*Container Transport International Inc* v. *Oceanus Mutual Underwriting Association (Bermuda) Ltd* [1984] 1 Lloyd's Rep 476). Policies on related but separate risks need not be disclosed (*Wilson, Holgate & Co Ltd* v. *Lancashire & Cheshire Insurance Corporation Ltd* (1922) 13 Ll LR 486).

(c) The master's qualifications or previous conduct are immaterial (*Anon* (1699) 12 Mod Rep 325; *Thames & Mersey Marine Insurance Co Ltd* v. *Gunford Ship Co* [1911] AC 529) unless they relate directly to the hazard. The master's past criminal conduct may be material if it increases the risk of the vessel's seizure (*"The Dora"* [1989] 1 Lloyd's Rep 69).

(d) There is authority for the proposition that the nationality of the shipowner or the vessel may be a material fact (*Steel* v. *Lacy* (1810) 3 Taunt 285; *Campbell* v. *Innes* (1821) 4 B & Ald 423; *Associated Oil Carriers Ltd* v. *Union Insurance Society of Canton Ltd* [1917] 2 KB 184; *Demetriades & Co* v. *Northern Assurance Co, "The Spathari"* (1926) 21 Ll LR 265). *Quaere* whether it is now permissible under the Race Relations Act 1976 for an insurer to take the view that higher premiums are to be charged depending upon the assured's nationality, at least unless the assured is an enemy alien.

(e) The assured's criminal convictions are material (*Allden* v. *Raven, "The Kylie"* [1983] 2 Lloyd's Rep 444) as are those of the master (*"The Dora"* [1989] 2 Lloyd's Rep 69). It would also seem from *"The Dora"* criminal charges not heard at the date of the application, and criminal conduct which has not been the subject of any charge, are also material facts. Criminal convictions are, however, to be disregarded if they are spent under the Rehabilitation of Offenders Act 1974.

(f) General dishonesty on the assured's part is material, e.g., where the assured has fraudulently prepared invoices intended to be used to defraud its bankers: *Insurance Corporation of the Channel Islands* v. *Royal Hotel* [1998] Lloyd's Rep IR 151.

(3) Facts which do not form part of the physical or moral hazard, but which affect the amount of premium paid, are material.

(a) The amount of vessels to be declared to the insurer is material, as this affects the premium charged for each vessel (*"The Dora"* [1989] 1 Lloyd's Rep 69).

(b) The fact that the assured has not personally signed the proposal is material, as the proposal is a personal undertaking by the assured (*Sharp* v. *Sphere Drake Insurance Co Ltd, "The Moonacre"* [1992] 2 Lloyd's Rep 501).

(4) Matters held to be immaterial include the following.

(a) The assured under a marine policy does not have to disclose rejections of cover by other insurers (*Lebon & Co* v. *Straits Insurance Co* (1894) 10 TLR 517; *Glasgow Assurance Corporation Ltd* v. *William Symondson & Co* (1911) 16 Com Cas 109; *North British Fishing Boat Insurance Co* v. *Starr* (1922) 13 Ll LR 206) or the fact that he has previously been guilty of non-disclosure (*Container Transport International* v. *Oceanus Mutual Underwriting Association (Bermuda) Ltd* [1982] 2 Lloyd's Rep 178, reversed on other grounds [1984] 1 Lloyd's Rep 476), but previous claims against other insurers are material.

(b) Assuming that there are no facts affecting the moral hazard, the identity of the assured is not a material fact, so that an agent can insure on behalf of the assured and the assured may take the benefit of the policy on the basis of the undisclosed principal doctrine (*National Oilwell (UK) Ltd* v. *Davy Offshore Ltd* [1993] 2 Lloyd's Rep 582; *Siu* v. *Eastern Insurance Ltd* [1994] 1 Lloyd's Rep 213).

(c) The nature of the assured's interest is not material (see the note to s 4 of the 1906 Act, page 6).

(d) Fraud by the assured's agent perpetrated on the assured himself is a material fact only if it relates directly to the risk: it cannot form part of the moral hazard if unconnected to the risk in question (*Deutsche Ruckversicherung Akt* v. *Walbrook Insurance Co Ltd* [1996] 1 Lloyd's Rep 345).

Subs (3) (a) An illustration is *Inversiones Manria SA* v. *Sphere Drake Insurance Co plc, "The Dora"* [1989] 1 Lloyd's Rep 69 (vessel insured against marine risks not completed when risk attached).

Subs (3) (b) The insurer need not be told what he actually knows. There is some authority for the proposition that each branch or department of an insurer is a distinct entity for the purpose of ascertaining its knowledge—*Stone* v. *Reliance Mutual Insurance Association* [1972] 1 Lloyd's Rep 469; *Malhi* v. *Abbey Life Assurance Co Ltd* [1996] LRLR 237; *Gunns* v. *Par Insurance Brokers* [1997] 1 Lloyd's Rep 173—but these cases should be treated with some caution. Two forms of information are presumed to be known to the insurer.

(1) Matters of general knowledge (*Planche* v. *Fletcher* (1779) 1 Doug KB 251; *Bates* v. *Hewitt* (1867) LR 2 QB 595; *Schloss Brothers* v. *Stevens* [1906] 2 KB 665).

(2) Matters relating specifically to the class of business insured under the policy and to the nature of the subject-matter insured (*Noble* v. *Kennaway* (1780) 2 Doug 510; *Moxon* v. *Atkins* (1812) 3 Camp 200; *Da Costa* v. *Edmonds* (1815) 4 Camp 142; *Stewart* v. *Bell* (1821) 5 B & Ald 238; *Gandy* v. *Adelaide Insurance Co* (1871) LR 6 QB 746; *"The Bedouin"* [1894] P 1; *Cantiere Meccanico Brindisino* v. *Janson* [1912] 3 KB 452; *British and Foreign Marine Insurance Co* v. *Gaunt* [1921] 2 AC 41; *North British Fishing Boat Insurance Co Ltd* v. *Starr* (1922) 13 Ll LR 206; *George Cohen, Sons & Co* v. *Standard Marine Insurance Co Ltd* (1925) 21 Ll LR 30; *Kingscroft* v. *Nissan Fire and Marine Insurance Co (No 2)* 1999, unreported). There is a conflict of authority on whether

that information appears in Lloyd's lists containing shipping information dis-
with the duty of disclosure. This was held to be so in some cases (*Friere* v.
use (1817) Holt NP 572) but not in others (*Elton* v. *Larkins* (1832) 8 Bing 198;
sal Marine Insurance Co v. *Morrison* (1873) LR 8 Exch 197; *London General
nce Co* v. *General Marine Underwriters Association* [1921] 1 KB 104). The true
ple would appear to be that a misrepresentation is not overridden by the availability
of the information from Lloyd's (*Mackintosh* v. *Marshall* (1843) 11 M & W 116).

Falling within this heading are matters which are deemed to be known to the insurer due to
trade usage relating, eg, to route to be taken or method of loading cargo: a series of decisions
has raised the question whether a practice was sufficiently widespread and notorious to
amount to a usage (*Salvador* v. *Hopkins* (1765) 3 Burr 1707; *Noble* v. *Kennaway* (1780) 2
Doug KB 510; *Vallance* v. *Dewar* (1808) 1 Camp 503; *Tennant* v. *Henderson* (1813) 1 Dow
324; *Da Costa* v. *Edmonds* (1815) 4 Camp 142; *Stewart* v. *Bell* (1821) 5 B & Ald 238).

Subs (3)(c) Waiver may arise in the following ways:

(1) disclaimer by the insurer of the relevance of the facts at issue, particularly by policy
terms (*Cantiere Meccanico Brindisino* v. *Janson* [1912] 3 KB 452; *Kumar* v. *AGF Insurance
Ltd* [1998] 4 All ER 788; *Rothschild* v. *Collyear* [1999] Lloyd's Rep IR 6) or by an
authorised agent (*Allden* v. *Raven, "The Kylie"* [1983] 2 Lloyd's Rep 444);

(2) limited request by the insurer for information which excludes facts otherwise material, although not all limited express questions amount to waiver (*Svenska Handelsbanken*
v. *Sun Alliance & London Insurance plc* [1996] 1 Lloyd's Rep 519);

(3) failure by the insurer to seek further information when alerted by existing disclosures
(*Court* v. *Martineau* (1782) 2 Doug KB 161; *Freeland* v. *Glover* (1806) 7 East 457; *Weir*
v. *Aberdeen* (1819) 2 B & Ald 320; *Inman SS Co* v. *Bischoff* (1882) 7 App Cas 670; *Asfar
& Co* v. *Blundell* [1896] 1 QB 123; *Cantiere Meccanico Brindisino* v. *Janson* [1912] 3 KB
452; *Mann, MacNeal and Steeves Ltd* v. *General Marine Underwriters Ltd* [1921] 2 KB
300; *J Kirkaldy & Sons* v. *Walker* [1999] Lloyd's Rep IR 410).

There is no waiver by failure to ask a material question (*Marc Rich & Co AG* v. *Portman*
[1996] 1 Lloyd's Rep 430, but *contra GMA* v. *Unistorebrand* [1995] LRLR 333).

Subs (3)(d) If the matter is covered by a warranty, the insurer is discharged from liability
as from the date of the breach, and thus need not rely upon utmost good faith. The cases are
largely concerned with the failure of the assured under a voyage policy to disclose the
unseaworthiness of the vessel (*Haywood* v. *Rodgers* (1804) 4 East 590; *Gandy* v. *Adelaide
Insurance Co* (1871) LR 6 QB 746; *"The Dora"* [1989] 1 Lloyd's Rep 69; *Cape plc* v. *Iron
Trades Employers Insurance Association Ltd* 1999, unreported).

Disclosure by agent effecting insurance

19. Subject to the provisions of the preceding section as to circumstances which
need not be disclosed, where an insurance is effected for the assured by an agent,
the agent must disclose to the insurer—

(a) Every material circumstance which is known to himself, and an agent to
insure is deemed to know every circumstance which in the ordinary course
of business ought to be known by, or to have been communicated to, him;
and

(b) Every material circumstance which the assured is bound to disclose, unless
it come to his knowledge too late to communicate it to the agent.

NOTES

Subs (a) An "agent to insure" is an agent authorised by the assured to obtain insurance, as opposed to a general agent of the assured: In *PCW Syndicates* v. *PCW Insurers* [1996] 1 Lloyd's Rep 241 and *Group Josi Re* v. *Walbrook Insurance* [1996] 1 Lloyd's Rep 345 Saville LJ held that an agent to insure is the placing broker. A fact need be disclosed by an agent to insure only if he is in possession of it in his capacity as agent, and in particular if the agent has defrauded the assured, the agent's knowledge of that fraud need not be disclosed to the insurer for the policy to be valid: *Simner* v. *New India Insurance* [1995] LRLR 240; *SAIL* v. *Farex Gie* [1995] LRLR 116; *PCW Syndicates* v. *PCW Insurers* [1996] 1 Lloyd's Rep 241; *Group Josi Re* v. *Walbrook Insurance* [1996] 1 Lloyd's Rep 345; *Arab Bank* v. *Zurich Insurance Co.* [1999] 1 Lloyd's Rep 262. For an illustration of the situation in which information is in the possession of the agent but is not passed to the insurer by the agent when placing the insurance, see *Russell* v. *Thornton* (1860) 6 H & N 140.

Subs (b) For an illustration of the situation in which information known to the assured is not passed on to the broker, see *Republic of Bolivia* v. *Indemnity Mutual Assurance Co* [1909] 1 KB 785.

Representations pending negotiation of contract

20.—(1) Every material representation made by the assured or his agent to the insurer during the negotiations for the contract, and before the contract is concluded, must be true. If it be untrue the insurer may avoid the contract.

(2) A representation is material which would influence the judgment of a prudent insurer in fixing the premium, or determining whether he will take the risk.

(3) A representation may be either a representation as to a matter of fact, or as to a matter of expectation or belief.

(4) A representation as to matter of fact is true, if it be substantially correct, that is to say, if the difference between what is represented and what is actually correct would not be considered material by a prudent insurer.

(5) A representation as to a matter of expectation or belief is true if it be made in good faith.

(6) A representation may be withdrawn or corrected before the contract is concluded.

(7) Whether a particular representation be material or not is, in each case, a question of fact.

NOTES

This section reflects ordinary principles of misrepresentation, a position confirmed by *Pan Atlantic Insurance Co Ltd* v. *Pine Top Insurance Co Ltd* [1994] 3 All ER 581, in which it was held—overruling earlier authority—that the insurer himself must have been influenced by the misrepresentation. Any statement by the assured has to be construed reasonably. Thus if the assured insures a vessel with an English name, he is not taken to be representing that it is an English vessel (*Clapham* v. *Cologan* (1813) 3 Camp 382). As is the case with the general law, a misstatement may be material irrespective of the representor's state of mind (*Dennistoun* v. *Lillie* (1821) 3 Bli 202; *Hamilton & Co* v. *Eagle Star and British Dominions Insurance Co Ltd* (1924) 19 Ll LR 242).

Subs (1) See also the note to s 18, page 17. If there is a misrepresentation, the insurer's right to avoid is not removed by the fact that the truth of the matter could have been discovered by the insurer by consulting Lloyd's lists (*Mackintosh* v. *Marshall* (1843) 11 M & W 116). Not every pre-contractual statement is a representation: *Kingscroft* v. *Nissan Fire and Marine Insurance Co Ltd (No 2)* 1999, unreported.

The insurer's right to avoid is tempered by s 2(2) of the Misrepresentation Act 1967, which authorises the court to refuse to avoid the contract and instead to award damages to the innocent party. The section is for the benefit of the misrepresentor, and is intended to mitigate the hardships of avoidance. It has been held that s 2(2) of the 1967 Act ought not in principle to be used in reinsurance cases (*Highland Insurance Co* v. *Continental Insurance Co* [1987] 1 Lloyd's Rep 109), although its use in marine insurance remains possible.

There is some difficulty in applying this provision to insurances formed at Lloyd's, as the slip presented to successive underwriters gives rise to a fresh contract on each occasion on which an underwriter subscribes to it. The practice at Lloyd's is that any exchange of information takes place primarily between the leading underwriter and the broker and that subsequent underwriters do not ask questions in the same amount of detail. Consequently, it is likely that any false statements will be made to the leading underwriter only. In such a case, the leading underwriter can clearly avoid liability, but it is unclear whether the subsequent underwriters are the deemed recipients of false information or whether they remain bound by the contract. There is old authority for the proposition that all underwriters can avoid the policy (*Pawson* v. *Watson* (1778) 2 Cowp 785; *Barber* v. *Fletcher* (1779) 1 Doug KB 305; *Marsden* v. *Reid* (1803) 3 East 572; *Bell* v. *Carstairs* (1810) 2 Camp 543), but this approach was not universally approved (*Forrester* v. *Pigou* (1813) 1 M & S 9; *Robertson* v. *Marjoribanks* (1819) 2 Stark 573). The most recent authority indicates that an underwriter can avoid liability only when he has personally been given false information by the broker (*General Accident, Fire and Life Assurance Corporation* v. *Tanter, "The Zephyr"* [1985] 2 Lloyd's Rep 529; *Bank Leumi Le Israel BM* v. *British National Insurance Co Ltd* [1988] 1 Lloyd's Rep 71). See, however *Aneco Reinsurance Underwriting Ltd* v. *Johnson & Higgins* [1998] 1 Lloyd's Rep 565, where it was decided that the fact that a false statement has been made to the leading underwriter is a material fact which has to be disclosed to the following market.

Subs (2) For the general meaning of materiality, see s 18(2), page 16. A post-contractual misrepresentation is immaterial (*Ionides* v. *Pacific Insurance Co* (1871) LR 6 QB 674). There is authority for the proposition that a fraudulent misrepresentation always gives the insurer the right to avoid, whether or not it is material (*Sibbald* v. *Hill* (1814) 2 Dow 263; *"The Bedouin"* [1894] P 1), but this principle has not been incorporated into the statute and did not form part of the actual decisions.

Subs (3) The distinction between a representation of fact and one of expectation is hard to draw, but in general, an unequivocal statement is likely to be construed as one of fact (*Dennistoun* v. *Lillie* (1821) 3 Bli 202; *Highland Insurance* v. *Continental Insurance* [1987] 1 Lloyd's Rep 108; *Sirius International Insurance Corporation* v. *Oriental Assurance Corporation* [1999] Lloyd's Rep IR 343) whereas a statement as to a matter over which the assured has no control is more likely to be construed as a matter of expectation (*Bowden* v. *Vaughan* (1809) 10 East 415; *Hubbard* v. *Glover* (1812) 3 Camp 313). As far as opinions are concerned, see: *Brine* v. *Featherstone* (1813) 4 Taunt 869.

Subs (4) This is based on, eg, *Pawson* v. *Watson* (1778) 2 Cowp 785 and *Nonnen* v. *Kettlewell* (1812) 16 East 176. The meaning of the assured's statement must be judged in accordance with the custom and practice of the trade in question (*Chaurand* v. *Angerstein* (1791) Peake 43).

Subs (5) For illustrations of this provision, see: *Brine* v. *Featherstone* (1813) 4 Taunt 869; *Grant* v. *Aetna Insurance Co* (1862) 15 Moo PC 516; *Anderson* v. *Pacific Fire and Marine Insurance Co* (1872) LR 7 CP 65. It was confirmed in *Economides* v. *Commercial Union* [1997] 3 All ER 636 that if the assured is required to answer a question to the best of his knowledge and belief, and does so, the fact that he is objectively mistaken provides no defence to the insurer.

Subs (6) See, eg, *Edwards* v. *Footner* (1808) 1 Camp 530.

When contract is deemed to be concluded

21. A contract of marine insurance is deemed to be concluded when the proposal of the assured is accepted by the insurer, whether the policy be then issued or not; and, for the purpose of showing when the proposal was accepted, reference may be made to the slip or covering note or other customary memorandum of the contract,

. . .

NOTES

Section 21 was amended by the Finance Act 1959, Sched 8.

A slip is a binding contract in its own right (*Cory* v. *Patton* (1874) LR 9 QB 577), which cannot be varied by the policy itself. The contract is made as soon as the slip is initialled (*Ionides* v. *Pacific Insurance Co* (1871) LR 6 QB 674; *Morrison* v. *Universal Marine Insurance Co* (1873) LR 8 Ex 194; *Citizens' Insurance Co of Canada* v. *Parsons* (1881) 7 App Cas 96; *Thompson* v. *Adams* (1889) 23 QBD 361; *Tyser* v. *Shipowners' Syndicate* [1896] 1 QB 135; *Eagle Star Insurance Co Ltd* v. *Spratt* [1971] 2 Lloyd's Rep 116; *American Airlines Inc* v. *Hope* [1974] 2 Lloyd's Rep 301; *General Reinsurance Corporation* v. *Forskringsaktiebolaget Fennia Patria* [1983] 2 Lloyd's Rep 287; *Roadworks (1952) Ltd* v. *Charman* [1994] 2 Lloyd's Rep 99). This means that the slip cannot be varied once it has been initialled, although there is a customary exception to this where the slip has been oversubscribed, in which case a proportionate signing down of the underwriters' liabilities is permissible: the custom was recognised in *General Accident Fire and Life Assurance Corporation* v. *Tanter, "The Zephyr"* [1985] 2 Lloyd's Rep 529. In practice Lloyd's slips contain leading underwriter clauses, authorising the leading underwriter to accept amendments to the slip and thereby to bind all of the signatories to the slip: a leading underwriter clause in suitably wide terms authorises the leader to vary the risk or alter conditions laid down for the inception of the risk (*Barlee Marine Corporation* v. *Mountain, "The Leegas"* [1987] 1 Lloyd's Rep 471; *Roadworks (1952) Ltd* v. *Charman* [1994] 2 Lloyd's Rep 99). For the relationship between slip and policy, see the note to s 89 of the Marine Insurance Act 1906, page 92.

It is unclear whether a slip can be used in evidence to clarify an ambiguity in the policy itself. The slip was admitted for this purpose in *Lower Rhine & Wurtenburg Insurance Association* v. *Sedgwick* [1899] 1 QB 179, but the Court of Appeal's decision in *Youell* v. *Bland Welch (No 1)* [1992] 2 Lloyd's Rep 127 indicates that the slip probably cannot be admitted for this purpose, and cf *Punjab National Bank* v. *De Boinville* [1992] 1 Lloyd's Rep 7).

The Policy

Contract must be embodied in policy

22. Subject to the provisions of any statute, a contract of marine insurance is inadmissible in evidence unless it is embodied in a marine policy in accordance with this Act. The policy may be executed and issued either at the time when the contract is concluded, or afterwards.

NOTES

Although a contract of insurance may exist independently of a policy, eg where a slip has been initialled, the contract is unenforceable until a policy has been issued, as only the policy itself may be sued upon in the court (*Fisher* v. *Liverpool Marine Insurance Co* (1874) LR 9 QB 418; *Genforsikrings & Co* v. *Da Costa* [1911] 1 KB 137; *Re National Benefit Assurance Co Ltd* [1931] 1 Ch 46). However, there are cases in which an action has been heard at the instance of an assured not in possession of the policy (*Swan* v. *Maritime Insurance Co* [1907] 1 KB 116) and in *Eide UK Ltd* v. *Lowndes Lambert Group Ltd, The Sun Tender* [1998] 1 Lloyd's Rep 389 the Court of Appeal left open the question whether s 22 has the effect of rendering a marine contract unenforceable if the assured cannot produce the policy unless the policy itself so provided. The point is of the greatest significance where the broker has retained possession of the policy as security for premiums advanced by him on the assured's behalf in accordance with s 53 of the 1906 Act (see page 50). It is the practice of an insurer who has not issued a policy at the date of the loss not to plead s 22 as a defence but to issue a policy in order to allow the assured the right to commence proceedings (*Mead* v. *Davison* (1835) 3 Ad & El 303).

Section 22 does not apply to contracts of reinsurance or insurance falling within ss 1 and 2 of the Marine and Aviation (War Risks) Insurance Act 1952: see s 7 of the 1952 Act, page 112.

What policy must specify

23. A marine policy must specify—

(1) The name of the assured, or of some person who effects the insurance on his behalf:

(2)–(5) . . .

NOTES

Section 23 was amended by the Finance Act 1959, Sched 8. The section recognises the practice of a broker insuring in his own name on behalf of various persons interested in the policy (*Bell* v. *Gibson* (1798) 1 Bos & P 345). Where a policy is procured by an agent, the mere fact that a person is named in the policy as an assured is not sufficient to make him such: a person in this position may claim the benefit of the insurance only by demonstrating that the agent was authorised to insure on his behalf and intended to do so (*Sutherland* v. *Pratt* (1843) 12 M & W 16; *Boston Fruit Co* v. *British and Foreign Marine Insurance Co* [1905] 1 KB 637; *National Oilwell (UK) Ltd* v. *Davy Offshore Ltd* [1993] 2 Lloyd's Rep 582). Conversely, where the agent is authorised to act on the assured's behalf, the assured's name need not appear in the policy and the assured is entitled to the benefit of the policy on the basis of the undisclosed principal doctrine provided that the agent intended to effect the policy on the assured's behalf (*Yangtse Insurance Association* v. *Lukmanjee* [1918] AC 585; *National Oilwell (UK) Ltd* v. *Davy Offshore Ltd* [1993] 2 Lloyd's Rep 582).

Signature of insurer

24.—(1) A marine policy must be signed by or on behalf of the insurer, provided that in the case of a corporation the corporate seal may be sufficient, but nothing in this section shall be construed as requiring the subscription of a corporation to be under seal.

(2) Where a policy is subscribed by or on behalf or two or more insurers, each subscription, unless the contrary be expressed, constitutes a distinct contract with the assured.

NOTES

Subs (2) The notion that a policy constitutes a bundle of individual contracts was confirmed by the House of Lords in *Touche Ross* v. *Baker* [1992] 2 Lloyd's Rep 207, where it was held that each subscribing underwriter was separately bound by the obligations in the policy. The point is further illustrated by the Lloyd's rule that each separate "scratching" of the slip constitutes a separate contract, made when the slip is scratched (see the note to s 21, page 25).

Voyage and time policies

25.—(1) Where the contract is to insure the subject-matter "at and from", or from one place to another or others, the policy is called a "voyage policy", and where the contract is to insure the subject-matter for a definite period of time the policy is called a "time policy". A contract for both voyage and time may be included in the same policy.

(2) . . .

NOTES

Section 25 was amended by the Finance Act 1959, Sched 8.

The distinction between voyage and time policies is important for the following reasons:

   (a) a voyage policy is subject to the warranty of seaworthiness in s 39(1), whereas a time policy is subject to the rather lesser seaworthiness constraints of s 39(5) (see page 37);

   (b) different rules apply to the commencement and termination of the risk under the two types of policy (see s 42 of the Marine Insurance Act 1906, page 41);

   (c) voyage policies are avoided where the assured deviates, delays or changes the voyage (Marine Insurance Act 1906, ss 44–49, pages 44 *et seq*, whereas no such limits are placed upon time policies.

A policy may contain both time and voyage elements (*Way* v. *Modigliani* (1787) 2 TR 30), eg where a policy is for a fixed time but the assured is held covered if the voyage has not been completed by the expiry of the policy (Institute Time Clauses Hulls, cl 2): such a policy is to be treated as "mixed" and takes effect as a time policy followed by a voyage policy, so that, for example, rules as to deviation do not apply once the policy has been converted from voyage to time (*Gambles* v. *Ocean Insurance Co* (1876) 1 Ex D 141; *Maritime Insurance Co* v. *Alianza Insurance Co of Santander* (1907) 13 Com Cas 46; *Royal Exchange Assurance Corporation* v. *Sjoforsakrings Aktibolaget Vega* [1902] 2 KB 384).

A policy remains a time policy despite the fact that it is renewable and that it may be determined by notice prior to the stated date of termination (*Compania Maritima San Basilio SA* v. *Oceanus Mutual Underwriting Association (Bermuda) Ltd, "The Eurysthenes"* [1976] 2 Lloyd's Rep 171). Equally, it is perfectly consistent for a time policy to contain geographical restrictions on the area of trading, so that a relaxation of those restrictions does not give rise to a voyage policy (*Kim Yuen Co Pte Ltd* v. *Lombard Insurance Co Ltd* (1995) *Lloyd's List*, 26 April).

Designation of subject-matter

26.—(1) The subject-matter insured must be designated in a marine policy with reasonable certainty.

(2) The nature and extent of the interest of the assured in the subject-matter insured need not be specified in the policy.

(3) Where the policy designates the subject-matter insured in general terms, it shall be construed to apply to the interest intended by the assured to be covered.

(4) In the application of this section regard shall be had to any usage regulating the designation of the subject-matter insured.

NOTES

Subs (1) For illustrations, see: *Le Mesurier* v. *Vaughan* (1805) 6 East 382; *Ionides* v. *Pacific Insurance Co* (1871) LR 6 QB 674; *Denoon* v. *Home and Colonial Assurance Co* (1872) LR 7 CP 341; *Mackenzie* v. *Whitworth* (1875) 1 Ex D 36; *Overseas Commodities Ltd* v. *Style* [1958] 1 Lloyd's Rep 546 (cover applying only to subject-matter complying with policy description).

Subs (2) Neither is such interest a material fact: see the note to s 4 of the 1906 Act, page 6.

Subs (3) The effect of this subsection is unclear, as in some cases the intention of the assured has overriden policy wording (*Janson* v. *Poole* (1915) 20 Com Cas 232) whereas in others the assured has been allowed the benefit of the wording despite want of intention to insure that widely (*Reliance Marine Insurance Co* v. *Duder* [1913] 1 KB 265). In the case of a floating policy which designates the subject-matter in general terms, subs (3) confines the assured's recovery to his own interest (*Stephens* v. *Australasian Insurance Co* (1872) LR 8 CP 18; *Scott* v. *Globe Marine Insurance Co* (1896) 1 Com Cas 370; *Dunlop Brothers* v. *Townend* [1919] 2 KB 127). The subsection does not have the effect of making a named person a party to the policy, in the absence of the necessary agency relationship between the agent taking out the policy and that person (*National Oilwell (UK) Ltd* v. *Davy Offshore Ltd* [1993] 2 Lloyd's Rep 582).

Valued policy

27.—(1) A policy may be either valued or unvalued.

(2) A valued policy is a policy which specifies the agreed value of the subject-matter insured.

(3) Subject to the provisions of this Act, and in the absence of fraud, the value fixed by the policy is, as between the insurer and assured, conclusive of the insurable value of the subject intended to be insured, whether the loss be total or partial.

(4) Unless the policy otherwise provides, the value fixed by the policy is not conclusive for the purpose of determining whether there has been a constructive total loss.

NOTES

Subs (1) The validity of valued policies was confirmed by *Lewis* v. *Rucker* (1761) 2 Burr 1167, where it was held that an agreement by the parties as to the basis of indemnity did not render the contract void as a wager. In practice most marine policies are valued. It is now clear that a valued policy is perfectly valid even though the indemnity given to the assured is far from perfect (*Irving* v. *Manning* (1847) 1 HL Cas 287).

Subs (2) Under a valued policy the value of the subject-matter is agreed and the premium is calculated on that value (*Bousfield* v. *Barnes* (1815) 4 Camp 228). A policy is not valued merely because the assured is required to state the value of the insured subject-matter (*Wilson* v. *Nelson* (1864) 33 LJQB 220).

Subs (3) Once the insurer has accepted the premium based on the agreed value, it is not open to the insurer to contest the valuation for any reason (*Barker* v. *Janson* (1868) LR 3 CP 303; *Herring* v. *Janson* (1895) 1 Com Cas 177; *Muirhead* v. *Forth & North Sea Steamboat Mutual Insurance Association* [1894] 2 AC 72; *"The Main"* [1894] P 320) unless:

    (a) the assured has been guilty of fraud in presenting the valuation (*Lewis* v. *Rucker* (1761) 2 Burr 1167, *Haigh* v. *De La Cour* (1812) 3 Camp 319—overvaluation is not enough, as is demonstrated by *General Shipping and Forwarding Co* v. *British General*

Insurance Co Ltd (1923) 15 Ll LR 175 and *Papademetriou* v. *Henderson* (1939) 64 Ll LR 345); or

(b) the assured has overvalued the subject-matter in a material fashion and has failed to disclose, or has misrepresented, the valuation (see the note to s 18(2) of the Marine Insurance Act 1906, page 16); or

(c) in the case of a floating policy, the value of each declaration has not been honestly stated (Marine Insurance Act 1906, s 29(3), below).

In the event of a total loss, the assured recovers the full value of the subject-matter, subject to policy limits (*Steamship Balmoral Co* v. *Marten* [1902] AC 511). If the assured is over-insured by double insurance, he recovers only a sum representing the agreed value (Marine Insurance Act 1906, s 32(2)(a)). In the event of a partial loss, the assured recovers the proportion of the agreed value representing the degree of loss. Thus, if subject-matter valued at £100,000 suffers a 50 per cent loss, the assured recovers £50,000, irrespective of the actual market value of the subject-matter (*Thompson* v. *Reynolds* (1857) 26 LJQB 93; *"The Main"* [1894] P 320). This measure is, however, subject to the other provisions of the 1906 Act: see in particular s 69 of the Act, page 72, which lays down market value rules for calculating indemnity for a damaged vessel. The agreed value is also disregarded in determining the insurer's subrogation rights: see the note to s 79, page 82.

Subs (4) The definition of constructive total loss in s 60 of the 1906 Act, page 62, refers to repaired and unrepaired values. The effect of subs (4) is to require market values rather than the agreed value to be used as the basis of calculation. See: *Irving* v. *Manning* (1847) 1 HL Cas 287; *Woodside* v. *Globe Marine Insurance Co Ltd* [1896] 1 QB 105; *Helmville Ltd* v. *Yorkshire Insurance Co Ltd, "The Medina Princess"* [1965] 1 Lloyd's Rep 361, and Marine Insurance Act 1906, s 60(2)(ii).

Unvalued policy

28. An unvalued policy is a policy which does not specify the value of the subject-matter insured, but, subject to the limit of the sum insured, leaves the insurable value to be subsequently ascertained, in the manner herein-before specified.

NOTES

A policy which imposes financial limits on the amount recoverable is not a valued policy for the purposes of this section (*Continental Illinois National Bank and Trust Co of Chicago* v. *Bathurst* [1985] 1 Lloyd's Rep 625). The amount recoverable in the absence of a valuation for indemnity purposes is based on the insurable value, as set out in s 16 of the Marine Insurance Act 1906 (see page 13).

Floating policy by ship or ships

29.—(1) A floating policy is a policy which describes the insurance in general terms, and leaves the name of the ship or ships and other particulars to be defined by subsequent declaration.

(2) The subsequent declaration or declarations may be made by indorsement on the policy, or in other customary manner.

(3) Unless the policy otherwise provides, the declarations must be made in the order of dispatch or shipment. They must, in the case of goods, comprise all consignments within the terms of the policy, and the value of the goods or other property must be honestly stated, but an omission or erroneous declaration may be

rectified even after loss or arrival, provided the omission or declaration was made in good faith.

(4) Unless the policy otherwise provides, where a declaration of value is not made until after notice of loss or arrival, the policy must be treated as an unvalued policy as regards the subject-matter of that declaration.

NOTES

Subs (1) A floating policy is a framework agreement under which the insurer agrees to insure subject-matter of a given description which is subsequently at the assured's risk. A floating cover will become exhausted when the financial limits are reached, and it is common for the assured to arrange a further policy covering excess risks. The assured merely has to declare each risk as and when it incepts, and the insurer is liable for any loss following declaration. In the absence of any declaration, the insurer is not on risk in respect of that particular subject-matter (*Union Insurance Society of Canton Ltd* v. *Wills & Co* [1916] 1 AC 281). Floating policies are used primarily for cargo insurance, and may be procured by warehousemen and carriers.

The application of the doctrine of utmost good faith depends upon the nature of the policy. If the insurer is obliged to cover any risk declared by the assured, the assured's duty of utmost good faith attaches to the open cover itself but not to subsequent declarations (*Glasgow Assurance Corporation Ltd* v. *William Symondson & Co* (1911) 16 Com Cas 109), but if the floating policy gives the insurer the right to reject individual declarations the duty of utmost good faith is relevant only at declaration stage (*SAIL* v. *Farex Gie* [1995] LRLR 116). Cf the note to s 17 of the 1906 Act, page 14.

Subs (3) As to the common law basis for the rule as to the order of declaration, see: *Henchman* v. *Offley* (1782) 3 Doug KB 135; *Kewley* v. *Ryan* (1794) 2 Hy Bl 343; *Gledstanes* v. *Royal Exchange Assurance Co* (1864) 5 B & S 797; *Ionides* v. *Pacific Fire and Marine Insurance Co Ltd* (1871) LR 6 QB 674; *Dunlop Bros & Co* v. *Townend* [1919] 2 KB 127. The right to rectify a declaration, even after a loss, is based upon: *Robinson* v. *Touray* (1811) 3 Camp 158; *Stephens* v. *Australasian Insurance Co* (1872) LR 8 CP 18; *Imperial Marine Insurance Co* v. *Fire Insurance Corporation* (1879) 4 CPD 166.

Subs (4) See: *Harman* v. *Kingston* (1811) 3 Camp 150; *Gledstanes* v. *Royal Exchange Assurance Corporation* (1864) 34 LJQB 30; *Union Insurance Society of Canton Ltd* v. *George Wills & Co* [1916] 1 AC 281.

Construction of terms in policy

30.—(1) A policy may be in the form in the First Schedule to this Act.

(2) Subject to the provisions of this Act, and unless the context of the policy otherwise requires, the terms and expressions mentioned in the First Schedule to this Act shall be construed as having the scope and meaning in that schedule assigned to them.

NOTES

The form of policy set out in the First Schedule was abandoned in the UK in 1983, after usage of some 200 years. The modern practice is to attach to a simple front-sheet a set of standard terms published by the Institute of London Underwriters (modified where appropriate).

The construction of a marine policy is governed by a series of well developed rules, which indicate that the starting point is that the intentions of the parties must prevail. The meaning of individual words or phrases may depend upon context, the *ejusdem generis* rule and the principle that legal terms of art are afforded their technical meaning by way of exception to the general rule that the ordinary and natural meaning of words should prevail. Further, where a term has acquired a recognised meaning in the courts, the doctrine of precedent will apply in order to ensure consistency, and it will be permissible to introduce evidence of custom and usage for the construction of particular terminology provided it can be shown that both parties were aware of the custom or usage of the market and that the parties have not expressly agreed to the contrary (*Brough* v. *Whitmore* (1791) 4 TR 206; *Blackett* v. *Royal Exchange Assurance Co* (1832) 2 Cr & J 244; *Gabay* v. *Lloyd* (1825) 3 B & C 793, and cf s 87 of the Marine Insurance Act 1906, page 91). Within an individual policy, the courts will give priority to added words as opposed to printed words (*Robertson* v. *French* (1803) 4 East 130; *Dudgeon* v. *Pembroke* (1877) 2 App Cas 284). In the event of a genuine ambiguity the doctrine of *contra proferentem* will be applied (as in *Lawrence* v. *Aberdein* (1821) 5 B & Ald 107), although this is likely to be of little import in commercial cases (cf *Youell* v. *Bland Welch (No 1)* [1990] 2 Lloyd's Rep 423), and it should also be remembered that if the ambiguity arises in wording proposed by the assured or his broker the ambiguity is to be construed in favour of the insurer (*A/S Ocean* v. *Black Sea & Baltic General Insurance Co Ltd* (1935) 51 Ll LR 305; *Abrahams* v. *Mediterranean Insurance and Reinsurance Co Ltd* [1991] 1 Lloyd's Rep 216).

For the significance of the "factual matrix" as an aid to construction, see *Investors Compensation Scheme* v. *West Bromwich Building Society* [1998] 1 WLR 896.

Premium to be arranged

31.—(1) Where an insurance is effected at a premium to be arranged, and no arrangement is made, a reasonable premium is payable.

(2) Where an insurance is effected on the terms that an additional premium is to be arranged in a given event, and that event happens but no arrangement is made, then a reasonable additional premium is payable.

NOTES

The principle of s 31, that in the absence of agreement a reasonable premium is payable, is one familiar in the English law of sale of goods (Sale of Goods Act 1979, s 8) and the supply of services (Supply of Goods and Services Act 1982, s 15). What is reasonable is a question of fact (Marine Insurance Act 1906, s 88). If the premium due is not paid, the insurer is not obliged to issue the policy (Marine Insurance Act 1906, s 52, page 50).

Subs (1) This deals with the case in which the premium is not agreed at the outset.

Subs (2) This deals with the case in which the insurer agrees, under a "held covered" clause, to accept an additional risk during the currency of the policy, eg where the policy has expired before the voyage has been completed (Institute Cargo Clauses, cl 9, Institute Time Clauses Hulls, cl 2), or where the assured has broken a warranty (Institute Time Clauses Hulls, cl 3) or has deviated or changed voyage (Institute Cargo Clauses, cl 10; Institute Voyage Clauses Hulls, cl 2). In the case of extension of cover, it is usual for the insurer to agree to be held covered on payment of a *pro rata* premium, but in other cases the held covered clause requires the assured to meet two conditions.

  (a) To give prompt notice of the event bringing the clause into operation (the old contractual requirement to give notice within a reasonable time having been discontinued in 1983 in the light of decisions to the effect that notice could be given after loss: *Mentz, Decker & Co* v. *Maritime Insurance Co* (1909) 15 Com Cas 17; *Hewitt* v. *London General Insurance Co* (1925) 23 Ll LR 243)—for a discussion of the meaning of "prompt", see *Liberian Insurance Agency* v. *Mosse* [1977] 2 Lloyd's Rep 560.

  (b) To agree on an additional premium or, in the case of the continuation of an existing policy for an additional period, a *pro rata* premium. If additional premium has to be agreed upon, and no agreement is reached, the court will look to the market rate for the risk as affected by the variation (*Greenock SS Co* v. *Maritime Insurance Co Ltd* [1903] 1 KB 367). If there is no market rate for the risk, the held covered clause cannot operate (*Liberian Insurance Agency* v. *Mosse* [1977] 2 Lloyd's Rep 560).

Double Insurance

Double insurance

32.—(1) Where two or more policies are effected by or on behalf of the assured on the same adventure and interest or any part thereof, and the sums insured exceed the indemnity allowed by this Act, the assured is said to be over-insured by double insurance.

(2) Where the assured is over-insured by double insurance—

(a) The assured, unless the policy otherwise provides, may claim payment from the insurers in such order as he may think fit, provided that he is not entitled to receive any sum in excess of the indemnity allowed by this Act;

(b) Where the policy under which the assured claims is a valued policy, the assured must give credit as against the valuation for any sum received by him under any other policy without regard to the actual value of the subject-matter insured;

(c) Where the policy under which the assured claims is an unvalued policy he must give credit, as against the full insurable value, for any sum received by him under any other policy;

(d) Where the assured receives any sum in excess of the indemnity allowed by this Act, he is deemed to hold such sum in trust for the insurers, according to their right of contribution among themselves.

NOTES

Subs (1) A distinction has to be drawn between double insurance as here defined (based on *Godin* v. *London Assurance Co* (1758) 1 Burr 489 and *North British & Mercantile Insurance Co* v. *London, Liverpool & Globe Insurance Co* (1877) 5 Ch D 569) and the issue of one policy in substitution for another, as in *Union Marine Insurance* v. *Martin* (1866) 35 LJCP 181. Equally, an increased value policy does not overlap with the original policy (*Boag* v. *Economic Insurance Co Ltd* [1954] 2 Lloyd's Rep 581).

Subs (2)(a) The purpose of this provision is to allow the assured the benefit of double insurance in the event that one of the insurers becomes insolvent (*Newby* v. *Reed* (1763) 1 W Bl 416; *Bousfield* v. *Barnes* (1815) 4 Camp 228; *Morgan* v. *Price* (1849) 4 Exch 615; *Bruce* v. *Jones* (1863) 1 H & C 769). Where the assured has claimed a disproportionate sum from one of the insurers, that insurer has a right of contribution from the others, so that each will ultimately pay its proportionate part of the loss (see s 80 of the Marine Insurance Act 1906, page 86). As is anticipated by subs (2)(a), policies commonly provide that the assured is unable to recover from the insurer in the event that some other policy covers the loss. Alternatively, a policy may contain a rateable proportion clause, under which the assured is restricted to recovering from that insurer its own proportion of the loss, ie, the amount which it would have paid net of contribution recoveries (*Legal & General Assurance Society* v. *Drake Insurance Co Ltd* [1992] 1 All ER 283).

Subs (2)(b) The effect here is that if the assured is underinsured under a valued policy, and first claims part of his loss from another valued or unvalued policy, the amount recoverable under the valued policy is the difference between the agreed value and the sum previously recovered, thereby leaving a potential shortfall. This is based on: *Irving* v. *Richardson* (1831) 2 B & Ad 193; *Bruce* v. *Jones* (1863) 1 H & C 769 (*contra Bousfield* v. *Barnes* (1815) 4 Camp 228). To avoid this, the first claim must be made on any valued policy.

Subs (2)(c) See the note to subs (2)(b) above.

Subs (2)(d) For the right of contribution, see Marine Insurance Act 1906, s 80, page 86.

Warranties, etc

Nature of warranty

33.—(1) A warranty, in the following sections relating to warranties, means a promissory warranty, that is to say, a warranty by which the assured undertakes that some particular thing shall or shall not be done, or that some condition shall be fulfilled, or whereby he affirms or negatives the existence of a particular state of facts.

(2) A warranty may be express or implied.

(3) A warranty, as above defined, is a condition which must be exactly complied with, whether it be material to the risk or not. If it be not so complied with, then, subject to any express provision in the policy, the insurer is discharged from liability as from the date of the breach of warranty, but without prejudice to any liability incurred by him before that date.

NOTES

Subs (1) The word "promissory" encompasses both warranties as to existing facts or intentions (present warranties), and warranties as to future conduct (continuing warranties). In the absence of clear wording, a warranty will not be construed as relating to the assured's future conduct (*Hussain* v. *Brown* [1996] 1 Lloyd's Rep 627). Again, if the warranty is in the nature of an opinion or statement of intention by the assured, breach of warranty depends upon whether the assured held that opinion or intention and not on the assured's actual conduct at a later date; *Gerling-Konzern General Insurance Co* v. *Polygram Holdings*, 1998, unreported; *Arab Bank* v. *Zurich Insurance Ltd* [1999] 1 Lloyd's Rep 262. There is no need for a warranty to relate in any way to the likelihood of loss or the nature of the risk (*Woolmer* v. *Muilman* (1763) 1 Wm Bl 427; *Rich* v. *Parker* (1798) 7 TR 705; *Yorkshire Insurance Co Ltd* v. *Campbell* [1917] AC 218). A warranty on its proper construction may be restricted to material facts (see the discussion in *Unipac (Scotland) Ltd* v. *Aegon Insurance Co (UK) Ltd* [1997] Lloyd's Rep IR 502) or to a specific part of the policy (*Printpak* v. *AGF Insurance* [1999] Lloyd's Rep IR 542).

It is also necessary to distinguish a warranty proper from the description of the insured subject-matter in the policy. If the subject-matter fails to comply with its description the insurer is off risk for the duration of the default, whereas if a warranty is involved the insurer's liability is discharged and cannot be reinstated (cf s 33(3), below, and see *Provincial Insurance Co* v. *Morgan* [1933] AC 240 and *Kler Knitwear Ltd* v. *Lombard General Insurance Co Ltd* 1999, unreported, for the distinction).

The law on express warranties was developed in a series of old cases—now largely redundant in the light of the modern Institute wordings—concerning matters such as the number of crew (*Bean* v. *Stupart* (1778) 1 Doug 11; *De Hahn* v. *Hartley* (1786) 1 TR 343), the safety of the ship when the risk was to commence (*Kenyon* v. *Berthon* (1778) 1 Doug 12n; *Macdowell* v. *Fraser* (1779) 1 Doug 260; *Blackhurst* v. *Cockell* (1789) 3 TR 360; *Colby* v. *Hunter* (1827) 3 C & P 7), the time by or after which the vessel was to sail (as to which, see s 42 and the note thereto, page 41), the course of the voyage (*Colledge* v. *Harty* (1851) 6 Exch 205, and cf the rules on deviation and change of voyage, in ss 44–49, pages 44 *et seq*) and the requirement for the vessel to sail in convoy (*Hibbert* v. *Pigou* (1783) 3 Doug KB 224; *Anderson* v. *Pitcher* (1800) 2 Bos & P 164; *Sanderson* v. *Busher* (1814) 4 Camp 54n; *Warwick* v. *Scott* (1814) 4 Camp 62). The assured may also be required to warrant that he will retain part of the risk for his own account, thereby reducing the incentive for him to bring about his own loss: the retention remains important, particularly in reinsurance, and the assured or rein-sured will be in breach of the warranty by obtaining cover for that part of the risk to be retained by him (*Muirhead* v. *Forth & North Sea Steamboat Mutual Insurance Association* [1894] AC 72; *Roddick* v. *Indemnity Mutual Marine Insurance Co* [1895] 2 QB 380; *Samuel & Co Ltd* v. *Dumas* [1924] AC 431, but contrast *Lishman* v. *Northern Maritime Insurance Co* (1875) LR 10 CP 179, *General Insurance Co of Trieste* v. *Cory* [1897] 1 QB 335 and *General Shipping and Forwarding Co* v. *British General Insurance Co Ltd* (1923) 15 Ll LR 175 in each of which the warranty was not broken). The old method of excluding war risks from a marine policy was by means of a "free of capture and seizure" (fcs) warranty, but this wording has now fallen into disuse. For illustrations of the old wording, see: *Maydhew* v. *Scott* (1811) 3 Camp 205; *Dalgleish* v. *Brooke* (1812) 15 East 295.

Subs (2) Implied warranties are peculiar to marine insurance (*Euro-Diam Ltd* v. *Bathurst* [1988] 2 All ER 23), and are set out in ss 39–41 of the Marine Insurance Act 1906. See pages 37 *et seq*.

Subs (3) The doctrine of exact compliance means that if there is only a minor deviation from what is required by the warranty, the insurer is discharged from liability (*Bond* v. *Nutt* (1777) 2 Cowp 601; *Hore* v. *Whitmore* (1778) 2 Cowp 784; *Earle* v. *Harris* (1780) 1 Doug KB 357; *Sanderson* v. *Busher* (1814) 4 Camp 54n; *De Hahn* v. *Hartley* (1786) 1 TR 343; *Hart* v. *Standard Marine Insurance Co* (1889) 22 QBD 499; *Union Insurance Society of Canton* v. *George Wills & Co* [1916] AC 281; *Simons* v. *Gale* [1958] 2 All ER 504; *Overseas Commodities* v. *Style* [1958] 1 Lloyd's Rep 546). The strictness of the doctrine is tempered by a willingness in the courts to construe narrowly the obligations imposed by warranties. Thus a warranty that the vessel is carrying a particular cargo does not preclude the assured from carrying additional cargo (*Muller* v. *Thompson* (1811) 2 Camp 610). See also: *Hide* v. *Bruce* (1783) 3 Doug 213; *Laing* v. *Glover* (1813) 5 Taunt 49; *Hart* v. *Standard Marine Insurance Co Ltd* (1889) 22 QBD 499.

The saving in the case in which the policy provides otherwise, reflects "held covered" clauses, presently found in the Institute Clauses, under which the assured is held covered despite a breach of warranty provided that the assured gives prompt notice to the insurer and pays an additional premium. See the note to s 31, page 31.

The principle that the insurer is discharged from liability on breach, whether or not the insurer is aware of the breach at that date, was established by the House of Lords in *Bank of Nova Scotia* v. *Hellenic Mutual War Risks Association (Bermuda) Ltd, "The Good Luck"* [1991] 3 All ER 1, relying on *Provincial Insurance Co of Canada* v. *Leduc* (1874) LR 6 PC 224). Losses which have accrued prior to the date of the assured's breach remain payable under the policy. This necessarily applies only to breaches of a continuing warranty, as in the case of a present warranty the insurer never comes on risk as in *Arab Bank* v. *Zurich Insurance Ltd* [1999] 1 Lloyd's Rep 262. If the loss occurs prior to breach, the insurer remains liable (*Woolmer* v. *Muilman* (1763) 2 Burr 1419; *Simpson SS Co Ltd* v. *Premier Underwriting Association Ltd* (1905) 92 LT 730). Equally, once a warranty has been broken, the insurer is off risk and the assured cannot reinstate the risk by complying with the warranty following its breach (*De Hahn* v. *Hartley* (1786) 1 TR 343; *Forshaw* v. *Chabert* (1821) 3 Brod & Bing 158; *Foley* v. *Tabor* (1861) 2 F & F 663; *Quebec Marine Insurance Co* v. *Commercial Bank of Canada* (1870) LR 3 PC 234). The point is graphically illustrated by *J A Chapman & Co Ltd* v. *Kadirga*

Denizcilik Ve Ticaret [1998] Lloyd's Rep IR 377, in which the late payment of an instalment of premium put the assured in breach of a premium warranty clause, putting an end to the risk under the policy but leaving untouched the assured's liability to pay the full amount of the premium.

There must be actual breach of warranty before the insurer is discharged, and not merely an anticipated or intended breach (*Baines* v. *Holland* (1855) 10 Exch 802; *Simpson SS Co* v. *Premier Underwriting Association* (1905) 10 Com Cas 198).

A policy may oust the right of an insurer to rely upon breach of warranty as giving rise to automatic termination of the risk: in such a case, the insurer retains a right to claim damages for breach of contract (*Kumar* v. *AGF Insurance Ltd* [1998] 4 All ER 788).

When breach of warranty excused

34.—(1) Non-compliance with a warranty is excused when, by reason of a change of circumstances, the warranty ceases to be applicable to the circumstances of the contract, or when compliance with the warranty is rendered unlawful by any subsequent law.

(2) Where a warranty is broken, the assured cannot avail himself of the defence that the breach has been remedied, and the warranty complied with, before loss.

(3) A breach of warranty may be waived by the insurer.

NOTES

Subs (1) For illustrations of these situations, see: *Hore* v. *Whitmore* (1778) 2 Cowp 784; *Esposito* v. *Bowden* (1857) 7 E & B 763.

Subs (2) There are many reported instances of this: *De Hahn* v. *Hartley* (1786) 1 TR 343 (warranty as to number of crew); *Quebec Marine Insurance Co* v. *Commercial Bank of Canada* (1870) LR 3 PC 234 (seaworthiness).

Subs (3) Waiver arises where the insurer, having become aware of the assured's breach of duty, equivocally represents by word or conduct that he does not intend to rely on the breach of warranty (*Weir* v. *Aberdeen* (1819) 2 B & Ald 320; *Samuel & Co Ltd* v. *Dumas* [1924] AC 431). Contrast *Sleigh* v. *Tyser* [1900] 2 QB 333. In particular, the insurer is taken to have waived a breach when he accepts a notice of abandonment in full knowledge of the breach (*Quebec Marine Insurance Co* v. *Commercial Bank of Canada* (1870) LR 3 PC 234; *Provincial Insurance Co* v. *Leduc* (1874) LR 6 PC 224; *Samuel & Co* v. *Dumas* [1924] AC 431). It is not possible to waive breach of the implied warranty of legality (Marine Insurance Act 1906, s 41—see page 40), as the issue is one of public policy rather than private contract (*Gedge* v. *Royal Exchange Assurance Corporation* [1900] 2 QB 214). Waiver by the insurer leaves the risk intact, but exposes the assured to an action for damages for breach of contract (*Kumar* v. *AGF Insurance* [1998] 4 All ER 788). As a result of the doctrine of automatic termination, "waiver" in the present context requires positive affirmation by the insurer: *J Kirkaldy & Sons* v. *Walker* [1999] Lloyd's Rep IR 410.

Standard policy wording waives certain breaches of warranty: the warranty of seaworthiness is waived in relation to cargo policies unless the assured was privy to the unseaworthiness (Institute Cargo Clauses, cl 5.2).

Express warranties

35.—(1) An express warranty may be in any form of words from which the intention to warrant is to be inferred.

(2) An express warranty must be included in, or written upon, the policy, or must be contained in some document incorporated by reference into the policy.

(3) An express warranty does not exclude an implied warranty, unless it be inconsistent therewith.

NOTES

Subs (1) The use of the word warranty is not essential for the creation of a warranty (*Union Insurance Society of Canton Ltd* v. *George Wills & Co* [1916] AC 281). Equally, the fact that a term is described as a warranty does not make it one without more (*CTN Cash & Carry* v. *General Accident Fire and Life Assurance Corporation* [1989] 1 Lloyd's Rep 299).

Subs (2) The most common method of creating warranties is by means of a declaration on the proposal form to the effect that the proposal form is to be the "basis of the contract" between the parties, a form of wording which is settled as creating a warranty (*Yorkshire Insurance Co* v. *Campbell* [1917] AC 218; *Samuel & Co Ltd* v. *Dumas* [1924] AC 431) providing that it is not limited to material facts, in which case the warranty adds nothing to s 20 of the Act (*Fowkes* v. *Manchester & London Life Assurance Co* (1863) 3 B & S 917; *Hemmings* v. *Sceptre Life Association* [1905] 1 Ch 365; *Unipac (Scotland) Ltd* v. *Aegon Insurance Co* [1999] Lloyd's Rep IR 502). Warranties were in earlier times attached to standard policy wordings, and it was ultimately established that this form of attachment did not preclude a term from becoming a warranty (*Bensuade* v. *Thames and Mersey Marine Insurance Co* [1897] AC 609, doubting *Pawson* v. *Watson* (1778) 1 Doug KB 12n).

Subs (3) This is illustrated by *Sleigh* v. *Tyser* [1900] 2 QB 333.

Warranty of neutrality

36.—(1) Where insurable property, whether ship or goods, is expressly warranted neutral, there is an implied condition that the property shall have a neutral character at the commencement of the risk, and that, so far as the assured can control the matter, its neutral character shall be preserved during the risk.

(2) Where a ship is expressly warranted "neutral" there is also an implied condition that, so far as the assured can control the matter, she shall be properly documented, that is to say, that she shall carry the necessary papers to establish her neutrality, and that she shall not falsify or suppress her papers, or use simulated papers. If any loss occurs through breach of this condition, the insurer may avoid the contract.

NOTES

Subs (1) There is no common law implied warranty of neutrality (*Tyson* v. *Gurney* (1789) 3 TR 477; *Baring* v. *Claggett* (1802) 3 B & P 201; *Lothian* v. *Henderson* (1803) 3 B & P 499). An express warranty of neutrality imposes an absolute obligation as regards the position when the risk incepts (*Tabbs* v. *Bendelack* (1801) 3 Bos & P 207n; *Baring* v. *Christie* (1804) 5 East 398), and thereafter the warranty is subject to the ability of the assured to control the matter. If a vessel loses its neutrality for reasons beyond the assured's control, such as outbreak of war, there is no breach of warranty (*Eden* v. *Parkinson* (1781) 2 Doug 732), whereas if neutrality is lost due to the assured's fault, eg because the vessel has disobeyed the rules of neutrality, the warranty is broken (*Garrels* v. *Kensington* (1799) 8 TR 230). Many of the cases concern the question, generally answered in the affirmative, whether the ruling of a foreign prize court as to the neutrality of a vessel can be regarded as conclusive evidence as to neutrality for the purposes of a warranty (*Baring* v. *Claggett* (1802) 3 Bos & P 201; *Lothian* v. *Henderson* (1803) 3 Bos & P 499; *Bolton* v. *Gladstone* (1809) 2 Taunt 85).

Subs (2) For the common law basis, see: *Barzillai* v. *Lewis* (1782) 3 Doug KB 126; *Rich* v. *Parker* (1798) 7 TR 705; *Steel* v. *Lacy* (1810) 3 Taunt 285). The insurer is required to show that the documents carried by the vessel were inappropriate (*Le Cheminant* v. *Pearson* (1812) 4 Taunt 367). As to seizure while carrying simulated papers, see: *Oswell* v. *Vigne* (1812) 15 East 70; *Bell* v. *Bromfield* (1812) 15 East 364. The warranty may be waived by prior permission given by the insurer (*Bell* v. *Bromfield* (1812) 15 East 364).

The warranty applies only to the vessel, so that cargo lost as a result of improper documentation may be claimed for under a cargo policy (*Dawson* v. *Atty* (1806) 7 East 367; *Bell* v. *Carstairs* (1811) 14 East 374; *Carruthers* v. *Gray* (1811) 3 Camp 142).

The warranty is unique in that, by the terms of s 36(2) itself, the insurer is able to avoid the policy only where the breach has caused the loss.

No implied warranty of nationality

37. There is no implied warranty as to the nationality of a ship, or that her nationality shall not be changed during the risk.

NOTES

This is based on: *Eden* v. *Parkinson* (1781) 2 Doug KB 732; *Tyson* v. *Gurney* (1789) 3 TR 477; *Clapham* v. *Cologan* (1813) 3 Camp 382; *Dent* v. *Smith* (1869) LR 4 QB 414. In *Seavision Investment SA* v. *Evennett and Clarkson Puckle, "The Tiburon"* [1990] 2 Lloyd's Rep 418 it was held that the warranty refers to the nationality of the legal owner of the vessel and not to the beneficial owner (eg, the main shareholder in the assured company).

Warranty of good safety

38. Where the subject-matter insured is warranted "well" or "in good safety" on a particular day, it is sufficient if it be safe at any time during that day.

NOTES

This is based on *Blackhurst* v. *Cockell* (1789) 3 TR 360.

Warranty of seaworthiness of ship

39.—(1) In a voyage policy there is an implied warranty that at the commencement of the voyage the ship shall be seaworthy for the purpose of the particular adventure insured.

(2) Where the policy attaches while the ship is in port, there is also an implied warranty that she shall, at the commencement of the risk, be reasonably fit to encounter the ordinary perils of the port.

(3) Where the policy relates to a voyage which is performed in different stages, during which the ship requires different kinds of or further preparation or equipment, there is an implied warranty that at the commencement of each stage the ship is seaworthy in respect of such preparation or equipment for the purposes of that stage.

(4) A ship is deemed to be seaworthy when she is reasonably fit in all respects to encounter the ordinary perils of the seas of the adventure insured.

(5) In a time policy there is no implied warranty that the ship shall be seaworthy at any stage of the adventure, but where, with the privity of the assured, the ship is sent to sea in an unseaworthy state, the insurer is not liable for any loss attributable to unseaworthiness.

NOTES

Section 39 draws a distinction between voyage and time policies (as to which, see *Biccard* v. *Shepherd* (1861) 14 Moo PCC 471). Under a voyage policy there is a full warranty of seaworthiness of the vessel (s 39(1)–(4)). By contrast, under a time policy, there is no warranty of seaworthiness as such and the assured is precluded from recovering only where the assured was aware of the unseaworthiness and the loss was to some extent the result of that unseaworthiness. In all cases the seaworthiness must be assessed at the commencement of the voyage, so that the insurer is not discharged when a vessel subsequently becomes unseaworthy (*Dixon* v. *Sadler* (1841) 8 M & W 895—negligent conduct by crew, and see the note to s 55 of the 1906 Act, page 53). In practice, insurers require condition surveys of vessels prior to the inception of risk; as to what constitutes a proper survey, see *Zeus Tradition (Marine)* v. *Bell* [1999] 1 Lloyd's Rep 703 and *J Kirkaldy & Sons Ltd* v. *Walker* [1999] Lloyd's Rep IR 410.

The burden of proving unseaworthiness rests on the insurer (*Pickup* v. *Thames and Mersey Marine Insurance Co Ltd* (1878) 3 QBD 594; *Ajum Goolam Hossen & Co* v. *Union Marine Insurance Co* [1901] AC 362). The mere fact that a vessel goes down may in some cases be *prima facie* evidence of unseaworthiness (*Parker* v. *Potts* (1815) 3 Dow 23; *Douglas* v. *Scougall* (1816) 4 Dow 276), although this is a secondary question as the assured will not be able to claim unless he can demonstrate that an insured peril was operative at the time of the loss (*Rhesa Shipping Co* v. *Edmunds, "The Popi M"* [1985] 2 Lloyd's Rep 1; *Lamb Head Shipping Co Ltd* v. *Jennings, "The Marel"* [1992] 1 Lloyd's Rep 402).

Seaworthiness may relate to: the condition of the vessel (*Wilkie* v. *Geddes* (1815) 3 Dow 57; *Quebec Marine Insurance Co Ltd* v. *Commercial Bank of Canada* (1870) LR 3 PC 234; *Turnbull* v. *Janson* (1877) 36 LT 635; *Hoffman & Co* v. *British General Insurance Co* (1922) 10 Ll LR 434; *Neue Fischmehl Vertriebs-Gesellschaft Haselhorst mbH* v. *Yorkshire Insurance Co Ltd* (1934) 50 Ll LR 151; *Silcock & Sons Ltd* v. *Maritime Lighterage Co Ltd* (1937) 57 Ll LR 78; *Manifest Shipping Co Ltd* v. *Uni-Polaris Insurance Co Ltd, "The Star Sea"* [1995] 1 Lloyd's Rep 651); the vessel's failure to comply with the servicing requirements of its classification society (*Stewart* v. *Wilson* (1843) 2 M & W 11); the supplies carried by the vessel (*Woolf* v. *Claggett* (1800) 3 Esp 257; *Wilkie* v. *Geddes* (1815) 3 Dow 57; *Wedderburn* v. *Bell* (1807) 1 Camp 1; *Quebec Marine Insurance Co* v. *Commercial Bank of Canada* (1870) LR 3 PC 234); the number or competence of the crew (*Annen* v. *Woodman* (1810) 3 Taunt 299; *Tait* v. *Levi* (1811) 14 East 481; *Busk* v. *Royal Exchange Assurance Co* (1818) 2 B & Ald 73; *Forshaw* v. *Chabert* (1821) 3 Brod & Bing 158; *Clifford* v. *Hunter* (1827) 3 C & P 16; *Holdsworth* v. *Wise* (1828) 7 B & C 794; *Phillips* v. *Headlam* (1831) 2 B & Ad 383; *Thomas* v. *Tyne & Wear Insurance Association* [1917] 1 KB 938; *Thomas & Son Shipping Co Ltd* v. *London & Provincial Marine & General Insurance Co Ltd* (1914) 30 TLR 595; *The Star Sea* [1995] 1 Lloyd's Rep 651), including the use of a pilot to navigate the vessel into and out of port (*Phillips* v. *Headlam* (1831) 2 B & Ad 380); the method in which the cargo is stowed, including the overloading of the vessel (*Weir* v. *Aberdeen* (1819) 2 B & Ald 320; *Foley* v. *Tabor* (1861) 2 F & F 663; *Biccard* v. *Shepherd* (1861) 14 Moo PCC 471; *Daniels* v. *Harris* (1874) LR 10 CP 1); or the sufficiency of the vessel's fuel supplies (*Greenock SS Co* v. *Maritime Insurance Co* [1903] 2 KB 657; *"The Vortigern"* [1899] P 140; *Cohen Sons & Co* v. *Standard Marine Insurance Co Ltd* (1925) 21 Ll LR 30; *Harocopus* v. *Mountain* (1934) 49 Ll LR 267). If a defect can be cured easily and without great expense, it is unlikely to be regarded as giving rise to unseaworthiness (*Ajum Goolam Hossen & Co* v. *Union Marine Insurance Co* [1901] AC 362).

In all cases, the burden is on the insurer to prove unseaworthiness (*Davidson* v. *Burnand* (1868) LR 4 CP 117).

Subs (1) This is based on *Christie* v. *Secretan* (1799) 8 TR 192. The section is concerned only with the seaworthiness of the vessel, but provides a defence in all forms of marine policies, whether on ships, cargo or freight. Seaworthiness does not involve an absolute standard, but relates merely to the particular adventure insured. Moreover, the vessel need only be reasonably fit to withstand sea perils (subs (4)).

The seaworthiness warranty may be excluded by agreement, and in practice does not apply in cargo policies in the form of the Institute Cargo Clauses: cl 5 excludes liability for loss "arising from" unseaworthiness, but only where the assured was privy to the unseaworthiness. Older policies excluded the warranty by means of "seaworthiness admitted", "held covered" and similar clauses (*Parfitt* v. *Thompson* (1844) 13 M & W 392; *Phillips* v. *Nairne* (1847) 4 CB 343; *Sleigh* v. *Tyser* [1900] 2 QB 333; *Cantiere Meccanico Brindisino* v. *Janson* [1912] 3 KB 452).

The implied warranty of seaworthiness operates at the inception of the voyage only (*Bermon* v. *Woodbridge* (1781) 2 Doug KB 781; *Holdsworth* v. *Wise* (1828) 7 B & C 794; *Hollingworth* v. *Brodrick* (1837) 7 Ad & E 40; *Dixon* v. *Sadler* (1841) 8 M & W 895; *Gibson* v. *Small* (1853) 4 HL Cas 353; *Biccard* v. *Shepherd* (1861) 14 Moo PC 471), which means that the insurer may be put in the position of proving that a vessel lost in an unseaworthy state was unseaworthy at the earlier date at which the voyage commenced (*Watson* v. *Clark* (1813) 1 Do 336; *Parker* v. *Potts* (1815) 3 Dow 23): unseaworthiness at inception may nevertheless be presumed if the vessel is found to be unseaworthy within a short period thereafter (*Pickup* v. *Thames & Mersey Marine Insurance Co Ltd* (1878) 3 QBD 594). It also operates irrespective of the assured's knowledge of the condition of the vessel (*Douglas* v. *Scougall* (1816) 4 Dow 269). A breach of warranty cannot be repaired, so that if the vessel is unseaworthy when the voyage commences the insurer is off risk and the fact that repairs are effected does not reinstate the insurer's liability (*Forshaw* v. *Chabert* (1821) 3 Brod & Bing 458). The warranty extends to the vessel itself, but not to lighters used to transport cargo to and from the dock, even if the policy is in warehouse to warehouse form (*Lane* v. *Nixon* (1866) LR 1 CP 412).

Subs (2) For port perils, see: *Parmeter* v. *Cousins* (1809) 2 Camp 235; *Annen* v. *Woodman* (1810) 3 Taunt 299; *Gibson* v. *Small* (1853) 4 HL Cas 353; *Buchanan & Co* v. *Faber* (1899) 4 Com Cas 223.

Subs (3) The doctrine of stages requires a vessel to be seaworthy for each successive stage. This may require refitting (*Bouillon* v. *Lupton* (1863) 33 LJCP 37; *Quebec Marine Insurance Co* v. *Commercial Bank of Canada* (1870) LR 3 PC 234; *Buchanan & Co* v. *Faber* (1899) 4 Com Cas 223), additional crew or additional fuel (*Greenock SS Co* v. *Maritime Insurance Co* [1903] 2 KB 657; *"The Vortigern"* [1899] P 140). Where a vessel is delayed as a result of compliance with subs (3), the insurer cannot plead delay as a defence (Marine Insurance Act 1906, s 49(1)(c)).

Subs (4) Seaworthiness, as is clear from subs (1) and subs (4) taken together, is a variable standard based upon what is reasonably necessary for the voyage in question (*Hibbert* v. *Martin* (1808) Park's Marine Insurances 473; *Burges* v. *Wickham* (1863) 3 B & S 669; *Clapham* v. *Langton* (1864) 5 B & S 729; *Turnbull* v. *Janson* (1877) 36 LT 635; *Steel* v. *State Line SS Co* (1877) 3 App Cas 72).

Subs (5) In the case of a time policy, the unseaworthiness of the vessel when she commences her voyage is not an absolute defence, but rests on the "privity of the assured" (*Gibson* v. *Small* (1853) 4 HL Cas 353; *Thompson* v. *Hopper* (1856) 6 E & B 172; *Fawcus* v. *Sarsfield* (1856) 6 E & B 192; *Dudgeon* v. *Pembroke* (1877) 2 App Cas 284; *Thomas & Son Shipping Co Ltd* v. *London & Provincial Marine & General Insurance Co Ltd* (1914) 30 TLR 595; *George Cohen, Sons & Co* v. *Standard Marine Insurance Co* (1924) 20 Ll LR 133; *Harocopus* v. *Mountain* (1934) 49 Ll LR 267; *Wilmott* v. *General Accident Fire and Life Assurance Corporation Ltd* (1935) 53 Ll LR 156; *Compania Naviera Vascongada* v. *British and Foreign Marine Insurance Co Ltd* (1936) 54 Ll LR 35; *"The Star Sea"* [1995] 1 Lloyd's Rep 651, reversed on the application of the "blind-eye" test [1997] 1 Lloyd's Rep 360). This phrase means that the assured must be aware that the vessel is unseaworthy, or must have acted recklessly in that regard, and must have sent the vessel to sea in that state (*Compania Maritima San Basilio SA* v. *Oceanus Mutual Underwriting Association (Bermuda) Ltd, "The Eurysthenes"* [1976] 2 Lloyd's Rep 171; *Frangos* v. *Sun Life Insurance Office Ltd* (1934) 49 Ll LR 354). Moreover, s 39(5) operates to defeat the assured only when the loss is attributable to unseaworthiness of which he was aware (*Thomas* v. *Tyne & Wear Insurance Association* [1917] 1 KB 938; "*The Star Sea*" [1997] 1 Lloyd's Rep 360). This contrasts with the position under s 39(1) in relation to voyage policies, where there is no causation element.

There may be express provision for the seaworthiness of a vessel. In *Martin Maritime Ltd* v. *Provident Capital Indemnity Fund Ltd*, "*The Lydia Flag*" [1998] 2 Lloyd's Rep 652 the warranty was construed as requiring the vessel to be seaworthy at the inception of the policy unless the unseaworthiness resulted from a latent defect or crew/repairer negligence and the assured had exercised due diligence.

It is common practice in the London market for a vessel to be required to undergo a survey as a condition of the attachment of the policy. What constitutes a survey of the required type is a question of fact in every case: *Zeus Tradition Marine Ltd* v. *Bell*, "*The Zeus V*" [1999] 1 Lloyd's Rep 703; *J Kirkaldy & Sons* v. *Walker* [1999] Lloyd's Rep IR 410.

No implied warranty that goods are seaworthy

40.—(1) In a policy on goods or other moveables there is no implied warranty that the goods or moveables are seaworthy.

(2) In a voyage policy on goods or other moveables there is an implied warranty that at the commencement of the voyage the ship is not only seaworthy as a ship, but also that she is reasonably fit to carry the goods or other moveables to the destination contemplated by the policy.

NOTES

Subs (1) See *Koebel* v. *Saunders* (1864) 33 LJCP 310.

Subs (2) See, for illustrations: *Daniels* v. *Harris* (1874) LR 10 CP 1; *Sleigh* v. *Tyser* [1900] 2 QB 333; "*The Maori King*" [1895] 2 QB 550: *Blackett* v. *National Benefit Insurance Co* (1921) 8 Ll LR 293. It is the practice to exclude this particular warranty, under the Institute Cargo Clauses, cl 5, and to restrict the exception to cases in which the assured was privy to the unseaworthiness.

Warranty of legality

41. There is an implied warranty that the adventure insured is a lawful one, and that, so far as the assured can control the matter, the adventure shall be carried out in a lawful manner.

NOTES

This section, like s 36(1), contemplates two different situations.

(a) If the adventure is illegal from the outset, the policy insuring the adventure is void, and this is so irrespective of the ignorance or otherwise of the parties (*Johnston* v. *Sutton* (1779) Doug 254; *Farmer* v. *Legg* (1797) 7 TR 186; *Marryat* v. *Wilson* (1799) 1 Bos & P 430; *Parkin* v. *Dick* (1809) 11 East 502; *Gray* v. *Lloyd* (1812) 4 Taunt 136; *Camelo* v. *Britten* (1820) 4 B & Ald 184; *Redmond* v. *Smith* (1844) 7 Man & G 457; *Cunard* v. *Hyde* (1859) 2 E & E 1; *Australian Insurance Co* v. *Jackson* (1875) 33 LT 286).

(b) If the adventure is not illegal from the outset, the position is governed by the ordinary principles of law applicable to illegal contracts. If the statute specifically provides that the performance of a contract contrary to its terms is illegal, the court has no discretion in the matter and the policy will be rendered unenforceable. If, as is nearly always the case, the statute is silent as to the effects of illegality, the position is governed by the principles laid down by the Court of Appeal in *Euro-Diam Ltd* v. *Bathurst* [1988] 2 All ER 23. This case holds that not every act of illegality will render the entire contract illegal as formed (*Atkinson* v. *Abbott* (1809) 11 East 135; *Waugh* v. *Morris* (1873) LR 8 QB 202; *Dudgeon* v. *Pembroke* (1874) LR 9 QB 581). An act of illegality committed with the connivance of the assured renders the adventure illegal in its performance only if the illegality goes to the core of the adventure. Thus, the warranty is broken if the vessel is used for smuggling (*Pipon* v. *Cope* (1808) 1 Camp 434) or if regulatory legislation is disregarded (*Cunard* v. *Hyde* (1859) 29 LJQB 6; *James Yachts Ltd* v. *Thames and Mersey Marine Insurance Co Ltd* [1977] 1 Lloyd's Rep 206) but not merely because the assured has made an illegal payment: *Royal Boskalis Westminster NV* v. *Mountain* [1997] 2 All ER 929.

To be relevant, the illegality must arise under English law and must not merely be the contravention of a foreign statute, although in some cases it may be contrary to English public policy to enforce a contract to break foreign law (*Planche* v. *Fletcher* (1779) 1 Doug 251; *Euro-Diam Ltd* v. *Bathurst* [1988] 2 All ER 23).

If an act of illegality is committed contrary to the assured's instructions or wishes, and a loss occurs, the assured will be unaffected by the illegality and can recover as long as the loss was caused by an insured peril (*Carstairs* v. *Allnutt* (1813) 3 Camp 497; *Wilson* v. *Rankin* (1865) LR 1 QB 162). Moreover, if the illegality was on the part of the master or crew, the assured is entitled to recover on the basis of the insured peril of barratry. For barratry, see Marine Insurance Act 1906, Sched, r 11, page 101.

It is not possible to waive breach of the warranty of illegality (*Gedge* v. *Royal Exchange Assurance Corporation* [1900] 2 QB 214).

Independently of s 41, a policy will be illegal if its enforcement would be contrary to public policy, eg, if trading with the enemy is involved (*Gamba* v. *Le Mesurier* (1803) 4 East 407; *Brandon* v. *Curling* (1803) 4 East 410). Contrast the position if the policy was valid in its inception, and war was declared after the loss has occurred: in such a case, an action may be maintained after war has ceased (*Janson* v. *Driefontein Consolidated Gold Mines Ltd* [1902] AC 484).

The Voyage

Implied condition as to commencement of risk

42.—(1) Where the subject-matter is insured by a voyage policy "at and from" or "from" a particular place, it is not necessary that the ship should be at that place when the contract is concluded, but there is an implied condition that the adventure shall be commenced within a reasonable time, and that if the adventure be not so commenced the insurer may avoid the contract.

(2) The implied condition may be negatived by showing that the delay was caused by circumstances known to the insurer before the contract was concluded, or by showing that he waived the condition.

NOTES

Subs (1) See *Moxon* v. *Atkins* (1812) 3 Camp 200. Section 42 applies only to a voyage policy.

Duration of time policies: The date at which the risk attaches and determines under a time policy is a matter for the wording of the policy itself. The risk may, for example, attach when the vessel leaves port (*Sea Insurance Co* v. *Blogg* [1898] 2 QB 398). A time policy expressed to be from a stated day to or until another stated day excludes the first day but includes the last day (*Johnson & Co Ltd* v. *Bryant* (1896) 1 Com Cas 363; *Heinrich Hirdes GmbH* v. *Edmunds, "The Kiel"* [1991] 2 Lloyd's Rep 546). In all cases the loss must take place during the currency of the time policy (*Bushell* v. *Faith* (1850) 15 QB 649; *Hough & Co* v. *Head* (1885) 55 LJQB 43; *Lidgett* v. *Secretan* (1870) LR 5 CP 190; *Anderson* v. *Martin* [1908] AC 334). London market hulls policies terminate on the stated day, but there is provision for automatic early termination where the vessel changes its classification or flag (Institute Time Clauses Hulls, cl 4).

Commencement of risk under voyage policies: The risk under a voyage policy "from" a particular place (port risks excluded) attaches when the vessel commences the voyage unless the policy contemplates some earlier date, eg, before the goods have been allocated to a particular voyage (*Wunsche International* v. *Tai Ping Insurance* [1998] 2 Lloyd's Rep 8). Some difficulty may here exist in determining whether the vessel has left port when the loss occurred (*Hunting & Son* v. *Boulton* (1895) 1 Com Cas 120). The risk under a voyage policy "at and from" a particular place (port risks included) attaches as soon as the contract is concluded (Marine Insurance Act 1906, Sched, rr 2 and 3, page 96). The main concern which this section addresses is that a delayed start to the voyage may risk adverse seasonal weather conditions. For illustrations, see: *Chitty* v. *Selwyn & Martyn* (1742) 2 Atk 359; *Grant* v. *King* (1802) 4 Esp 175; *Hull* v. *Cooper* (1811) 14 East 479; *Mount* v. *Larkins* (1831) 8 Bing 108; *Palmer* v. *Marshall* (1832) 8 Bing 317; *Palmer* v. *Fenning* (1833) 9 Bing 460; *De Wolf* v. *Archangel Insurance Co* (1874) LR 9 QB 451; *Maritime Insurance Co* v. *Stearns* [1901] 2 KB 912; *Bah Lias Tobacco and Rubber Estates* v. *Volga Insurance Co* (1920) 3 Ll LR 155. Reasonableness is a matter of fact (Marine Insurance Act 1906, s 88), and external causes for the delay may be taken into account (*Smith* v. *Surridge* (1801) 4 Esp 25).

In practice, cargo policies governed by the Institute Cargo Clauses, cl 8, are written on a "warehouse to warehouse" basis. The risk commences when the goods leave the warehouse, (although in some cases cover may commence from a factory rather than a warehouse—*Wunsche International* v. *Tai Ping Insurance Co* [1998] 2 Lloyd's Rep 8) and terminates on delivery to the consignee's warehouse, subject to a 60-day maximum period running from the completion of the discharge of the goods from the vessel. There are numerous authorities on earlier versions of the transit clause. See, eg: *Allagar Rubber Estates Ltd* v. *National Benefit Assurance Co Ltd* (1922) 10 Ll LR 564 (risk terminating on safe delivery to purchaser—subject to unreasonable delay by purchaser); *Safadi* v. *Western Assurance Co* (1933) 46 Ll LR 140 (risk terminating 30 days after discharge—period to be regarded as extended if moving goods would expose them to danger but not if goods are retained for commercial reasons). For the authorities on the old standard provision whereby cover terminated when the goods were "safely landed" (see Marine Insurance Act 1906, Sched, r 5, page 97). Where a policy specifies the name and address of the warehouseman, it is sufficient if the goods are stored in any warehouse controlled by that person: they need not be stored at the stated address (*Cecom Trade BV* v. *Bishop* (1995) *Lloyd's List*, 14 October).

Termination of risk under a voyage policy: There is nothing in the 1906 Act dealing with the termination of the risk under a voyage policy (for cargo, see Sched, r 5, page 97, in practice superseded by the warehouse to warehouse clause). The policy may terminate on arrival (which refers to arrival at the part of the port where discharge takes place: *Lindsay* v. *Janson* (1859) 4 H & N 699; *Samuel* v. *Royal Exchange Assurance* (1828) 8 B & C 19; *Stone* v. *Marine Insurance Co of Gothenburg* (1876) 1 Ex D 81) at the port (which must be a friendly port—*Brown* v. *Vigne* (1810) 12 East 283) of final discharge or destination (see *Marten* v. *Vestey Brothers Ltd* [1920] AC 307, although the addition of the words "however employed" extend the assured's cover to ports subsequently visited: *Crocker* v. *Sturge* [1897] 1 QB 330; *Crocker* v. *General Insurance Co Ltd* (1897) 3 Com Cas 22; *Kynance SS Co* v. *Young* (1911) 16 Com Cas 123).

Nevertheless, some form of extension is usual. The cases have considered policies expressed to terminate:

(a) a specified period (normally 30 days) following arrival (see the note to s 25, page 27, as to the nature of the extended policy in such a case) and it is here established that the extension runs for consecutive periods of 24 hours from the exact time of arrival, so that in the case of a 30-day extension the risk will terminate exactly 30 days from the time of arrival and not midnight on the last day—*Mercantile Marine Insurance Co v. Titherington* (1864) 5 B & S 765; *Cornfoot v. Royal Exchange Assurance Corporation* [1904] 1 KB 40);

(b) after 24 hours following mooring in good safety (as to which see: *Lockyer v. Offley* (1786) 1 TR 252; *Minett v. Anderson* (1794) Peake 212; *Shawe v. Felton* (1801) 2 East 109; *Horneyer v. Lushington* (1812) 15 East 46; *Samuel v. Royal Exchange Assurance Co* (1828) 8 B & C 119; *Whitwell v. Harrison* (1848) 2 Exch 127); *Lidgett v. Secretan* (1870) LR 5 CP 190).

Sailing warranties: Old forms of policy, whether time or voyage, commonly contained sailing warranties by which the assured was required to sail by or after a specified date. These cases gave rise to the need to define "sail" or "depart". They established that a vessel had sailed if she had left the port with an intention on the part of the master of going to sea even if she was subsequently prevented from sailing by external causes (*Earle v. Harris* (1780) 1 Doug KB 357; *Lang v. Anderdon* (1824) 3 B & C 495; *Cockrane v. Fisher* (1835) 1 C, M & R 809) but not if she had left port:

(a) without being fully equipped to sail (*Ridsdale v. Newnham* (1815) 3 M & S 456; *Pittegrew v. Pringle* (1832) 3 B & Ad 514; *Graham v. Barras* (1834) 5 B & Ad 1011; *Thompson v. Gillespy* (1855) 5 E & B 209; *Hudson v. Bilton* (1856) 2 Jur NS 784; *Price v. Livingstone* (1882) 9 QBD 679, but contrast *Bouillon v. Lupton* (1863) 15 CBNS 113), or

(b) without any intention on the master's part to head for open sea (*Lang v. Anderdon* (1824) 3 B & C 495; *Fisher v. Cochran* (1835) 5 Tyr 496; *Sea Insurance Co v. Blogg* [1898] 2 QB 398).

Failure to leave port, even if prevented from doing so by external causes, constituted a breach of warranty (*Hore v. Whitmore* (1778) 2 Cowp 784; *Nelson v. Salvador* (1829) Mood & M 309; *Graham v. Barras* (1834) 5 B & Ad 1011; and cf *Moir v. Royal Exchange Assurance Co* (1815) 3 M & S 461, where the wording was slightly different).

Subs (2) If the insurer is aware of the delay and accepts the risk of it, eg by taking a supplementary premium, there is waiver (*Bah Lias Tobacco and Rubber Estates v. Volga Insurance Co Ltd* (1920) 3 Ll LR 155).

Alteration of port of departure

43. Where the place of departure is specified by the policy, and the ship instead of sailing from that place sails from any other place, the risk does not attach.

NOTES

This section is applicable to voyage policies (as the risk under a time policy will normally have attached at some earlier date), and is based on *Way v. Modigliani* (1787) 2 TR 30. Compare *Driscol v. Passmore* (1798) 1 Bos & P 200, where the assured was held to be justified in adopting a different route to the port of commencement of risk due to fear of capture at an intermediate port.

Sailing for different destination

44. Where the destination is specified in the policy, and the ship, instead of sailing for that destination, sails for any other destination, the risk does not attach.

NOTES

This section is applicable to voyage policies (as the risk under a time policy will normally have attached at some earlier date). For the basis of the rule, see *Woolridge* v. *Boydell* (1778) 1 Doug KB 16; *Sellar* v. *McVicar* (1804) 1 B & PNR 23; *Simon, Israel & Co* v. *Sedgwick* [1893] 1 QB 303. The fact that the assured has the intention to change the voyage before the risk commences does not discharge the insurer if the voyage is in fact properly commenced (*Hare* v. *Travis* (1827) 7 B & C 14; *Simon, Israel & Co* v. *Sedgwick* [1893] 1 QB 303; *Hewitt* v. *London General Insurance Co Ltd* (1925) 23 Ll LR 243). Equally, there is no deviation on such facts (see s 46(3), page 45). Section 44 deals with the case in which the destination is changed *before* the voyage has commenced: for the situation in which the voyage is changed *after* the voyage is commenced, see section 45, below.

Change of voyage

45.—(1) Where, after the commencement of the risk, the destination of the ship is voluntarily changed from the destination contemplated by the policy, there is said to be a change of voyage.

(2) Unless the policy otherwise provides, where there is a change of voyage, the insurer is discharged from liability as from the time of change, that is to say, as from the time when the determination to change it is manifested; and it is immaterial that the ship may not in fact have left the course of voyage contemplated by the policy when the loss occurs.

NOTES

Section 45, which applies to voyage policies, operates on the basis that the voyage has been validly commenced, and that the intention to change voyage arises after commencement (for change of port of commencement, see s 43, page 43, and for pre-commencement change of destination, see s 44, above). It should be noted that s 45 is concerned with the case in which the ultimate destination is changed: if there is merely a deviation from the agreed route to that destination, the matter is governed by ss 46–47 and 49, pages 45 *et seq*).

Subs (1) For illustrations, see: *Woolridge* v. *Boydell* (1778) 1 Doug KB 16; *Bottomley* v. *Bovill* (1826) 5 B & C 210; *Tasker* v. *Cunningham* (1819) 1 Bligh HL 87; *Fraser Shipping Ltd* v. *Colton* [1997] 1 Lloyd's Rep 586. Resumption of the original voyage does not reinstate the policy (*Way* v. *Modigliani* (1787) 2 TR 30). There are no statutory excuses for change of voyage comparable with those for deviation (see Marine Insurance Act 1906, s 49, page 47), although the effect of some aspects of s 49 is reproduced by the requirement that the change of voyage must be voluntary and not forced on the assured by, eg, governmental action (*Phelps* v. *Auldjo* (1809) 2 Camp 350; *British and Foreign Marine Insurance Co* v. *Samuel Sanday & Co* [1916] 1 AC 650; *Rickards* v. *Forestal Land, Timber and Railway Co* [1942] AC 50).

Subs (2) Under this provision, which is based on *Tasker* v. *Cunningham* (1819) 1 Bligh HL 87 (and cf *Bottomley* v. *Bovill* (1826) 5 B & C 210), the insurer is discharged as soon as there is sufficient evidence of an intention to change voyage. The evidence in that case was found in statements by the agents of the shipowner that the voyage would be changed. Contrast the position of deviation, where actual deviation is required (Marine Insurance Act 1906, s 46(3)).

In practice change of voyage is not an automatic discharging event, and will be protected by a "held covered" clause requiring prompt notice to the insurers and payment of additional premium if requested (Institute Cargo Clauses, cl 10; Institute Voyage Clauses Hulls, cl 2).

Deviation

46.—(1) Where a ship, without lawful excuse, deviates from the voyage contemplated by the policy, the insurer is discharged from liability as from the time of deviation, and it is immaterial that the ship may have regained her route before any loss occurs.

(2) There is a deviation from the voyage contemplated by the policy—

(a) Where the course of the voyage is specifically designated by the policy, and that course is departed from; or

(b) Where the course of the voyage is not specifically designated by the policy, but the usual and customary course is departed from.

(3) The intention to deviate is immaterial; there must be a deviation in fact to discharge the insurer from his liability under the contract.

NOTES

Deviation, unlike change of voyage, contemplates no change in the ultimate destination but rather a change of route to that destination (*Thames & Mersey Marine Insurance Co* v. *Van Laun & Co* [1917] 1 KB 48n (decided in 1905). The rule set out in s 46 must be read subject to the list of excuses contained in s 49, page 47. Deviation is confined to voyage policies, although time policies may contain terms or warranties restricting the limits of navigation (see Institute Time Clauses Hulls, cl 1, lesser restrictions also being found in Institute Voyage Clauses Hulls, cl 1). Thus the vessel may be confined to port (*Pearson* v. *Commercial Union Assurance Co* (1876) 1 App Cas 498; *Mountain* v. *Whittle* [1921] 1 AC 615) or to particular geographic regions (*Birrell* v. *Dryer* (1884) 9 App Cas 345; *Simpson SS Co Ltd* v. *Premier Underwriting Association Ltd* (1905) 10 Com Cas 198).

Subs (1) Losses incurred prior to the deviation are recoverable (*Green* v. *Young* (1702) 2 Ld Raym 840; *Hare* v. *Travis* (1827) 7 B & C 14), but post-deviation losses are irrecoverable whatever the subsequent cause of the loss (*Elliot* v. *Wilson* (1766) 4 Bro PC 470; *Davis* v. *Garrett* (1830) 6 Bing 716; *Thompson* v. *Hopper* (1856) 6 E & B 172) and even though the vessel had resumed its course prior to the loss (*Way* v. *Modigliani* (1787) 2 TR 30). The fact that the risk has not increased as a result of the deviation is immaterial (*Hartley* v. *Buggin* (1781) 3 Doug KB 39).

Subs (2) As to (a), see: *Phyn* v. *Royal Exchange Assurance Co* (1798) 7 TR 505; *Tait* v. *Levi* (1811) 14 East 481; *Brown* v. *Tayleur* (1835) 4 A & E 241; *Wingate* v. *Foster* (1878) 3 QBD 582; *Difiori* v. *Adams* (1884) 53 LJQB 437. The policy overrides any customary route (*Elliot* v. *Wilson* (1766) 4 Bro PC 470). As to (b), see: *Salvador* v. *Hopkins* (1765) 3 Burr 1707; *Gregory* v. *Christie* (1784) 3 Doug 419; *Middlewood* v. *Blakes* (1797) 7 TR 162; *Ougier* v. *Jennings* (1808) 1 Camp 505n; *Vallance* v. *Dewar* (1808) 1 Camp 503; *Cormack* v. *Gladstone* (1809) 11 East 347; *Davis* v. *Garrett* (1830) 6 Bing 716; *Thompson* v. *Hopper* (1858) EB & E 1038; *Morrison (James) & Co Ltd* v. *Shaw, Savill and Albion Co Ltd* [1916] 2 KB 783. Whether a usual and customary course is established is a matter of fact, and it may be possible for the assured to sustain a claim by establishing a customary route involving deviation: *Reardon Smith Lines Ltd* v. *Black Sea and Baltic General Insurance Co Ltd, "The Indian City"* [1939] AC 562; *Frenkel* v. *MacAndrews & Co Ltd* [1929] AC 545.

Subs (3) This rule is based on *Foster* v. *Wilmer* (1746) 2 Str 1249; *Woolridge* v. *Boydell* (1778) 1 Doug KB 16; *Thellusson* v. *Fergusson* (1780) 1 Doug KB 360; *Kewley* v. *Ryan* (1794)

2 H Bl 343; *Heselton* v. *Allnutt* (1813) 1 M & S 46. An intention to deviate which is not put into operation is, therefore, immaterial (*Kingston* v. *Phelps* (1793) 1 Peake 299). For a post-Act illustration, see *Hewitt* v. *London General Insurance Co Ltd* (1925) 23 Ll LR 243, where the intention to deviate was formed prior to the commencement of the voyage, and cf the note to s 44, page 44. Contrast the position with change of voyage, where a manifest intention is sufficient to discharge the insurer (Marine Insurance Act 1906, s 45(2), page 44). If the deviation has occurred before the policy has incepted, the risk never attaches unless the insurer can be shown to have been aware of the deviation and to have agreed to it (*Redman* v. *Lowdon* (1814) 5 Taunt 462).

Deviation has traditionally been waived by insurers, under a "liberty to touch and stay" clause, on which there are numerous authorities (see, eg: *Violett* v. *Allnutt* (1813) 3 Taunt 419; *Leathley* v. *Hunter* (1831) 7 Bing 517, and Marine Insurance Act 1906, Sched, r 6, page 98). A rather more extensive waiver appears in the Institute Clauses, whereby deviation is permitted subject to prompt notice to the insurer and the payment of any required additional premium (Institute Voyage Clauses Hulls, cl 2).

Several ports of discharge

47.—(1) Where several ports of discharge are specified by the policy, the ship may proceed to all or any of them, but, in the absence of any usage or sufficient cause to the contrary, she must proceed to them, or such of them as she goes to, in the order designated by the policy. If she does not there is a deviation.

(2) Where the policy is to "ports of discharge", within a given area, which are not named, the ship must, in the absence of any usage or sufficient cause to the contrary, proceed to them, or such of them as she goes to, in their geographical order. If she does not there is a deviation.

NOTES

Subs (1) For examples, see: *Beatson* v. *Haworth* (1796) 6 TR 531; *Marsden* v. *Reid* (1803) 3 East 572; *Metcalf* v. *Parry* (1814) 4 Camp 123; *Kynance Sailing Ship Co Ltd* v. *Young* (1911) 16 Com Cas 123. If there is only one port at a place, there is no deviation by visiting different bays (*Warre* v. *Miller* (1825) 4 B & C 538). There is equally no deviation if the vessel does not visit all of the ports specified in the policy (*Marsden* v. *Reid* (1803) 3 East 572).

Subs (2) For examples, see: *Clason* v. *Simmonds* (1741) cited in 6 TR at p 533, 101 ER 687; "*The Dunbeth*" [1897] P 133; *Marten* v. *Vestey Bros* [1920] AC 307. The obligation on the assured to visit ports in geographical order is not overriden by a "liberty to touch and stay" clause (*Gairdner* v. *Senhouse* (1810) 3 Taunt 16).

Delay in voyage

48. In the case of a voyage policy, the adventure insured must be prosecuted throughout its course with reasonable dispatch, and, if without lawful excuse it is not so prosecuted, the insurer is discharged from liability as from the time when the delay became unreasonable.

NOTES

At common law, delay was regarded as a form of deviation, although the two concepts were separated out by s 48. The excuses for delay and deviation remain identical under s 49, page 47. The insurer is discharged from liability where delay becomes unreasonable, but even where delay is not unreasonable the insurer will not be liable for a loss proximately caused by delay (see Marine Insurance Act 1906, s 55(2)(b), page 52). The Institute Clauses provide insurance on a held covered basis where there has been delay, although this is limited to cases of delay beyond the assured's control, so that little is added to the common law (Institute Cargo Clauses, cl 18). Whether or not delay has been undue is a question of fact, taking into account the length of the delay, the nature of the voyage and the purpose of the delay (*Langhorn* v. *Allnutt* (1812) 4 Taunt 511). For illustrations of undue delay, see: *Mount* v. *Larkins* (1831) 8 Bing 108; *Doyle* v. *Powell* (1832) 4 B & Ad 267; *Hamilton* v. *Sheddon* (1837) 3 M & W 49; *Company of African Merchants* v. *British Insurance Co* (1873) LR 8 Ex 154; *Pearson* v. *Commercial Union Assurance Co* (1876) 1 App Cas 498; *Phillips* v. *Irving* (1884) 7 Man & G 325; *Hyderabad (Deccan) Co* v. *Willoughby* [1899] 2 QB 530. Contrast cases of acceptable delay: *Smith* v. *Surridge* (1801) 4 Esp 25; *Grant* v. *King* (1802) 4 Esp 175; *Schroder* v. *Thompson* (1817) 7 Taunt 462; *Samuel* v. *Royal Exchange Assurance* (1828) 8 B & C 119; *Bain* v. *Case* (1829) 3 C & P 496; *British American Tobacco* v. *Poland* (1921) 7 Ll LR 108; *Niger Co Ltd* v. *Guardian Assurance Co* (1922) 13 Ll LR 75.

Excuses for deviation or delay

49.—(1) Deviation or delay in prosecuting the voyage contemplated by the policy is excused—

(a) Where authorised by any special term in the policy; or

(b) Where caused by circumstances beyond the control of the master and his employer; or

(c) Where reasonably necessary in order to comply with an express or implied warranty; or

(d) Where reasonably necessary for the safety of the ship or subject-matter insured; or

(e) For the purpose of saving human life, or aiding a ship in distress where human life may be in danger; or

(f) Where reasonably necessary for the purpose of obtaining medical or surgical aid for any person on board the ship; or

(g) Where caused by the barratrous conduct of the master or crew, if barratry be one of the perils insured against.

(2) When the cause excusing the deviation or delay ceases to operate, the ship must resume her course, and prosecute her voyage, with reasonable dispatch.

NOTES

Subs (1)(a) It is standard practice for marine policies to contain held covered provisions in the event of deviation. Such a clause does not apply where the assured's intention to deviate was formed prior to the making of the contract (*Laing* v. *Union Marine Insurance Co* (1895) 1 Com Cas 11). The modern wording replaced the old form of policy which conferred upon the assured "liberty to touch and stay" at ports of his choice. See Marine Insurance Act 1906, Sched, r 6, page 98.

Subs (1)(b) Relevant factors include government or belligerent action (*Scott* v. *Thompson* (1805) 1 Bos & PNR 181; *Blackenhagen* v. *London Assurance Co* (1808) 1 Camp 454; *Phelps* v. *Auldjo* (1809) 2 Camp 350; *Schroder* v. *Thompson* (1817) 7 Taunt 462; *Rickards* v. *Forestal Land, Timber and Railway Co Ltd* [1942] AC 50), weather conditions (*Harrington* v. *Halkeld* (1778) 2 Park's Marine Insurances 639; *Kingston* v. *Phelps* (1795) 7 TR 165n; *Delany* v. *Stoddart* (1785) 1 TR 22; *Samuel* v. *Royal Exchange Assurance Co* (1828) 8 B & C 119) and conduct of the crew (*Elton* v. *Brogden* (1747) 2 Str 1264; *Driscol* v. *Bovil* (1798) 1 Bos & P 313). The mere fact that the vessel deviated due to the master's lack of knowledge of the geography of an area is no excuse (*Tait* v. *Levi* (1811) 14 East 481).

Subs (1)(c) this primarily relates back to s 39(3) of the 1906 Act. The combined effect of the two sections is that delay in order to make a vessel seaworthy for the next stage of its voyage is excused. For the common law origin, see: *Motteux* v. *London Assurance* (1739) 1 Atk 545; *Bouillon* v. *Lupton* (1863) 15 CBNS 113.

Subs (1)(d) This ground overlaps with (b) above. The carrying out of necessary repairs to or refitting of the ship is a defence under this head (*Clason* v. *Simmons* (1741) 6 TR 533n; *Smith* v. *Surridge* (1801) 4 Esp 25; *Weir* v. *Aberdeen* (1819) 2 B & Ald 320), as is the taking on of provisions (*Raine* v. *Bell* (1808) 9 East 195). Deviating to avoid uninsured risks does not suffice (*Scott* v. *Thompson* (1805) 1 Bos & PNR 181).

Subs (1)(e) See *Lawrence* v. *Sydebotham* (1805) 6 East 45. There is no excuse for delay or deviation to save third party property (*Company of African Merchants* v. *British Insurance Co* (1873) LR 8 Ex 154; *Scaramanga* v. *Stamp* (1880) 5 CPD 295).

Subs (1)(f) See *Woolf* v. *Claggett* (1800) 3 Esp 257.

Subs (1)(g) Barratry is conduct by the master or crew in breach of the assured's instructions or wishes (see Marine Insurance Act 1906, Sched, r 11), and is an insured peril in its own right. Where barratry results in delay or deviation, the assured remains covered. For the origins of this principle, see *Ross* v. *Hunter* (1790) 4 TR 33. Negligence by the master and crew which results in deviation or delay is outside this provision (*Tait* v. *Levi* (1811) 14 East 481; *Mentz, Decker & Co* v. *Maritime Insurance Co* [1910] 1 KB 132). For barratry in general, see Marine Insurance Act 1906, Sched, r 11, page 101.

Subs (2) For the origins and illustrations of this principle, see: *Harrington* v. *Halkeld* (1778) 2 Park on Marine Insurance 639; *Lavabre* v. *Wilson* (1779) 1 Doug KB 284; *Delany* v. *Stoddart* (1785) 1 TR 22. The subsection is probably superfluous, under the general prohibition on unreasonable delay under s 48, page 46.

Assignment of Policy

When and how policy is assignable

50.—(1) A marine policy is assignable unless it contains terms expressly prohibiting assignment. It may be assigned either before or after loss.

(2) Where a marine policy has been assigned so as to pass the beneficial interest in such policy, the assignee of the policy is entitled to sue thereon in his own name; and the defendant is entitled to make any defence arising out of the contract which he would have been entitled to make if the action had been brought in the name of the person by or on behalf of whom the policy was effected.

(3) A marine policy may be assigned by indorsement thereon or in other customary manner.

NOTES

Subs (1) The assignability of marine policies is necessary to facilitate commercial practice in the sale of cargoes under CIF and related arrangements. Policies governed by the Institute of London Underwriters terms do not prohibit assignment, although notice must be given to the insurer where a policy on a vessel is assigned (Institute Time Clauses Hulls, cl 5, Institute Voyage Clauses Hulls, cl 3); if notice is not given the assignment is void (*Laurie* v. *West Hartlepool SS Thirds Indemnity Association and David* (1899) 4 Com Cas 322). See also s 15 of the Marine Insurance Act 1906, page 13, which provides that the assignment of the subject-matter of the policy does not carry with it the policy itself, and that a separate assignment is necessary; moreover, the assignment of the policy and the subject-matter must be contemporaneous (s 51, page 49).

For the principle that assignment is possible after loss, see: *Sparkes* v. *Marshall* (1836) 2 Bing NC 761; *Lloyd* v. *Fleming* (1872) LR 7 QB 299; *Aron & Co Inc* v. *Miall* (1928) 34 Com Cas 18, confirmed by Marine Insurance Act 1906, s 51, proviso, page 49.

Subs (2) The section, replacing s 1 of the Policies of Marine Insurance Act 1868 (and thus predating the general right to assign choses in action at law first conferred by the Judicature Act 1873—now s 136 of the Law of Property Act 1925), gives the assignee a right to sue in his own name only where the policy itself has been assigned so as to transfer to the assignee the entire beneficial interest in the policy (*Williams* v. *Atlantic Assurance Co Ltd* [1933] 1 KB 81).

The assignment is subject to equities, so that the insurer can plead against the assignee any defence which may have been pleaded against the original assured, eg non-disclosure (*Pickersgill* v. *London and Provincial Marine Insurance Co* [1912] 3 KB 614), scuttling by the assignor prior to the assignment (*Graham Joint Stock Shipping Co Ltd* v. *Merchants' Marine Insurance Co Ltd* (1923) 17 Ll LR 44, a case of an equitable mortgage), the absence of loss due to indemnification of the assured by a third party (*Colonia Versicherung AG* v. *Amoco Oil Co* [1995] 1 Lloyd's Rep 570 affirmed [1997] 1 Lloyd's Rep 261) or the fact that the policy is illegal because the assignor was an enemy alien (*Bank of New South Wales* v. *South British Insurance Co Ltd* (1920) 4 Ll LR 266). The insurer is not, however, given the right to set off claims under the policy against other sums owed to him by the assignee (*Baker* v. *Adam* (1910) 15 Com Cas 227), unless either party is insolvent in which case all mutual debts can be set off against each other. (Insolvency Rules 1986, SI 1986 No 1925, r 4.90). Equally, the insurer cannot claim a set off in respect of post-assignment debts owed by the original assignor (*Pellas* v. *Neptune Marine Insurance Co Ltd* (1879) 5 CPD 34).

If the policy is subject to a lien in favour of the broker, the assignment of the policy is subject to the lien (*Man* v. *Shiffner* (1802) 2 East 523).

The fact of assignment which is effective to pass the entire beneficial interest does not remove the right of the assignor to rely upon policy terms inserted for his benefit, eg subrogation waiver provisions: "*The Surf City*" [1995] 2 Lloyd's Rep 242.

Subs (3) This subsection reproduces s 2 of the Policies of Marine Insurance Act 1868, which permitted assignment by indorsement (*Aron & Co Inc* v. *Miall* (1928) 34 Com Cas 18). A marine policy may, therefore, be assigned without notice to the insurer (unless the policy otherwise provides, as in the case of hull insurance). Mere delivery is not, however, a customary assignment (*Baker* v. *Adam* (1910) 15 Com Cas 227; *Safadi* v. *Western Assurance Co* (1933) 46 Ll LR 140). Where this section cannot be used, it will be necessary to comply with the formalities of s 136 of the Law of Property Act 1925, under which the assignee can sue in his own name if the assignment is in writing, for value, and notified to the insurer.

The section does not deal with the possibility of the assignment of the right to claim under the policy, as opposed to the policy itself, although a claim is a chose in action which can be assigned at law or in equity (*Swann & Cleland's Graving Dock & Slipway Co* v. *Maritime Insurance Co* [1907] 1 KB 116).

Assured who has no interest cannot assign

51. Where the assured has parted with or lost his interest in the subject-matter insured, and has not, before or at the time of so doing, expressly or impliedly agreed to assign the policy, any subsequent assignment of the policy is inoperative:

Provided that nothing in this section affects the assignment of a policy after loss.

NOTES

Under s 15 of the 1906 Act, page 13, the assignment of the subject-matter does not carry with it the policy, and contemporaneous assignment of both is required. If the subject-matter is assigned first, the policy lapses (although s 51 does not say this in terms) and there is nothing left to assign at any future date (*North of England Oil-Cake Co* v. *Archangel Insurance*

Co (1875) LR 10 QB 249; *Powles* v. *Innes* (1843) 11 M & W 10). If, however, the subject-matter has been lost by reason of an insured peril, the assured may assign the policy to a third party after loss (*Lloyd* v. *Fleming* (1872) LR 7 QB 299; cf Marine Insurance Act 1906, s 50(1), page 48).

The Premium

When premium payable

52. Unless otherwise agreed, the duty of the assured or his agent to pay the premium, and the duty of the insurer to issue the policy to the assured or his agent, are concurrent conditions, and the insurer is not bound to issue the policy until payment or tender of the premium.

NOTES

This is based on *Burges* v. *Wickham* (1863) 33 LJCP 17. The section does not make the attachment of the risk dependent upon the payment of the premium, so that losses incurred prior to payment can be recovered (subject to contract): the significance of the issue of the policy is that no action can be brought in a marine case other than on the policy itself (Marine Insurance Act 1906, s 22, page 25). The insurer may additionally sue for the amount of the premium (although the liability is borne by the broker—s 53(1), below). Failure to pay premiums will rarely give the insurer the right to treat the contract as repudiated by the assured (*Fenton Insurance Co Ltd* v. *Gothaer Verischerungsbank VVag* [1991] 1 Lloyd's Rep 172, *Figre Ltd* v. *Mander* [1999] Lloyd's Rep IR 193, but contrast *Pacific & General* v. *Hazell* [1997] LRLR 65, where the assured was insolvent).

(For the amount of premium, see Marine Insurance Act 1906, s 31, page 31.)

Policy effected through broker

53.—(1) Unless otherwise agreed, where a marine policy is effected on behalf of the assured by a broker, the broker is directly responsible to the insurer for the premium, and the insurer is directly responsible to the assured for the amount which may be payable in respect of losses, or in respect of returnable premium.

(2) Unless otherwise agreed, the broker has, as against the assured, a lien upon the policy for the amount of the premium and his charges in respect of effecting the policy; and, where he has dealt with the person who employs him as a principal, he has also a lien on the policy in respect of any balance on any insurance account which may be due to him from such person, unless when the debt was incurred he had reason to believe that such person was only an agent.

NOTES

Subs (1) The responsibility of the broker for the premiums, a principle which applies to marine policies but not to Lloyd's insurances and apparently not other forms of cover (*Pacific & General Insurance* v. *Hazell* [1997] LRLR 65) is of some antiquity (*Airy* v. *Bland* (1774) 2 Park 811; *Edgar* v. *Fowler* (1803) 3 East 222; *Edgar* v. *Bumstead* (1809) 1 Camp 411; *Power* v. *Butcher* (1829) 10 B & C 329), and was rationalised by the Court of Appeal in *Universo Insurance Co of Milan* v. *Merchants' Marine Insurance Co* [1897] 2 QB 93 by the fiction that the premium has been paid by the assured and has been lent back to the broker by the insurer. The rule imposing personal liability for premiums upon the broker under a marine policy may be ousted by express agreement, as is stated by the opening words of s 53(1). However, the rule will not be ousted lightly. In *J A Chapman & Co. Ltd* v. *Kadirga Denizcilik Ve Ticaret* [1998] Lloyd's Rep IR 377, the Court of Appeal held that a premium warranty, whereby each instalment of the premium was warranted to be paid by given dates, did not operate to make the assured personally liable but rather retained the broker's personal liability even though it meant that the assured had no control over the payment of premiums and thus potential loss of cover in the event of delay. If the Lloyd's broker is acting as a sub-broker, to place risks on behalf of a non-Lloyd's broker, the Lloyd's broker remains liable to the underwriters for the premium although he will have a right of indemnity against the original broker (*Harris and Dixon (Insurance Brokers) Ltd* v. *Graham (Run-Off) Ltd* 1989, unreported, *Prentis Donegan & Partners Ltd* v. *Leeds & Leeds Co Inc* [1998] 2 Lloyd's Rep 326). Section 53(1) may be overriden by agreement, including net accounting arrangements, but only if such arrangements are expressly entered into (see the note to s 54, page 52). The broker's liability to pay the premium is brought to an end in the event of the assured's provisional liquidation, as this terminates the broker's authority to act for the assured. *Pacific & General* v. *Hazell* [1997] LRLR 65.

The concluding words of subs (1) impose upon the insurer the obligation to pay losses to the assured. The cases illustrate that the loss may be paid to a broker acting as the assured's agent as long as the loss is paid in a manner authorised by the assured (*Hine Bros* v. *Steamship Insurance Syndicate Ltd, "The Netherholme"* (1895) 72 LT 79). In particular, the broker is not deemed to have been paid by the insurer by means of set off under a net accounting system and the assured thus remains free to bring proceedings against the insurer (*Jell* v. *Pratt* (1817) 2 Stark 67; *Todd* v. *Reid* (1821) 4 B & Ald 210; *Russell* v. *Bangley* (1821) 4 B & Ald 395; *Scott* v. *Irving* (1830) 1 B & Ad 605; *Bartlett* v. *Pentland* (1830) 10 B & C 760; *McGowin Lumber & Export Co Inc* v. *Pacific Marine Insurance Co Ltd* (1922) 12 Ll LR 496) unless the assured has given specific authority to the broker (*Stewart* v. *Aberdein* (1838) 4 M & W 211) or was aware of the custom when the broker was engaged (*Sweeting* v. *Pearce* (1861) 9 CBNS 534). Once the broker has been paid, directly or notionally on account, he must account to the assured for the proceeds (*Andrew* v. *Robinson* (1812) 3 Camp 199; *Wilkinson* v. *Clay* (1815) 6 Taunt 110). It is only where the broker is insolvent that it becomes necessary to consider whether the broker has been paid in a fashion authorised by the assured so that the insurer may be called upon to pay the assured whatever the insurer's arrangement with the broker may have been.

The broker is under no legal duty to the assured to pay losses, and if the broker does so without the insurer's express authorisation, such payment is to be regarded as a gift to the assured, which leaves intact the assured's right to sue the insurer for the full amount of the loss: *Merrett* v. *Capitol Indemnity Corporation* [1991] 1 Lloyd's Rep 169. If authority is given to a broker to make payments, it may be withdrawn: *A A Mutual Insurance Co* v. *Bradstock Blunt & Crawley Ltd* [1996] LRLR 161.

Subs (2) Two distinct liens are involved here. As regards the lien on the premium and charges, see: *Godin* v. *London Assurance Co* (1758) 1 Burr 489; *Mildred, Goyeneche & Co* v. *Maspons* (1883) 8 App Cas 874; *Fairfield Shipbuilding & Engineering Co Ltd* v. *Gardner, Mountain & Co Ltd* (1912) 104 LT 288. As regards the general lien, see *Olive* v. *Smith* (1815) 5 Taunt 56. The broker's right of lien, ie, to retain the policy until the assured has indemnified the broker, is a necessary corollary of the rule in s 53(1). If the broker parts with possession of the policy and then regains possession, the lien reattaches (*Levy* v. *Barnard* (1818) 8 Taunt 149). The lien attaches also to the proceeds of the policy as a matter of market usage flowing from the existence of a lien on the policy itself: *Eide UK Ltd* v. *Lowndes Lambert Group Ltd, The Sun Tender* [1998] 1 Lloyd's Rep 389. In this case the Court of Appeal held that if the broker receives the proceeds of the policy, he is entitled to retain them as security for any premium owed to him by the assured, and can set off the sum due against the proceeds. However, the lien does not apply where the policy is composite, as it may be that the premium is owed by co-assured A while the policy moneys are payable to co-assured

B, and in line with the general rule that composite insurance involves distinct contracts the broker cannot treat the policy moneys as indivisible.

A sub-broker has a lien on the policy as against the head broker even though the head broker has received his commission and charges from the assured (*Mann* v. *Forrester* (1814) 4 Camp 60; *Westwood* v. *Bell* (1815) 4 Camp 349), provided that the sub-broker was unaware that the head broker was himself an agent (*Maanss* v. *Henderson* (1801) 1 East 335; *Man* v. *Shiffner* (1802) 2 East 523; *Snook* v. *Davidson* (1809) 2 Camp 218; *Lanyon* v. *Blanchard* (1811) 2 Camp 597; *Mann* v. *Forrester* (1814) 4 Camp 60; *Fisher* v. *Smith* (1878) 4 App Cas 1; *Near East Relief* v. *King, Chausseur & Co Ltd* [1930] 2 KB 40).

Effect of receipt on policy

54. Where a marine policy effected on behalf of the assured by a broker acknowledges the receipt of the premium, such acknowledgment is, in the absence of fraud, conclusive as between the insurer and the assured, but not as between the insurer and broker.

NOTES

See *Dalzell* v. *Mair* (1808) 1 Camp 532; *Du Gaminide* v. *Pigou* (1812) 4 Taunt 246. It is market practice at Lloyd's for the premium not to be paid by the broker, but rather for the broker and the underwriters to operate a quarterly accounting system under which the broker receives the premiums and pays the losses, subject to quarterly settlement with the insurer. To facilitate this, the policy may state that the premium has been received by the underwriter even when this is not the case. For that reason, the statement prevents the underwriter from proceeding against the assured for a premium which he may have paid to the broker. It does not, however, create an estoppel as between underwriter and broker. Net accounting has not been recognised as a custom by the courts, so that in the absence of a net accounting agreement the broker remains liable for the premium under s 53(1), page 50 above, and cannot rely upon net accounting as a defence (*Grand Union Insurance Co Ltd* v. *Evans-Lombe Ashton & Co* 1989, unreported).

Loss and Abandonment

Included and excluded losses

55.—(1) Subject to the provisions of this Act, and unless the policy otherwise provides, the insurer is liable for any loss proximately caused by a peril insured against, but, subject as aforesaid, he is not liable for any loss which is not proximately caused by a peril insured against.

(2) In particular,—

    (a) The insurer is not liable for any loss attributable to the wilful misconduct of the assured, but, unless the policy otherwise provides, he is liable for any loss proximately caused by a peril insured against, even though the loss would not have happened but for the misconduct or negligence of the master or crew;

    (b) Unless the policy otherwise provides, the insurer on ship or goods is not liable for any loss proximately caused by delay, although the delay be caused by a peril insured against;

    (c) Unless the policy otherwise provides, the insurer is not liable for ordinary wear and tear, ordinary leakage and breakage, inherent vice or nature of the subject-matter insured, or for any loss proximately caused by rats or vermin, or for any injury to machinery not proximately caused by maritime perils.

NOTES

Subs (1) The modern development of the doctrine of proximate cause can be traced back to *Leyland Shipping Co* v. *Norwich Union Fire Insurance Society* [1918] AC 350, in which a vessel holed by a torpedo was lost in a storm after being refused entry to a nearby port for repairs. In holding that the proximate cause of the loss was the torpedo rather than sea perils, the House of Lords emphasised that the last cause is not necessarily the proximate cause. The question of proximate cause has arisen in a large number of cases and in a large number of contexts. In freight cases, for example, there may be an issue as to whether loss of freight is due to a marine peril affecting the vessel or to a fall in the market for the chartering of vessels (*Continental Grain Co Inc* v. *Twitchell* (1945) 78 Ll LR 251, and cf *Cepheus Shipping Corporation* v. *Guardian Royal Exchange Assurance plc* [1995] 1 Lloyd's Rep 622, where the loss of earnings was due to the vessel being off-hire and would have occurred independently of damage to the vessel). Three of the most problematic are the following.

(1) A vessel may be lost by a combination of its unseaworthiness and perils of the sea. Assuming that the matter is unaffected by s 39 of the Marine Insurance Act 1906, page 37, its resolution depends upon whether perils of the sea or unseaworthiness was the proximate cause. See: *Dudgeon* v. *Pembroke* (1877) 2 App Cas 284; *Ballantyne* v. *Mackinnon* [1896] 2 QB 455; *Sassoon & Co Ltd* v. *Western Assurance Co* [1921] AC 561; *Grant, Smith & Co & McDonnell* v. *Seattle Construction & Dry Dock Co* [1920] AC 162; *Lloyd Instruments Ltd* v. *Northern Star Insurance Co Ltd, "The Miss Jay Jay"* [1987] 1 Lloyd's Rep 32.

(2) There is frequently a difficulty in distinguishing between marine and war perils. In some cases this may be a matter of proximate cause. The mere fact that a war exists, for example, does not mean that all losses occurring in the territory affected by the war are proximately caused by the war: the state of affairs is generally not regarded as sufficient to amount to proximate cause (*France, Fenwick & Co Ltd* v. *North of England Protection and Indemnity Association* [1917] 2 KB 522; *Moor Line* v. *R* (1920) 4 Ll LR 208; *Green* v. *British India Steam Navigation Co, "The Matiana"* [1921] 1 AC 99; *Harrison* v. *Shipping Controller, "The Inkonka"* [1921] 1 KB 122; *Adelaide SS Co* v. *R, "The Warilda"* (1923) 14 Ll LR 41; *Mazarakis Bros* v. *Furness, Withy & Co* (1924) 17 Ll LR 113; *Clan Line Steamers Ltd* v. *Board of Trade, "The Clan Matheson"* [1929] AC 514; *Hain SS Co* v. *Board of Trade* [1929] AC 534). Other wordings may, however, be involved. Where the policy excludes "all consequences of" war and related risks, the doctrine of proximate cause is ousted and the insurer is not liable for negligent navigation or other marine perils which have resulted or been encountered because of the existence of a war. Equally, where the policy covers "all consequences of hostilities or warlike operations", the insurer is liable for losses directly or indirectly caused by such operations, including collisions with vessels involved in warlike operations (*Atlantic Transport Co* v. *R, "The Maryland"* (1921) 9 Ll LR 208; *Charente SS Co* v. *Director of Transport* (1922) 10 Ll LR 514; *Ard Coasters* v. *Attorney General* [1921] 2 AC 141; *Liverpool & London War Risks Insurance Association* v. *Marine Underwriters of SS Richard de Larringa* [1921] 2 AC 144; *Peninsular and Oriental Branch Service* v. *Commonwealth Shipping Representative, "The Geelong"* [1922] 1 KB 766) and loss while providing ancillary assistance to the war effort, eg refuelling and conveying casualties (*"The Caroline"* (1921) 7 Ll LR 56; *Hindustan SS Co* v. *Admiralty Commissioners* (1921) 8 Ll LR

230; *Ocean Steamship Co Ltd* v. *Liverpool & London War Risks Insurance Association,* *"The Priam"* [1948] AC 243; *Yorkshire Dale Steamship Co* v. *Minister of War Transport, "The Coxwold"* [1942] AC 691). The modern wording in the Institute Clauses narrows the liability of war risks insurers to the situation in which the loss is directly caused by a war risk.

(3) If the voyage is abandoned due to an anticipated peril, the insurer's liability depends upon whether the abandonment was justifiable or premature. In the latter case, the proximate cause of any loss is the assured's own conduct. In the former case, there is a total loss and no notice of abandonment is required (see Marine Insurance Act 1906, s 62(7) and the note thereto, page 71). The principle applies to hulls, cargo and freight policies alike: (*Milles* v. *Fletcher* (1779) 1 Doug KB 231; *Lubbock* v. *Rowcroft* (1803) 5 Esp 50; *Hadkinson* v. *Robinson* (1803) 3 Bos & P 388; *Forster* v. *Christie* (1809) 11 East 205; *Parkin* v. *Tunno* (1809) 11 East 22; *Mordy* v. *Jones* (1825) 4 B & C 394; *Philpott* v. *Swann* (1861) 11 CBNS 270; *Mercantile Steamship Co Ltd* v. *Tyser* (1881) 7 QBD 73; *Inman Steamship Co* v. *Bischoff* (1882) 7 App Cas 670; *"The Alps"* [1893] P 109; *Nickels & Co* v. *London & Provincial Marine & General Insurance Co Ltd* (1900) 6 Com Cas 15; *Manchester Liners Ltd* v. *British & Foreign Marine Insurance Co Ltd* (1901) 7 Com Cas 26; *Williams & Co* v. *Canton Insurance Office Ltd* [1901] AC 462; *Kacianoff* v. *China Traders Insurance Co Ltd* [1914] 3 KB 1121; *Becker, Gray & Co* v. *London Assurance Corporation* [1918] AC 101). A similar situation may arise under a hull or cargo policy, where the master (assuming that he is unable to communicate with the assured—*Australasian Steam Navigation Co* v. *Morse* (1872) LR 4 PC 222) determines in the case of an emergency to sell the subject-matter following damage: if the sale is unjustified in that there is no actual total loss, the assured will be confined to claiming for a partial loss (*Tanner* v. *Bennett* (1825) Ry & M 182; *Somes* v. *Sugrue* (1830) 4 C & P 276; *Roux* v. *Salvador* (1836) 3 Bing NC 266; *Knight* v. *Faith* (1850) 15 QB 649; *Navone* v. *Hadden* (1859) 9 CB 30; *Kaltenbach* v. *Mackenzie* (1878) 3 CPD 467, and cf the note to s 57(1), page 59). In the case of freight policies, the common law established the principle that where a vessel was lost and abandoned to hull insurers, there could be no claim for loss of freight if the freight was subsequently earned by the hull insurers—the loss of freight to the assured was caused not by a peril of the sea but rather by abandonment of the vessel to the hull insurer (*M'Carthy* v. *Abel* (1804) 5 East 388; *Scottish Marine Insurance Co* v. *Turner* (1853) 4 HL Cas 312n). Under the Institute Hulls Clauses, hulls underwriters now waive their right to freight: see the note to s 63(2), page 68.

Steps taken to avoid loss form an insured peril, which result in loss in a different form, will not break the chain of causation from the original peril (*"The Thruscoe"* [1897] P 301; *"The Knight of St Michael"* [1898] P 30; *Symington & Co* v. *Union Insurance Society of Canton* (1928) 31 Ll LR 179; *Canada Rice Mills Ltd* v. *Union Marine & General Insurance Co Ltd* [1941] AC 55; *Quinta Communications SA* v. *Warrington* 1999, unreported). However, an insurer on cargo is not liable where the cargo is sold to pay for repairs to the vessel, rendered necessary by perils of the sea, as in such a case the loss of the cargo is proximately caused not by perils of the sea but by reason of the assured's impecuniosity (*Powell* v. *Gudgeon* (1816) 5 M & S 431; *Sarquy* v. *Hobson* (1827) 4 Bing 131; and cf *Greer* v. *Poole* (1880) 5 QBD 272).

In some cases it may not be possible to disentangle the proximate cause from two distinct causes, so that the causes are concurrent. The rule here is that if one of the causes is insured and one is uninsured, the assured may recover, whereas if one of the causes is insured and the other excluded, the exclusion takes priority (*Wayne Tank and Pump Co Ltd* v. *Employers*

Liability Assurance Corporation Ltd [1974] QB 57; *Kuwait Airways Corporation* v. *Kuwait Insurance Co SAK* [1999] 1 Lloyd's Rep 803). This has significance, for Institute of London Underwriters marine policies and war risks policies are drafted in mutually exclusive terms.

The doctrine of proximate cause is nevertheless merely a rule of construction which may be ousted by express agreement, eg where the policy states that a risk is covered only if it is the sole and direct cause of the loss (*Merchants' Marine Insurance Co Ltd* v. *Liverpool Marine and General Insurance Co Ltd* (1928) 31 Ll LR 45), or where the policy excludes liability for a loss if it is in any way caused or contributed to by an excluded peril (*Coxe* v. *Employers' Liability Insurance Corporation* [1916] 2 KB 629; *American Tobacco Co* v. *Guardian Assurance Co* (1925) 22 Ll LR 37). A policy which insures against the "consequences of" a peril has been held to reflect exactly the doctrine of proximate cause (*Ionides* v. *Universal Marine Insurance Association* (1863) 14 CBNS 259; *The Nassau Bay* [1979] 1 Lloyd's Rep 395), although an exclusion for all consequences of a peril may oust the doctrine (see above, in relation to war risks).

The burden of proving that a loss was caused by an insured peril is borne by the assured, so that if there is no evidence as to how a loss was caused the assured will lose (*Rhesa Shipping* v. *Edmunds, "The Popi M"* [1985] 2 All ER 712; *Lamb Head Shipping Co Ltd* v. *Jennings, "The Marel"* [1994] 1 Lloyd's Rep 624). Thus, it is not enough for the assured to show that cargo has suffered water damage, as he must go on to show that the loss was caused by sea water and was attributable to a peril of the sea (*Cobb & Jenkins* v. *Volga Insurance Co Ltd of Petrograd* (1920) 4 Ll LR 130; *Miceli* v. *Union Marine and General Insurance Co Ltd* (1938) 60 Ll LR 275). However, if the policy is "all risks" it is enough for the assured to show that a loss has occurred (*British and Foreign Marine Insurance Co* v. *Gaunt* [1921] 2 AC 41, and see Institute Cargo Clauses A, which are written on an "all risks" basis, unlike clauses B and C). If the assured has proved his loss, the burden then switches to the insurer to demonstrate that the peril proximately causing the loss was uninsured or that some other defence exists (*Munro, Brice & Co* v. *War Risks Association Ltd* [1918] 2 KB 78). It is permissible for an insurer to seek to reverse the burden of proof by express wording to the effect that the assured must disprove any allegation by the insurer that the loss was proximately caused by an excepted cause. However, in order to benefit from this type of clause, the insurer must produce *prima facie* evidence demonstrating that the loss was caused by an excepted peril, and only then is the assured required to rebut that evidence (*Spinney's (1948) Ltd* v. *Royal Insurance Co* [1980] 1 Lloyd's Rep 406).

Subs (2)(a) "Wilful misconduct" requires a deliberate act by the assured which is designed to cause loss, or which is committed recklessly with a blind eye to its consequences, and in respect of which he intends to make an insurance claim (*Forder* v. *Great Western Railway Co* [1905] 2 KB 532; *National Oilwell (UK) Ltd* v. *Davy Offshore Ltd* [1993] 2 Lloyd's Rep 582). Most of the marine cases on wilful misconduct involve the deliberate casting away of the vessel by or with the privity of the assured, the main issue being the insurer's ability to prove the assured's complicity: the standard of proof increases in proportion to the seriousness of the allegations against the assured. Relevant factors in wilful misconduct cases include the level of insurance on the vessel, the assured's financial position, the conduct of the assured immediately following the loss (eg, in accepting or refusing offers of salvage), whether the crew have managed to salvage all of their possessions or whether they have escaped with the bare minimum of possessions, and the condition of the vessel and its equipment—the many authorities are considered in *National Justice Compania Naviera SA* v. *Prudential Assurance Co, "The Ikarian Reefer"* [1993] 2 Lloyd's Rep 68, and include: *Bowring* v. *Elmslie* (1790) 7 TR 216n; *Visscherij Maatschappij Nieuwe Onderneming* v. *Scottish Metropolitan Assurance Co* (1922) 10 Ll LR 579; *Coulouras* v. *British General Insurance Co Ltd* (1922) 12 Ll LR 220; *Dorigo Y Sanudo* v. *Royal Exchange Assurance Corporation* (1922) 13 Ll LR 126; *Ansoleaga Y Cia* v. *Indemnity Mutual Marine Insurance Co* (1922) 13 Ll LR 231; *Issaias (Elfie)* v. *Marine Insurance*

Co Ltd (1923) 15 Ll LR 186; *Comunidad Naviera Baracaldo v. Norwich Union Fire Insurance Society* (1923) 16 Ll LR 45; *Anghelatos* v. *Northern Assurance Co* (1924) 19 Ll LR 255; *Compania Martiartu* v. *Royal Exchange Assurance* [1923] 1 KB 650; *Compania Naviera Martiartu* v. *Royal Exchange Assurance Corporation* (1924) 18 Ll LR 247; *Société d'Avances Commerciales* v. *Merchants' Marine Insurance Co* (1924) 20 Ll LR 74; *Domingo Mumbru SA* v. *Laurie* (1924) 20 Ll LR 122; *Banco de Barcelona* v. *Union Marine Insurance Co Ltd* (1925) 22 Ll LR 209; *Empire SS Co Inc* v. *Threadneedle Insurance Co* (1925) 22 Ll LR 437; *Lemos* v. *British and Foreign Marine Insurance Co Ltd* (1931) 39 Ll LR 275; *Piper* v. *Royal Exchange Assurance* (1932) 42 Ll LR 103; *Pateras* v. *Royal Exchange Assurance* (1934) 49 Ll LR 400; *Grouds* v. *Dearsley* (1935) 51 Ll LR 203; *Maris* v. *London Assurance* (1935) 52 Ll LR 211; *Compania Naviera Vascongada* v. *British and Foreign Marine Insurance Co Ltd* (1936) 54 Ll LR 35; *Canning* v. *Maritime Insurance Co Ltd* (1936) 56 Ll LR 91; *Bank of Athens* v. *Royal Exchange Assurance* (1937) 59 Ll LR 67; *Compania Naviera Santi SA* v. *Indemnity Mutual Marine Assurance Co Ltd, "The Tropaioforos"* [1960] 2 Lloyd's Rep 469; *Astrovlanis Compania Naviera SA* v. *Linard, "The Gold Sky"* [1972] 2 Lloyd's Rep 187; *Michalos & Sons Maritime SA* v. *Prudential Assurance Co Ltd, "The Zinovia"* [1984] 2 Lloyd's Rep 264; *Continental Illinois National Bank of Chicago* v. *Alliance Assurance Co Ltd* [1986] 2 Lloyd's Rep 470. If the loss was deliberately caused by the master or crew, and the insurer cannot establish that the assured was involved (*"The Ikarian Reefer"* [1995] 1 Lloyd's Rep 445), the loss is covered under the insured peril of barratry (see Marine Insurance Act 1906, Sched, r 11, page 101 and the notes thereto for the burden of proof in barratry cases). For pleadings in relation to wilful misconduct, see: *Astrovlanis Compania Naviera SA* v. *Linard, "The Gold Sky"* [1972] 2 QB 611; *Palamisto General Enterprises SA* v. *Ocean Marine Insurance Co Ltd* [1972] 2 QB 625. It is not possible for a policy to insure against loss by wilful misconduct, as such a loss falls outside the contingency requirement of insurance. There is a fine line between wilful misconduct, which bars a claim, and negligence, which does not bar a claim—the running of a risk is the latter rather than the former (*Papademetriou* v. *Henderson* (1939) 64 Ll LR 345).

If there are co-assureds, the effect of wilful misconduct by one of them depends upon whether the policy is joint (same interests) or composite (different interests). In the case of a joint policy, neither party can recover. By contrast, if the policy is composite, each assured has a distinct contract with the insurer and can recover independently of any defence that the insurer may have against any other co-assured. Thus if the mortgagor of the vessel scuttles it, the mortgagor cannot recover although the mortgagee's rights are unaffected, provided that scuttling by the mortgagor is an insured peril (*Samuel & Co.* v. *Dumas* [1924] AC 421). Again, if the builder of a vessel is guilty of wilful misconduct in relation to its construction, and the employer suffers loss, the employer but not the builder is able to recover from the insurers under a composite policy: it was held in *State of Netherlands* v. *Youell* [1997] 2 Lloyd's Rep 440 (aff'd on other grounds [1998] 1 Lloyd's Rep 236) that the insurer remains liable to pay the employer in these circumstances even if, under the building contract, the insurance moneys are to be handed to the builder by the employer.

"Negligence", whether of the assured himself or of the master or crew, is neutral in its effect. If the loss is caused by an insured peril, it is irrelevant that the peril was brought about by negligence (*Busk* v. *Royal Exchange Assurance Co* (1818) 2 B & Ald 73; *Walker* v. *Maitland* (1821) 5 B & Ald 171; *Hahn* v. *Corbett* (1824) 2 Bing 205; *Bishop* v. *Pentland* (1827) 7 B & C 219; *Shore* v. *Bentall* (1828) 7 B & C 798n; *Dixon* v. *Sadler* (1839) 5 M & W 405; *Redman* v. *Wilson* (1845) 14 M & W 476; *Thompson* v. *Hopper* (1856) 6 E & B 172; *Trinder Anderson & Co* v. *Thames and Mersey Marine Insurance Co* [1898] 2 QB 114; *Blackburn* v. *Liverpool, Brazil and River Plate Steam Navigation Co* [1902] 1 KB 290; *Cohen, Sons & Co* v. *National Benefit Assurance Co Ltd* (1924) 18 Ll LR 199; *Lind* v. *Mitchell* (1928) 32 Ll LR 70). These cases also decide that the warranty of seaworthiness in s 39 of the Marine Insurance Act 1906 applies only to the commencement of the voyage, so that any subsequent negligence by the master and crew does not provide a defence under that section (see page 37). Equally, if the loss is not caused by an insured peril, the fact that the peril was brought about by negligence cannot give the assured the right to recover. Policies may require the assured to take all reasonable steps to avoid a loss, but such clauses have been construed as requiring the assured only to avoid recklessness (*Sofi* v. *Prudential Assurance Co* [1993] 2 Lloyd's Rep 559) and are subjective in that the assured's conduct must be assessed in the light of his own experience and qualifications (*Stephen* v. *Scottish Boatowners Mutual Insurance Association, "The Talisman"* [1989] 1 Lloyd's Rep 535).

There is some overlap, as yet unresolved, between the principle that negligence does not defeat a claim and the obligation of the assured under s 78(4) of the Marine Insurance Act 1906 to sue and labour, ie, to take reasonable steps to avoid or mitigate a loss. This conflict is discussed in the note to s 78, page 79.

Subs (2)(b) It was usual under the Lloyd's SG policy to exclude delay as an insured peril in respect of the vessel and its cargo (*Gregson* v. *Gilbert* (1783) 3 Doug 232; *Tatham* v. *Hodgson* (1796) 6 TR 656; *Taylor* v. *Dunbar* (1869) LR 4 CP 206; *Pink* v. *Fleming* (1890) 25 QBD 396; *St Margaret's Trust Ltd* v. *Navigators and General Insurance Co Ltd* (1949) 82 Ll LR 752). This is codified by s 55(2)(b). The exclusion was not extended to freight (*Jackson* v. *Union Marine Insurance Co* (1874) LR 10 CP 125; *"The Bedouin"* [1894] P 1), although the "time charter" clause now in operation (Institute Time Clauses (Freight), cl 14; Institute Voyage Clauses (Freight), cl 12) excludes freight claims "consequent on loss of time". This wording was held by the House of Lords in *Naveria de Canarias SA* v. *Nacional Hispanica Asequradora SA* [1978] AC 873 to mean that any delay, whether or not the proximate cause of the loss, precluded recovery. After this decision, it is clear that loss of freight as a result of delay is recoverable only where the adventure has been frustrated, delay being the inevitable consequence of frustration: the position is that if the assured has to show delay independently of frustration he will be unable to claim. For illustrations of frustration, see: *Re Jamieson and Newcastle SS Freight Insurance Association* [1895] 2 QB 90; *Roura & Forgas* v. *Townend* [1919] 1 KB 189; *Carras* v. *London and Scottish Assurance Corp Ltd* [1936] 1 KB 291; *Petros M Nomikos* v. *Robertson* [1939] AC 371; *Atlantic Maritime Co Inc* v. *Gibbon* [1954] 1 QB 88. Contrast: *Bensuade & Co* v. *Thames & Mersey Marine Insurance Co* [1897] AC 609; *Turnbull, Martin & Co* v. *Hull Underwriters Association* [1900] 2 QB 242; *Russian Bank for Foreign Trade* v. *Excess Insurance Co* [1918] 2 KB 123.

Subs (2)(c) The perils listed in this section relate to the nature of the subject-matter insured, and reflect the exclusions found in the Institute of London Underwriters Cargo Clauses, cl 4. However, as long as loss is not inevitable (eg, in the case of perishable goods which are not appropriately stored), it is possible to insure against these perils. The point is illustrated by a series of inherent vice cases (*Traders and General Insurance Association* v. *Bankers & General Insurance Co* (1921) 9 Ll LR 223; *Maignen & Co* v. *National Benefit Assurance Co* (1922) 10 Ll LR 30; *Sassoon & Co Ltd* v. *Yorkshire Insurance Co* (1923) 16 Ll LR 129; *Dodwell & Co Ltd* v. *British Dominions General Insurance Co Ltd* [1955] 2 Lloyd's Rep 391n (decided in 1918); *Overseas Commodities Ltd* v. *Style* [1958] 1 Lloyd's Rep 546; *Soya GmbH* v. *White* [1983] 1 Lloyd's Rep 122; *Wunsche International* v. *Tai Ping Insurance Co* [1998] 2 Lloyd's Rep 8).

"Ordinary wear and tear": For illustrations, see: *Harrison* v. *Universal Marine Insurance Co* (1862) 3 F & F 190; *Wadsworth Lighterage and Coaling Co Ltd* v. *Sea Insurance Co Ltd* (1929) 35 Com Cas 1. The exclusion does not extend to design defects (*Prudent Tankers Ltd SA* v. *Dominion Insurance Co Ltd, "The Caribbean Sea"* [1980] 1 Lloyd's Rep 338).

"Leakage or breakage": For the common law position, see *Crofts* v. *Marshall* (1836) 7 C & P 597. This peril is nevertheless insurable where the policy so states, as loss from this source is not inevitable (*Traders & General Insurance Association Ltd* v. *Bankers & General Insurance*

Co Ltd (1921) 38 TLR 94; *Maignen & Co* v. *National Benefit Assurance Co Ltd* (1922) 10 Ll LR 30; *De Monchy* v. *Phoenix Insurance Co of Hartford* (1929) 34 Ll LR 201; *Dodwell & Co Ltd* v. *British Dominions General Insurance Co Ltd* [1955] 2 Lloyd's Rep 391n).

"Inherent vice" involves a non-external cause of loss, arising from the nature of the subject-matter, eg, sweating, mildew, natural deterioration or the method by which it has been transported (*Gregson* v. *Gilbert* (1783) 3 Doug KB 232; *Tatham* v. *Hodgson* (1796) 6 TR 656; *Boyd* v. *Dubois* (1811) 3 Camp 133; *Koebel* v. *Saunders* (1864) 17 CBNS 71; *Blower* v. *Great Western Railway Co* (1872) LR 7 CP 655; *Bird's Cigarette Manufacturing Co Ltd* v. *Rouse* (1924) 19 Ll LR 301; *Bowring & Co Ltd* v. *Amsterdam London Insurance Co Ltd* (1930) 36 Ll LR 309; *Gee & Garnham Ltd* v. *Whittall* [1955] 2 Lloyd's Rep 562; *Berk & Co Ltd* v. *Style* [1955] 2 Lloyd's Rep 382; *Biddle, Sawyer & Co Ltd* v. *Peters* [1957] 2 Lloyd's Rep 339; *Noten BV* v. *Harding* [1990] 2 Lloyd's Rep 527; *Wunsche International* v. *Tai Ping Insurance Co Ltd* [1998] 2 Lloyd's Rep 8). By contrast, if the loss is externally caused and not inevitable from the nature of the subject-matter, it is covered (*Wilson, Holgate & Co Ltd* v. *Lancashire and Cheshire Insurance Corporation Ltd* (1922) 13 Ll LR 486; *Sassoon & Co Ltd* v. *Yorkshire Insurance Co* (1923) 16 Ll LR 129; *Whiting* v. *New Zealand Insurance Co Ltd* (1932) 44 Ll LR 179).

"Rats or vermin": This exclusion is based on: *Rohl* v. *Parr* (1796) 1 Esp 445; *Hunter* v. *Potts* (1815) 4 Camp 203; *Laveroni* v. *Drury* (1852) 22 LJ Ex 2. See also *Hamilton* v. *Pandorf* (1887) 12 App Cas 518, where the proximate cause of the loss was perils of the sea due to the entry of sea water caused by rats gnawing at the side of the vessel, although this decision is now open to doubt: see the note to Marine Insurance Act 1906, Sched, r 7, page 98. Cf the position as regards insects (*Schloss Brothers* v. *Stevens* [1906] 2 KB 665).

"Injury to machinery": In *Thames and Mersey Marine Marine Insurance Co* v. *Hamilton, Fraser & Co, "The Inchmaree"* (1887) 12 App Cas 484, the House of Lords held that mechanical failure was not a peril of the sea, as it could occur on land. The market responded with the "Inchmaree Clause", presently cl 6.2 of the Institute Time Clauses Hulls and cl 4.2 of the Institute Voyage Clauses Hulls, under which the assured is covered for, *inter alia*, bursting of boilers, breakage of shafts or any latent defect in the machinery or hull. The clause covers external or additional damage resulting from a latent defect, as opposed to a latent defect merely becoming patent without causing any further damage to the machinery or to other property. For this point, and the meaning of latent defect, see: *Jackson* v. *Mumford* (1904) 9 Com Cas 114; *Oceanic SS Co* v. *Faber* (1907) 13 Com Cas 28; *Hutchins Bros* v. *Royal Exchange Corporation* [1911] 2 KB 398; *Stott (Baltic) Steamers Ltd* v. *Marten* [1916] 1 AC 304; *Scindia SS (London) Ltd* v. *London Assurance* (1936) 56 Ll LR 136; *Wills & Sons* v. *World Marine Insurance Ltd, "The Mermaid"* [1980] 1 Lloyd's Rep 350n; *Prudent Tankers Ltd SA* v. *Dominion Insurance Co Ltd, "The Caribbean Sea"* [1980] 1 Lloyd's Rep 338. The leading authority on defects is now *Promet Engineering (Singapore) Pte Ltd* v. *Sturge, The Nukila* [1997] 2 Lloyd's Rep 146, in which the footings of an oil rig, which were defective, caused severe cracking in the oil rig's legs. The Court of Appeal held that if there is merely a defect which becomes apparent or patent, the insurer is not liable. However, in the present case, the defect had caused further damage, and that additional damage was recoverable under the policy.

Partial and total loss

56.—(1) A loss may be either total or partial. Any loss other than a total loss, as hereinafter defined, is a partial loss.

(2) A total loss may be either an actual total loss, or a constructive total loss.

(3) Unless a different intention appears from the terms of the policy, an insurance against total loss includes a constructive, as well as an actual, total loss.

(4) Where the assured brings an action for a total loss and the evidence proves only a partial loss, he may, unless the policy otherwise provides, recover for a partial loss.

(5) Where goods reach their destination in specie, but by reason of obliteration of marks, or otherwise, they are incapable of identification, the loss, if any, is partial, and not total.

NOTES

Whatever the form of loss, the six year limitation period for the issue of a writ against the insurer runs from the date of the casualty (*Chandris* v. *Argo Insurance Co Ltd* [1963] 2 Lloyd's Rep 65; *Castle Insurance Co Ltd* v. *Hong Kong Islands Shipping Co Ltd* [1983] 2 Lloyd's Rep 376; *Bank of America National Trust and Savings Corporation* v. *Chrismas, "The Kyriaki"* [1993] 1 Lloyd's Rep 137). This period may be reduced by contract, eg by a clause providing that an action may be brought against the insurer only within one year running from the date of the loss (*Phoenix Assurance Co of Hartford* v. *De Monchy* (1929) 34 Ll LR 201).

Subs (1) The distinction between total and partial loss is relevant for the measure of indemnity, as defined in Marine Insurance Act 1906, ss 67–72, pages 71 *et seq.*

Subs (2) For the definition of actual total loss, see s 57, below. For the definition of constructive total loss, see s 60, page 62. In general terms, a constructive total loss (which is confined to marine insurance—*Moore* v. *Evans* [1918] AC 185—is an economic rather than physical loss, in that the subject-matter remains in existence but is not worth repairing or capable of retrieval. Where there has been a constructive total loss, the assured is entitled to seek indemnity on the basis of an actual total loss by giving a notice of abandonment to the insurer (ss 61–62, pages 65 *et seq*). If the assured fails to serve a notice of abandonment, his loss remains a constructive total loss but is held to an indemnity based on partial loss only: thus, a policy term restricting cover to total losses will not prevent recovery for a constructive total loss despite the lack of a notice of abandonment (*Bank of America National Trust and Savings Association* v. *Chrismas, "The Kyriaki"* [1993] 1 Lloyd's Rep 137).

Subs (3) This provision is illustrated by *Adams* v. *Mackenzie* (1863) 13 CBNS 442. Policies rarely provide to the contrary.

Subs (4) See, for illustrations: *Gardiner* v. *Croasdale* (1760) 2 Burr 904; *King* v. *Walker* (1864) 2 H & C 384; *Helmville Ltd* v. *Yorkshire Insurance Co Ltd, "The Medina Princess'* [1965] 1 Lloyd's Rep 361. Some policies are confined to total loss only (*Continental Grain Co Inc* v. *Twitchell* (1945) 78 Ll LR 251—freight), as to which see Marine Insurance Act 1906, s 76, page 77.

Subs (5) This is based on *Spence* v. *Union Marine Insurance Co* (1868) LR 3 CP 427.

Actual total loss

57.—(1) Where the subject-matter insured is destroyed, or so damaged as to cease to be a thing of the kind insured, or where the assured is irretrievably deprived thereof, there is an actual total loss.

(2) In the case of an actual total loss no notice of abandonment need be given.

NOTES

Subs (1) There are many instances in the cases of actual total loss, relating to vessels, cargo and freight.

(1) In the case of a vessel there will be an actual total loss where the vessel is fatally damaged (*Cambridge* v. *Anderton* (1824) 2 B & C 691; *Cossman* v. *West* (1887) 13 App Cas 160), where it is unable to sail in order for repairs to be effected (*Barker* v. *Janson* (1868) LR 3 CP 303) or where it is seized with no reasonable prospect of recovery (*Stringer* v. *English and Scottish Marine Insurance Co Ltd* (1870) LR 5 QB 599; *Panamanian Oriental Steamship Corporation* v. *Wright* [1970] 2 Lloyd's Rep 365—no actual total loss on the facts). If the vessel continues to exist *in specie* (*Bell* v. *Nixon* (1816) Holt NP 423), or is capable of salvage (*Captain JA Cates Tug and Wharfage Co Ltd* v. *Franklin Insurance Ltd* [1927] AC 698) or, where seized or stranded, is not irretrievable (*Kemp* v. *Halliday* (1865) LR 1 QB 520; *George Cohen Sons & Co* v. *Standard Marine Insurance Co Ltd* (1925) 21 Ll LR 30; *Marstrand Fishing Co Ltd* v. *Beer, "The Girl Pat"* (1937) 56 Ll LR 163; *St Margaret's Trust Ltd* v. *Navigators and General Insurance Co Ltd* (1949) 82 Ll LR 752; *Fraser Shipping Ltd* v. *Colton* [1997] 1 Lloyd's Rep 586), there is no actual total loss although there may be a constructive total loss.

(2) In the case of cargo there will be an actual total loss where the cargo ceases to meet its description (*Cologan* v. *London Assurance Co* (1816) 5 M & S 447; *Montoya* v. *London Assurance Co* (1851) 6 Exch 451; *Garrett* v. *Melhuish* (1858) 4 Jur NS 943; *Duthie* v. *Hilton* (1868) LR 4 CP 138; *Asfar* v. *Blundell* [1896] 1 QB 123; *Montreal Light, Heat & Power Co* v. *Sedgwick* [1910] AC 598; *Berger and Light Diffusers Pty Ltd* v. *Pollock* [1973] 2 Lloyd's Rep 442), where it is damaged and will be unable to meet its description by the time of its arrival at its destination (*Dyson* v. *Rowcroft* (1803) 3 Bos & P 474; *Roux* v. *Salvador* (1836) 3 Bing 266; *Farnworth* v. *Hyde* (1865) LR 2 CP 204; *Saunders* v. *Baring* (1876) 34 LT 419) or where it is seized with no reasonable prospect of recovery (*Mullett* v. *Shedden* (1811) 13 East 304; *Mellish* v. *Andrews* (1812) 15 East 13; *Stringer* v. *English & Scottish Marine Insurance Co* (1870) LR 5 QB 599; *De Mattos* v. *Saunders* (1872) LR 7 CP 570). If the cargo is merely damaged, but retains its essential character, there is no actual total loss (*Cocking* v. *Foster* (1785) 4 Doug KB 295; *M'Andrews* v. *Vaughan* (1793) 1 Park on Marine Insurances 252; *Anderson* v. *Royal Exchange Assurance Co* (1805) 7 East 38; *Glennie* v. *London Assurance* (1814) 2 M & S 371; *Navone* v. *Hadden* (1859) 9 CB 30; *Francis* v. *Boulton* (1895) 65 LJQB 153). Where part of a cargo is damaged, there is generally a partial loss only, and not a total loss either of the whole or of the part lost. See the note to s 76, page 77. If there is a mere paper loss of cargo, eg, because the amount shipped has been overstated, such loss does not fall within a marine policy at all (*Coven SpA* v. *Hong Kong Chinese Insurance Co* [1999] Lloyd's Rep IR 565).

(3) In the case of freight or profits, there is a total loss when the operation of an insured peril affecting the vessel or cargo, rendering it an actual or total constructive loss or causing delay, prevents the assured from earning freight or profits. Whether or not freight has been lost depends upon the allocation of the risk of non-arrival of or damage to the cargo as laid down by the contract of carriage. The general principle is that freight is earned only when the cargo is delivered, but that damage to the cargo, short of its total loss, does not discharge liability for freight. For illustrations, see, in addition to the authorities on loss of cargo cited above and in the note to s 60, page 62: *Atty* v. *Lindo* (1805) 1 Bos & PNR 236; *Horncastle* v. *Suart* (1807) 7 East 400; *Mackenzie* v. *Shedden* (1810) 2 Camp 431; *Devaux* v. *J'Anson* (1839) 5 Bing NC 519; *De Cuadra* v. *Swann* (1864) 16 CBNS 772; *Byrne* v. *Schiller* (1871) LR 6 Ex 319; *Rankin* v. *Potter* (1873) LR 6 HL 83; *Jackson* v. *Union Marine Insurance Co* (1874) LR 10 CP 125; *Metcalfe* v. *Britannia Iron Works Co* (1877) 2 QBD 423; *Asfar* v. *Blundell* [1896] 1 QB 123; *Price* v. *Maritime Insurance Co* [1901]

2 KB 412; *French Marine* v. *Compagnie Napolitaine d'Eclairage et de Chauffage par le Gaz* [1921] 2 AC 494. In the case of a damaged or delayed vessel, freight will be lost if the vessel is unable to proceed and transhipment is not possible, whether or not the vessel is an actual or constructive total loss within the meaning of the hull policy (*Shipton* v. *Thornton* (1838) 9 A & E 314; *Carras* v. *London and Scottish Assurance Corporation Ltd* [1936] 1 KB 291; *Kulukundis* v. *Norwich Union Fire Insurance Society* [1937] 1 KB 1), although the policy may provide that freight is deemed to be lost only where the vessel itself has been lost within the meaning of the 1906 Act (*Petros M Nomikos Ltd* v. *Robertson* [1939] AC 371; *Papadimitriou* v. *Henderson* (1939) 64 Ll LR 345; *Vrondissis* v. *Stevens* [1940] 2 KB 90). The Institute Freight Clauses appear to be in the latter form, as they require the subject-matter insured (which seems to be a reference to the vessel rather than to the freight) to be lost.

There will commonly be a causation issue as to whether the loss of freight was caused by loss of the vessel due to an insured peril or by some act of the master or assured. If the cargo is sold en route, following the occurrence of an insured peril, on the basis that it will not survive the voyage, there is a loss of freight. However, if the sale is precipitate, the loss is not caused by an insured peril (*Milles* v. *Fletcher* (1779) 1 Doug KB 231; *Parmeter* v. *Todhunter* (1808) 1 Camp 541; *Everth* v. *Smith* (1814) 2 M & S 278; *Green* v. *Royal Exchange Assurance Co* (1815) 6 Taunt 68; *Mordy* v. *Jones* (1825) 4 B & C 394; *Guthrie* v. *North China Insurance Co Ltd* (1902) 7 Com Cas 130; *Vrondissis* v. *Stevens* [1940] 2 KB 90). The loss in such a case is an actual total loss and no notice of abandonment is required. See the note to s 55(1), page 52, and also the note to s 62(7), page 66.

Subs (2) This was so held in *Cossman* v. *West* (1887) 13 App Cas 160. In practice it is always sensible to give a notice of abandonment, as the assured's right to claim an indemnity based on total loss is preserved in the event of a later ruling that the loss was a constructive, rather than an actual, total loss. Where there is a constructive total loss in respect of which no notice of abandonment has been given, and it is followed by an actual total loss, the assured is not precluded from claiming for the latter because of his failure in relation to the former (*Mellish* v. *Andrews* (1812) 5 East 13).

Missing ship

58. Where the ship concerned in the adventure is missing, and after the lapse of a reasonable time no news of her has been received, an actual total loss may be presumed.

NOTES

Section 58 is based on: *Green* v. *Brown* (1743) 2 Str 1199; *Cohen* v. *Hinkley* (1809) 2 Camp 51; *Koster* v. *Reed* (1826) 6 B & C 19. What constitutes a reasonable time is a question of fact: Marine Insurance Act 1906, s 88. The section gives rise to questions of proof which it does not resolve. If a vessel disappears, and is not heard of for, say, six months, in which time the policy has run off, is it to be assumed not only that the vessel has been lost but that the loss occurred during the currency of the policy? The issue was treated as one of fact in *Reid* v. *Standard Marine Insurance Co Ltd* (1886) 2 TLR 807 and *Houstman* v. *Thornton* (1816) Holt NP 242. The presumption is in any event rebuttable by evidence of some other cause of the disappearance (*Compania Martiartu* v. *Royal Exchange Assurance* [1923] 1 KB 650).

Once the insurer has paid for an actual total loss, he is entitled to take over the vessel by way of salvage in the event that it subsequently reappears (Marine Insurance Act 1906, s 79, page 82).

The disappearance of a vessel in time of war may give rise to problems of determining whether the claim should be met by marine or war risks underwriters. The presumption applies in time of war: *British & Burmese Steam Navigation Co Ltd* v. *Liverpool & London War Risks Association Ltd* (1917) 34 TLR 140; *Compania Maritima of Barcelona* v. *Wishart* (1918) 23 Com Cas 264. However, if the vessel is lost in a war zone, the presumption that the loss is by marine perils would seem to be somewhat weaker (*General Steam Navigation Co Ltd* v. *Commercial Union Assurance Co Ltd* (1915) 31 TLR 630; *Macbeth & Co* v. *King* (1916) 32 TLR 581; *Euterpe SS Co Ltd* v. *North of England Protecting & Indemnity Association Ltd* (1917) 33 TLR 540; *Munro, Brice & Co* v. *Marten* [1920] 3 KB 94; *Zachariessen* v. *Importers and Exporters Marine Insurance Co* (1924) 29 Com Cas 202; *United Scottish Insurance Co Ltd* v. *British Fishing Vessels Mutual War Risks Association Ltd, "The Braconbush"* (1944) 78 Ll LR 70).

Effect of transhipment, etc

59. Where, by a peril insured against, the voyage is interrupted at an intermediate port or place, under such circumstances as, apart from any special stipulation in the contract of affreightment, to justify the master in landing and re-shipping the goods or other moveables, or in transhipping them, and sending them on to their destination, the liability of the insurer continues, notwithstanding the landing or transhipment.

NOTES

For transhipment generally, see: *Platamour* v. *Staples* (1781) 3 Doug KB 1; *Oliverson* v. *Brightman* (1846) 8 QB 781; *De Cuadra* v. *Swann* (1864) 16 CBNS 772; *Hansen* v. *Dunn* (1906) 11 Com Cas 100. Where transhipment is required as the result of the operation of an insured peril, cl 12 of the Institute Cargo Clauses provides that the insurer is liable for the costs of transhipment (including unload, storing and reloading).

Constructive total loss defined

60.—(1) Subject to any express provision in the policy, there is a constructive total loss where the subject-matter insured is reasonably abandoned on account of its actual total loss appearing to be unavoidable, or because it could not be preserved from actual total loss without an expenditure which would exceed its value when the expenditure had been incurred.

(2) In particular, there is a constructive total loss—

    (i) Where the assured is deprived of the possession of his ship or goods by a peril insured against, and (a) it is unlikely that he can recover the ship or goods, as the case may be, or (b) the cost of recovering the ship or goods, as the case may be, would exceed their value when recovered; or

    (ii) In the case of damage to a ship, where she is so damaged by a peril insured against that the cost of repairing the damage would exceed the value of the ship when repaired.

        In estimating the cost of repairs, no deduction is to be made in respect of general average contributions to those repairs payable by other interests, but account is to be taken of the expense of future salvage operations and of any future general average contributions to which the ship would be liable if repaired; or

(iii) In the case of damage to goods, where the cost of repairing the damage and forwarding the goods to their destination would exceed their value on arrival.

NOTES

The definitions in this section are reproduced with some modifications in cl 13 of the Institute Cargo Clauses, cl 19 of the Institute Time Clauses Hulls, cl 19 and the Institute Voyage Clauses Hulls, cl 17.

Subs (1) Two forms of constructive total loss are set out in the general provisions of subs (1).

(a) Reasonable abandonment of subject-matter. See: *Anderson* v. *Wallis* (1813) 2 M & S 240; *Rowland and Marwood's Steamship Co Ltd* v. *Maritime Insurance Co Ltd* (1901) 6 Com Cas 160. If the subject-matter is abandoned prematurely, the loss is caused by the abandonment rather than by an insured peril and the assured cannot recover (*Becker, Gray & Co* v. *London Assurance Corporation* [1918] AC 101; *Lind* v. *Mitchell* (1928) 32 Ll LR 70, and cf the position when the vessel is sold prematurely as the master erroneously believes that the vessel is a total loss—*Gardner* v. *Salvador* (1831) 1 Moo & Rob 116). A vessel is not abandoned merely because the master and crew leave due to the vessel's damaged state (*Court Line* v. *R, "The Lavington Court"* (1945) 78 Ll LR 390). See also the note to s 55, page 52.

(b) Expenditure to avoid actual total loss greater than salvaged value. For the calculation of expenditure and salvaged value, see the note to subs (2)(c), below.

Subs (2) The situations set out in subs (2) are stated to be illustrations of subs (1), but as drafted appear to be rather different in nature (cf the comments of Lord Wright in *Rickards* v. *Forestal Land, Timber and Railway Co Ltd* [1942] AC 50). Four different forms of constructive total loss are identified.

(a) Deprivation of possession of ship or goods, it being unlikely that they can be recovered. In *Polurrian Steamship Co* v. *Young* [1915] 1 KB 922 and in *Kuwait Airways Corporation* v. *Kuwait Insurance Co SAK* [1996] 1 Lloyd's Rep 664 it was pointed out that the test was "unlikely" and not the more generous "uncertain". For illustrations, see: *Goss* v. *Withers* (1758) 2 Burr 683; *Rotch* v. *Edie* (1795) 6 TR 413; *Brown* v. *Smith* (1813) 1 Dow 349; *Forster* v. *Christie* (1809) 11 East 205; *Rodocanachi* v. *Elliott* (1874) LR 9 CP 518; *Roura & Forgas* v. *Townend* [1919] 1 KB 189; *Captain J A Cates Tug & Wharfage Co Ltd* v. *Franklin Insurance Co* [1927] AC 698; *Société Belge des Bétons SA* v. *London and Lancashire Insurance Co Ltd* (1938) 60 Ll LR 225; *Czarnikow Ltd* v. *Java Sea and Fire Insurance Co Ltd* (1941) 70 Ll LR 319; *Court Line* v. *R, "The Lavington Court"* (1945) 78 Ll LR 390; *Marstrand Fishing Co Ltd* v. *Beer, "The Girl Pat"* (1937) 56 Ll LR 163; *Czarnikow Ltd* v. *Java Sea and Fire Insurance Co Ltd* (1940) 70 Ll LR 319; *Rickards* v. *Forestal Land, Timber and Railway Co Ltd* [1942] AC 50; *Panamanian Oriental Steamship Co* v. *Wright* [1970] 2 Lloyd's Rep 365. The word "unlikely" means in practice that if the assured is likely to be deprived of his property for a period of 12 months, there is a constructive total loss (*"The Bamburi"* [1982] 1 Lloyd's Rep 312), although some policies may specify a lesser period (*Rowland & Marwood SS Co Ltd* v. *Maritime Insurance Co Ltd* (1901) 6 Com Cas 160). If the vessel is captured and recovered by the assured on payment of a sum of money to the captors, the loss is the sum paid and the vessel itself cannot be regarded as totally lost (*M'Masters* v. *Shoolbred* (1794) 1 Esp 236; *Wilson* v. *Forster* (1815) 6 Taunt 25). In *"The Bamburi"* [1982] 1 Lloyd's Rep 312 it was pointed out that loss of possession means loss of the right to use the subject-matter, so that the detention of a vessel or cargo while in the physical possession of the master is nevertheless a loss of possession for insurance purposes. Cf: *Rodocanachi* v. *Elliott* (1874) LR 9 CP 518; *Fooks* v. *Smith* [1924] 2 KB 508; *Czarnikow Ltd* v. *Java Sea and Fire Insurance Co Ltd* [1941] 3 All ER 256; *Kuwait Airways Corporation* v. *Kuwait Insurance Co SAK* [1996] 1 Lloyd's Rep 664. By contrast if the assured is allowed to retain possession and use, there is no constructive total loss, although a sum paid (or debt waived) to avoid capture, by way of ransom, is an effective war risks loss (*A* v. *B* 1996, unreported).

(b) Deprivation of possession of ship or goods, the cost of recovery exceeding recovered value. For illustrations, see: *Rodocanachi* v. *Elliott* (1874) LR 9 CP 518; *Sailing Ship Blaimore* v. *Macredie* [1898] AC 593. There is no constructive total loss where the subject-matter is sold by order of a foreign court and the proceeds are swallowed up by costs or by expenses incurred by the master (*De Mattos* v. *Saunders* (1872) LR 7 CP 570; *Meyer* v. *Ralli* (1876) 1 CPD 358).

(c) Damage to vessel, the cost of repair exceeding repaired value. See: *Allen* v. *Sugrue* (1828) 8 B & C 561; *Phillips* v. *Nairne* (1847) 4 CB 343; *Irving* v. *Manning* (1847) 1 HL Cas 287; *Moss* v. *Smith* (1850) 19 LJCP 225. Contrast: *Gardner* v. *Salvador* (1831) 1 Moo & Rob 116, in which the repaired value exceeded the cost of repair; and *Grainger* v. *Martin* (1863) 4 B & S 9 (cf *"The Harmonides"* [1903] P 1), where the special nature of the vessel meant that no market comparison was possible and thus made repair the only real option even though the cost of repair exceeded the repaired value. In determining the cost of repairs, the common law reached the conclusion that the value of the wreck must be added to the cost of repairs (*Macbeth & Co* v. *Maritime Insurance Co Ltd* [1908] AC 144, overruling *Angel* v. *Merchants' Marine Insurance Co* [1903] 1 KB 811 and reinstating *Young* v. *Turing* (1841) 2 Man & G 593), but the *Macbeth* case reached the House of Lords only after the passing of the 1906 Act, which has subsequently been construed as requiring the value of the wreck to be disregarded (*Hall* v. *Hayman* [1912] 2 KB 5). The Institute Hulls Clauses, cl 17 (voyage) and 19 (hulls), confirm s 60(2)(ii) and require the value of the wreck to be disregarded. The repairs must restore the vessel more or less to her pre-casualty condition (*North Atlantic SS Co Ltd* v. *Bure* (1904) 9 Com Cas 164). In considering the repaired value for determining whether there has been a constructive total loss, the market and not the agreed value must be taken into account (*Irving* v. *Manning* (1847) 1 HL Cas 287, operating as an exception to Marine Insurance Act 1906, s 27(3)—see s 27(4), page 78). The Institute Clauses reverse the statutory rule, and provide that the agreed value is the relevant measure: Institute Voyage Clauses Hulls, cl 17; Institute Time Clauses Hulls, cl 19. The proviso relating to general average contributions is based on *Kemp* v. *Halliday* (1866) LR 1 QB 520.

(d) Damage to goods, the cost of repair and forwarding exceeding arrived value. See: *Boyfield* v. *Brown* (1736) 2 Str 1065; *Glennie* v. *London Assurance Co* (1814) 2 M & S 371; *Parry* v. *Aberdein* (1829) 9 B & C 411; *Reimer* v. *Ringrose* (1851) 6 Exch 263. It was held in *Rosetto* v. *Gurney* (1851) 11 CB 176 and *Farnworth* v. *Hyde* (1866) LR 2 CP 204 that the forwarding cost must be considered net of the original freight, but the section apparently reverses the common law rule by providing that all the forwarding costs must be taken into account.

No mention is made in the section of constructive total loss of freight, presumably on the basis that freight is either lost or not lost. The possibility of constructive total loss of freight was recognised at common law in *Rankin* v. *Potter* (1873) LR 6 HL 83, but doubted in *Carras* v. *London & Scottish Assurance Corporation Ltd* [1936] 1 KB 291.

Equally, s 60 does not refer to the possibility of constructive total loss of goods by frustration of the voyage, a pre-Act concept (illustrated by: *Barker* v. *Blakes* (1808) 9 East 283; *Anderson* v. *Wallis* (1813) 2 M & S 240; *Cologan* v. *London Assurance Co* (1816) 5 M &

S 447; *Miller* v. *Law Accident Insurance Co* [1903] 1 KB 712; *Mansell & Co* v. *Hoade* (1903) 20 TLR 150) which was held by the House of Lords in *British and Foreign Marine Insurance Co* v. *Samuel Sanday & Co* [1916] 1 AC 650, *Becker, Gray & Co* v. *London Assurance Corporation* [1918] AC 101 and *Rickards* v. *Forestal Land, Timber and Railway Co* [1942] AC 50 to have survived the Act. There is no loss of voyage if the master has abandoned the voyage prematurely: *Wilson Bros Bobbin Co Ltd* v. *Green* (1915) 31 TLR 605. Loss of voyage is normally caused by a war risk, and frustration and loss of voyage are now excluded by the Institute War Clauses for cargo (cl 3.7, applied in *Atlantic Maritime Co Inc* v. *Gibbon* [1953] 2 Lloyd's Rep 294).

Finally, s 60 does not contemplate the possibility that the policy may deem particular events as constituting a constructive total loss, although this may be done. Thus, in the case of seizure, the subject-matter may be deemed by the contract to be a constructive total loss if it has not been returned to the assured at the end of a specified period (*Fowler* v. *English and Scottish Marine Insurance Co Ltd* (1865) 18 CBNS 818; *Rowland and Marwood SS Co* v. *Maritime Insurance Co* (1901) 6 Com Cas 160).

These exceptional situations apart, the definition of constructive total loss in s 60 is exhaustive. Thus, if a vessel cannot be repaired due to the assured's inability to obtain a licence, there is no constructive total loss (*Irvin* v. *Hine* [1950] 1 KB 555).

In all cases the question whether there has been a constructive total loss has to be determined both at the date of the loss and at the date at which the writ against the insurer is issued by the assured (*Bainbridge* v. *Nielson* (1808) 10 East 329; *Paterson* v. *Ritchie* (1815) 4 M & S 393; *M'Iver* v. *Henderson* (1816) 4 M & S 576; *Brotherston* v. *Barber* (1816) 5 M & S 418; *Naylor* v. *Taylor* (1829) 9 B & C 718; *Lozano* v. *Janson* (1859) 2 E & E 160; *Shepherd* v. *Henderson* (1881) 7 App Cas 49; *Ruys* v. *Royal Exchange Assurance Corporation* [1897] 2 QB 135; *Sailing Ship Blaimore* v. *Macredie* [1898] AC 593; *Roura and Forgas* v. *Townend* [1919] 1 KB 189), so that if what appears to be a loss at the date of loss proves not to be by the date of the writ, there is no total loss. However, as a matter of practice, insurers accept that the date at which the notice of abandonment is rejected is the relevant date for determining whether there is a constructive total loss so that a change of circumstances after the issue of the writ is to be disregarded (*Barque Robert S Besnard Co Ltd* v. *Murton* (1909) 14 Com Cas 267; *Pollurian Steamship Co* v. *Young* (1913) 19 Com Cas 143; *Panamanian Oriental Steamship Corporation* v. *Wright* [1970] 2 Lloyd's Rep 365; "*The Bamburi*" [1982] 1 Lloyd's Rep 312). Cf the situation in which the policy states that the loss is deemed to be that which it appears to be on a given day, referred to above and illustrated by *Fowler* v. *English & Scottish Marine Insurance Co Ltd* (1865) 18 CBNS 818.

Effect of constructive total loss

61. Where there is a constructive total loss the assured may either treat the loss as a partial loss, or abandon the subject-matter insured to the insurer and treat the loss as if it were an actual total loss.

NOTES

For the mechanics of the exercise of this option, see s 62, page 65. The effect of the assured's decision to treat the loss as a partial loss is merely to affect the measure of indemnity, and the loss remains a total loss for all other purposes (*Petros M Nomikos Ltd* v. *Robertson* [1939] AC 371; *Bank of America National Trust and Savings Corporation* v. *Chrismas, "The Kyriaki"* [1993] 1 Lloyd's Rep 137, discussed in the note to s 56(1), page 58). Once the assured has elected to claim for a partial loss only, he cannot alter his approach and claim for a total loss even though relevant evidence has later come to light (*Martin* v. *Crokatt* (1811) 14 East 465; *Fleming* v. *Smith* (1848) 1 HL Cas 513).

Notice of abandonment

62.—(1) Subject to the provisions of this section, where the assured elects to abandon the subject-matter insured to the insurer, he must give notice of abandonment. If he fails to do so the loss can only be treated as a partial loss.

(2) Notice of abandonment may be given in writing, or by word of mouth, or partly in writing and partly by word of mouth, and may be given in terms which indicate the intention of the assured to abandon his insured interest in the subject-matter insured unconditionally to the insurer.

(3) Notice of abandonment must be given with reasonable diligence after the receipt of reliable information of the loss, but where the information is of a doubtful character the assured is entitled to a reasonable time to make inquiry.

(4) Where notice of abandonment is properly given, the rights of the assured are not prejudiced by the fact that the insurer refuses to accept the abandonment.

(5) The acceptance of an abandonment may be either express or implied from the conduct of the insurer. The mere silence of the insurer after notice is not an acceptance.

(6) Where notice of abandonment is accepted the abandonment is irrevocable. The acceptance of the notice conclusively admits liability for the loss and the sufficiency of the notice.

(7) Notice of abandonment is unnecessary where, at the time when the assured receives information of the loss, there would be no possibility of benefit to the insurer if notice were given to him.

(8) Notice of abandonment may be waived by the insurer.

(9) Where an insurer has re-insured his risk, no notice of abandonment need be given by him.

NOTES

This section is concerned only with preserving the assured's right, following a constructive total loss, to recover an indemnity based on total rather than partial loss; this is achieved by the service of a notice of abandonment. The policy may independently contain notice of loss provisions, which, if expressed as conditions precedent to the insurer's liability have to be complied with whatever the form of the loss (see Institute Time Clauses, cl 10; Institute Voyage Clauses, cl 8), failing which the insurer is not liable for the loss in question. This is so even if the insurer is not prejudiced by the breach of condition. Failure by the assured to disclose all material facts on making the claim may amount to breach of the assured's duty of utmost good faith, allowing the insurer to avoid liability: see the note to s 17, page 14.

Subs (1) See *"The Kyriaki"* [1993] 1 Lloyd's Rep 137, which emphasises that whether or not a notice of abandonment is served, a loss cannot lose its character as a total loss other than for the purpose of the measure of indemnity. For illustrations of the consequences of failure to give notice of abandonment, see *Goldsmid* v. *Gillies* (1813) 4 Taunt 803.

The rationale of the notice of abandonment was discussed by Cotton LJ in *Kaltenbach* v. *Mackenzie* (1878) 3 CPD 467:

(a) the assured is required to make a decision and to inform the insurers of that decision by means of a notice of abandonment, thereby preventing the assured from changing his mind if circumstances should alter;

(b) the underwriters, following receipt of a notice of abandonment, are able to decide what approach to adopt with respect to the property abandoned to them.

Subs (2) The principle that the word "abandon" need not be used as long as the assured's intentions are clear, comes from *M'Masters* v. *Shoolbred* (1794) 1 Esp 236, *King* v. *Walker*

(1864) 3 H & C 209 and *Currie & Co* v. *Bombay Native Insurance Co* (1869) LR 3 PC 72. Several documents may be joined for this purpose (*Panamanian Oriental Steamship Corporation* v. *Wright* [1971] 1 Lloyd's Rep 487). A claim may constitute a valid notice of abandonment (*Cohen Sons & Co* v. *Standard Marine Insurance Co Ltd* (1925) 21 Ll LR 30). A request or proposal to the insurer is not a notice of abandonment (*Parmeter* v. *Todhunter* (1808) 1 Camp 541; *Martin* v. *Crokatt* (1811) 14 East 465; *Russian Bank for Foreign Trade* v. *Excess Insurance Co* [1919] 1 KB 39; *Vacuum Oil Co* v. *Union Insurance Society of Canton Ltd* (1926) 25 Ll LR 546). A notice of abandonment, to be valid, must be given to a person authorised by the insurer to receive it, and not merely to the assured's own agent (*Vacuum Oil Co* v. *Union Insurance Society of Canton Ltd* (1926) 25 Ll LR 546). It may be given by a co-assured in respect of his own interest only or on behalf of all interested parties (*Hunt* v. *Royal Exchange Assurance* (1816) 5 M & S 47), but not by a person with a mere security interest in the insured subject-matter (*Jardine* v. *Leathley* (1863) 32 LJQB 132).

Subs (3) The first part of this provision reflects the justification of a notice of abandonment, that the assured, having become aware of the loss, cannot wait to see how things develop (*Kaltenbach* v. *Mackenzie* (1878) 3 CPD 467). See also: *Mitchell* v. *Edie* (1797) 1 TR 608; *Anderson* v. *Royal Exchange Assurance Co* (1805) 7 East 38; *Barker* v. *Blakes* (1808) 9 East 283; *Kelly* v. *Walton* (1808) 2 Camp 155; *Hunt* v. *Royal Exchange Assurance Co* (1816) 5 M & S 47; *Aldridge* v. *Bell* (1816) 1 Stark 498; *Hudson* v. *Harrison* (1821) 3 B & B 97; *Fleming* v. *Smith* (1848) 1 HL Cas 513; *Grainger* v. *Martin* (1863) 4 B & S 9; *King* v. *Walker* (1864) 3 H & C 209; *Potter* v. *Campbell* (1867) 17 LT 474; *Currie* v. *Bombay Native Assurance Co* (1869) LR 3 PC 72. Under s 88 of the Marine Insurance Act 1906, what is a reasonable time is a question of fact. For the second part of the section, delay pending confirmation of the extent of the loss, see *Gernon* v. *Royal Exchange Assurance* (1815) 6 Taunt 383.

Subs (4) See *Brooks* v. *MacDonnell* (1835) 1 Y & C Ex 500. One consequence of this provision is that the assured can withdraw a notice of abandonment before acceptance (*Pesquerias y Secaderos de Bacalao de España SA* v. *Beer* (1947) 80 Ll LR 318) and this may be done by conduct, eg, in operating the vessel (*A* v. *B* 1996, unreported).

Subs (5) The position is illustrated by *Provincial Insurance Co of Canada* v. *Leduc* (1874) LR 6 PC 224, where silence on the part of the insurers, coupled with their taking over the abandoned subject-matter, was held to be acceptance. See also: *Bainbridge* v. *Nielson* (1808) 10 East 329; *Hudson* v. *Harrison* (1821) 3 B & B 97, where inactivity for a lengthy period was held to be acceptance; *Sailing Ship Blaimore* v. *Macredie* [1898] AC 593. Contrast: *Thelluson* v. *Fletcher* (1793) 1 Esp 73; *Shepherd* v. *Henderson* (1881) 7 App Cas 49, where there was no acceptance by underwriters taking possession only in order to effect repairs and informing the assured accordingly, *Captain JA Cates Tug and Wharfage Co Ltd* v. *Franklin Insurance Co* [1927] AC 698, where salvage was effected but coupled with a rejection of the assured's notice of abandonment. The Institute Cargo Clauses make it clear that any action taken by the insurers to preserve the subject-matter shall not be taken as any acceptance of a notice of abandonment (cl 17).

Subs (6) This is based on: *Da Costa* v. *Firth* (1766) 4 Burr 1966; *Smith* v. *Robertson* (1814) 2 Dow 474. For an illustration of waiver of insufficiency of notice, see *Provincial Insurance Co of Canada* v. *Leduc* (1874) LR 6 PC 224. Subs (6) has been held not to preclude an insurer from revoking a binding acceptance on subsequently discovering that the loss had been caused by an uninsured peril (*Norwich Union Fire Insurance Society* v. *Price Ltd* [1934] AC 455) or that the policy was voidable for non-disclosure (*Fraser Shipping Ltd* v. *Colton* [1997] 1 Lloyd's Rep 586). In the same way an insurer who accepts an adjustment may set it aside if the loss proves to have been caused by an uninsured peril or if the insurer possessed some other defence under the policy which had not been waived (*Shepherd* v. *Chewter* (1808) 1 Camp 274; *Steel* v. *Lacy* (1810) 3 Taunt 285; *Scottish Metropolitan Assurance Co* v. *Samuel & Co* [1923] 1 KB 348; and cf *Holland* v. *Russell* (1863) 4 B & S 14, where the underwriters failed to obtain a return of the insurance moneys from the assured's broker who had transmitted the money to the assured). An adjustment is in any event presumed not to be binding on the insurer until it has been accepted (*Castle Insurance Co* v. *Hong Kong Islands Shipping Co* [1983] 2 Lloyd's Rep 376; *Attaleia Marine Co Ltd* v. *Iran Insurance Co, "The Zeus"* [1993] 2 Lloyd's Rep 497).

Subs (7) This provision is narrow in its impact on losses affecting vessels and cargo, as it is based on the notion that the insurer is entitled to insist upon notice unless no further useful action can be taken by him in relation to the subject-matter: such a possibility is unlikely unless there has been an actual total loss (cf: *Associated Oil Carriers Ltd* v. *Union Insurance Society of Canton Ltd* [1917] 2 KB 184; *Vacuum Oil Co* v. *Union Insurance Society of Canton* (1926) 25 Ll LR 546). Justifiable emergency sale by the master for the benefit of the underwriters may, however, excuse the need for a notice of abandonment, as no benefit can accrue to them (*Farnworth* v. *Hyde* (1865) 18 CBNS 835; *Cobequid Marine Insurance Co* v. *Barteaux* (1875) LR 6 PC 319; *Trinder, Anderson & Co* v. *Thames and Mersey Marine Insurance Co* [1898] 2 QB 114).

There is much authority for the proposition that no notice of abandonment is necessary in the case of lost freight, which may be another way of saying that there cannot be a constructive total loss of freight (*Green* v. *Royal Exchange Assurance* (1815) 6 Taunt 68; *Mount* v. *Harrison* (1827) 4 Bing 388; *Rankin* v. *Potter* (1873) LR 6 HL 83; *Trinder, Anderson & Co* v. *Thames and Mersey Marine Insurance Co* [1898] 2 QB 114; *Associated Oil Carriers Ltd* v. *Union Insurance Society of Canton Ltd* [1917] 2 KB 184).

Subs (8) For waiver, see: *Houstman* v. *Thornton* (1816) Holt NP 242; *Rickards* v. *Forestal Land, Timber and Railway Co Ltd* [1942] AC 50.

Subs (9) This is based on *Uzielli* v. *Boston Marine Insurance Co* (1884) 15 QBD 11.

Effect of abandonment

63.—(1) Where there is a valid abandonment the insurer is entitled to take over the interest of the assured in whatever may remain of the subject-matter insured, and all proprietary rights incidental thereto.

(2) Upon the abandonment of a ship, the insurer thereof is entitled to any freight in course of being earned, and which is earned by her subsequent to the casualty causing the loss, less the expenses of earning it incurred after the casualty; and, where the ship is carrying the owner's goods, the insurer is entitled to a reasonable remuneration for the carriage of them subsequent to the casualty causing the loss.

NOTES

Subs (1) The insurer is given the right to take over property abandoned to him in the case of a total loss, a right which is retroactive to the date of the loss and not merely from the acceptance of the notice of abandonment (*Cammell* v. *Sewell* (1858) 3 H & N 617). The insurer may, therefore, take over the remains of a vessel or cargo, or of a ship presumed lost which has been discovered safe and sound (*Houstman* v. *Thornton* (1816) Holt NP 242). The assured is divested of ownership as from the date of the loss following the acceptance of a notice of abandonment (*Arrow Shipping Co* v. *Tyne Improvement Commissioners* [1894] AC 508; *Barraclough* v. *Brown* [1897] AC 615). Earlier liabilities incurred by the assured remain with him (*"The Ella"* [1915] P 111; *Dee Conservancy Board* v. *McConnell* [1928] 2 KB 159). It is unclear whether the insurer can refuse to take over property having accepted a notice of abandonment. Prior to the 1906 Act the point was unresolved (and was expressly left open in *Arrow Shipping Co* v. *Tyne Improvement Commissioners* [1894] AC 508), but the wording of the 1906 Act indicates that the matter is optional as far as the insurer is concerned, and it has been said that if the insurer declines to take over abandoned property, it becomes *res nullius* (*Boston Corporation* v. *Fenwick & Co Ltd* (1923) 15 Ll LR 85; *Allgemeine Versicherungs-Gesellschaft Helvetia* v. *Administrator of German Property* [1931] 1 KB 672), but in later cases the view has been expressed that the property vests in the insurer irrespective of the insurer's wishes (*Oceanic Steam Navigation Co Ltd* v. *Evans* (1934) 50 Ll LR 1; *Blane Steamships Ltd* v. *Minister of Transport* [1951] 2 KB 965).

Salvage is not available to the insurer in the event of a partial loss (*Tunno* v. *Edwards* (1810) 12 East 488; *Goldsmid* v. *Gillies* (1813) 4 Taunt 803; *Brooks* v. *Macdonnell* (1835) 1 Y & C Ex 500).

Subs (2) The principle that the hull insurer is entitled to freight in the course of being earned was settled by *Sea Insurance Co* v. *Hadden* (1884) 13 QBD 706. Cf also: *Luke* v. *Lyde* (1759) 2 Burr 882; *Barclay* v. *Stirling* (1816) 5 M & S 6; *Davidson* v. *Case* (1820) 2 Brod & Bing 379; *Stewart* v. *Greenock Insurance Co* (1848) 2 HL Cas 159; *Keith* v. *Burrows* (1877) 2 App Cas 636; *"The Red Sea"* [1896] P 20, and see the note to s 55(1), page 52. This rule necessarily did not apply where the assured transhipped the cargo and earned freight in so doing (*Hickie & Borman* v. *Rodocanachi* (1859) 4 H & N 455). The practice is for the hull insurer to waive freight in favour of the freight insurer (Institute Time Clauses Hulls, cl 20; Institute Voyage Clauses Hulls, cl 18, and see: *United Kingdom Mutual SS Assurance* v. *Boulton* (1898) 3 Com Cas 330; *Coker* v. *Bolton* [1912] 3 KB 315). As to the right of the insurer to claim reasonable remuneration for carriage of goods, see: *Miller* v. *Woodfall* (1857) 27 LJQB 120; *Keith* v. *Burrows* (1877) 2 App Cas 636.

Partial Losses (including Salvage and General Average and Particular Charges)

Particular average loss

64.—(1) A particular average loss is a partial loss of the subject-matter insured, caused by a peril insured against, and which is not a general average loss.

(2) Expenses incurred by or on behalf of the assured for the safety or preservation of the subject-matter insured, other than general average and salvage charges, are called particular charges. Particular charges are not included in particular average.

NOTES

Subs (1) A particular average loss is simply a partial loss, excluding any general average contributions which the assured has to make to any person who has sacrificed expenditure or property for common good (Marine Insurance Act 1906, s 66, page 70). General average contributions are covered separately by a standard marine policy.

Subs (2) "Particular charges" are losses incurred by the assured in preserving the subject-matter, other than by way of general average contributions. Particular charges also exclude "salvage charges", defined by s 65, below, as charges payable to a salvor in the absence of contract. See *Kidston* v. *Empire Marine Insurance Co* (1867) LR 2 CP 357. Consequently, particular charges will include contractual salvage charges, and will be recoverable under the suing and labouring clause (Marine Insurance Act 1906, s 78, page 79).

Salvage charges

65.—(1) Subject to any express provision in the policy, salvage charges incurred in preventing a loss by perils insured against may be recovered as a loss by those perils.

(2) "Salvage charges" means the charges recoverable under maritime law by a salvor independently of contract. They do not include the expenses of services in the nature of salvage rendered by the assured or his agents, or any person employed for hire by them, for the purpose of averting a peril insured against. Such expenses, where properly incurred, may be recovered as particular charges or as a general average loss, according to the circumstances under which they were incurred.

NOTES

Salvage charges—defined by subs (2) as excluding salvage under contract—are recoverable under the policy as marine losses (*Nourse* v. *Liverpool SS Owners' Mutual Protection and Indemnity Association* [1896] 2 QB 21; *Grand Union Shipping Ltd* v. *London SS Owners' Mutual Insurance Association Ltd*, *"The Bosworth"* [1962] 1 Lloyd's Rep 483). Contractual salvage, which in practice accounts for most salvage (under the Lloyd's Open Form), is recoverable under the suing and labouring clause (Marine Insurance Act 1906, s 78, page 79). The distinction between contractual and maritime salvage was drawn by the House of Lords in *Aitchison* v. *Lohre* (1879) 4 App Cas 755, where their Lordships held that salvage under maritime law did not fall within the suing and labouring clause, on the basis that a voluntary salvor was not the agent of the assured for the purposes of a suing and labouring clause. The most significant difference between contractual and maritime salvage charges is that the former, as they fall within the suing and labouring clause, are recoverable independently of the insurance contract and without reference to the maximum sum insured under the policy, while the latter form part of the cover provided by the policy and must thus be added to the loss under the policy itself which may be subject to a maximum figure.

Salvage charges are recoverable only where the salvage is in consequence of the operation of an insured peril (*Ballantyne* v. *Mackinnon* [1896] 2 QB 455). The same principle applies to contractual salvage under the suing and labouring clause.

General average loss

66.—(1) A general average loss is a loss caused by or directly consequential on a general average act. It includes a general average expenditure as well as a general average sacrifice.

(2) There is a general average act where any extraordinary sacrifice or expenditure is voluntarily and reasonably made or incurred in time of peril for the purpose of preserving the property imperilled in the common adventure.

(3) Where there is a general average loss, the party on whom it falls is entitled, subject to the conditions imposed by maritime law, to a rateable contribution from the other parties interested, and such contribution is called a general average contribution.

(4) Subject to any express provision in the policy, where the assured has incurred a general average expenditure, he may recover from the insurer in respect of the proportion of the loss which falls upon him; and, in the case of a general average sacrifice, he may recover from the insurer in respect of the whole loss without having enforced his right of contribution from the other parties liable to contribute.

(5) Subject to any express provision in the policy, where the assured has paid, or is liable to pay, a general average contribution in respect of the subject insured, he may recover therefor from the insurer.

(6) In the absence of express stipulation, the insurer is not liable for any general average loss or contribution where the loss was not incurred for the purpose of avoiding, or in connexion with the avoidance of, a peril insured against.

(7) Where ship, freight, and cargo, or any two of those interests, are owned by the same assured, the liability of the insurer in respect of general average losses or contributions is to be determined as if those subjects were owned by different persons.

NOTES

The rules laid down in s 66(1)–(3) and (7) are general common law principles. In practice, general average is adjusted in accordance with the York Antwerp Rules, which contain detailed definitions of general average acts as well as rules for making adjustments. Insurance aspects of general average are dealt with by s 66(4)–(7).

Subs (4) If the assured has suffered a loss in the form of a general average expenditure his proportion of the loss is recoverable from the insurer (*Carisbrook Steamship Co Ltd* v. *London and Provincial Marine and General Insurance Co Ltd* (1901) 6 Com Cas 291; *Brandeis, Goldschmidt & Co Ltd* v. *Economic Insurance Co Ltd* (1922) 11 Ll LR 42; *Green Star Shipping Co Ltd* v. *London Assurance* [1933] 1 KB 378). However, the right of contribution from third parties must be enforced before recovery from insurers is possible: *Comatra Ltd* v. *Lloyd's Underwriters* 1999, unreported. If the assured has suffered a loss in the form of a general average sacrifice the full amount of the loss (disregarding any contributions due to him) is recoverable from the insurer who is then subrogated to the assured's rights against persons liable to make contributions (*Dickinson* v. *Jardine* (1868) LR 3 CP 639: *Steamship Balmoral Co* v. *Marten* [1901] 2 KB 896), These principles are repeated in the Institute Time Clauses Hulls, cl 11.1 and the Institute Voyage Clauses Hulls, cl 9.1. The measure of loss under a general average sacrifice is not subject to the one-third customary deduction for repaired vessels laid down by the common law under s 69, page 72 (*Henderson Brothers* v. *Shankland* [1896] 1 QB 525).

Subs (5) General average contributions payable by the assured to a person incurring a general average expenditure or general average sacrifice are themselves recoverable under the policy. See the Institute Cargo Clauses, cl 2. The amount recoverable is regulated by Marine Insurance Act 1906, s 73, page 76.

Subs (6) General average losses and contributions are recoverable only where an insured peril has led to the general average act. If the assured mistakenly believes that there is a peril in operation, and a sacrifice is made accordingly, the insurers are not liable (*Watson & Son Ltd* v. *Firemen's Fund Insurance Co of San Francisco* [1922] 2 KB 355). Standard London market policies do not provide to the contrary: Institute Time Clauses Hulls, cl 11.4, Institute Voyage Clauses Hulls, cl 9.4, Institute Cargo Clauses, cl 2 (which covers general average contributions as long as the event was not specifically excluded from coverage).

Subs (7) This is based on *Montgomery & Co* v. *Indemnity Mutual Marine Insurance Co* [1902] 1 KB 734.

Measure of Indemnity

Extent of liability of insurer for loss

67.—(1) The sum which the assured can recover in respect of a loss on a policy by which he is insured, in the case of an unvalued policy to the full extent of the insurable value, or, in the case of a valued policy to the full extent of the value fixed by the policy, is called the measure of indemnity.

(2) Where there is a loss recoverable under the policy, the insurer, or each insurer if there be more than one, is liable for such proportion of the measure of indemnity as the amount of his subscription bears to the value fixed by the policy in the case of a valued policy, or to the insurable value in the case of an unvalued policy.

NOTES

The measure of indemnity laid down in this and the succeeding sections is exhaustive. Losses falling outside these sections, other than interest, are irrecoverable. An assured may not, therefore, recover damages for distress or disturbance resulting from the insurer's late payment. The policy may, however, extend the range of sums available, eg in respect of exemplary damages (see the note to s 74, page 76). A claim under an insurance policy is in any event a claim for unliquidated damages (*Boddington* v. *Castelli* (1853) 1 E & B 879; *Pellas* v. *Neptune Marine Insurance Co* (1879) 5 CPD 34) so that late payment cannot be a breach of contract, the insurer being in deemed breach as from the date of loss (*Ventouris* v. *Mountain, The Italian Express* [1992] 2 Lloyd's Rep 281; *Sprung* v. *Royal Insurance Co (UK)* [1999] Lloyd's Rep IR 111 (where it was accepted that it was arguable that a policy of insurance contained an implied term that payment would be made within a reasonable time; and see also *Pride Valley Foods Ltd* v. *Independent Insurance Co Ltd* [1999] Lloyd's Rep IR 120).

Subs (1) The measure of indemnity is calculated, in the case of a valued policy by reference to the agreed value and in the case of an unvalued policy by reference to the insurable value as calculated in accordance with s 16 of the 1906 Act, page 13.

Subs (2) The insurer is liable only for the proportion of the insurable value which he has insured. Thus, if the agreed or insurable value is £100,000, and the insured sum is £50,000, the insurer is liable for one-half of the amount of any loss. It follows that, in the event of underinsurance, the assured is deemed to be his own insurer for the uninsured sum and is deemed to be required to contribute the uninsured proportion. Where more than one insurer is involved, the same principle applies, so that if the agreed or insurable value is £150,000 and the assured is insured for £50,000 with each of two insurers, a loss of £75,000 would require contributions of £25,000 from each of the insurers while the assured is deemed to be his own insurer for the uninsured amount.

Total loss

68. Subject to the provisions of this Act and to any express provision in the policy, where there is a total loss of the subject-matter insured,—

    (1) If the policy be a valued policy, the measure of indemnity is the sum fixed by the policy:

    (2) If the policy be an unvalued policy, the measure of indemnity is the insurable value of the subject-matter insured.

NOTES

This section is relatively straightforward. If there is a total loss under a valued policy, the assured receives the agreed value, subject to any excess or financial ceiling in the policy (*Lidgett* v. *Secretan* (1871) LR 6 CP 616). Actual values are disregarded, so that the assured may make a profit or suffer a shortfall (*Barker* v. *Janson* (1868) LR 3 CP 303; *Steamship Balmoral Co* v. *Marten* [1902] AC 511). If there is a total loss under an unvalued policy, the assured receives the insurable value as defined by s 16 of the 1906 Act, page 13, subject to any excess or financial ceiling in the policy.

Partial loss of ship

69. Where a ship is damaged, but is not totally lost, the measure of indemnity, subject to any express provision in the policy, is as follows:—

    (1) Where the ship has been repaired, the assured is entitled to the reasonable cost of the repairs, less the customary deductions, but not exceeding the sum insured in respect of any one casualty:

(2) Where the ship has been only partially repaired, the assured is entitled to the reasonable cost of such repairs, computed as above, and also to be indemnified for the reasonable depreciation, if any, arising from the unrepaired damage, provided that the aggregate amount shall not exceed the cost of repairing the whole damage, computed as above:

(3) Where the ship has not been repaired, and has not been sold in her damaged state during the risk, the assured is entitled to be indemnified for the reasonable depreciation arising from the unrepaired damage, but not exceeding the reasonable cost of repairing such damage, computed as above.

NOTES

In the event of the partial loss of a ship, the agreed or insurable values of the ship remain the basis of the calculation of the assured's indemnity, and the measure of indemnity is based on the three situations set out in s 69. In each case, the maximum amount recoverable is the sum insured under the policy (*Goole and Hull Steam Towing Co Ltd* v. *Ocean Marine Insurance Co Ltd* (1927) 29 Ll LR 242).

Subs (1) (full repair by the assured). Here, the assured obtains the reasonable cost of repairs, subject to customary deductions. The reasonable cost of repairs will include docking and surveyors' costs (*Ruabon SS Co* v. *London Assurance* [1900] AC 6; *Agenoria SS Co* v. *Merchants' Marine Insurance Co* (1903) 8 Com Cas 212; *Helmville Ltd* v. *Yorkshire Insurance Co Ltd, "The Medina Princess"* [1965] 1 Lloyd's Rep 361, but contrast *Marine Insurance Co* v. *China Transpacific SS Co* (1886) 11 App Cas 573 where dock expenses were incurred for the assured's own purposes) and the cost of towing the vessel to the port of repair (*"The Medina Princess"* [1965] 1 Lloyd's Rep 361), but excludes costs incurred in relation to the cargo (*Field SS Co* v. *Burr* [1899] 1 QB 579; *Polurrian SS Co* v. *Young* (1913) 9 Com Cas 142) and other consequential losses such as the wages of the crew and loss of profit (*Robertson* v. *Ewer* (1786) 1 TR 127; *Sharp* v. *Gladstone* (1805) 7 East 24; *Everth* v. *Smith* (1814) 2 M & S 278; *De Vaux* v. *Salvador* (1836) 4 Ad & El 420; *Shelbourne & Co* v. *Law Investment and Insurance Corporation* [1898] 2 QB 626). The customary deduction referred to was the old "two-thirds" rule under which the assured would lose one-third of reasonable repair costs (*Da Costa* v. *Newnham* (1788) 2 TR 407; *Poindestre* v. *Royal Exchange Corporation* (1826) Ry & M 378; *Aitchison* v. *Lohre* (1879) 4 App Cas 755). This rule did not extend to a vessel on its first voyage (*Fenwick* v. *Robinson* (1828) 3 C & P 323), to an iron vessel (*Lidgett* v. *Secretan* (1871) LR 6 CP 616), to a vessel which was not restored to the assured following repair (*Da Costa* v. *Newnham* (1788) 2 TR 407), and to the cost of a general average sacrifice (*Henderson Brothers* v. *Shankland & Co* [1896] 1 QB 525) and is no longer applied in practice (see the Institute Time Clauses Hulls, cl 14 and the Institute Voyage Clauses Hulls, cl 12, which give the assured full recovery on a "new for old" basis).

Subs (2) (partial repair by the assured). Here, the assured obtains the reasonable cost of the repairs effected, plus depreciation flowing from the unrepaired damage, subject to a maximum recovery of the reasonable cost of full repairs as calculated under subs (1). The assured may not, therefore, profit by effecting only partial repairs. It is unclear how, in the case of a valued policy, depreciation is to be calculated under this provision: see the discussion in *Irvin* v. *Hine* [1950] 1 KB 555, where the court refused to choose between agreed value minus actual damaged value, and the proportion of the agreed value given by the proportion of actual depreciation. See also Institute Time Clauses Hulls, cl 18 and Institute Voyage Clauses Hulls, cl 16. For the earlier common law, see *Lidgett* v. *Secretan* (1871) LR 6 CP 616. The point was considered by Colman J in *Kusel* v. *Atkin, "The Catariba"* [1997] 2 Lloyd's Rep

749, where it was held that depreciation is the reduced value of the damaged vessel as against the insured value.

Subs (3) (no repair). Here, the assured recovers the depreciation flowing from the unrepaired damage (as to which see *Irvin* v. *Hine* [1950] 1 KB 555, subs (2) above and *Manifest Shipping & Co Ltd* v. *Uni-Polaris Insurance Co Ltd, "The Star Sea"* [1995] 1 Lloyd's Rep 651, affirmed [1997] 1 Lloyd's Rep 360), subject to a maximum recovery of the reasonable cost of full repair had the repairs been carried out, as calculated under subs (1). The date at which the amount of depreciation is to be assessed is, under a voyage policy, when the voyage is abandoned, and, under a time policy, when the policy expires (*Helmville Ltd* v. *Yorkshire Insurance Co, "The Medina Princess"* [1965] 1 Lloyd's Rep 361; *"The Catariba"* [1997] 2 Lloyd's Rep 749).

Section 69 does not deal in express terms with a fourth possibility, namely, the case in which the vessel has not been repaired but has been sold. In *Pitman* v. *Universal Marine Insurance Co* (1882) 9 QBD 192 the Court of Appeal ruled that the correct measure was the reasonable cost of repairs, as calculated under subs (1), but subject to a ceiling represented by depreciation.

Partial loss of freight

70. Subject to any express provision in the policy, where there is a partial loss of freight, the measure of indemnity is such proportion of the sum fixed by the policy in the case of a valued policy, or of the insurable value in the case of an unvalued policy, as the proportion of freight lost by the assured bears to the whole freight at the risk of the assured under the policy.

NOTES

Where freight is partially lost, the agreed or insurable value is the basis of the calculation, the assured recovering such proportion of that value as the amount of freight lost bears to the total freight. This is based on: *Forbes* v. *Cowie* (1808) 1 Camp 520; *Forbes* v. *Aspinall* (1811) 13 East 323; *Denoon* v. *Home & Colonial Assurance* (1872) LR 7 CP 341. Contrast *"The Main"* [1894] P 320, in which part of the freight had ceased to be at risk.

At common law the assured is entitled to recover gross freight, ie, without deduction for savings in wages and other costs which would have been incurred had the vessel completed its voyage (*Palmer* v. *Blackburn* (1822) 1 Bing 61; *United States Shipping Co* v. *Empress Assurance Corporation* [1907] 1 KB 259). The Institute Freight Clauses maintain gross freight recovery, subject to deduction for other insurance recoveries: Institute Time Clauses (Freight), cl 13; Institute Voyage Clauses (Freight), cl 11.

Partial loss of goods, merchandise, etc

71. Where there is a partial loss of goods, merchandise, or other moveables, the measure of indemnity, subject to any express provision in the policy, is as follows:—

(1) Where part of the goods, merchandise or other moveables insured by a valued policy is totally lost, the measure of indemnity is such proportion of the sum fixed by the policy as the insurable value of the part lost bears to the insurable value of the whole, ascertained as in the case of an unvalued policy:

(2) Where part of the goods, merchandise, or other moveables insured by an unvalued policy is totally lost, the measure of indemnity is the insurable value of the part lost, ascertained as in case of total loss:

(3) Where the whole or any part of the goods or merchandise insured has been delivered damaged at its destination, the measure of indemnity is such proportion of the sum fixed by the policy in the case of a valued policy, or of the insurable value in the case of an unvalued policy, as the difference between the gross sound and damaged values at the place of arrival bears to the gross sound value:

(4) "Gross value" means the wholesale price, or, if there be no such price, the estimated value, with, in either case, freight, landing charges, and duty paid beforehand; provided that, in the case of goods or merchandise customarily sold in bond, the bonded price is deemed to be the gross value. "Gross proceeds" means the actual price obtained at a sale where all charges on sale are paid by the sellers.

NOTES

Subs (1) In the case of a valued policy, the assured recovers the proportion of the agreed value that the actual value (ie, insurable value calculated under s 16) lost bears to the actual (insurable) value of the whole. This is based on: *Lewis* v. *Rucker* (1761) 2 Burr 1167; *Johnson* v. *Sheddon* (1802) 2 East 581; *Goldsmid* v. *Gillies* (1813) 4 Taunt 803; *Irving* v. *Manning* (1847) 1 HL Cas 287; *Anstey* v. *Ocean Marine Insurance Co* (1913) 19 Com Cas 8. If the insurable value cannot be ascertained, the assured is entitled to recover the full amount of the loss (*Tobin* v. *Harford* (1863) 13 CBNS 791). If the remainder of the cargo is undamaged but is devalued as a result of the loss, the insurer is not liable for the depreciation (*Cator* v. *Great Western Insurance Co of New York* (1873) LR 8 CP 552; *Lysaght Ltd* v. *Coleman* [1895] 1 QB 49; but contrast *Brown Bros* v. *Fleming* (1902) 7 Com Cas 245).

Subs (2) In the case of an unvalued policy, the assured simply recovers the proportion of the insured value which the sum lost bears to the full insurable value.

Subs (3) This provision lays down a special rule for cargo which is delivered at its destination in a damaged state. If the policy is valued, the assured recovers the proportion of the agreed value that the actual diminution in value bears to the actual value. Thus, if cargo with an agreed value of £90,000 would have been worth £120,000 at its destination had it arrived in a sound condition,, and in its damaged condition was worth at its destination only £40,000, the assured recovers 80:120 of £90,000, ie, £60,000.

In the case of an unvalued policy, the same calculation is carried out, using the insurable value as determined under s 16 of the 1906 Act.

The subsection is based on: *Lewis* v. *Rucker* (1761) 2 Burr 1167; *Johnson* v. *Sheddon* (1802) 2 East 581; *Hurry* v. *Royal Exchange Assurance* (1802) 3 Bos & P 308; *Francis* v. *Boulton* (1895) 65 LJQB 153. For an application of the subsection, see *Whiting* v. *New Zealand Insurance Co* (1932) 44 Ll LR 179.

Apportionment of valuation

72.—(1) Where different species of property are insured under a single valuation, the valuation must be apportioned over the different species in proportion to their respective insurable values, as in the case of an unvalued policy. The insured value of any part of a species is such proportion of the total insured value of the same as the insurable value of the part bears to the insurable value of the whole, ascertained in both cases as provided by this Act.

(2) Where a valuation has to be apportioned, and particulars of the prime cost of each separate species, quality, or description of goods cannot be ascertained, the division of the valuation may be made over the net arrived sound values of the different species, qualities, or descriptions of goods.

NOTES

This section deals with the situation in which different types of property are insured under a single valued policy.

Subs (1) provides that if just one type of property is damaged, the assured's measure of indemnity is based on the relationship between the insurable value (ie, actual value at the inception of risk, in accordance with s 16, page 13) of the property damaged and the total sum insured. Thus, if the assured procures a valued policy for £16,000 covering property A with an insurable value of £10,000 and property B with an insurable value of £10,000, and property A is destroyed, the assured recovers £8,000 and not £10,000. The purpose is to protect the insurer in the event of underinsurance. The above process operates automatically in the case of an unvalued policy.

Subs (2) If, for the purposes of the above calculation the insurable value cannot be ascertained, then in the case of goods the net arrived sound value is to be taken as the basis of measurement.

General average contributions and salvage charges

73.—(1) Subject to any express provision in the policy, where the assured has paid, or is liable for, any general average contribution, the measure of indemnity is the full amount of such contribution, if the subject-matter liable to contribution is insured for its full contributory value; but, if such subject-matter be not insured for its full contributory value, or if only part of it be insured, the indemnity payable by the insurer must be reduced in proportion to the under insurance, and where there has been a particular average loss which constitutes a deduction from the contributory value, and for which the insurer is liable, that amount must be deducted from the insured value in order to ascertain what the insurer is liable to contribute.

(2) Where the insurer is liable for salvage charges the extent of his liability must be determined on the like principle.

NOTES

Subs (1) This section carries over the proportionate recovery principle, which operates in respect of underinsurance, to general average contributions (see s 66 of the 1906 Act, page 70). If the assured is liable for general average contributions, the insurer need indemnify him only for a sum representing the proportion of cover obtained by the assured. Thus, if the assured is 50 per cent underinsured, the insurer will be liable only for 50 per cent of the assured's general average contributions. This rule is based on *SS Balmoral Co v. Marten* [1902] AC 511. The same principle applies to cases in which the assured's own property has been partially lost.

Subs (2) The principle applicable to general average contributions applies equally to salvage charges (see s 65, page 69).

The insurer's obligation to indemnify the assured for suing and labouring costs—in accordance with s 78 of the Marine Insurance Act 1906, page 79—is in practice also restricted to the proportion of primary cover which the assured has obtained.

Liabilities to third parties

74. Where the assured has effected an insurance in express terms against any liability to a third party, the measure of indemnity, subject to any express provision in the policy, is the amount paid or payable by him to such third party in respect of such liability.

NOTES

The insurer's obligation to indemnify the assured against liability is a separate type of undertaking to insurance on property, even though it appears in the same policy. Consequently, if the assured is underinsured as regards the hull and machinery, the amount payable by the insurer under the liability section is not reduced proportionately (*Joyce* v. *Kennard* (1871) LR 7 QB 78; *Cunard SS Co* v. *Marten* [1902] 2 KB 624). The London Hulls clauses do cover collision liability on this basis. A liability policy may legitimately indemnify the assured for exemplary damages awarded against him (*Lancashire County Council* v. *Municipal Mutual Insurance Ltd* [1995] LRLR 293).

There may on occasion be some difficulty in distinguishing between a first party property policy and a third party liability policy, particularly where the assured is a bailee and is entitled to insure for the full value of the cargo as well as or as an alternative to insuring against his own liability. There is a presumption that a bailee's policy covers the property rather than liability (*Hepburn* v. *Tomlinson (Hauliers)* [1966] AC 451).

General provisions as to measure of indemnity

75.—(1) Where there has been a loss in respect of any subject-matter not expressly provided for in the foregoing provisions of this Act, the measure of indemnity shall be ascertained, as nearly as may be, in accordance with those provisions, in so far as applicable to the particular case.

(2) Nothing in the provisions of this Act relating to the measure of indemnity shall affect the rules relating to double insurance, or prohibit the insurer from disproving interest wholly or in part, or from showing that at the time of the loss the whole or any part of the subject-matter insured was not at risk under the policy.

NOTES

Subs (1) The subsection extends the principles of indemnity set out in the Act to forms of cover which are marine in nature but which are not caught by the Act, as in the case of share certificates (which are not within the definition of cargo) despatched by sea (*Baring Brothers & Co* v. *Marine Insurance Co* (1894) 10 TLR 276.

Subs (2) The obvious point here made is that the measure of indemnity is subject to other provisions of the Act which may operate to reduce the insurer's liability, eg, double insurance (s 32), want of insurable interest (s 6) or the fact that the subject-matter was not at risk—for any one of a variety of factual or legal reasons—when the loss occurred. Equally, if part of the subject-matter was not at risk, the insurer's liability is reduced proportionately (*Forbes* v. *Aspinall* (1811) 13 East 323; *Rickman* v. *Carstairs* (1833) 5 B & Ad 651; *Tobin* v. *Harford* (1864) 34 LJCP 37).

Particular average warranties

76.—(1) Where the subject-matter insured is warranted free from particular average, the assured cannot recover for a loss of part, other than a loss incurred by a general average sacrifice unless the contract contained in the policy be apportionable; but, if the contract be apportionable, the assured may recover for a total loss of any apportionable part.

(2) Where the subject-matter insured is warranted free from particular average, either wholly or under a certain percentage, the insurer is nevertheless liable for

salvage charges, and for particular charges and other expenses properly incurred pursuant to the provisions of the suing and labouring clause in order to avert a loss incurred against.

(3) Unless the policy otherwise provides, where the subject-matter insured is warranted free from particular average under a specified percentage, a general average loss cannot be added to a particular average loss to make up the specified percentage.

(4) For the purpose of ascertaining whether the specified percentage has been reached, regard shall be had only to the actual loss suffered by the subject-matter insured. Particular charges and the expenses of and incidental to ascertaining and proving the loss must be excluded.

NOTES

Subs (1) Under a particular average warranty, where the vessel is warranted "fpa" (free from particular average) the insurer is liable only for a total loss (*Lawther* v. *Black* (1901) 6 Com Cas 196; *Wait & James* v. *British & Foreign Marine Insurance Co* (1921) 9 Ll LR 552), although the policy may allow particular average in respect of specific perils (*Great Indian Peninsula Railway Co* v. *Saunders* (1862) 2 B & S 266; *Otago Farmers Co-Operative Association of New Zealand* v. *Thompson* [1910] 2 KB 145; *Renton & Co Ltd* v. *Cornhill Insurance Co Ltd* (1933) 46 Ll LR 14; *"The Glenlivet"* [1894] P 48). The old form of fpa excluded loss by stranding and burning, in which cases a partial loss was recoverable. See the note to Marine Insurance Act 1906, Sched, r 14, page 102.

The fpa terminology is relatively uncommon, and it is more usual for the insurer expressly to confine cover to arranged or compromised total loss. Where the assured has suffered a constructive total loss, and has failed to give notice of abandonment, his loss remains a total loss for the purposes of a particular average warranty even though his measure of indemnity is as for partial loss (*Unirise Development Ltd and Noble Resources Ltd* v. *Greenwood, "The Vasso"* [1993] 2 Lloyd's Rep 309).

Where part of the cargo has been lost, the assured's claim depends upon whether or not the lost part is apportionable from the remainder of the subject-matter. If the lost part is apportionable, the assured may claim for a total loss of that part (*Duff* v. *Mackenzie* (1857) 3 CBNS 16; *Wilkinson* v. *Hyde* (1858) 3 CBNS 30; *General Insurance Co Ltd of Trieste* v. *Royal Exchange Assurance* (1897) 2 Com Cas 144; *La Fabrique de Produits Chimiques SA* v. *Large* [1923] 1 KB 203). If, however, the lost part is not apportionable, the assured will be treated as suffering a partial loss of the whole (*Hills* v. *London Assurance Corporation* (1839) 5 M & W 569; *Ralli* v. *Janson* (1856) 6 E & B 422; *Entwisle* v. *Ellis* (1857) 2 H & N 549, and therefore unable to recover if there is a fpa warranty) and will generally be unable to recover for a total loss of the whole unless the undamaged part is *de minimis* in comparison to the lost part (*Hedburg* v. *Pearson* (1816) 7 Taunt 154, and see also the note to s 60, page 62, on the possibility of a total loss of cargo where a substantial part is lost).

Subs (2) The insurer's liability for suing and labouring costs was established by *Kidston* v. *Empire Marine Insurance Co* (1866) LR 1 CP 535. See also s 78(1), page 79.

Subs (3) This provision is based on *Price & Co* v. *Al Ships Small Damage Insurance Association* (1889) 22 QBD 580. It does not preclude the aggregation of partial losses occurring on the same voyage (*Blackett* v. *Royal Exchange Asssurance Co* (1832) 2 Cr & J 244) although it is not permissible to aggregate partial losses on different voyages (*Stewart* v. *Merchants' Marine Insurance Co* (1885) 16 QBD 619, but see *Portvale SS Co Ltd* v. *Royal Exchange Assurance Corporation* (1932) 43 Ll LR 161 in which there was an extended definition of "voyage").

Subs (4) In determining the "actual loss" here referred to, dock dues are included, but there is proportionate deduction in respect of uninsured repairs effected while the vessel is in dry dock: *Marine Insurance Co v. China Transpacific SS Co* (1886) 11 App Cas 573; *Ruabon SS Co v. London Assurance* [1900] AC 6; *"The Haversham Grange"* [1905] P 307.

Successive losses

77.—(1) Unless the policy otherwise provides, and subject to the provisions of this Act, the insurer is liable for successive losses, even though the total amount of such losses may exceed the sum insured.

(2) Where, under the same policy, a partial loss, which has not been repaired or otherwise made good, is followed by a total loss, the assured can only recover in respect of the total loss:

Provided that nothing in this section shall affect the liability of the insurer under the suing and labouring clause.

NOTES

Subs (1) The principle that the insurer is liable for successive partial losses whatever their aggregate cost is derived from *Le Cheminant v. Pearson* (1812) 4 Taunt 367 and *Lidgett v. Secretan* (1871) LR 6 CP 616. See also *"The Dora Foster"* [1900] P 241. The subsection applies only to successive repaired losses, so that where a vessel has been damaged but has not been repaired, and is damaged again, the assured cannot recover more than the total sum insured under the policy: *Kusel v. Atkins, "The Catariba"* [1997] 2 Lloyd's Rep 749.

Subs (2) This section codifies the common law doctrine of merger, whereby an unrepaired partial loss merges into, and is extinguished by, a subsequent independently caused total loss. The assured's claim in such a case is, therefore, only for total loss (*Barker v. Janson* (1868) LR 3 CP 303). The rule means that the assured will be unable to recover if the total loss is caused by an uninsured peril (*Livie v. Janson* (1810) 12 East 648; *British and Foreign Insurance Co v. Wilson Shipping Co Ltd* [1921] 1 AC 188) or if the total loss occurs after the policy has run off (*Rankin v. Potter* (1873) LR 6 HL 83, doubting the decision to the contrary in *Knight v. Faith* (1850) 15 QB 649). See also Institute Time Clauses Hulls, cl 18.2 and Institute Voyage Clauses Hulls, cl 16.2. If the subsequent total loss is the natural consequence of the event giving rise to the original partial loss, with no break in the chain of causation, there is a total loss (*Anderson v. Royal Exchange Assurance* (1805) 7 East 38; *Mellish v. Andrews* (1812) 15 East 13; *Fooks v. Smith* [1924] 2 KB 508).

Section 77 does not deal with the case in which a constructive total loss for which a notice of abandonment has not been served is followed by an actual total loss. In *Woodside v. Globe Marine Insurance Co Ltd* [1896] 1 QB 105 it was held that the first loss is to be treated as a partial loss, with the result that the doctrine of merger applies to it and it is subsumed by the total loss. *Woodside* would seem not to be able to stand alongside *"The Kyriaki"* [1993] 1 Lloyd's Rep 137, where it was held that a constructive loss in respect of which no notice of abandonment is served is nevertheless to be treated as a total loss for all purposes other than the calculation of the measure of indemnity, and not a partial loss (see s 61, page 65).

Suing and labouring clause

78.—(1) Where the policy contains a suing and labouring clause, the engagement thereby entered into is deemed to be supplementary to the contract of insurance, and the assured may recover from the insurer any expenses properly incurred pursuant to the clause, notwithstanding that the insurer may have paid for a total loss, or that the subject-matter may have been warranted free from particular average, either wholly or under a certain percentage.

(2) General average losses and contributions and salvage charges, as defined by this Act, are not recoverable under the suing and labouring clause.

(3) Expenses incurred for the purpose of averting or diminishing any loss not covered by the policy are not recoverable under the suing and labouring clause.

(4) It is the duty of the assured and his agents, in all cases, to take such measures as may be reasonable for the purpose of averting or minimising a loss.

NOTES

Subs (1) The suing and labouring clause is universal in English policies (Institute Cargo Clauses, 15; Institute Time Clauses, cl 13; Institute Voyage Clauses Hulls, cl 11), although it is arguable that even in the absence of the clause the assured would be able to recover expenses properly incurred in averting or minimising a loss (but *contra Cunard SS Co* v. *Marten* [1903] 2 KB 511 and *Yorkshire Water* v. *Sun Alliance & London Insurance Ltd* [1997] 1 Lloyd's Rep 1). To this extent, subs (1) is the mirror of the assured's obligation in s 78(4) to take such action.

The separability of the suing and labouring obligation has long been established, most importantly in *Aitchison* v. *Lohre* (1879) 4 App Cas 755, and cf *Dixon* v. *Whitworth* (1880) 49 LJQB 408. The main effect of separability is that the financial limits of the policy relate only to the marine loss itself, and not to the suing and labouring claim: to this extent, the suing and labouring clause is a distinct contract (*Kuwait Airways Corporation* v. *Kuwait Insurance Co SAK* [1996] 1 Lloyd's Rep 664, reversed on the wording of the clause itself [1999] 1 Lloyd's Rep 803.) If, however, the assured is underinsured, he is under standard London wording deemed to be his own insurer for the uninsured sum and must bear that proportion of any suing and labouring expense (*Cunard SS Co* v. *Marten* [1903] 2 KB 511).

The sums recoverable under the clause are those properly incurred in averting or minimising a loss. This will include, eg, the costs of preserving perishable cargo or repairing damaged cargo (*Meyer* v. *Ralli* (1876) 1 CPD 358; *"The Pomeranian"* [1895] P 349; *Wilson Brothers Bobbin Co* v. *Green* [1917] 1 KB 860), the costs of transhipment (*Kidston* v. *Empire Marine Insurance Co* (1867) LR 2 CP 357; *Francis* v. *Boulton* (1895) 1 Com Cas 217), salvage and related costs other than those incurred under maritime law (*St Margaret's Trust Ltd* v. *Navigators and General Insurance Co Ltd* (1949) 82 Ll LR 752) and the costs involved in retaking cargo which is in danger of being seized (*Integrated Container Service Inc* v. *British Traders Insurance Co Ltd* [1984] 1 Lloyd's Rep 154). Payment to a third party to secure release of the insured subject-matter, or waiver of a sum owing by the third party to the assured, are potentially suing and labouring expenses, although if payment or waiver are by way of ransom and the agreement is either illegal or voidable, the assured is not to be treated as having suffered any loss as the sums involved can be reclaimed: *Royal Boskalis Westminster NV* v. *Mountain* [1997] 2 All ER 929. The clause does not extend to expenses incurred by the assured after the loss has occurred (*Xenos* v. *Fox* (1869) LR 4 CP 665; *Dixon* v. *Whitworth* (1880) 49 LJQB 408), including legal expenses incurred in pursuing a third party who has wrongfully taken possession of the insured property (*Kuwait Airways Corporation* v. *Kuwait Insurance Co SAK* [1996] 1 Lloyd's Rep 664, [1999] 1 Lloyd's Rep 803).

The amount recoverable is reasonable rather than actual expenditure (*Lee* v. *Southern Insurance Co* (1870) LR 5 CP 397; *Integrated Containers Service Inc* v. *British Traders Insurance Co Ltd* [1984] 1 Lloyd's Rep 154). In determining what is reasonable, the test is that the assured can recover those expenses which a reasonable person would have incurred in the absence of insurance in order to preserve his property, ie, the test under s 78(4) (*Integrated Container Service Inc* v. *British Traders Insurance Co Ltd* [1984] 1 Lloyd's Rep 154).

Suing and labouring expenses paid by an insurer are not recoverable from the reinsurer unless the reinsurance agreement expressly provides (*Uzielli* v. *Boston Marine Insurance Co* (1884) 15 QBD 11).

When an assured takes steps to avoid or mitigate a loss, the result may be that the loss occurs despite his efforts, possibly in some other form. As long as the steps taken are reasonable, the assured's conduct will not be regarded as having broken the chain of causation from the original peril (*Gordon* v. *Rimmington* (1807) 1 Camp 123; *Butler* v. *Wildman* (1820) 3 B & Ald 398, and cf the note to s 55(2)(a), page 52).

Subs (2) This subsection stems from the distinction drawn in *Aitchison* v. *Lohre* (1879) 4 App Cas 755 (and cf: *Dixon* v. *Whitworth* (1880) 49 LJQB 408; *Ballantyne* v. *Mackinnon* [1896] 2 QB 455) between contractual salvage charges, which are recoverable under the suing and labouring clause, and maritime salvage charges which are recoverable under the policy (and thus are subject to policy financial limits) but not under the suing and labouring clause. See s 65 of the 1906 Act, page 69. The distinction is based upon the wording of the old suing and labouring clause, under which the assured was liable for costs incurred by his agents, factors and assigns: an independent salvor not working under contract did not fit into any of these categories.

Subs (3) See: *Great Indian Peninsula Railway Co* v. *Saunders* (1862) 2 B & S 266; *Booth* v. *Gair* (1863) 15 CBNS 291 (cost of transhipping insured goods which were undamaged despite loss of vessel); *Weissberg* v. *Lamb* (1950) 84 Ll LR 509 (loss proximately caused by excluded peril, delay); *Berk & Co Ltd* v. *Style* [1955] 2 Lloyd's Rep 382 (loss proximately caused by excluded peril, inherent vice). If the assured is underinsured, and the assured incurs expenditure which does not reduce the loss to a level within the policy, the assured has no right to recover that expenditure under s 78 (*Kuwait Airways Corporation* v. *Kuwait Insurance Co SAK* [1996] 1 Lloyd's Rep 664, varied [1999] 1 Lloyd's Rep 803).

As long as an insured peril has operated, the insurers are liable under the suing and labouring clause even where non-insured subject-matter is also preserved, although apportionment may be appropriate. It was held in *Royal Boskalis Westminster* v. *Mountain* [1997] 2 All ER 929 that if uninsured lives are also saved, there is no apportionment and the insurer is liable for the full sum. If there is no risk to the goods when the expenditure is incurred, the assured cannot recover it from the insurer (*Hadkinson* v. *Robinson* (1803) 3 B & P 388; *Lubbock* v. *Rowcroft* (1803) 5 Esp 50; *Blackenhagen* v. *London Assurance Co* (1808) 1 Camp 454; *Forster* v. *Christie* (1809) 11 East 205; *Great Indian Peninsula Railway Co* v. *Saunders* (1862) 2 B & S 266; *Nickels & Co* v. *London and Provincial Marine and General Insurance Co Ltd* (1906) 17 TLR 54, but contrast: *"The Knight of St Michael"* [1898] P 30; *Pyman SS Co* v. *Lords Commissioners of the Admiralty* [1919] 1 KB 49; *Green* v. *British India Steam Navigation Co* [1921] 1 AC 99; *Atlantic Maritime Co* v. *Gibbon* [1954] 1 QB 88; *Integrated Container Service Inc* v. *British Traders General Insurance Co Ltd* [1984] 1 Lloyd's Rep 154).

If a vessel is, following the occurrence of an insured peril, preserved from being a constructive total loss and the insurer is liable only for total losses, the salvage costs are nevertheless recoverable under the suing and labouring clause (*Crouan* v. *Stanier* [1904] 1 KB 87, where the underwriters unsuccessfully sought to recover salvage costs incurred by them from the assured).

Subs (4) The obligation to avert or minimise a loss arises independently of any suing and labouring clause, although in practice the obligation is spelt out in contractual provisions in more or less the same language, and it is made clear that, where a third party is potentially liable for the assured's loss, the assured is under a duty to take steps to preserve his action against the third party (eg, by issuing a writ within the limitation period or seeking a Mareva injunction freezing the third party's assets). See Institute Cargo Clauses, cl 17.

The phrase "avert or minimise a loss" cannot, in the absence of additional words, extend to a failure by the assured to take steps to ascertain the extent of a loss (*Irvin* v. *Hine* [1949] 2 All ER 1089).

The test of what constitutes reasonable behaviour by the assured seems to be that the assured must act as if he were uninsured (*Integrated Container Service Inc* v. *British Traders Insurance Co Ltd* [1984] 1 Lloyd's Rep 154; *"The Vasso"* [1993] 2 Lloyd's Rep 309). The test is subjective to the extent that the assured is not expected to possess skill beyond that attributable to his actual knowledge and experience (*Stephen* v. *Scottish Boatowners Mutual Insurance Association, "The Talisman"* [1989] 1 Lloyd's Rep 535).

The nature of the duty is problematic, and has given rise to two particular difficulties.

(a) What is the relationship between s 78(4) and s 55(2)(a) of the 1906 Act? Under s 55(2)(a) the assured is entitled to recover despite the negligence of the master or crew (and, at common law, his own negligence), whereas under s 78(4) the assured and his agents are in effect under a duty to take reasonable care. In *Astrovlanis* v. *Linard, "The Gold Sky"* [1972] 2 Lloyd's Rep 187 it was suggested that the phrase "agents" in s 78(4) excluded the master and crew, so that the duty to sue and labour applied only to the assured personally and to other (unspecified) agents: failure by the master and crew to take reasonable steps to avert or minimise a loss would not, therefore, fall within s 78(4) and would be governed by s 55(2)(a). However, in *National Oilwell (UK) Ltd* v. *Davy Offshore Ltd* [1993] 2 Lloyd's Rep 582 Colman J expressed the view that the matter was one of causation, and that if the assured or his agents (including master and crew) failed to take steps to avert or minimise a loss, s 78(4) stated that the loss would be proximately caused by their conduct and not by any insured peril. On this reasoning, s 55(2)(a) has little role to play. In *State of Netherlands* v. *Youell* [1998] 1 Lloyd's Rep 236, Phillips LJ held that s 78(4) was applicable after the occurrence of the insured peril, whereas s 35(2)(a) applied prior to the occurrence of the peril: on this view, s 78(4) would provide a defence only where the assured's failure to sue and labour was of itself the proximate cause of the loss, a situation likely to be extremely rare.

(b) What is the insurer's remedy if the assured fails to sue and labour? This depends upon the view taken of the nature of the suing and labouring obligation. If, as indicated in *National Oilwell*, the matter is one of causation, the assured's failure to sue and labour means that there is no insured loss and thus the assured cannot recover (and cf *Currie & Co* v. *Bombay Native Insurance Co* (1869) LR 3 PC 72). However, if the duty to sue and labour is seen as an implied contract term, the assured's breach means that the insurer is liable in damages, but subject to set-off to the extent that the assured's neglect has contributed to the loss: this was the view accepted in *"The Vasso"* [1993] 2 Lloyd's Rep 309. In *State of Netherlands* v. *Youell* [1998] 1 Lloyd's Rep 236, Phillips LJ commented that as the duty to sue and labour constituted a separate obligation a failure by the assured to act would not give the insurer a defence under the policy.

Right of Insurer on Payment

Right of subrogation

79.—(1) Where the insurer pays for a total loss, either of the whole, or in the case of goods of any apportionable part, of the subject-matter insured, he thereupon becomes entitled to take over the interest of the assured in whatever may remain of the subject-matter so paid for, and he is thereby subrogated to all the rights and remedies of the assured in and in respect of that subject-matter as from the time of the casualty causing the loss.

(2) Subject to the foregoing provisions, where the insurer pays for a partial loss, he acquires no title to the subject-matter insured, or such part of it as may remain, but he is thereupon subrogated to all rights and remedies of the assured in and in respect of the subject-matter insured as from the time of the casualty causing the loss, in so far as the assured has been indemnified, according to this Act, by such payment for the loss.

NOTES

General: The section deals with two separate issues: salvage and subrogation. Salvage is the right of an insurer who has paid for a total loss (actual or constructive) to assert proprietary rights over whatever remains of the insured subject-matter. This overlaps with s 63(1), page 68. The principle of s 79 is that the insurer is subrogated to the rights of the assured as against any person who has caused the assured's loss and in respect of any payments made by a third party to the assured to meet his loss. Subrogation is an equitable doctrine (*Napier and Ettrick v. Hunter* [1993] 1 All ER 385) and can thus be refused on equitable grounds, (*Morris v. Ford Motor Co* [1973] QB 792, *per* Lord Denning MR; *The Surf City* [1995] 2 Lloyd's Rep 242) but not where the policy contemplates subrogation (*Woolwich Building Society v. Brown* 1996, unreported). For the basis of subrogation, see *Banque Financière de la Cité v. Parc (Battersea) Ltd* [1998] 1 All ER 737, at p 744. Payments by the third party which are intended not to diminish the assured's loss as such but to compensate him for ancillary uninsured losses (*Sea Insurance v. Hadden* (1884) 13 QBD 706; *Attorney General v. Glen Line* (1930) 37 Ll LR 55) or for personal discomfort (*Burnand v. Rodocanachi Sons & Co* (1882) 7 App Cas 33) do not fall to be counted in determining whether the assured has received an indemnity and cannot be claimed by the insurer. However, a sum which does go towards reducing the assured's loss is to be taken into account, even if it has been paid *ex gratia* by the third party (*Randal v. Cockran* (1748) 1 Ves Sen 98; *Blaaupot v. Da Costa* (1758) 1 Eden 130; *Stearns v. Village Main Reef Gold Mining Co* (1905) 21 TLR 236; *Colonia Versicherung AG v. Amoco Oil Co* [1995] 1 Lloyd's Rep 570, affirmed [1997] 1 Lloyd's Rep 261.

If the assured has received payment from a third party, he has suffered no loss to that extent and the insurer can deduct that payment from the amount of its own liability (*Goole and Hull Steam Towing Co v. Ocean Marine Insurance Co Ltd* [1928] 1 KB 589). By contrast, if the assured has yet to be paid by the third party, the insurer is liable for the full amount but, having paid the assured, is subrogated to his rights against the third party. For the origins of the doctrine, see: *Randal v. Cockran* (1748) 1 Ves Sen 98; *Blaaupot v. Da Costa* (1758) 1 Eden 130; *Mason v. Sainsbury* (1782) 3 Doug 61.

Subrogation is reliant on the rule that payment by the insurer does not discharge the liability of the third party who has caused the assured's loss (*Yates v. White* (1838) 1 Arnold 85). This proposition was to some extent doubted by the Court of Session in *Elf Enterprises (Caledonia) Ltd v. London Bridge Engineering Ltd* (1997) *The Times*, 28 November, where it was held that where an insurer had paid the assured's losses, it had no subrogation rights against a third party which had caused the loss and which was obliged under its contract with the assured to provide an indemnity for its losses: the court's view was that the insurer and the third party were co-indemnifiers and that the insurer was merely entitled to contribution (see the Marine Insurance Act 1906, s 80, discussed on page 86) rather than subrogation: the correctness of this decision is open to severe doubt. Subrogation is in its origins an equitable doctrine, but is modified by terms implied into the contract of insurance (*Napier and Ettrick v. Hunter* [1993] 1 All ER 385). The right of subrogation may be conferred upon an insurer by the express terms of the policy, but this is not necessary for its operation. As an alternative to subrogation, it is open to an insurer to seek an assignment of the assured's rights against the third party, in which case the insurer can sue the third party in his own name without having paid the assured and may retain for his own account a nominal sum in excess of the amount paid to the assured (*Compania Columbiana de Seguros* v. *Pacific Steam Navigation Co* [1965] 1 QB 101).

Provision of an indemnity: The insurer may exercise subrogation rights only after it has indemnified the assured, and until that date the insurer has no rights against the wrongdoing third party and it is doubtful whether the insurer has any rights against the assured. This means that the insurer must at least have made payment to the limits of the policy in respect of the loss. It is doubtful whether the payment must be made under legal liability, and it may be that an *ex gratia* payment by the insurer will suffice (as was assumed in *Napier and Ettrick* v. *Hunter* [1993] 1 All ER 385, and cf *King* v. *Victoria Insurance Co* [1896] AC 250), although there is no subrogation under a ppi policy as such a contract is by its terms not to be regarded as one of indemnity (*John Edwards & Co* v. *Motor Union Insurance Co Ltd* [1922] 2 KB 249. The sum which constitutes the assured's indemnity is the amount of his loss, including sums reasonably incurred by the assured in bringing successful legal proceedings against a third party: *England* v. *Guardian Insurance* [1999] 2 All ER (Comm) 481.

Prior to making payment, the insurer has no subrogation rights as such. If the assured is underinsured (other than by virtue of an excess, which is deemed not to be any part of the loss—*Napier and Ettrick* v. *Hunter* [1993] 1 All ER 385), the assured retains the right to control any proceedings against the third party (*Commercial Union Assurance Co* v. *Lister* (1874) LR 9 Ch App 483) and the insurer is limited to claiming its share of the sum recovered from the third party.

Exercise of subrogation rights by action: If the insurer has fully indemnified the assured, the insurer may commence proceedings against the third party in the assured's name (*Esso Petroleum Co Ltd* v. *Hall Russell & Co* [1988] 3 WLR 730). The insurer's claim is, therefore, subject to any defences which the third party may have against the assured, including a time-bar or an express agreement between the assured and the third party restricting the former's rights against the latter. One benefit of the use of the assured's name is that interest is payable to the assured by the third party on the full amount of his loss, even if by the date of payment the insurer has indemnified the assured, and in such a case the insurer will be subrogated to the interest from the date of their payment to the assured (*Cousins & Co* v. *D & C Carriers Ltd* [1970] 2 Lloyd's Rep 397). If the assured himself brings the action, it is arguably subject to an equitable charge in favour of the insurer (*Napier and Ettrick* v. *Hunter* [1993] 1 All ER 385).

Sums recovered by way of subrogation: Where the assured has recovered sums from the third party, and the insurer has a subrogation claim, the assured holds those sums subject to an equitable lien or charge in favour of the insurer, so that in the event of the assured's insolvency the insurer has a prior claim (*Napier and Ettrick* v. *Hunter* [1993] 1 All ER 385, confirming *Re Miller, Gibb & Co* [1957] 2 All ER 266). See also *England* v. *Guardian Insurance Ltd* [1999] 2 All ER (Comm) 481, where the insurers' lien was held to attach to moneys paid into court by the third party, giving the insurers priority over the Legal Aid Board which had funded the assured's action against the third party. The moneys are also traceable into the hands of third parties (*Elgood* v. *Harris* [1896] 2 QB 491—broker) and the insurer can restrain the third party from making payment to the assured (*White* v. *Dobinson* (1844) 14 Sim 273). If the insurer has effected recovery from the third party, any sums in excess of the amount paid by the insurer to the assured, or which is otherwise the assured's entitlement, are similarly held on trust by the insurer for the assured: *Lonrho Exports Ltd* v. *Export Credit Guarantee Department* [1996] 4 All ER 673.

The amount which may be recovered and retained by the insurer from the third party may not exceed the nominal amount which the insurer has paid to the assured, a principle which may cause the insurer loss if there have been adverse currency movements (*Yorkshire Insurance Co* v. *Nisbet Shipping Co* [1962] 2 QB 330, not following *North of England Iron Steamship Insurance Association* v. *Armstrong* (1870) LR 5 QB 244). Any excess borne by the assured is to be disregarded in allocating subrogation recoveries, and in non-marine insurance law any moneys are distributed on a recover down basis. Thus, if the assured under a policy for loss up to £500 bears an excess of £100, and suffers a loss of £800, a recovery from the third party of £750 would be distributed in the following order: £200 to the assured for the top layer uninsured loss; £500 to the insurer in respect of its payment; and the remaining £50 to the assured in respect of his excess. The same principle applies to insurances arranged in layers (*Napier and Ettrick* v. *Hunter* [1993] 1 All ER 385, but contra *Boag* v. *Standard Marine Insurance Ltd* [1937] 1 All ER 714, which was not cited in *Napier and Ettrick*). In *Boag* a cargo was insured with primary insurers in the sum of £685 and with increased value insurers in the sum of £215. A total loss occurred, for which both insurers made payment, and a subrogation recovery of £532 was obtained. The Court of Appeal held that the sum belonged in its entirety to the primary insurers. This decision has been reversed by cl 14 of the Cargo Clauses, which provides for a pro rata apportionment of recoveries. In marine insurance in a case where the assured is underinsured, the assured is deemed to be his own insurer for the uninsured sum (see Marine Insurance Act 1906, s 81). Thus, assume that the assured bears an excess of £100 under a policy for £500, and suffers a loss of £800. If only £400 is recoverable from the third party, that sum must be allocated between the insurer and assured in proportion to their respective insurances: the £400 would thus be allocated in the proportions 300/800 to the assured and 500/800 to the insurer (*"The Commonwealth"* [1907] P 216; *"The Welsh Girl"* (1906) 22 TLR 475; *Kuwait Airways Corporation* v. *Kuwait Insurance Co SAK* [1996] 1 Lloyd's Rep 664). The excess continues to be ignored unless the sum recovered from the third party exceeds the insured and uninsured totals. If the policy is a valued policy, the relevant figure for determining the amount of the assured's loss is the agreed rather than actual value (*Thames & Mersey Marine Insurance Co* v. *British & Chilian SS Co* [1916] 1 KB 30).

No subrogation against an insured party: A person who is insured under a policy cannot have subrogation rights exercised against him (*Simpson* v. *Thompson* (1877) 3 App Cas 279, although see the modification of this in respect of sisterships in the Institute Time Clauses Hulls, cl 9 and the Institute Voyage Clauses Hulls, cl 7, which treat vessels under common ownership or management as separately owned in the event of a collision). In the case of co-insurance, the insurer cannot, having paid one co-assured, seek to exercise subrogation rights against the other unless that other was uninsured in respect of the loss in question or was guilty of wilful misconduct which caused the loss (*"The Yasin"* [1979] 2 Lloyd's Rep 45, explained in *National Oilwell (UK) Ltd* v. *Davy Offshore Ltd* [1993] 2 Lloyd's Rep 582). This immunity is based on an implied term in the insurance contract. The insurer may also be prevented from exercising subrogation rights against a third party who is not insured as such but for whose benefit the contract was made, eg where the third party has indirectly paid the premiums under a contract with the assured (*Mark Rowlands Ltd* v. *Berni Inns Ltd* [1985] 3 All ER 473, followed in *National Oilwell*). Subrogation is not, however, ousted, if the policy is not for the third party's benefit, even if he has paid the premium: *Woolwich Building Society* v. *Brown* 1996, unreported; *Europe Mortgage Ltd* v. *Halifax Estate Agencies* 1996, unreported. London market cargo clauses make it clear that the benefit of the policy does not extend to the carrier or other bailee (Institute Cargo Clauses, cl 15).

Subrogation waiver clause: Under a subrogation waiver clause the insurer agrees with the assured not to pursue the assured's rights against a third party. The clause is of no value to the third party: if the third party is a party to the insurance contract by way of co-insurance or agency, he is immune from a subrogation action, and if he is not a party then the doctrine of privity of contract prevents his reliance on the clause. Moreover, if he is a party to the insurance contract in respect of some risks but not others, he cannot rely upon the subrogation waiver clause as regards uninsured risks, and he has no need to rely upon it in respect of insured risks (*National Oilwell (UK) Ltd* v. *Davy Offshore Ltd* [1993] 2 Lloyd's Rep 582). However, in *Enimont Supply SA* v. *Chesapeake Shipping Inc, The Surf City* [1995] 2 Lloyd's Rep 242, Clarke J held that, as subrogation is an equitable doctrine, it could be refused by a court where appropriate, eg where the insurer sought to exercise it in the face of a subrogation waiver clause. The assured himself may be able to insist upon the insurer adhering to a subrogation waiver clause, but presumably only if the assured has a sufficient interest in so doing, eg where the assured is obliged to indemnify the third party where subrogation rights have been exercised.

Prejudice to subrogation rights: Although the insurer has no subrogation rights prior to indemnifying the assured, the law confers various rights upon an insurer who loses subrogation rights by virtue of the assured's dealings with the third party. If the assured has entered into an agreement with the third party prior to taking out the insurance, under which the third party is exempted from any liability in the event that loss is caused to the assured, that agreement may be a material fact requiring disclosure to the insurer: the policy may therefore be voidable under s 18 of the 1906 Act, page 16 (*Tate & Sons* v. *Hyslop* (1885) 15 QBD 368; *Thomas & Co* v. *Brown* (1891) 4 Com Cas 186). If the assured, having suffered a loss, enters into an agreement with the third party to restrict or discharge the third party's liability, the insurer may hold the assured accountable for the loss of subrogation rights at least in so far as the assured's agreement with the third party was not entered into as a *bona fide* compromise of a doubtful liability (*Commercial Union Assurance Co* v. *Lister* (1874) LR 9 Ch App 483).

Subs (2) This is based on *Brooks* v. *MacDonnell* (1835) 1 Y & C Ex 500.

Right of contribution

80.—(1) Where the assured is over-insured by double insurance, each insurer is bound, as between himself and the other insurers, to contribute rateably to the loss in proportion to the amount for which he is liable under his contract.

(2) If any insurer pays more than his proportion of the loss, he is entitled to maintain an action for contribution against the other insurers, and is entitled to the like remedies as a surety who has paid more than his proportion of the debt.

NOTES

There is double insurance only where there are concurrent policies by the same assured and on the same interest (*North British and Mercantile Insurance Co* v. *London, Liverpool and Globe Insurance Co* (1877) 5 Ch D 569). As to double insurance generally, see Marine Insurance Act 1906, s 32, page 32. In *Elf Enterprises (Caledonia) Ltd* v. *London Bridge Engineering Ltd*, (1997) *The Times*, 28 November, the Court of Session held that an insurer and a contractual indemnifier were to be regarded as being in the same position as two insurers, so that if the insurer indemnified the assured the insurer would be entitled to contribution from the contractual indemnifier, but had no subrogation rights. This reasoning seems to give the contractual indemnifier the benefit of the insurance policy, and in particular leads to the situation in which the contractual indemnifier is entitled to seek contribution from the insurer if the former has paid the assured first.

The right of contribution is an equitable right, but is nevertheless governed by the contract of insurance in that an insurer who has a defence against the assured (eg breach of duty of utmost good faith) cannot be liable to contribute. In assessing whether a right of contribution exists in favour of the paying insurer, it is necessary to look at the position of the insurers not when the loss occurs but at the date of judgment against the paying insurer: if by that time the other insurer has acquired a defence against the assured (eg breach of a condition precedent such as a loss notification clause or arbitration clause) that insurer cannot be called upon to contribute to the paying insurer (*Eagle Star Insurance Co Ltd* v. *Provincial Insurance plc* [1993] 2 Lloyd's Rep 143, doubting *Legal and General Assurance Society* v. *Drake Insurance Co* [1992] 2 QB 887 to the opposite effect).

Where contribution is possible, the amount will generally be determined on an independent liability basis (*North British & Mercantile Insurance Co* v. *London, Liverpool and Globe Insurance Co* (1877) 5 Ch D 569; *Commercial Union Assurance Co Ltd* v. *Hayden* [1977] QB 804), whereby the liability of each insurer for the loss is calculated, and each then pays that proportion of the loss. Thus, if the subject-matter is insured by insurer A for £50,000, and by insurer B for £100,000, then:

(i) a loss of £50,000 would be met by them equally, as each is independently liable for the entire loss;

(ii) a loss of £75,000 would be met by them in the proportions of A 50/125 and B 75/125.

Effect of under insurance

81. Where the assured is insured for an amount less than the insurable value or, in the case of a valued policy, for an amount less than the policy valuation, he is deemed to be his own insurer in respect of the uninsured balance.

NOTES

The principle of average expressed in this section operates automatically where there is a total loss, for in such a case the assured recovers to the financial limits of the policy and must carry any uninsured loss himself. Average is of real significance in the case of a partial loss, for here the assured is treated as an insurer and is required to share the loss with the insurer in proportion to their respective shares of the value of the subject-matter. The principle is enshrined in ss 70–71 of the 1906 Act, pages 74 *et seq* (partial loss of cargo and freight).

Return of Premium

Enforcement of return

82. Where the premium or a proportionate part thereof is, by this Act, declared to be returnable,—

(a) If already paid, it may be recovered by the assured from the insurer; and

(b) If unpaid, it may be retained by the assured or his agent.

NOTES

For the circumstances in which all or a part of the premium is returnable, see ss 83–84, pages 88 *et seq*. Under the Act, the premium is returnable to the assured and not to the broker, unless the broker is authorised to receive it on the assured's behalf. This is so even though the obligation to pay the premium under a contract of marine insurance is on the broker: see s 53(1), page 50.

It was decided in *Velos Group Ltd* v. *Harbour Insurance Services Ltd* [1997] 2 Lloyd's Rep 461 that if the premium is returned to the broker, he may set off against the return premium any commission which is owed to him by the assured. The case further decides (although perhaps the point is open to doubt) that the broker's commission is fully earned as soon as the policy is effected, so that if it is subsequently cancelled and premium is returned to the broker, he can deduct the full amount of the commission from the proportion of premium returned to him.

Return by agreement

83. Where the policy contains a stipulation for the return of the premium, or a proportionate part thereof, on the happening of a certain event, and that event happens, the premium, or, as the case may be, the proportionate part thereof, is thereupon returnable to the assured.

NOTES

This is simply a declaratory provision, and its operation turns upon the proper construction of the policy to determine whether an event giving rise to proportionate return has occurred (see, eg: *Simond* v. *Boydell* (1779) 1 Doug KB 268; *Aguilar* v. *Rodgers* (1797) 7 TR 421; *Audley* v. *Duff* (1800) 2 Bos & P 111: *Hunter* v. *Wright* (1830) 10 B & C 714; *Gorsedd SS Co Ltd* v. *Forbes* (1900) 5 Com Cas 413; *Pyman* v. *Marten* (1906) 13 Com Cas 64; *North Shipping Co Ltd* v. *Union Marine Insurance Co Ltd* (1919) 24 Com Cas 161). The premium is returnable under a hulls time policy as the contract is terminated automatically when the vessel changes its classification or flag (Institute Time Clauses Hulls, cl 4) or when the vessel is laid up or the contract terminated by agreement (Institute Time Clauses Hulls, cl 22).

Return for failure of consideration

84.—(1) Where the consideration for the payment of the premium totally fails, and there has been no fraud or illegality on the part of the assured or his agents, the premium is thereupon returnable to the assured.

(2) Where the consideration for the payment of the premium is apportionable and there is a total failure of any apportionable part of the consideration, a proportionate part of the premium is, under the like conditions, thereupon returnable to the assured.

(3) In particular—

(a) Where the policy is void, or is avoided by the insurer as from the commencement of the risk, the premium is returnable, provided that there has been no fraud or illegality on the part of the assured; but if the risk is not apportionable, and has once attached, the premium is not returnable;

(b) Where the subject-matter insured, or part thereof, has never been imperilled, the premium, or, as the case may be, a proportionate part thereof, is returnable:

Provided that where the subject-matter has been insured "lost or not lost" and has arrived in safety at the time when the contract is concluded, the premium is not returnable unless, at such time, the insurer knew of the safe arrival.

(c) Where the assured has no insurable interest throughout the currency of the risk, the premium is returnable, provided that this rule does not apply to a policy effected by way of gaming of wagering;

(d) Where the assured has a defeasible interest which is terminated during the currency of the risk, the premium is not returnable;

(e) Where the assured has over-insured under an unvalued policy, a proportionate part of the premium is returnable;

(f) Subject to the foregoing provisions, where the assured has over-insured by double insurance, a proportionate part of the several premiums is returnable:

Provided that, if the policies are effected at different times, and any earlier policy has at any time borne the entire risk, or if a claim has been paid on the policy in respect of the full sum insured thereby, no premium is returnable in respect of that policy, and when the double insurance is effected knowingly by the assured no premium is returnable.

NOTES

Section 84 is founded on the twin principles of *Tyrie* v. *Fletcher* (1777) 2 Cowp 666 (cf *Bermon* v. *Woodbridge* (1781) 2 Doug KB 781; *Gale* v. *Mitchell* (1781) Park on Insurance 797; *Stone* v. *Marine Insurance Co of Gothenburg* (1876) 1 Ex D 81): the premium is returnable if there is total failure of consideration, but the premium is not apportionable so that once the risk has attached—even only momentarily—the insurer has earned the full amount of the premium and no part of it is returnable. Thus, if there has been a deviation or change of voyage, the insurer is discharged only from that date and the unearned part of the premium is not recoverable (*Tait* v. *Levi* (1811) 14 East 481; *Moses* v. *Pratt* (1815) 4 Camp 297). Thus in *J A Chapman & Co. Ltd* v. *Kadirga Denizcilik Ve Ticaret* [1998] Lloyd's Rep IR 377, the assured's failure to pay an instalment of the premium amounted to breach of a premium warranty clause, thereby putting an end to the risk under the policy but as the risk had commenced, the assured remained liable to pay outstanding and future instalments of the premium.

Subs (1) This sets out the first principle in *Tyrie* v. *Fletcher*. If the assured has been guilty of fraudulent non-disclosure or misrepresentation, or if the policy is on an illegal adventure, the right to recover the premium will be lost (*Tyler* v. *Horne* (1785) Marshall on Marine Insurances 525; *Andree* v. *Fletcher* (1789) 3 TR 266; *Vandyck* v. *Hewitt* (1800) 1 East 96; *Morck* v. *Abel* (1802) 3 Bos & P 35; *Lubbock* v. *Potts* (1806) 7 East 449; *Feise* v. *Parkinson* (1812) 4 Taunt 640; *Rivaz* v. *Gerussi* (1880) 6 QBD 222; *Re National Benefit Assurance Co Ltd* [1931] 1 Ch 46). The assured will, however, be entitled to a return of the premium despite the illegality if he repents in good time (*Lowry* v. *Bordieu* (1780) 2 Doug KB 468; *Palyart* v. *Leckie* (1817) 6 M & S 290) or if he was unaware of the facts which rendered the adventure illegal (*Oom* v. *Bruce* (1810) 12 East 225). Equally, if the policy provides for the forfeiture of the premium, the assured will not be entitled to return of the premium despite the fact that the risk has not attached.

Subs (2) The subsection assumes the application of the second principle of *Tyrie* v. *Fletcher*, and deals with the case in which the premium can be apportioned to divisible parts of the risk. It will rarely be the case that the risk under a single policy can be subdivided in this way (*Meyer* v. *Gregson* (1784) 3 Doug KB 402; *Loraine* v. *Thomlinson* (1781) 2 Doug KB 585; *Annen* v. *Woodman* (1810) 3 Taunt 299; *Moses* v. *Pratt* (1815) 4 Camp 297), although exceptional cases may exist (*Stevenson* v. *Snow* (1761) 3 Burr 1237; *Rothwell* v. *Cooke* (1797) 1 Bos & P 172—policy covering distinct voyages).

Subs (3) contains a list of illustrations of the principles in subs (1) and (2). The list is not exhaustive and does not cover, for example, cases of deviation, change of voyage, delay or breach of warranty, where the risk has attached but has subsequently lapsed due to the assured's conduct (*Annen* v. *Woodman* (1810) 3 Taunt 299).

Subs (3)(a) See generally: *Hogg* v. *Horner* (1797) 2 Park on Marine Insurance 782; *Duffell* v. *Wilkinson* (1808) 1 Camp 401; *Tait* v. *Levi* (1811) 14 East 481; *Feise* v. *Parkinson* (1812) 4 Taunt 640; *Anderson* v. *Thornton* (1853) 8 Exch 425. For an illustration of illegality, see *Vandyck* v. *Hewitt* (1800) 1 East 96 (trading with the enemy).

Subs (3)(b) This provision operates where the risk has not attached, fully or in part: *Henkle* v. *Royal Exchange Assurance Co* (1749) 1 Ves Sen 317; *Stevenson* v. *Snow* (1761) 3 Burr 1237; *Forbes* v. *Aspinall* (1811) 13 East 323; *Colby* v. *Hunter* (1827) 3 C & P 7; *Rickman* v. *Carstairs* (1833) 5 B & Ad 651; *Tobin* v. *Harford* (1864) 17 CBNS 528; *"The Main"* [1894] P 320. The proviso is illustrated by *Bradford* v. *Symondson* (1881) 7 QBD 456.

Subs (3) (c) A number of different possibilities are contained in this section. First, if the assured has a reasonable expectation of acquiring insurable interest, but fails to do so, the policy is valid but the risk never attaches, and the premium is recoverable for total failure of consideration (*Routh* v. *Thompson* (1809) 11 East 428). Secondly, if the assured has no expectation of acquiring an insurable interest and is gambling from the outset (in accordance with s 4(2)(a), page 6), the policy is void and the assured forfeits his premium (*Lowry* v. *Bordieu* (1780) 2 Doug KB 468; *M'Culloch* v. *Royal Exchange Assurance Co* (1813) 3 Camp 406; *Allkins* v. *Jupe* (1877) 2 CPD 375). Thirdly, if the assured has an insurable interest but the policy is deemed to be a wagering policy by s 4(2)(b) of the 1906 Act because it is made "ppi", the premium is returnable despite the express wording of s 84(3)(c) (*Re London County Commercial Reinsurance Office Ltd* [1922] 2 Ch 67, but *contra Allkins* v. *Jupe* (1877) 2 CPD 375). Fourthly, if the assured has an insurable interest at the outset, but loses his interest during the currency of the policy, the premium is not returnable as the risk has to some extent been run (*Boehm* v. *Bell* (1799) 8 TR 154).

Subs (3) (d) See *Boehm* v. *Bell* (1799) 8 TR 154.

Subs (3) (e) This rule does not apply in non-marine insurance.

Subs (3) (f) The proviso is based on *Fisk* v. *Masterman* (1841) 8 M & W 165.

Mutual Insurance

Modification of Act in case of mutual insurance

85.—(1) Where two or more persons mutually agree to insure each other against marine losses there is said to be a mutual insurance.

(2) The provisions of this Act relating to the premium do not apply to mutual insurance, but a guarantee, or such other arrangement as may be agreed upon, may be substituted for the premium.

(3) The provisions of this Act, is so far as they may be modified by the agreement of the parties, may in the case of mutual insurance be modified by the terms of the policies issued by the association, or by the rules and regulations of the association.

(4) Subject to the exceptions mentioned in this section, the provisions of this Act apply to a mutual insurance.

NOTES

Mutual insurance, the earliest form of marine insurance and a type which continues to operate in the marine market, particularly for liability risks through the Protection and Indemnity Clubs, differs from insurance provided by the private company market and Lloyd's in a number of respects.

    (a) Insurance is based not on a policy but on membership of the Club. The cover granted to members is laid down by the rule book. A duty of disclosure identical in its nature to that owed to an insurer is owed by a member when applying for membership.

    (b) Club rules do not give the member a right to recover in the event of loss, but confer a discretion on those administering the rules as to whether or not payment should be made. Decisions must be reached on the basis of natural justice. This feature of club rules renders it uncertain whether membership of a club amounts to a contract of insurance, as a mere discretion to pay would appear not to create insurance.

    (c) Club rules are normally framed on a "pay to be paid" basis, thereby preventing the member from recovering from the club until he has actually paid the sum owing to his victim. One side effect of this feature is that the Third Parties (Rights against Insurers) Act 1930, which transfers insurance rights to the victim of an insolvent assured, cannot apply to P & I Clubs, as the club is not liable until the assured has made payment, with the result that there are no rights to be transferred to the victims. See *Firma C-Trade* v. *Newcastle Protection and Indemnity Association ("The Fanti")* [1990] 2 Lloyd's Rep 191.

(d) Clubs are formed not for profit but to provide a fund to meet claims by members. The premiums paid to an insurer are fixed at the outset, and thereafter the risk of loss or chance of profit accrues to shareholders. By contrast, under P & I rules any shortfalls in the fund must be made up by members (by means of calls) and any profits accrue to the members (by means of lower contributions in the following year). This difference forms the basis of subs (2).

The subject is given detailed treatment by Hazelwood, *P & I Clubs Law and Practice*, 2nd edn 1994, Lloyd's of London Press.

Supplemental

Ratification by assured

86. Where a contract of marine insurance is in good faith effected by one person on behalf of another, the person on whose behalf it is effected may ratify the contract even after he is aware of a loss.

NOTES

There are many illustrations of this point in the early cases, for the most part involving brokers insuring without authority but on behalf of the assured. See: *Lucena* v. *Craufurd* (1808) 1 Taunt 325; *Routh* v. *Thompson* (1812) 13 East 274. It is a prerequisite to ratification that the agent intended to insure on behalf of the assured. In the case of a broker this is relatively easy to establish, but if the agent has an insurable interest in his own right it may be difficult for a third party to establish that the agent intended to insure on the third party's behalf as well as his own: this point was explored in *National Oilwell (UK) Ltd* v. *Davy Offshore Ltd* [1993] 2 Lloyd's Rep 582 (construction of an oil rig) where it was held that if the agent is under an obligation to the third party to insure on the third party's behalf, the necessary intention to do so will be presumed. See also: *Grant* v. *Hill* (1812) 4 Taunt 380; *Hagedorn* v. *Oliverson* (1814) 2 M & S 485; *Watson* v. *Swann* (1862) 11 CBNS 756; *Byas* v. *Miller* (1897) 3 Com Cas 39; *Boston Fruit Co* v. *British and Foreign Marine Insurance Co* [1906] AC 336.

If the assured is not identified in the policy as the intended beneficiary, ratification is in any event not possible, in line with the rule in *Keighley, Maxsted & Co* v. *Durant* [1901] AC 240 that an undisclosed principal cannot ratify.

The rule that the assured can ratify after knowledge of loss was laid down in *Williams* v. *North China Insurance Co* (1876) 1 CPD 757, but has been rejected for non-marine insurance (*Grover and Grover Ltd* v. *Matthews* [1910] 2 KB 401). However, in the *National Oilwell* case Colman J doubted the non-marine rule.

Implied obligations varied by agreement or usage

87.—(1) Where any right, duty, or liability would arise under a contract of marine insurance by implication of law, it may be negatived or varied by express agreement, or by usage, if the usage be such as to bind both parties to the contract.

(2) The provisions of this section extend to any right, duty, or liability declared by this Act which may be lawfully modified by agreement.

NOTES

Subs (1) A usage is binding on the parties only if its existence is established by evidence and if both parties were aware of it. Many usages recognised by the common law are found in the 1906 Act itself, eg s 53(1), page 50 (liability of the broker for the premium), and other sections are expressly made subject to usages, eg s 47 (deviation where there are several ports of discharge).

Subs (2) Few of the provisions of the 1906 Act are not subject to contrary agreement. The two clearest examples are s 41, page 40 (warranty of legality) and s 55(2)(a), page 52 (loss caused by wilful misconduct).

Reasonable time, etc, a question of fact

88. Where by this Act any reference is made to reasonable time, reasonable premium, or reasonable diligence, the question what is reasonable is a question of fact.

NOTES

This definition is relevant for a number of sections of the 1906 Act, eg s 58, page 61 (missing ship) s 42, page 41 (commencement of voyage) and Sched, r 5, page 97 (cargo safely landed).

Slip as evidence

89. Where there is a duly stamped policy, reference may be made, as heretofore, to the slip or covering note, in any legal proceeding.

NOTES

In the event of inconsistency between the slip and the policy, the policy may be rectified to conform to the slip (*Mackenzie* v. *Coulson* (1869) LR 8 Eq 368; *Ionides* v. *Pacific Marine Insurance Co Ltd* (1872) LR 7 QB 517; *Cory* v. *Patton* (1872) LR 7 QB 304; *Empress Assurance Corporation* v. *Bowring* (1905) 11 Com Cas 107; *Spalding* v. *Crocker* (1897) 13 TLR 396; *Wilson, Holgate & Co Ltd* v. *Lancashire and Cheshire Insurance Corporation Ltd* (1922) 13 Ll LR 486; *Eagle Star and British Dominions Insurance Co Ltd* v. *Reiner* (1927) 27 Ll LR 173). Rectification is available only where the slip represents the actual agreement between the parties and the policy has incorrectly recorded that agreement (*Henkle* v. *Royal Exchange Assurance* (1749) 1 Ves Sen 317; *British and Foreign Marine Insurance Co Ltd* v. *Sturge* (1897) 2 Com Cas 244; *Scottish Metropolitan Assurance Co* v. *Stewart* (1923) 15 Ll LR 55; *Pindos Shipping Corporation* v. *Raven, "The Mata Hari"* [1983] 2 Lloyd's Rep 449), and it is doubtful whether the underwriters can seek rectification of the policy as the Lloyd's Policy Signing Office—which issues the policy—is the authorised agent of underwriters and policy wordings issued by it will bind them.

The section deals only with rectification of the policy to conform with the slip. However, rectification is not confined to cases in which the policy is preceded by a slip: any form of agreement or common understanding prior to the issue of the policy can be used as a basis for rectification, although a mere misunderstanding of the arrangements by one part will not justify rectification (*Motteux* v. *London Assurance* (1739) 1 Atk 545; *Collett* v. *Morrison* (1851) 9 Hare 162; *Lowlands SS Co* v. *North of England Protecting and Indemnity Association* (1921)

6 Ll LR 230; *Gagniere & Co Ltd* v. *Eastern Co of Warehouses Insurance* (1921) 8 Ll LR 365).

It is not open to either party unilaterally to vary the terms of the policy once they have been agreed. There is a series of cases in which the assured has attempted to do this, and the courts have ruled that a material variation has the effect of avoiding the policy as from the date of variation (*Laird* v. *Robertson* (1791) 4 Bro Parl Cas 488; *Fairlie* v. *Christie* (1817) 7 Taunt 416; *Campbell* v. *Christie* (1817) 2 Stark 64; *Forshaw* v. *Chabert* (1821) 6 Moo CP 369; *Norwich Union Fire Insurance Co* v. *Colonial Mutual Fire Insurance Co Ltd* (1922) 12 Ll LR 94), although immaterial variations are of no effect (*Clapham* v. *Cologan* (1813) 3 Camp 382; *Sanderson* v. *Symonds* (1819) 4 Moo CP 42; *Sanderson* v. *M'Cullom* (1819) 4 Moo CP 5).

Despite the possibility of rectification of the policy to conform to the slip, it might be thought that the slip could be used as an aid to the interpretation of the policy in the event of any inconsistency between the two. This, however, is not the case, and it is generally not permissible to have regard to the slip in the event of any ambiguity in the policy (*Youell* v. *Bland Welch (No 1)* [1992] 2 Lloyd's Rep 127).

Given that the slip is a binding contract, it follows that the assured's duty of disclosure comes to an end as regards any underwriter when the slip has been initialled by that underwriter: see the note to s 17 of the Marine Insurance Act 1906, page 14.

Interpretation of terms

90. In this Act, unless the context or subject-matter otherwise requires,—
 "Action" includes counter-claim and set off:
 "Freight" includes the profit derivable by a shipowner from the employment of his ship to carry his own goods or moveables, as well as freight payable by a third party, but does not include passage money:
 "Moveables" means any moveable tangible property, other than the ship, and includes money, valuable securities, and other documents:
 "Policy" means a marine policy.

NOTES

Freight: See the note to Sched, r 16.

Moveables: The definition of moveables in the Act is somewhat wider than the definition of "goods": see Sched, r 17. Securities and money are moveables (*Baring Brothers & Co* v. *Marine Insurance Co* (1894) 10 TLR 276) but are not goods.

Savings

91.—(1) Nothing in this Act, or in any repeal effected thereby, shall affect—
 (a) The provisions of the Stamp Act 1891, or any enactment for the time being in force relating to the revenue;
 (b) The provisions of the Companies Act 1862, or any enactment amending or substituted for the same;
 (c) The provisions of any statute not expressly repealed by this Act.
 (2) The rules of the common law including the law merchant, save in so far as they are inconsistent with the express provisions of this Act, shall continue to apply to contracts of marine insurance.

Section 92

[Repealed by the Statute Law Revision Act 1927.]

Section 93

[*Repealed by the Statute Law Revision Act 1927.*]

Short title

94. This Act may be cited as the Marine Insurance Act 1906.

SCHEDULES

FIRST SCHEDULE   SECTION 30

Form of Policy

BE IT KNOWN THAT   as well in   own name as for and in the name and names of all and every other person or persons to whom the same doth, may, or shall appertain, in part or in all doth make assurance and cause   and them, and every of them, to be insured lost or not lost, at and from

Upon any kind of goods and merchandises, and also upon the body, tackle, apparel, ordnance, munition, artillery, boat, and other furniture, of and in the good ship or vessel called the   whereof is master under God, for this present voyage,   or whosoever else shall go for master in the said ship, or by whatsoever other name or names the said ship, or the master thereof, is or shall be named or called; beginning the adventure upon the said goods and merchandises from the loading thereof aboard the said ship.

upon the said ship, etc

and so shall continue and endure, during her abode there, upon the said ship, etc

And further, until the said ship, with all her ordnance, tackle, apparel, etc, and goods and merchandises whatsoever shall be arrived at

upon the said ship, etc, until she hath moored at anchor twenty-four hours in good safety; and upon the goods and merchandises, until the same be there discharged and safely landed. And it shall be lawful for the said ship, etc, in this voyage, to proceed and sail to and touch and stay at any ports or places whatsoever

without prejudice to this insurance. The said ship, etc, goods and merchandises, etc, for so much as concerns the assured by agreement between the assured and assurers in this policy, are and shall be valued at

Touching the adventures and perils which we the assurers are contented to bear and do take upon us in this voyage: they are of the seas, men of war, fire, enemies, pirates, rovers, thieves, jettisons, letters of mart and counterpart, surprisals, takings at sea, arrests, restraints, and detainments of all kings, princes, and people, of what nation, condition, or quality soever, barratry of the master and mariners, and of all other perils, losses, and misfortunes, that have or shall come to the hurt, detriment, or damage of the said goods and merchandises, and ship, etc, or any part thereof. And in case of any loss or misfortune it shall be lawful to the assured, their factors, servants and assigns, to sue, labour, and travel for, in and about the defence, safeguards, and recovery of the said goods and merchandises, and ship, etc, or any part thereof, without prejudice to this insurance; to the charges whereof we, the assurers, will contribute each one according to the rate and quantity of his sum herein assured. And it is especially declared and agreed that no acts of the insurer or insured in recovering, saving, or preserving the property insured shall be considered as a waiver, or acceptance of abandonment. And it is agreed by us, the insurers, that this writing or policy of assurance shall be of as much force and effect as the surest writing or policy of assurance heretofore made in Lombard Street, or in the Royal Exchange, or elsewhere in London. And so we, the assurers, are contented, and do hereby promise and bind ourselves, each one for his own part, our heirs, executors, and goods to the assured, their executors, administrators, and assigns, for the true performance of the premises, confessing ourselves paid the consideration due unto us for this assurance by the assured, at and after the rate of

IN WITNESS whereof we, the assurers, have subscribed our names and sums assured in London.

N.B.—Corn, fish, salt, fruit, flour, and seed are warranted free from average, unless general, or the ship be stranded—sugar, tobacco, hemp, flax, hides and skins are warranted free from average, under five pounds per cent, and all other goods, also the ship and freight, are warranted free from average, under three pounds per cent unless general, or the ship be stranded.

GENERAL NOTES

Form of policy: The Lloyd's SG (Ship and Goods) policy, which had existed since 1779, was superseded in 1983 after frequent instances of judicial criticism, "absurd and incoherent" being the description by Buller J as early as *Brough* v. *Whitmore* (1791) 4 TR 206. The practice was for amendments to the policy to be written in the margins or gummed to the policy. The following rules are intended to give guidance to the meaning of words used in the Lloyd's policy. Many of these words are used in the new forms of policy, although various of the definitions are now obsolete, eg rr 6 (touch and stay), 10 (restraint of princes) and 12 (all other perils). For general principles of construction, see s 30 and the note thereto, page 30.

Rules for Construction of Policy

The following are the rules referred to by this Act for the construction of a policy in the above or other like form, where the context does not otherwise require:—

1. Where the subject-matter is insured "lost or not lost," and the loss has occurred before the contract is concluded, the risk attaches unless, at such time the assured was aware of the loss, and the insurer was not.

NOTES

This rule reflects the proviso to s 6(1) of the Marine Insurance Act 1906. See page 8.

2. Where the subject-matter is insured "from" a particular place, the risk does not attach until the ship starts on the voyage insured.

NOTES

A voyage policy "from" a particular place excludes port risks at the outward port. If the voyage does not commence within a reasonable time of the risk attaching, the insurer is discharged (Marine Insurance Act 1906, s 42, page 41).

3.— (a) Where a ship is insured "at and from" a particular place, and she is at that place, in good safety when the contract is concluded, the risk attaches immediately.

(b) If she be not at that place when the contract is concluded, the risk attaches as soon as she arrives there in good safety, and, unless the policy otherwise provides, it is immaterial that she is covered by another policy for a specified time after arrival.

(c) Where chartered freight is insured "at and from" a particular place, and the ship is at that place in good safety when the contract is concluded the risk attaches immediately. If she be not there when the contract is concluded, the risk attaches as soon as she arrives there in good safety.

(d) Where freight, other than chartered freight, is payable without special conditions and is insured "at and from" a particular place, the risk attaches pro rata as the goods or merchandise are shipped; provided that if there be cargo in readiness which belongs to the shipowner, or which some other person has contracted with him to ship, the risk attaches as soon as the ship is ready to receive such cargo.

NOTES

Rule 3(a) A voyage policy "at and from" a particular port includes the risks of that port, the risk attaching as soon as the vessel arrives at that port in good safety. As to what constitutes a port, see: *Camden* v. *Cowley* (1763) 1 Wm Bl 417; *Kingston* v. *Knibbs* (1808) 1 Camp 508n; *Cruickshank* v. *Janson* (1810) 2 Taunt 301; *Constable* v. *Noble* (1810) 2 Taunt 403; *Payne* v. *Hutchinson* (1810) 2 Taunt 405n; *Moxon* v. *Atkins* (1812) 3 Camp 200; *Cockey* v. *Atkinson* (1819) 2 B & Ald 460; *Warre* v. *Miller* (1825) 4 B & C 538; *Sea Insurance Co of Scotland* v. *Gavin* (1829) 4 Bli. NS 578; *Brown* v. *Tayleur* (1835) 4 Ad & El 241. The term "good safety" refers to the physical condition of the vessel. See: *Waples* v. *Eames* (1746) 2 Str 1243; *Lockyer* v. *Offley* (1786) 1 TR 252; *Minett* v. *Anderson* (1794) Peake 212; *Shawe* v. *Felton* (1801) 2 East 109; *Parmeter* v. *Cousins* (1809) 2 Camp 235; *Bell* v. *Bell* (1810) 2 Camp 475; *Annen* v. *Woodman* (1810) 3 Taunt 299; *Horneyer* v. *Lushington* (1812) 15 East 46; *Foley* v. *United Fire and Marine Insurance Co of Sydney* (1870) LR 5 CP 155; *Lidgett* v. *Secretan* (1870) LR 5 CP 190. Thereafter, the voyage must commence within a reasonable time (Marine Insurance Act 1906, s 42, page 41).

Rule 3(b) This is based on *Haughton* v. *Empire Marine Insurance Co* (1866) LR 1 Ex 206.

Rule 3(c) This is based on: *Horncastle* v. *Suart* (1806) 7 East 400; *Mackenzie* v. *Shedden* (1810) 2 Camp 431; *Davidson* v. *Willasey* (1813) 1 M & S 313; *Foley* v. *United Fire & Marine Insurance Co of Sydney* (1870) LR 5 CP 155.

Rule 3(d) For the *pro rata* rule, see: *Montgomery* v. *Eggington* (1789) 3 TR 362; *Patrick* v. *Eames* (1813) 3 Camp 441; *Davidson* v. *Willasey* (1813) 1 M & S 313; *Truscott* v. *Christie* (1820) 2 Brod & Bing 320. For the readiness rule, see: *Williamson* v. *Innes* (1831) 8 Bing 81n. The effect of rule 3(d) was frequently ousted in practice by policy wording which permitted the risk for freight to be earned on cargo to attach only "from the loading thereof" (*Beckett* v. *West of England Marine Insurance Co Ltd* (1871) 25 LT 739; *Jones* v. *Neptune Marine Insurance Co* (1872) LR 7 QB 702; *Hopper* v. *Wear Marine Insurance Co* (1882) 46 LT 107; *Hydarnes SS Co* v. *Indemnity Mutual Marine Assurance Co* [1895] 1 QB 500, and cf the note to r 4, below) or "from the time of the engagement of the goods" (*"The Copernicus"* [1896] P 237).

4. Where goods or other moveables are insured "from the loading thereof," the risk does not attach until such goods or moveables are actually on board, and the insurer is not liable for them while in transit from the shore to ship.

NOTES

This rule is concerned with cargo, although similar wording was found in freight policies (see r 3(d), page 96). The cases on this wording have established that the insurer is not liable for goods in transit prior to the date of the policy (*Robertson* v. *French* (1803) 4 East 130; *Spitta* v. *Woodman* (1810) 2 Taunt 416; *Nonnen* v. *Reid* (1812) 16 East 176; *Langhorn* v. *Hardy* (1812) 4 Taunt 628; *Mellish* v. *Allnutt* (1813) 2 M & S 166; *Carr* v. *Montefiore* (1864) 5 B & S 408). Contrast the position if the policy is the continuation of a previous insurance (*Bell* v. *Hobson* (1812) 16 East 240) or otherwise contemplates wider cover (*Gladstone* v. *Clay* (1813) 1 M & S 418).

5. Where the risk on goods or other moveables continues until they are "safely landed," they must be landed in the customary manner and within a reasonable time after arrival at the port of discharge, and if they are not so landed the risk ceases.

NOTES

This wording has been superseded by the warehouse to warehouse clause in the Institute Cargo Clauses. If landing is prevented by external forces, the policy remains effective (*Samuel* v. *Royal Exchange Assurance Co* (1828) 8 B & C 119). The wording does not cover a cargo which has actually been landed (*Deutsch-Australische Dampfschiffsgesellschaft* v. *Sturge* (1913) 109 LT 905), or which been left in barges pending use, as the assured is here regarded as having waived the need for landing (*Lindsay Blee Depots Ltd* v. *Motor Union Insurance Co Ltd* (1930) 37 Ll LR 220). If the goods have been removed from the vessel and into the consignee's own lighter the insurer is off risk, but the risk remains if the goods are put into a publicly-operated lighter (*Sparrow* v. *Carruthers* (1745) 2 Stra 1236; *Rucker* v. *London Assurance Co* (1784) 2 Bos & P 432n; *Hurry* v. *Royal Exchange Assurance Co* (1801) 3 Esp 289) or if the policy expressly covers "all risks of craft to and from the vessel" (*Paul Ltd* v. *Insurance Co of North America* (1899) 15 TLR 534). If the goods have been landed but are in the custody of Customs officials rather than the assured himself, they are nevertheless safely landed and the insurer is not liable for any loss after landing (*Brown* v. *Carstairs* (1811) 3 Camp 161; *Marten* v. *Nippon Sea & Land Insurance Co Ltd* (1898) 3 Com Cas 164). A policy which covers both cargo and loss of export refund in the event of rejection of the cargo is, absent contrary provision, to be construed as a cargo policy, so that if the cargo risk terminates following discharge then the risk in relation to the export subsidy terminates on the same date: *Hibernia Foods plc* v. *McAuslin, "The Joint Frost"* [1998] 1 Lloyd's Rep 310.

6. In the absence of any further license or usage, the liberty to touch and stay "at any port or place whatsoever" does not authorise the ship to depart from the course of her voyage from the port of departure to the port of destination.

NOTES

The "liberty to touch and stay" clause was the traditional method of excusing the assured's deviation, as to which see Marine Insurance Act 1906, ss 46–47, pages 45 *et seq*. The clause is no longer used, and has been superseded by "held covered" provisions. The "liberty to touch and stay" provision did not confer an absolute right on the assured to visit any port, and was subject to the limitation that even where the geographical region was not specifically indicated by the policy (as was common) the ports visited had to be within the contemplation of the policy and not wholly outside the scope of the voyage. Of the many illustrations, see: *Gairdner* v. *Senhouse* (1810) 3 Taunt 16; *Hammond* v. *Reid* (1820) 4 B & Ald 72; *Bottomley* v. *Bovill* (1826) 5 B & C 210.

7. The term "perils of the seas" refers only to fortuitous accidents or casualties of the seas. It does not include the ordinary action of the winds and waves.

NOTES

Perils of the sea is the most important of the marine perils. It is concerned only with fortuitous events, even though readily foreseeable (*Neter & Co* v. *Licences and General Insurance Co Ltd* (1944) 77 Ll LR 202), the burden of proving fortuity being borne by the assured (*Schiffshypothekenbank Zu Luebeck AG* v. *Compton, "The Alexion Hope"* [1988] 1 Lloyd's Rep 311; *National Justice Compania Naviera SA* v. *Prudential Assurance Co, "The Ikarian Reefer"* [1995] 1 Lloyd's Rep 455). If the vessel is cast away by the crew, there is no peril of the sea but there will be barratry (see r 11, page 101), and equally an innocent mortgagee who is party to the contract cannot plead peril of the sea where the vessel is cast away with the connivance of the owner (*Samuel & Co Ltd* v. *Dumas* [1924] AC 431).

The peril must be "of the sea", and this generally requires proof of adverse, but not necessarily abnormal, weather conditions (*Hagedorn* v. *Whitmore* (1816) 1 Stark 157; *Fletcher* v. *Inglis* (1819) 2 B & Ald 315; *Lawrence* v. *Aberdein* (1821) 5 B & Ald 107; *Gabay* v. *Lloyd* (1825) 3 B & C 793; *Montoya* v. *London Assurance Co* (1851) 6 Ex 451; *Magnus* v. *Buttemer* (1852) 11 CB 876; *Mountain* v. *Whittle* [1921] 1 AC 615; *Lind* v. *Mitchell* (1928) 32 Ll LR 70; *Baxendale* v. *Fane, "The Lapwing"* (1940) 66 Ll LR 174). However, the phrase also includes losses from perils in or on the sea, such as ice, rocks and other vessels, ie innocent or negligent collision losses (*Smith* v. *Scott* (1811) 4 Taunt 126; *Wilson, Sons & Co* v. *Xantho, "The Xantho"* (1887) 12 App Cas 503; *Popham* v. *St Petersburg Insurance Co* (1904) 10 Com Cas 31) but not deliberate collision or other wilful destruction by a third party. The Institute Clauses are based upon the assumption that collisions are covered, although earlier policies specifically included damage caused by collision with various objects (*Re Margetts and Ocean Accident & Guarantee Corporation* [1901] 2 KB 792; *Mancomunidad del Vapor Frumiz* v. *Royal Exchange Assurance* [1927] 1 KB 567).

Mechanical failure is not a peril of the sea, so held by the House of Lords in *Thames & Mersey Marine Insurance Co Ltd* v. *Hamilton, Fraser & Co, "The Inchmaree"* (1887) 12 App Cas 484, although losses caused by mechanical failure are in practice within hulls policies by virtue of the "Inchmaree" clause (see the note to s 55 of the 1906 Act, page 52).

Loss by stranding is a peril of the sea (*Fletcher* v. *Inglis* (1819) 2 B & Ald 315), although a vessel damaged by the sea while not at sea is not covered by this peril (*Rowcroft* v. *Dunsmore* (1810) 3 Taunt 228n; *Thompson* v. *Whitmore* (1810) 3 Taunt 227; *Phillips* v. *Barber* (1821) 5 B & Ald 161; *Magnus* v. *Buttemer* (1852) 11 CB 876, but see Marine Insurance Act 1906, Sched, r 12, page 102 and *Fletcher* v. *Inglis* (1819) 2 B & Ald 315).

Reasonable steps taken by the assured to avoid a peril of the sea, and which result in a loss by some other means, do not break the chain of causation from the peril of the sea. This follows from *Canada Rice Mills Ltd* v. *Union Marine & General Insurance Co Ltd* [1940] 4 All ER 169, where damage to cargo from overheating, resulting from the closing of valves to prevent the ingress of sea water, was held to be a peril of the sea. Cf *Redman* v. *Wilson* (1845) 14 M & W 476.

The ordinary action of the wind and the waves is not a peril of the sea (*Paterson* v. *Harris* (1861) 1 B & S 336), and unless the assured can demonstrate that weather conditions were adverse the insurer is not liable without having to raise any defence of its own, eg that the vessel was unseaworthy. If there is bad weather and the vessel is unseaworthy, then, assuming that the assured is not precluded from recovering by virtue of s 39 of the 1906 Act (see page 37) the claim will depend upon which of the two causes of loss was the proximate cause (*Fawcus* v. *Sarsfield* (1856) 6 E & B 192; *Lloyd Instruments Ltd* v. *Northern Star Insurance Co Ltd, "The Miss Jay Jay"* [1987] 1 Lloyd's Rep 32).

If there has been a peril of the sea, and loss occurs subsequently, eg loss of cargo by theft or seizure following the stranding of the vessel, it is a question of fact as to whether there is a break in the chain of causation from the peril of the sea (*Bondrett* v. *Hentigg* (1816) Holt NP 149; *Hahn* v. *Corbett* (1824) 2 Bing 205; *Dent* v. *Smith* (1869) LR 4 QB 414). Equally, causation issues arise where an uninsured peril results in the exposure of the vessel to perils of the sea (*Hodgson* v. *Malcolm* (1806) 2 Bos & PNR 336, and cf the war risks cases discussed in the note to s 55(1), page 52).

It is to be stressed that the mere ingress of water is not a peril of the sea: what is required is that the ingress was caused by a peril of the sea as opposed to, say, a war risk (*Leyland Shipping Co Ltd* v. *Norwich Union Fire Insurance Society Ltd* [1918] AC 350), scuttling (*Samuel & Co Ltd* v. *Dumas* [1924] AC 431) or unseaworthiness (*Sassoon & Co Ltd* v. *Western Assurance Co* [1921] AC 561; *Grant Smith & Co* v. *Seattle Construction & Dry Dock Co* [1920] AC 162; *Lamb Head Shipping Co Ltd* v. *Jennings, "The Marel"* [1992] 1 Lloyd's Rep 402). If a vessel is in a rusty condition, and water enters as a result, there is no peril of the sea in the absence of abnormal action of the wind and waves (*Sassoon & Co* v. *Western Assurance Co* [1912] AC 561). A contrary decision is *Hamilton, Fraser & Co* v. *Pandorf & Co* (1887) 12 App Cas 518, where water entered the vessel due to action by vermin and the loss was held to have been caused by perils of the sea. The decision appears to be unsupportable on this point, and vermin damage is now presumed to be excluded (Marine Insurance Act 1906, s 55(2)(c), page 52). See also *Cohen, Sons & Co* v. *National Benefit Assurance Co Ltd* (1924) 18 Ll LR 199, where Bailhache J came close to saying that any unintended ingress of water constituted a peril of the sea.

8. The term "pirates" includes passengers who mutiny and rioters who attack the ship from the shore.

NOTES

The reference in the definition to passengers is based on *Palmer* v. *Naylor* (1854) 10 Exch 382 and *Kleinwort* v. *Shepherd* (1859) 1 E & E 447, and the reference to attacks from shore is based on *Nesbitt* v. *Lushington* (1792) 4 TR 783. Piracy may also be committed by the crew (*Brown* v. *Smith* (1813) 1 Dow 349), although in practice the claim in these circumstances will normally be for barratry (see Rule 11, page 101). Piracy requires robbery or attempted robbery (*Re Piracy Jure Gentium* [1934] AC 586) effected with the use of violent rather than clandestine conduct (*Shell International Petroleum Co Ltd* v. *Gibbs, "The Salem"* [1982] QB 946; *Athens Maritime Enterprises Corporation* v. *Hellenic Mutual War Risks Association (Bermuda) Ltd, "The Andreas Lemos"* [1983] 1 All ER 591) for private rather than political gain (*Republic of Bolivia* v. *Indemnity Mutual Marine Assurance Co Ltd* [1909] 1 KB 785; *Banque Monetaca* v. *Motor Union Insurance Co Ltd* (1923) 14 Ll LR 48). It must take place on the high seas, tidal waters or in a port or harbour, but not on a mere inland waterway (*The Magellan Pirates* (1852) 1 Ecc & Ad 81; *Republic of Bolivia* v. *Indemnity Mutual Marine Assurance Co Ltd* [1909] 1 KB 785; *United Africa Co* v. *NV Tolten* [1946] P 135n; *"The Andreas Lemos"* [1983] 1 All ER 591).

Seizure by pirates is to be regarded as at least a constructive total loss (*Dean* v. *Hornby* (1854) 3 E & B 180).

For the reference to riot, see the Public Order Act 1986, ss 1 and 10, page 115.

9. The term "thieves" does not cover clandestine theft or a theft committed by any one of the ship's company, whether crew or passengers.

NOTES

The word "theft" generally bears its statutory meaning (under s 1 of the Theft Act 1968) in insurance policies (*Dobson* v. *General Accident Fire and Theft Assurance Co* [1989] 3 All ER 927; *Deutsche Genossenschaftsbank* v. *Burnhope* [1995] 4 All ER 717). That meaning is modified in marine insurance to encompass only non-clandestine theft and theft by strangers (*Harford* v. *Maynard* (1785) 1 Park on Marine Insurances 36; *Taylor* v. *Liverpool and Great Western Steam Co* (1874) LR 9 QB 546; *Nishina Trading Co Ltd* v. *Chiyoda Fire & Marine Insurance Co Ltd* [1969] 2 QB 449). Some element of violence is required, but that may be violence towards property, eg the smashing down of doors (*La Fabrique de Produits Chimiques SA* v. *Large* (1922) 13 Ll LR 269) or even the turning of a key in the lock of a door (*Dino Services Ltd* v. *Prudential Assurance Co Ltd* [1989] 1 Lloyd's Rep 379) rather than violence towards persons.

Where a vessel is shipwrecked and her cargo is stolen, the loss is to be regarded as one by perils of the sea and not theft (*Bondrett* v. *Hentigg* (1816) Holt NP 149, and see the note to rule 7, page 98).

10. The term "arrests, etc, of kings, princes, and people" refers to political or executive acts, and does not include a loss caused by riot or by ordinary judicial process.

NOTES

The terminology of the "restraint of princes" clause appeared in the Lloyd's SG Policy which was abandoned in 1983, and the clause is now obsolete. The most recent authorities on the clause are *Rickards* v. *Forestal Land, Timber and Railway Co Ltd* [1942] AC 50 (seizure of cargo by agents of government is restraint of princes) and *Panamanian Oriental SS Corporation* v. *Wright* [1970] 2 Lloyd's Rep 365 (decision of customs officials to detain a ship was restraint of princes despite subsequent judicial proceedings). Where a policy covers the peril of "seizure", the term is to be taken to include both belligerent and non-belligerent seizure: *Kuwait Airways Corporation* v. *Kuwait Insurance Co SAK* [1999] 1 Lloyd's Rep 803.

For the reference to riot, see the Public Order Act 1986, ss 1 and 10, page 115.

11. The term "barratry" includes every wrongful act wilfully committed by the master or crew to the prejudice of the owner, or, as the case may be, the charterer.

NOTES

Barratry consists of fraud by the master (*Arcangelo* v. *Thompson* (1811) 2 Camp 620) or crew (*Elton* v. *Brogden* (1747) 2 Str 1264) against the owner of the vessel (*Nutt* v. *Bordieu* (1768) 1 TR 323; *Bradford* v. *Levy* (1825) 2 C & P 137). There can be no barratry where the master and crew have failed to understand the assured's instructions or otherwise have innocently disobeyed the assured (*Phyn* v. *Royal Exchange Assurance Co* (1798) 7 TR 505; *Hibbert* v. *Martin* (1808) 1 Camp 538; *Todd* v. *Ritchie* (1816) 1 Stark 240; *Bottomley* v. *Bovill* (1826) 5 B & C 210). If the assured or his agent (*Hobbs* v. *Hannam* (1811) 3 Camp 93) is implicated in the conduct, either because he has authorised it (*Stamma* v. *Brown* (1743) 2 Str 1173; *Ross* v. *Hunter* (1790) 4 TR 33; *Everth* v. *Hannam* (1815) 6 Taunt 375; *Soares* v. *Thornton* (1817) 7 Taunt 627; *Visscherij Maatschappij Nieuw Onderneming* v. *Scottish Metropolitan Assurance Co Ltd* (1922) 10 Ll LR 579) or because he was aware of it and took no steps to prevent further conduct of that type (*Pipon* v. *Cope* (1808) 1 Camp 434; *Panamanian Oriental Steamship Co* v. *Wright* [1971] 1 Lloyd's Rep 487), there is no barratry. The burden of proving barratry rests on the assured, with the burden switching to the insurer if there is an allegation that the assured was party to the barratry (*Elfie A Issaias* v. *Marine Insurance Co Ltd* (1923) 15 Ll LR 186; *Banco de Barcelona* v. *Union Marine Insurance Co Ltd* (1925) 22 Ll LR 209; *Piremay Shipping Co SA* v. *Chester*, *"The Michael"* [1979] 2 Lloyd's Rep 1; *Michalos & Sons Maritime SA* v. *Prudential Assurance Co Ltd*, *"The Zinovia"* [1984] 2 Lloyd's Rep 264; *Continental Illinois National Bank & Trust Co of Chicago* v. *Alliance Assurance Co Ltd* [1986] 2 Lloyd's Rep 470; *Houghton and Mancon Ltd* v. *Sunderland Marine Mutual Insurance Co*, *"The Ny-Eeasteyr"* [1988] 1 Lloyd's Rep 60; *National Justice Compania Naviera SA* v. *Prudential Assurance Co*, *"The Ikarian Reefer"* [1993] 2 Lloyd's Rep 68). There can be barratry by one co-owner against another (*Jones* v. *Nicholson* (1854) 10 Ex 28).

The definition of barratry in r 11 fails to reflect the common law in one important respect, namely, that an act of barratry need not be intended to operate contrary to the assured's interests: see *Earle* v. *Rowcroft* (1806) 8 East 126, which held that an act in breach of the assured's instructions but nevertheless intended to be in the assured's interests could be barratry (overruling on this point: *Knight* v. *Cambridge* (1724) 1 Str 581; *Stamma* v. *Brown* (1743) 2 Str 1173; *Vallejo* v. *Wheeler* (1774) 1 Cowp 143; *Nutt* v. *Bordieu* (1786) 1 TR 323; *Lockyer* v. *Offley* (1786) 1 TR 252).

Barratry may be committed against a charterer of the vessel as well as its owner (*Vallejo* v. *Wheeler* (1774) 1 Cowp 143; *Soares* v. *Thornton* (1817) 7 Taunt 627; *Ionides* v. *Pender* (1872) 27 LT 244; *Shell International Petroleum Co* v. *Gibbs*, *"The Salem"* [1982] 1 Lloyd's Rep 369). The mortgagee of a vessel may also recover for barratry (*Small* v. *United Kingdom Marine Mutual Insurance Association* [1897] 2 QB 311). Fraud by the crew authorised by the charterer is not barratry as far as the owner is concerned (*Hobbs* v. *Hannam* (1811) 3 Camp 93).

Barratry has typically taken the form of: deviation from the agreed voyage by the crew, for their own purposes (*Ross* v. *Hunter* (1790) 4 TR 33; *Moss* v. *Byrom* (1795) 6 TR 379; *Vallejo* v. *Wheeler* (1774) 1 Cowp 143; *Roscow* v. *Corson* (1819) 1 Taunt 684; *Mentz, Decker & Co* v. *Maritime Insurance Co Ltd* [1910] 1 KB 132); delay (*Roscow* v. *Corson* (1819) 8 Taunt 684); fraud in relation to the cargo, commonly involving sale of the cargo and scuttling of the vessel to disguise the fraud, misappropriation of the vessel or detention of the cargo (*Pole* v. *Fitzgerald* (1754) Amb 214; *Toulmin* v. *Inglis* (1808) 1 Camp 421; *Toulmin* v. *Anderson* (1808) 1 Taunt 227; *Heyman* v. *Parrish* (1809) 2 Camp 149; *Brown* v. *Smith* (1813) 1 Dow 349;

Falkner v. *Ritchie* (1814) 2 M & S 290; *Hucks* v. *Thornton* (1815) Holt NP 30; *Soares* v. *Thornton* (1817) 7 Taunt 627; *Dixon* v. *Reid* (1822) 5 B & Ald 597; *Ionides* v. *Pender* (1872) 27 LT 244; *Small* v. *UK Marine Insurance Association* [1897] 2 QB 311; *Compania Naviera Bachi* v. *Henry Hosegood & Co Ltd* [1938] 2 All ER 189; *Marstrand Fishing Co Ltd* v. *Beer, "The Girl Pat"* (1937) 56 Ll LR 163); or illegal trading (*Knight* v. *Cambridge* (1724) 1 Str 581; *Stamma* v. *Brown* (1742) 2 Str 1173; *Robertson* v. *Ewer* (1786) 1 TR 127; *Lockyer* v. *Offley* (1786) 1 TR 252; *Havelock* v. *Hancill* (1789) 3 TR 277; *Goldschmidt* v. *Whitmore* (1811) 3 Taunt 508; *Australian Insurance Co* v. *Jackson* (1875) 33 LT 286).

12. The term "all other perils" includes only perils similar in kind to the perils specifically mentioned in the policy.

NOTES

The phrase "all other perils" was the "sweeping up" provision in the old form of policy set out in the Sched to the 1906 Act, page 95. Rule 12 codifies a series of cases which held that the phrase did not greatly extend the specific cover provided by the policy, and was to be construed *ejusdem generis* (*Cullen* v. *Butler* (1816) 5 M & S 461; *Butler* v. *Wildman* (1820) 3 B & Ald 398; *Thames & Mersey Marine Insurance Co Ltd* v. *Hamilton, Fraser & Co, "The Inchmaree"* (1887) 12 App Cas 484). The assured has, under this principle, been held to be covered where the vessel was damaged by the sea while on a beach, a risk not constituting a peril of the sea (*Thompson* v. *Whitmore* (1810) 3 Taunt 227, and see also *Phillips* v. *Barber* (1821) 5 B & Ald 161).

13. The term "average unless general" means a partial loss of the subject-matter insured other than a general average loss, and does not include "particular charges".

NOTES

See s 64, page 69.

14. Where the ship has stranded, the insurer is liable for the excepted losses, although the loss is not attributable to the stranding, provided that when the stranding takes place the risk has attached and, if the policy be on goods, that the damaged goods are on board.

NOTES

The peril "stranding" no longer appears in standard marine policies. It was historically of greatest significance in policies warranted free of particular average (see s 76 and the note thereto, page 77), as the exclusion of partial losses was lifted where the vessel was "stranded". Rule 14 consolidates the common law, which had established that the assured could recover despite the fact that the cargo had not been damaged by the stranding (*Bowring* v. *Elmslie* (1790) 7 TR 216n; *Burnett* v. *Kensington* (1797) 7 TR 210; *Harman* v. *Vaux* (1813) 3 Camp 429), as long as it was on board at the time of the stranding (*"The Alsace Lorraine"* [1893] P 209; *Thames & Mersey Marine Insurance Co* v. *Pitts, Son & King* [1893] 1 QB 476).

Stranding, which should be distinguished from sinking (*Baker-Whiteley Coal Co* v. *Marten* (1910) 26 TLR 314) involves two elements.

(1) The vessel must be grounded by reason of an accident or fortuity rather than in the ordinary course of a voyage (*Burnett* v. *Kensington* (1797) 7 TR 210; *Thompson* v.

Whitmore (1810) 3 Taunt 227; *Harman* v. *Vaux* (1813) 3 Camp 429; *Carruthers* v. *Sydebotham* (1815) 4 M & S 77; *Hearne* v. *Edmunds* (1819) 1 Brod & Bing 388; *Rayner* v. *Godmond* (1821) 5 B & Ald 225; *Barrow* v. *Bell* (1825) 4 B & C 736; *Bishop* v. *Pentland* (1827) 7 B & C 219; *Wells* v. *Hopwood* (1832) 3 B & Ad 20; *Kingsford* v. *Marshall* (1832) 8 Bing 458; *Magnus* v. *Buttemer* (1852) 11 CB 876; *Corcoran* v. *Gurney* (1853) 1 E & B 456; *De Mattos* v. *Saunders* (1872) LR 7 CP 570; *Letchford* v. *Oldham* (1880) 5 QBD 538).

(2) Some form of settling on dry land is required (*M'Dougle* v. *Royal Exchange Assurance Co* (1816) 4 M & S 503; *Baker* v. *Towry* (1816) 1 Stark 436; *Wells* v. *Hopwood* (1832) 3 B & Ad 20; *Bryant & May Ltd* v. *London Assurance Corporation* (1886) 2 TLR 591).

See also r 7 and the note thereto, page 98.

15. The term "ship" includes the hull, materials and outfit, stores and provisions for the officers and crew, and, in the case of vessels engaged in a special trade, the ordinary fittings requisite for the trade, and also, in the case of a steamship, the machinery, boilers, and coals and engine stores, if owned by the assured.

NOTES

See the note to s 16, page 13.

16. The term "freight" includes the profit derivable by a shipowner from the employment of his ship to carry his own goods or moveables, as well as freight payable by a third party, but does not include passage money.

NOTES

This is based on *Flint* v. *Flemyng* (1830) 1 B & Ad 45 and *Denoon* v. *Home and Colonial Assurance Co* (1872) LR 7 CP 341. Expenses incidental to the voyage are outside the definition of freight (*Winter* v. *Haldimand* (1831) 2 B & Ad 649). The phrase "charges on cargo" includes freight (*Gulf & Southern SS Co Inc* v. *British Traders Insurance Co Ltd* [1930] 1 KB 451).

17. The term "goods" means goods in the nature of merchandise, and does not include personal effects or provisions and stores for use on board.

In the absence of any usage to the contrary, deck cargo and living animals must be insured specifically, and not under the general denomination of goods.

NOTES

"Goods" by this definition basically means cargo. Where effects are insured specifically, the term incorporates nautical instruments, clothes, books and furniture (*Duff* v. *Mackenzie* (1857) 3 CBNS 16). Whether the term "goods" includes the materials in which the goods are packed depends upon the description of the insured cargo. The cases are not fully consistent, but the principle appears to be that if it is contemplated from the agreement or from market practice that the goods are to be packaged rather than carried in bulk, the insurance covers the packaging, whereas if the packaging does not form part of the description of the risk it is not covered (*Brown Brothers* v. *Fleming* (1902) 7 Com Cas 245; *Berk* v. *Style* [1955] 2 Lloyd's Rep 383. Contrast *Vacuum Oil Co* v. *Union Insurance Society of Canton* (1925) 24 Ll LR 188).

The second paragraph of r 17 excludes cargo in the form of deck cargo and live animals from the term "goods". It is uncertain whether the deck cargo rule (illustrated by *Hood* v. *West*

End Motor Car Packing Co [1917] 2 KB 38) applies to inland voyages, the point being expressly left open in *Apollinaris Co* v. *Nord Deutsche Insurance Co* [1904] 1 KB 252.

Profits on goods must be insured separately (*Lucena* v. *Craufurd* (1806) 2 Bos & PNR 269; *Anderson* v. *Morice* (1875) LR 10 CP 609; *Royal Exchange Assurance Co* v. *M'Swiney* (1850) 14 QB 646, and see the note to s 3(2)(a), page 3).

Schedule 2

[Repealed by the Statute Law Revision Act 1927.]

Marine Insurance (Gambling Policies) Act 1909

(9 Edw 7 c 12)

An Act to prohibit Gambling on Loss by Maritime Perils

GENERAL NOTES

This Act superimposes criminal sanctions upon the civil consequences contained in the Marine Insurance Act 1906 of insuring under a marine policy where there is no insurable interest. The Act is to all effects redundant, and there are no reported prosecutions under the Act.

Prohibition of gambling on loss by maritime perils

1.—(1) If—

   (a) any person effects a contract of marine insurance without having any bona fide interest, direct or indirect, either in the safe arrival of the ship in relation to which the contract is made or in the safety or preservation of the subject-matter insured, or a bona fide expectation of acquiring such an interest; or

   (b) any person in the employment of the owner of a ship, not being a part owner of the ship, effects a contract of marine insurance in relation to the ship, and the contract is made "interest or no interest," or "without further proof of interest than the policy itself," or "without benefit of salvage to the insurer," or subject to any other like term,

the contract shall be deemed to be a contract by way of gambling on loss by maritime perils, and the person effecting it shall be guilty of an offence, and shall be liable, on summary conviction, to imprisonment, with or without hard labour, for a term not exceeding six months or to a fine not exceeding [level 3 on the standard scale], and in either case to forfeit to the Crown any money he may receive under the contract.

(2) Any broker or other person through whom, and any insurer with whom, any such contract is effected shall be guilty of an offence and liable on summary conviction to the like penalties if he acted knowing that the contract was by way of gambling on loss by maritime perils within the meaning of this Act.

(3) Proceedings under this Act shall not be instituted without the consent in England of the Attorney-General, in Scotland of the Lord Advocate, and in Ireland of the Attorney-General for Ireland.

(4) Proceedings shall not be instituted under this Act against a person (other than a person in the employment of the owner of the ship in relation to which the contract was made) alleged to have effected a contract by way of gambling on loss by maritime perils until an opportunity has been afforded him of showing that the contract was not such a contract as aforesaid, and any information given by that

person for that purpose shall not be admissible in evidence against him in any prosecution under this Act.

(5) If proceedings under this Act are taken against any person (other than a person in the employment of the owner of the ship in relation to which the contract was made) for effecting such a contract, and the contract was made "interest or no interest," or "without further proof of interest than the policy itself," or "without benefit of salvage to the insurer," or subject to any other like term, the contract shall be deemed to be a contract by way of gambling on loss by maritime perils unless the contrary is proved.

(6) For the purpose of giving jurisdiction under this Act, every offence shall be deemed to have been committed either in the place in which the same actually was committed or in any place in which the offender may be.

(7) Any person aggrieved by an order or decision of a court of summary jurisdiction under this Act, may appeal to [the Crown Court].

(8) For the purposes of this Act the expression "owner" includes charterer.

(9) Subsection (7) of this section shall not apply to Scotland.

NOTES

Subs (1) This subsection was amended by the Criminal Justice Act 1982, s 38. Subs (1)(a) corresponds to s 5(2) of the Marine Insurance Act 1906, page 7, and subs (1)(b) corresponds to s 4(2)(b) of the Marine Insurance Act 1906, page 6.

Subs (2) The imposition of criminal sanctions against a broker who arranges insurance by way of gambling is intended to prevent the creation of such contracts. The existence of this provision is virtually unknown in the broking industry.

Subs (7) This subsection was amended by the Courts Act 1971, s 56.

Short title

2.—This Act may be cited as the Marine Insurance (Gambling Policies) Act 1909, and the Marine Insurance Act 1906 and this Act may be cited together as the Marine Insurance Acts 1906 and 1909.

Marine and Aviation Insurance (War Risks) Act 1952

(15 & 16 Geo 6 & 1 Eliz 2 c 57)

An Act to make provision for authorising the Minister of Transport to undertake the insurance of ships, aircraft and certain other goods against war risks and, in certain circumstances, other risks; for the payment by him of compensation in respect of certain goods lost or damaged in transit in consequence of war risks; and for purposes connected with the matters aforesaid

GENERAL NOTES

In time of war commercial insurance or reinsurance against marine and aviation risks is virtually unobtainable. The purpose of the 1952 Act was to facilitate insurance arrangements by providing reinsurance to commercial insurers of British aircraft, vessels and cargo (s 1) or, in the absence of willing insurers, to provide insurance directly to assureds (s 2). The 1952 Act replaced the scheme originally contained in the War Risks Insurance Act 1939.

Agreements for re-insurance by Minister of Transport of war risks in respect of ships, aircraft and cargoes

1.—(1) The Minister of Transport (hereafter in this Act referred to as "the Minister") may, with the approval of the Treasury, enter into agreements with any authorities or persons—

(a) whereby he undertakes the liability of re-insuring any war risks against which a ship or aircraft is for the time being insured; and

(b) whereby he undertakes the liability of re-insuring any war risks against which the cargo carried in a ship or aircraft is for the time being insured:

Provided that the Minister shall not enter into an agreement whereby he undertakes the liability of re-insuring any war risks against which a ship or aircraft not being a British ship or British aircraft is for the time being insured, except in so far as they arise during the continuance of any war or other hostilities in which Her Majesty is engaged or arise after any such war or hostilities in consequence of things done or omitted during the continuance thereof.

(2) A copy of every agreement made in pursuance of this section shall, as soon as may be after the agreement is made, be laid before each House of Parliament; and if either House, within the period of fourteen days beginning with the day on which a copy of such an agreement is laid before it, resolves the agreement be annulled, the agreement shall thereupon become void except in so far as it confers rights or imposes obligations in respect of things previously done or omitted to be done, without prejudice, however, to the making of a new agreement.

In reckoning for the purposes of this subsection any such period of fourteen days as aforesaid, no account shall be taken of any time during which Parliament is dissolved or prorogued or during which both Houses are adjourned for more than four days.

(3) The reference in paragraph (a) of subsection (1) of this section to a ship or aircraft shall be construed as including a reference to any machinery, tackle, furniture or equipment of a ship or aircraft, and to any goods on board of a ship or aircraft, not being cargo carried therein, and the first reference in the proviso to that subsection to a ship or aircraft shall accordingly be similarly construed.

NOTES

The power to reinsure is confined to British ships and British aircraft, and their cargoes. Contracts need not conform to the requirement in s 22 of the Marine Insurance Act 1906 of embodiment in a policy: Marine and Aviation Insurance (War Risks) Act 1952, s 7, page 112.

Insurance by Minister of Transport of ships, aircraft and cargoes

2.—(1) The Minister may, with the approval of the Treasury, carry on business under and in accordance with all or any of the following provisions of this subsection, that is to say:—

    (a) at any time when it appears to him that reasonable and adequate facilities for the insurance of British ships or British aircraft against war risks, or any description of such risks, are not available, for the insurance by him of such ships, or as the case may be, such aircraft, against such risks or, as the case may be, that description thereof;

    (b) during the continuance of any war or other hostilities in which Her Majesty is engaged, for the insurance by him of ships and aircraft (whether British or not);

    (c) at any time when it appears to him that reasonable and adequate facilities for the insurance of cargoes carried in ships or aircraft against war risks, or any description of such risks, are not available, for the insurance by him of such cargoes against such risks or, as the case may be, that description thereof;

    (d) during the continuance of any war or other hostilities in which Her Majesty is engaged for the insurance by him of cargoes carried in ships or aircraft;

    (e) during the continuance of any such war or hostilities, for the insurance by him of goods consigned for carriage by sea or by air, while the goods are in transit between the premises from which they are consigned and the ship or aircraft or between the ship or aircraft and their destination:

Provided that the Minister shall not, by virtue of paragraph (b), (d) or (e) of this subsection, undertake the insurance of a ship, aircraft or cargo against risks other than war risks unless he is satisfied that, in the interests of the defence of the realm or the efficient prosecution of any such war or hostilities as aforesaid, it is necessary or expedient so to do.

(2) References in paragraphs (a) and (b) of the foregoing subsection to ships of any description and to aircraft of any description shall be construed as including references to any machinery, tackle, furniture or equipment of ships of that description and aircraft of that description respectively and to any goods on board of ships of that description and aircraft of that description respectively, not being cargo carried therein, and the reference in the proviso to that subsection to a ship or aircraft shall accordingly be similarly construed.

(3) In paragraph (e) of subsection (1) of this section the expression "the ship or aircraft", in relation to goods consigned for carriage by sea or by air, does not include a vessel from which the goods are discharged for the purpose of being carried by sea or by air or into which they are discharged for the purpose of being landed.

NOTES

This section contains the power to issue direct insurance where commercial cover is otherwise not available. Cover must normally be confined to war risks. Contracts need not conform to the requirement in s 22 of the Marine Insurance Act 1906 of embodiment in a policy: Marine and Aviation Insurance (War Risks) Act 1952, s 7, page 112.

Transitional provisions for compensation in respect of goods lost or damaged in transit after discharge or before shipment

3.—(1) Where a person satisfies the Minister with respect to any goods—
  (a) that the goods, having been consigned for carriage by sea or by air from a place outside any one of the countries to which this paragraph applies to a place in that country,—
    (i) were discharged in that country from the ship or aircraft before the expiration of the period of seven days beginning with such day as the Minister may declare to be the day as from which he will carry on business for the purpose mentioned in paragraph (e) of subsection (1) of the last foregoing section;
    (ii) were, after the beginning of that day and before the expiration of the appropriate period, lost or damaged in consequence of a war risk, being one which the Minister was, on that day, prepared to insure under the said paragraph (e); and
    (iii) were lost or damaged while in transit between the ship or aircraft and their destination;
    or, having been consigned for carriage by sea or by air from a place in any one of the countries to which this paragraph applies to a place outside that country before the expiration of the said period of seven days, were, after the beginning of the said day, lost or damaged in consequence of such a war risk as aforesaid while in transit between the premises from which they were consigned and the ship or aircraft; and
  (b) that the goods were not insured against the risk in consequence of which they were lost or damaged; and
  (c) that he and his agents exercised all due diligence for securing that no delay occurred while the goods were in such transit as aforesaid; and
  (d) that at the time when the loss or damage occurred the property in the goods was vested in him;
the Minister shall pay to him, by way of compensation for that loss or damage, an amount ascertained in accordance with the next following subsection.

(2) The amount of compensation payable under the foregoing subsection shall be—
  (a) in the case of lost goods, an amount equal to the insurable value of the goods;
  (b) in the case of damaged goods—
    (i) where the goods have been delivered at their destination, an amount equal to such proportion of the insurable value of the goods as the

difference between the gross sound and damaged values at the place of arrival bears to the gross sound value;

(ii) where the goods have not been so delivered, an amount equal to such proportion of the insurable value of the goods as the difference between the gross sound and damaged values at the premises from which they were consigned bears to the gross sound value.

(3) Where, at a time when the loss or damage for which compensation in respect of any goods has become payable under this section occurred, the goods were subject to a mortgage, charge or other similar obligation, the amount of the compensation shall be deemed to be comprised in that mortgage, charge or other obligation.

(4) The countries to which paragraph (a) of subsection (1) of this section applies are the United Kingdom, the Isle of Man and any of the Channel Islands.

(5) In this section—

(a) the expression "the ship or aircraft", in relation to goods consigned for carriage by sea or by air to or from a country to which paragraph (a) of subsection (1) of this section applies, does not include a vessel into which the goods are discharged at a port or place in that country for the purpose of being landed at that port or place, or from which the goods are discharged for the purpose of being carried by sea or by air from that country, as the case may be;

(b) the expression "the appropriate period" means—

(i) in a case where the destination of the goods is within the port or place at which they were discharged from the ship or aircraft, the period of fifteen days beginning with the day on which they were so discharged; or

(ii) in a case where the destination of the goods is outside the said port or place, the period of thirty days beginning with the day on which they were so discharged; and

(c) the expression "insurable value" means, in relation to goods consigned for carriage by sea or by air, the prime cost of the goods plus the expenses of and incidental to the carriage thereof as aforesaid and the charges of insurance upon the whole; and for the purposes of this section the gross value of goods shall be taken to be the wholesale price or, if there be no such price, the estimated value, with, in either case, the expenses of and incidental to the carriage of the goods.

NOTES

This section is purely transitional.

Liabilities of re-insurer in the event of insurer's insolvency

4. Where a sum becomes payable to a person (hereafter in this section referred to as "the insurer") in respect of any loss or damage arising from a risk against which the insurer has, either originally or by way of re-insurance, insured another person (hereafter in this section referred to as "the assured") and either—

(a) the sum has become payable by the Minister by virtue of an agreement under section one of this Act; or

(b) the sum has become payable under a contract of insurance by some person other than the Minister (hereafter in this section referred to as "the intermediate insurer") and the risk has been re-insured under such an agreement as aforesaid,

then, if before payment of that sum is made by the Minister or the intermediate insurer, the insurer becomes bankrupt or, in a case where the insurer is a company, the company commences to be wound up, or a receiver is appointed on behalf of the holders of any debentures of the company secured by a floating charge or possession is taken by or on behalf of the holders of such debentures of any property comprised in or subject to the charge, that sum shall cease to be payable to the insurer and the amount thereof shall be paid to the assured by the Minister or the intermediate insurer, as the case may be, and the right of the assured to receive payment in respect of the loss or damage from the insurer shall, to the extent to which the risk has been re-insured by the Minister, be extinguished.

NOTES

This section authorises a "cut-through" arrangement under which, in the event of the insolvency of an insurer who is reinsured directly or indirectly by the Minister under the Act, the reinsurance moneys are payable directly to the assured. Any moneys received by the assured go towards discharging the insurer's obligation, and any surplus over and above the reinsurance moneys payable to the assured must be recovered by the assured from the insurer's liquidator in the usual way. The section applies equally where the government is the retrocessionaire of a reinsurance arrangement and the reinsurer becomes insolvent: in such a case, the sums payable under the retrocession go directly to the reinsured.

It was necessary to legislate specifically for this result, as the Third Parties (Rights against Insurers) Act 1930 does not apply to reinsurance: see s 1(4) of the 1930 Act.

Establishment of fund for purposes of this Act

5.—(1) There shall be established under the control of the Minister a fund, to be called the "marine and aviation insurance (war risks) fund",—

    (a) into which shall be paid—

        (i) all sums received by the Minister by virtue of this Act; (ii), (iii) . . .

    (b) out of which shall be paid—

        (i) all sums required for the fulfilment by the Minister of any of his obligations under this Act; . . .

        (ii) . . .

(2) If, at any time when a payment falls to be made out of the marine and aviation insurance (war risks) fund, the sum standing to the credit of that fund is less than the sum required for the making of that payment, an amount equal to the deficiency shall be paid into that fund out of moneys provided by Parliament, but if and so far as that amount is not paid out of such moneys, it shall be charged on and issued out of the Consolidated Fund of the United Kingdom . . . (hereafter in this Act referred to as "the Consolidated Fund").

(3) If, at any time, the amount standing to the credit of the marine and aviation insurance (war risks) fund exceeds the sum which, in the opinion of the Minister and the Treasury, is likely to be required for the making of payments out of that fund, the excess shall be paid into the Exchequer . . .

(4) The Minister shall prepare, in such form and manner as the Treasury may direct, an account of the sums received into and paid out of the marine and aviation insurance (war risks) fund in each financial year, and shall, on or before the thirtieth

day of November in each year, transmit the account to the Comptroller and Auditor General, who shall examine and certify the account and lay copies thereof together with copies of his report thereon, before both Houses of Parliament:

Provided that if the Treasury certify that, in the interests of the defence of the realm or the efficient prosecution of any war or other hostilities in which Her Majesty is engaged, it is inexpedient that copies of the account for any year and of the report thereon should be laid before Parliament, a copy of the certificate shall be laid before both Houses of Parliament and, so long as the certificate remains in force, those copies of the account and of the report shall not be so laid.

NOTES

Subs (1) This was amended by the Statute Law (Reform) Act 1981.

Subs (2) This was amended by the Statute Law (Reform) Act 1963.

Subs (3) This was amended by the National Loans Act 1968, s 24(2).

Section 6

[*Repealed by the National Loans Act 1968, s 24.*]

Exemption of certain instruments from provisions of Stamp Act 1891 and Marine Insurance Act 1906

7.—(1) None of the following instruments shall . . . be inadmissible in evidence by reason only that it is not embodied in a marine policy in accordance with the Marine Insurance Act 1906, that is to say:—

    (a) an agreement for re-insurance made in pursuance of section one of this Act between the Minister and any other authority or person, and a policy of reinsurance issued by the Minister in pursuance of such an agreement;

    (b) an agreement entered into by a body to which this paragraph applies, being an agreement for the re-insurance of a risk insured by another person which may be again re-insured by the Minister, and a policy issued in pursuance of such an agreement, being a policy for the re-insurance only of such a risk as aforesaid;

    (c) a contract of insurance entered into by the Minister in exercise of the powers conferred on him by section two of this Act, and a policy of insurance and a certificate of insurance issued by the Minister in connection with any such contract.

(2), (3) . . .

(4) Paragraph (b) of subsection (1) of this section applies to any body of persons for the time being approved for the purposes of this Act by the Minister, being a body the objects of which are or include the carrying on of business by way of the re-insurance of risks which may be re-insured under any agreement for the purpose mentioned in paragraph (b) of subsection (1) of section one of this Act.

NOTES

Subs (1) This was amended by the Finance Act 1959, s 37. For the significance of this provision, see the notes to ss 1 and 2, pages 107 *et seq.*

Subs (2) This was repealed by the Finance Act 1970, s 36.

Subs (3) This was repealed by the Finance Act 1959, s 37 and the Finance Act 1970, s 36.

Section 8

[*See s 1(2)(b) of the Restriction of Advertisement (War Risks Insurance) Act 1939.*]

Expenses of the Minister of Transport

9. The expenses incurred for the purposes of this Act by the Minister shall, except in so far as they are required to be defrayed out of the marine and aviation insurance (war risks) fund, be defrayed out of moneys provided by Parliament.

Interpretation and savings

10.—(1) In this Act, unless the context otherwise requires, the following expressions have the meanings hereby respectively assigned to them, that is to say:–
"British aircraft" means aircraft registered in Her Majesty's dominions;
"goods" includes currency and any securities payable to bearer, not being either bills of exchange or promissory notes;
"war risks" means risks arising from any of the following events, that is to say, hostilities, rebellion, revolution and civil war, from civil strife consequent on the happening of any of those events, or from action taken (whether before or after the outbreak of any hostilities, rebellion, revolution or civil war) for repelling an imagined attack or preventing or hindering the carrying out of any attack, and includes piracy.
(2) The provisions of this Act relating to British ships shall apply also to ships of India and ships of the Republic of Ireland, and references in this Act to British ships shall be construed accordingly.
(3) The provisions of this Act relating to British aircraft shall apply also to aircraft registered in India, the Republic of Ireland, the Federation of Malaya, a protectorate, a protected state, a trust territory or a mandated territory, and references in this Act to British aircraft shall be construed accordingly.
The references in this subsection to a protectorate, a protected state, a trust territory and a mandated territory shall be construed as if they were references contained in the British Nationality Act 1948.
(4) . . .

NOTES

Subs (1) There are numerous authorities on the risks mentioned in the definition of war risks.
"Hostilities" This term refers to operations of war (*Britain Steamship Co* v. *R* [1921] AC 99).
"Rebellion" A rebellion is organised resistance to the government, the object being to supplant the government (*Spinney's (1948) Ltd v. Royal Insurance Co Ltd* [1980] 1 Lloyd's Rep 406).
"Revolution" There is no authority on the meaning of this term.
"Civil War" There are three elements of civil war (*Spinney's (1948) Ltd v. Royal Insurance Co Ltd* [1980] 1 Lloyd's Rep 406):

(i) there must be opposing sides rather than mere factional strife;
(ii) the objectives of the sides must be coherent, and must ultimately be political;
(iii) the violence must be on a scale in excess of mere outbreaks of strife, and must be judged in terms of the number of people involved, the duration of the conflict and the degree of civil dislocation.

"Civil strife" There is no authority on the meaning of this term.

"Piracy" See the definition in the Marine Insurance Act 1906, Sched, r 8, page 99.

Subs (4) This was repealed by the Statute Law (Reform) Act 1981.

Short title, extent and repeal

11.—(1) This Act may be cited as the Marine and Aviation Insurance (War Risks) Act 1952.

(2) It is hereby declared that this Act extends to Northern Ireland.

(3) . . .

NOTES

Subs (3) This was repealed by the Statute Law (Reform) Act 1974.

Schedule

[*Repealed by the Statute Law (Reform) Act 1974.*]

Public Order Act 1986

GENERAL NOTES

This Act redefined various common law public order offences. The only significant change for insurance purposes relates to riot, which was recognised as a crime at common law and constituted an excluded peril from most marine and other policies.

1.—(1) Where twelve or more persons who are present together use or threaten unlawful violence for a common purpose and the conduct of them (taken together) is such as would cause a person of reasonable firmness present at the scene to fear for his personal safety, each of the persons using unlawful violence for the common purpose is guilty of riot.

(2) It is immaterial whether or not the twelve or more use or threaten unlawful violence simultaneously.

(3) The common purpose may be inferred from conduct.

(4) No person of reasonable firmness need actually be, or be likely to be, present at the scene.

(5) Riot may be committed in private as well as in public places.

NOTES

At common law it was sufficient if three persons were involved (*Field* v. *Receiver of Metropolitan Police* [1907] 2 KB 853). In other respects, the definition follows the common law. See generally: *London and Manchester Plate Glass Co* v. *Heath* [1913] 3 KB 411; *London and Lancashire Fire Insurance Co* v. *Bolands* [1924] AC 836. See also the Riot (Damages) Act 1886.

10. In Schedule 1 to the Marine Insurance Act 1906 (form and rules for the construction of certain insurance policies) "rioters" in rule 8 and "riot" in rule 10 shall, in the application of the rules to any policy taking effect on or after the coming into force of this section, be construed in accordance with section 1 above unless a different intention appears.

NOTES

It is unclear whether the Act applies to non-marine policies, but it must be assumed—in line with the general rule of construction applicable to insurance policies—that the word "riot" when encountered in a non-marine policy must have been intended to have been used in its statutory sense.

Appendices*

* Reproduced with the kind permission of the International Underwriting Association of London.

Appendices

Institute Clauses for Builders' Risks

1/6/88—(FOR USE ONLY WITH THE NEW MARINE POLICY FORM)

(This insurance is subject to English law and practice)

VESSEL .... Contract or Yard No..............

BUILDERS ....

....

BUILDERS' YARDS ....

....

Subject of insurance

(Where more than one part of the subject-matter insured is described in Section I(A), Section I(B) or Section II below, then the respective wording of Section I(A), Section I(B) or Section II shall be applied to each part separately.)

SECTION I.   Provisional Period................from ....
but this insurance to terminate upon delivery to Owners if prior to expiry of Provisional Period.

   (A)   HULL and MACHINERY etc. under construction at the yard or other premises of the Builders.

Description	Contract or Yard No.	Provisionally valued at	To be built at/by

The subject-matter of this sub-section (A) is covered whilst at Builders' Yard and at Builders' premises elsewhere within the port or place of construction at which the Builders' Yard is

119

situated and whilst in transit between such locations. The Underwriters' liability in respect of each item of this sub-section (A) which is at such locations shall attach from the time:—

(i) of inception of this Section I if such item has already been allocated to the Vessel;

(ii) of delivery to Builders of such item (if allocated) when delivered after inception of this Section I;

(iii) of allocation by Builders if allocated after inception of this Section I.

(B)   MACHINERY etc. insured hereon whilst under construction by Sub-Contractors.

Description	Contract or Yard No.	Provisionally valued at	To be built at/by

The subject-matter of this sub-section (B) is covered whilst at Sub-Contractors' works and at Sub-Contractors' premises elsewhere within the port or place of construction at which the Sub-Contractors' works are situated and whilst in transit between such locations.

The Underwriters' liability in respect of each item of this sub-section (B) which is at such locations shall attach from the time:—

(i) of inception of this Section I if such item has already been allocated to the Vessel;

(ii) of delivery to the Sub-Contractors of such item (if allocated) when delivered after inception of this Section I;

(iii) of allocation by the Sub-Contractors if allocated after inception of this Section I.

The subject-matter of this sub-section (B) is also covered whilst:—

(a) in transit to Builders if the transit is within the port or place of construction at which the Builders' Yard is situated;

(b) at Builders' Yard and at Builders' premises elsewhere within the port or place of construction at which the Builders' Yard is situated and whilst in transit between such locations.

SECTION II.   Provisional Period...............from ....
            but this insurance to terminate upon delivery to Owners if prior to expiry of Provisional Period.

MACHINERY etc. insured hereon from delivery to Builders.

Description	Contract or Yard No.	Provisionally valued at	To be built at/by

The subject-matter of this Section II is covered whilst at Builders' Yard and at Builders' premises elsewhere within the port or place of construction at which the Builders' Yard is situated and whilst in transit between such locations. The Underwriters' liability in respect of each item on this Section II shall attach from the time of delivery to Builders.

1   Insured value

1.1   Whereas the value stated herein is provisional, it is agreed that the final contract price, or the total building cost plus .... % whichever is the greater, of the subject-matter of this insurance shall be the insured value.

1.2   Should the insured value, determined as above,

1.2.1   exceed the provisional value stated herein, the Assured agree to declare to the Underwriters hereon the amount of such excess and to pay premium thereon at the full policy rates, and the Underwriters agree to accept their proportionate shares of the increase,

or

1.2.2   be less than the provisional value stated herein, the sum insured by this insurance shall be reduced proportionately and the Underwriters agree to return premium at the full policy rates on the amounts by which their respective lines are reduced.

1.3   Nevertheless, should the insured value exceed 125% of the provisional value, then the limits of indemnity under this insurance shall be 125% of the provisional value, any one accident or series of accidents arising out of the same event.

1.4   Notwithstanding the above it is understood and agreed that any variation of the value for insurance on account of a material alteration in the plans or fittings of the Vessel or a change in type from that originally contemplated does not come within the scope of this clause and such a variation requires the specific agreement of the Underwriters.

2   Transit

Held covered at a premium to be arranged for transit not provided for in Section I or II above.

3   Delayed delivery

Held covered at a premium to be arranged in the event of delivery to Owners being delayed beyond the provisional period(s) mentioned above, but in no case shall any additional period of cover extend beyond 30 days from completion of Builders' Trials.

4   Deviation or change of voyage

Held covered in case of deviation or change of voyage, provided notice be given to the Underwriters immediately after receipt of advices and any amended terms of cover and any additional premium required by them be agreed.

5   Perils

5.1   SUBJECT ALWAYS TO ITS TERMS, CONDITIONS AND EXCLUSIONS this insurance is against all risks of loss of or damage to the subject-matter insured caused and discovered during the period of this insurance including the cost of repairing replacing or renewing any defective part condemned solely in

121

consequence of the discovery therein during the period of this insurance of a latent defect. In no case shall this insurance cover the cost of renewing faulty welds.

5.2   In case of failure of launch, the Underwriters to bear all subsequent expenses incurred in completing launch.

6   Earthquake and volcanic eruption exclusion

In no case shall this insurance cover loss damage liability or expense caused by earthquake or volcanic eruption. This exclusion applies to all claims including claims under Clauses 13, 17, 19 and 20.

7   Pollution hazard

This insurance covers loss of or damage to the Vessel caused by any governmental authority acting under the powers vested in it to prevent or mitigate a pollution hazard, or threat thereof, resulting directly from damage to the Vessel for which the Underwriters are liable under this insurance, provided such act of governmental authority has not resulted from want of due diligence by the Assured, the Owners, or Managers of the Vessel or any of them to prevent or mitigate such hazard or threat. Master, Officers, Crew or Pilots not to be considered Owners within the meaning of this Clause 7 should they hold shares in the Vessel.

8   Faulty design

Notwithstanding anything to the contrary which may be contained in the Policy or the clauses attached thereto, this insurance includes loss of or damage to the subject-matter insured caused and discovered during the period of this insurance arising from faulty design of any part or parts thereof but in no case shall this insurance extend to cover the cost or expense of repairing, modifying, replacing or renewing such part or parts, nor any cost or expense incurred by reason of betterment or alteration in design.

9   Navigation

9.1   With leave to proceed to and from any wet or dry docks, harbours, ways, cradles and pontoons within the port or place of construction and to proceed under own power, loaded or in ballast, as often as required, for fitting out, docking, trials or delivery, within a distance by water of 250 nautical miles of the port or place of construction, or held covered at a premium to be arranged in the event of such distance being exceeded.

9.2   Any movement of the Vessel in tow outside the port or place of construction held covered at a premium to be arranged, provided previous notice be given to the Underwriters.

10   Deductible

10.1   No claim arising from a peril insured against shall be payable under this insurance unless the aggregate of all such claims arising out of each separate accident or occurrence (including claims under Clauses 13, 17, 19 and 20) exceeds .... in which case this sum shall be deducted. Nevertheless the expense of sighting the bottom after stranding, if reasonably incurred specially for that purpose, shall be paid even if no damage be found. This Clause

10.1 shall not apply to a claim for total or constructive total loss of the Vessel or, in the event of such a claim, to any associated claim under Clause 20 arising from the same accident or occurrence.

10.2 Claims for damage by heavy weather occurring during a single sea passage between two successive ports shall be treated as being due to one accident. In the case of such heavy weather extending over a period not wholly covered by this insurance the deductible to be applied to the claim recoverable hereunder shall be the proportion of the above deductible that the number of days of such heavy weather falling within the period of this insurance bears to the number of days of heavy weather during the single sea passage.

The expression "heavy weather" in this Clause 10.2 shall be deemed to include contact with floating ice.

10.3 Excluding any interest comprised therein, recoveries against any claim which is subject to the above deductible shall be credited to the Underwriters in full to the extent of the sum by which the aggregate of the claim unreduced by any recoveries exceeds the above deductible.

10.4 Interest comprised in recoveries shall be apportioned between the Assured and the Underwriters, taking into account the sums paid by the Underwriters and the dates when such payments were made, notwithstanding that by the addition of interest the Underwriters may receive a larger sum than they have paid.

11 Unrepaired damage

11.1 The measure of indemnity in respect of claims for unrepaired damage shall be the reasonable depreciation in the market value of the Vessel at the time this insurance terminates arising from such unrepaired damage, but not exceeding the reasonable cost of repairs.

11.2 In no case shall the Underwriters be liable for unrepaired damage in the event of a subsequent total loss (whether or not covered under this insurance) sustained during the period covered by this insurance or any extension thereof.

11.3 The Underwriters shall not be liable in respect of unrepaired damage for more than the insured value at the time this insurance terminates.

12 Constructive total loss

12.1 In ascertaining whether the subject-matter insured is a constructive total loss, the insured value shall be taken as the repaired value and nothing in respect of the damaged or break-up value shall be taken into account.

12.2 No claim for constructive total loss based upon the cost of recovery and/or repair shall be recoverable hereunder unless such cost would exceed the insured value. In making this determination, only the cost relating to a single accident or sequence of damages arising from the same accident shall be taken into account.

13 General average and salvage

13.1 This insurance covers the Vessel's proportion of salvage, salvage charges and/or general average, reduced in respect of any under-insurance, but in case of general average sacrifice of the Vessel the Assured may recover in respect of the whole loss without first enforcing their right of contribution from other parties.

13.2   Adjustment to be according to the law and practice obtaining at the place where the adventure ends, as if the contract of affreightment contained no special terms upon the subject; but where the contract of affreightment so provides the adjustment shall be according to the York-Antwerp Rules.

13.3   When the Vessel sails in ballast, not under charter, the provisions of the York-Antwerp Rules, 1974 (excluding Rules XX and XXI) shall be applicable, and the voyage for this purpose shall be deemed to continue from the port or place of departure until the arrival of the Vessel at the first port or place thereafter other than a port or place of refuge or a port or place of call for bunkering only. If at any such intermediate port or place there is an abandonment of the adventure originally contemplated the voyage shall thereupon be deemed to be terminated.

13.4   No claim under this Clause 13 shall in any case be allowed where the loss was not incurred to avoid or in connection with the avoidance of a peril insured against.

14 Notice of claim

In the event of loss damage liability or expense which may result in a claim under this insurance, prompt notice shall be given to the Underwriters prior to repair and, if the subject-matter is under construction abroad, to the nearest Lloyd's Agent so that a surveyor may be appointed to represent the Underwriters should they so desire.

15 Change of interest

Any change of interest in the subject-matter insured shall not affect the validity of this insurance.

16 Assignment

No assignment of or interest in this insurance or in any moneys which may be or become payable thereunder is to be binding on or recognised by the Underwriters unless a dated notice of such assignment or interest signed by the Assured, and by the assignor in the case of subsequent assignment, is endorsed on the Policy and the Policy with such endorsement is produced before payment of any claim or return of premium thereunder.

17 Collision liability

17.1   The Underwriters agree to indemnify the Assured for any sum or sums paid by the Assured to any other person or persons by reason of the Assured becoming legally liable by way of damages for

17.1.1   loss of or damage to any other vessel or property on any other vessel

17.1.2   delay to or loss of use of any such other vessel or property thereon

17.1.3   general average of, salvage of, or salvage under contract of, any such other vessel or property thereon, where such payment by the Assured is in consequence of the Vessel hereby insured coming into collision with any other vessel.

17.2   The indemnity provided by this Clause 17 shall be in addition to the indemnity provided by the other terms and conditions of this insurance and shall be subject to the following provisions:

124

17.2.1   Where the insured Vessel is in collision with another vessel and both vessels are to blame then, unless the liability of one or both vessels becomes limited by law, the indemnity under this Clause 17 shall be calculated on the principle of cross-liabilities as if the respective Owners had been compelled to pay to each other such proportion of each other's damages as may have been properly allowed in ascertaining the balance or sum payable by or to the Assured in consequence of the collision.

17.2.2   In no case shall the Underwriters' total liability under Clause 17.1 and 17.2 exceed their proportionate part of the insured value of the Vessel hereby insured in respect of any one such collision.

17.3   The Underwriters will also pay the legal costs incurred by the Assured or which the Assured may be compelled to pay in contesting liability or taking proceedings to limit liability, with the prior written consent of the Underwriters.

EXCLUSIONS

17.4   Provided always that this Clause 17 shall in no case extend to any sum which the Assured shall pay for or in respect of

17.4.1   removal or disposal of obstructions, wrecks, cargoes or any other thing whatsoever

17.4.2   any real or personal property or thing whatsoever except other vessels or property on other vessels

17.4.3   the cargo or other property on, or the engagements of, the insured Vessel

17.4.4   loss of life, personal injury or illness

17.4.5   pollution or contamination of any real or personal property or thing whatsoever (except other vessels with which the insured Vessel is in collision or property on such other vessels).

18 Sistership

Should the Vessel hereby insured come into collision with or receive salvage services from another vessel belonging wholly or in part to the same Owners or under the same management, the Assured shall have the same rights under this insurance as they would have were the other vessel entirely the property of Owners not interested in the Vessel hereby insured; but in such cases the liability for the collision or the amount payable for the services rendered shall be referred to a sole arbitrator to be agreed upon between the Underwriters and the Assured.

19 Protection and indemnity

19.1   The Underwriters agree to indemnify the Assured for any sum or sums paid by the Assured to any other person or persons by reason of the Assured becoming legally liable, as Owner of the Vessel, for any claim, demand, damages and/or expenses, where such liability is in consequence of any of the following matters or things and arises from an accident or occurrence during the period of this insurance:

19.1.1   loss of or damage to any fixed or movable object or property or other thing or interest whatsoever, other than the Vessel, arising from any cause whatsoever in so far as such loss or damage is not covered by Clause 17

19.1.2 any attempted or actual raising, removal or destruction of any fixed or movable object or property or other thing, including the wreck of the Vessel, or any neglect or failure to raise, remove, or destroy the same

19.1.3 liability assumed by the Assured under contracts of customary towage for the purpose of entering or leaving port or manoeuvring within the port

19.1.4 loss of life, personal injury, illness or payments made for life salvage.

19.2 The Underwriters agree to indemnify the Assured for any of the following arising from an accident or occurrence during the period of this insurance:

19.2.1 the additional cost of fuel, insurance, wages, stores, provisions and port charges reasonably incurred solely for the purpose of landing from the Vessel sick or injured persons or stowaways, refugees, or persons saved at sea

19.2.2 additional expenses brought about by the outbreak of infectious disease on board the Vessel or ashore

19.2.3 fines imposed on the Vessel, on the Assured, or on any Master Officer crew member or agent of the Vessel who is reimbursed by the Assured, for any act or neglect or breach of any statute or regulation relating to the operation of the Vessel, provided that the Underwriters shall not be liable to indemnify the Assured for any fines which result from any act neglect failure or default of the Assured their agents or servants other than Master Officer or crew member

19.2.4 the expenses of the removal of the wreck of the Vessel from any place owned, leased or occupied by the Assured

19.2.5 legal costs incurred by the Assured, or which the Assured may be compelled to pay, in avoiding, minimising or contesting liability with the prior written consent of the Underwriters.

EXCLUSIONS

19.3 Notwithstanding the provisions of Clauses 19.1 and 19.2 this Clause 19 does not cover any liability cost or expense arising in respect of:

19.3.1 any direct or indirect payment of the Assured under workmen's compensation or employers' liability acts and any other statutory or common law, general maritime law or other liability whatsoever in respect of accidents to or illness of workmen or any other persons employed in any capacity whatsoever by the Assured or others in on or about or in connection with the Vessel or her cargo materials or repairs

19.3.2 liability assumed by the Assured under agreement expressed or implied in respect of death or illness of or injury to any person employed under a contract of service or apprenticeship by the other party to such agreement

19.3.3 punitive or exemplary damages, however described

19.3.4 cargo or other property carried, to be carried or which has been carried on board the Vessel but this Clause 19.3.4 shall not exclude any claim in respect of the extra cost of removing cargo from the wreck of the Vessel

19.3.5 loss of or damage to property, owned by builders or repairers or for which they are responsible, which is on board the Vessel

19.3.6	liability arising under a contract or indemnity in respect of containers, equipment, fuel or other property on board the Vessel and which is owned or leased by the Assured
19.3.7	cash, negotiable instruments precious metals or stones, valuables or objects of a rare or precious nature, belonging to persons on board the Vessel, or non-essential personal effects of any Master, Officer or crew member
19.3.8	fuel, insurance, wages, stores, provisions and port charges arising from delay to the Vessel while awaiting a substitute for any Master, Officer or crew member
19.3.9	fines or penalties arising from overloading or illegal fishing
19.3.10	pollution or contamination of any real or personal property or thing whatsoever.
19.4	The indemnity provided by this Clause 19 shall be in addition to the indemnity provided by the other terms and conditions of this insurance.
19.5	Where the Assured or the Underwriters may or could have limited their liability the indemnity under this Clause 19 in respect of such liability shall not exceed Underwriters' proportionate part of the amount of such limitation.
19.6	In no case shall the Underwriters' liability under this Clause 19 in respect of each separate accident or occurrence or series of accidents arising out of the same event, exceed their proportionate part of the insured value of the Vessel.
19.7	PROVIDED ALWAYS THAT
19.7.1	prompt notice must be given to the Underwriters of every casualty event or claim upon the Assured which may give rise to a claim under this Clause 19 and of every event or matter which may cause the Assured to incur liability costs or expenses for which he may be insured under this Clause 19
19.7.2	the Assured shall not admit liability for or settle any claim for which he may be insured under this Clause 19 without the prior written consent of the Underwriters.

20 Duty of assured (sue and labour)

20.1	In case of any loss or misfortune it is the duty of the Assured and their servants and agents to take such measures as may be reasonable for the purpose of averting or minimising a loss which would be recoverable under this insurance.
20.2	Subject to the provisions below and to Clause 10 the Underwriters will contribute to charges properly and reasonably incurred by the Assured their servants or agents for such measures. General average, salvage charges (except as provided for in Clause 20.4) collision defence or attack costs and costs incurred by the Assured in avoiding, minimising or contesting liability covered by Clause 19 are not recoverable under this Clause 20.
20.3	Measures taken by the Assured or the Underwriters with the object of saving, protecting or recovering the subject-matter insured shall not be considered as a waiver or acceptance of abandonment or otherwise prejudice the rights of either party.
20.4	When a claim for total loss of the subject-matter insured is admitted under this insurance and expenses have been reasonably incurred in saving or

attempting to save the subject-matter insured and other property and there are no proceeds, or the expenses exceed the proceeds, then this insurance shall bear its pro rata share of such proportion of the expenses, or of the expenses in excess of the proceeds, as the case may be, as may reasonably be regarded as having been incurred in respect of the subject-matter insured.

20.5   The sum recoverable under this Clause 20 shall be in addition to the loss otherwise recoverable under this insurance but shall in no circumstances exceed the amount insured under this insurance in respect of the Vessel.

The following clauses shall be paramount and shall override anything contained in this insurance inconsistent therewith.

21 War exclusion

In no case shall this insurance cover loss damage liability or expense caused by

21.1   war civil war revolution rebellion insurrection, or civil strife arising therefrom, or any hostile act by or against a belligerent power

21.2   capture seizure arrest restraint or detainment (barratry and piracy excepted), and the consequences thereof or any attempt thereat

21.3   derelict mines torpedoes bombs or other derelict weapons of war.

22 Strikes exclusion

In no case shall this insurance cover loss damage liability or expense caused by

22.1   strikers, locked-out workmen, or persons taking part in labour disturbances, riots or civil commotions

22.2   any terrorist or any person acting from a political motive.

23 Malicious acts exclusion

In no case shall this insurance cover loss damage liability or expense arising from

23.1   the detonation of an explosive

23.2   any weapon of war

and caused by any person acting maliciously or from a political motive.

24 Nuclear exclusion

In no case shall this insurance cover loss damage liability or expense directly or indirectly caused by or contributed to by or arising from

24.1   ionising radiations from or contamination by radioactivity from any nuclear fuel or from any nuclear waste from the combustion of nuclear fuel

24.2   the radioactive, toxic, explosive or other hazardous properties of any explosive nuclear assembly or nuclear component thereof

24.3   any weapon of war employing atomic or nuclear fission and/or fusion or other like reaction or radioactive force or matter.

128

Institute Deductible Clause
Builders' Risks

1/12/72

Notwithstanding anything to the contrary which may be contained in the Policy or the clauses attached thereto, no claim arising from a peril insured against shall be payable under this insurance unless the aggregate of all such claims arising out of each separate accident or occurrence (including claims under the Collision, Protection and Indemnity, Removal of Wreck, and Suing and Labouring Clauses) exceeds....................in which case this sum shall be deducted. Nevertheless the expense of sighting the bottom after stranding, if reasonably incurred specially for that purpose, shall be paid even if no damage be found. This paragraph shall not apply to a claim for total or constructive total loss of the subject matter insured.

Claims for damage by heavy weather occurring during a single sea passage between two successive ports shall be treated as being due to one accident. In the case of such heavy weather extending over a period not wholly covered by this insurance the deductible to be applied to the claim recoverable hereunder shall be the proportion of the above deductible that the number of days of such heavy weather falling within the period of this insurance bears to the number of days of heavy weather during the single sea passage.

The expression "heavy weather" in the preceding paragraph shall be deemed to include contact with floating ice.

Excluding any interest comprised therein, recoveries against any claim which is subject to the above deductible shall be credited to the Underwriters in full to the extent of the sum by which the aggregate of the claim unreduced by any recoveries exceeds the above deductible.

Interest comprised in recoveries shall be apportioned between the Assured and the Underwriters, taking into account the sums paid by Underwriters and the dates when such payments were made, notwithstanding that by the addition of interest the Underwriters may receive a larger sum than they have paid.

Builders' Risks Institute Clause for Limitation of Liability in Respect of Faulty Design & P & I Risks (Inst FD & P & I Clause)

1/6/88—(FOR USE ONLY WITH THE NEW MARINE POLICY FORM)

Notwithstanding anything to the contrary which may be contained in the Policy or the clauses attached thereto:—

(1) This insurance includes loss of or damage to the subject-matter insured caused and discovered during the period of this insurance arising from faulty design of any part or parts thereof but in no case shall this insurance extend to cover the cost or expense of repairing, modifying, replacing or renewing such part or parts, nor any cost or expense incurred by reason of betterment or alteration in design.

(2) The amount recoverable under the Protection and Indemnity Clause in respect of any one accident or series of accidents arising out of the same event shall in no case exceed the sum hereby insured.

Institute Cargo Clauses (A)

1/1/82—(FOR USE ONLY WITH THE NEW MARINE POLICY FORM)

Risks Covered

Risks Clause

1   This insurance covers all risks of loss of or damage to the subject-matter insured except as provided in Clauses 4, 5, 6 and 7 below.

General Average Clause

2   This insurance covers general average and salvage charges, adjusted or determined according to the contract of affreightment and/or the governing law and practice, incurred to avoid or in connection with the avoidance of loss from any cause except those excluded in Clauses 4, 5, 6 and 7 or elsewhere in this insurance.

"Both to Blame Collision" Clause

3   This insurance is extended to indemnify the Assured against such proportion of liability under the contract of affreightment "Both to Blame Collision" Clause as is in respect of a loss recoverable hereunder. In the event of any claim by shipowners under the said Clause the Assured agree to notify the Underwriters who shall have the right, at their own cost and expense, to defend the Assured against such claim.

Exclusions

General Exclusions Clause

4   In no case shall this insurance cover
    4.1   loss damage or expense attributable to wilful misconduct of the Assured
    4.2   ordinary leakage, ordinary loss in weight or volume, or ordinary wear and tear of the subject-matter insured
    4.3   loss damage or expense caused by insufficiency or unsuitability of packing or preparation of the subject-matter insured (for the purpose of this Clause 4.3 "packing" shall be deemed to include stowage in a container or liftvan but

131

only when such stowage is carried out prior to attachment of this insurance or by the Assured or their servants)

4.4 loss damage or expense caused by inherent vice or nature of the subject-matter insured

4.5 loss damage or expense proximately caused by delay, even though the delay be caused by a risk insured against (except expenses payable under Clause 2 above)

4.6 loss damage or expense arising from insolvency or financial default of the owners managers charterers or operators of the vessel

4.7 loss damage or expense arising from the use of any weapon of war employing atomic or nuclear fission and/or fusion or other like reaction or radioactive force or matter.

Unseaworthiness and Unfitness Exclusion Clause

5 5.1 In no case shall this insurance cover loss damage or expense arising from unseaworthiness of vessel or craft,
unfitness of vessel craft conveyance container or liftvan for the safe carriage of the subject-matter insured,
where the Assured or their servants are privy to such unseaworthiness or unfitness, at the time the subject-matter insured is loaded therein.

5.2 The Underwriters waive any breach of the implied warranties of seaworthiness of the ship and fitness of the ship to carry the subject-matter insured to destination, unless the Assured or their servants are privy to such unseaworthiness or unfitness.

War Exclusion Clause

6 In no case shall this insurance cover loss damage or expense caused by

6.1 war civil war revolution rebellion insurrection, or civil strife arising therefrom, or any hostile act by or against a belligerent power

6.2 capture seizure arrest restraint or detainment (piracy excepted), and the consequences thereof or any attempt thereat

6.3 derelict mines torpedoes bombs or other derelict weapons of war.

Strikes Exclusion Clause

7 In no case shall this insurance cover loss damage or expense

7.1 caused by strikers, locked-out workmen, or persons taking part in labour disturbances, riots or civil commotions

7.2 resulting from strikes, lock-outs, labour disturbances, riots or civil commotions

7.3 caused by any terrorist or any person acting from a political motive.

Duration

Transit Clause

8 8.1 This insurance attaches from the time the goods leave the warehouse or place of storage at the place named herein for the commencement of the transit, continues during the ordinary course of transit and terminates either

8.1.1	on delivery to the Consignees' or other final warehouse or place of storage at the destination named herein,
8.1.2	on delivery to any other warehouse or place of storage, whether prior to or at the destination named herein, which the Assured elect to use either
8.1.2.1	for storage other than in the ordinary course of transit or
8.1.2.2	for allocation or distribution, or
8.1.3	on the expiry of 60 days after completion of discharge overside of the goods hereby insured from the overseas vessel at the final port of discharge, whichever shall first occur.
8.2	If, after discharge overside from the oversea vessel at the final port of discharge, but prior to termination of this insurance, the goods are to be forwarded to a destination other than that to which they are insured here-under, this insurance, whilst remaining subject to termination as provided for above, shall not extend beyond the commencement of transit to such other destination.
8.3	This insurance shall remain in force (subject to termination as provided for above and to the provisions of Clause 9 below) during delay beyond the control of the Assured, any deviation, forced discharge, reshipment or tran-shipment and during any variation of the adventure arising from the exercise of a liberty granted to shipowners or charterers under the contract of affreightment.

Termination of Contract of Carriage Clause

9 If owing to circumstances beyond the control of the Assured either the contract of carriage is terminated at a port or place other than the destination named therein or the transit is otherwise terminated before delivery of the goods as provided for in Clause 8 above, then this insurance shall also terminate *unless prompt notice is given to the Under-writers and continuation of cover is requested when the insurance shall remain in force, subject to an additional premium if required by the Underwriters,* either

9.1	until the goods are sold and delivered at such port or place, or, unless otherwise specially agreed, until the expiry of 60 days after arrival of the goods hereby insured at such port or place, whichever shall first occur, or
9.2	if the goods are forwarded within the said period of 60 days (or any agreed extension thereof) to the destination named herein or to any other destina-tion, until terminated in accordance with the provisions of Clause 8 above.

Change of Voyage Clause

10 Where, after attachment of this insurance, the destination is changed by the Assured, *held covered at a premium and on conditions to be arranged subject to prompt notice being given to the Underwriters.*

Claims

Insurable Interest Clause

11	**11.1**	In order to recover under this insurance the Assured must have an insurable interest in the subject-matter insured at the time of the loss.

11.2 Subject to 11.1 above, the Assured shall be entitled to recover for insured loss occurring during the period covered by this insurance, notwithstanding that the loss occurred before the contract of insurance was concluded, unless the Assured were aware of the loss and the Underwriters were not.

Forwarding Charges Clause

12 Where, as a result of the operation a risk covered by this insurance, the insured transit is terminated at a port or place other than that to which the subject-matter is covered under this insurance, the Underwriters will reimburse the Assured for any extra charges properly and reasonably incurred in unloading storing and forwarding the subject-matter to the destination to which it is insured hereunder. This Clause 12, which does not apply to general average or salvage charges, shall be subject to the exclusions contained in Clauses 4, 5, 6 and 7 above, and shall not include charges arising from the fault negligence insolvency or financial default of the Assured or their servants.

Constructive Total Loss Clause

13 No claim for Constructive Total Loss shall be recoverable hereunder unless the subject-matter insured is reasonably abandoned either on account of its actual total loss appearing to be unavoidable or because the cost of recovering, reconditioning and forwarding the subject-matter to the destination to which it is insured would exceed its value on arrival.

Increased Value Clause

14 14.1 If any Increased Value insurance is effected by the Assured on the cargo insured herein the agreed value of the cargo shall be deemed to be increased to the total amount insured under this insurance and all Increased Value insurances covering the loss, and liability under this insurance shall be in such proportion as the sum insured herein bears to such total amount insured.

In the event of claim the Assured shall provide the Underwriters with evidence of the amounts insured under all other insurances.

14.2 **Where this insurance is on Increased Value the following clause shall apply:**

The agreed value of the cargo shall be deemed to be equal to the total amount insured under the primary insurance and all Increased Value insurances covering the loss and effected on the cargo by the Assured, and liability under this insurance shall be in such proportion as the sum insured herein bears to such total amount insured.

In the event of claim the Assured shall provide the Underwriters with evidence of the amounts insured under all other insurances.

Benefit of Insurance

Not to Inure Clause

15 This insurance shall not inure to the benefit of the carrier or other bailee.

Minimising Losses

Duty of Assured Clause

16 It is the duty of the Assured and their servants and agents in respect of loss recoverable hereunder
    16.1   to take such measures as may be reasonable for the purpose of averting or minimising such loss, and
    16.2   to ensure that all rights against carriers, bailees or other third parties are properly preserved and exercised

and the Underwriters will, in addition to any loss recoverable hereunder, reimburse the Assured for any charges properly and reasonably incurred in pursuance of these duties.

Waiver Clause

17 Measures taken by the Assured or the Underwriters with the object of saving, protecting or recovering the subject-matter insured shall not be considered as a waiver or acceptance of abandonment or otherwise prejudice the rights of either party.

Avoidance of Delay

Reasonable Despatch Clause

18 It is a condition of this insurance that the Assured shall act with reasonable despatch in all circumstances within their control.

Law and Practice

English Law and Practice Clause

19 This insurance is subject to English law and practice.

NOTE:

—It is necessary for the Assured when they become aware of an event which is "held covered" under this insurance to give prompt notice to the Underwriters and the right to such cover is dependent upon compliance with this obligation.

Institute Cargo Clauses (B)

1/1/82—(FOR USE ONLY WITH THE NEW MARINE POLICY FORM)

Risks Covered

Risks Clause

1   This insurance covers, except as provided in Clauses 4, 5, 6 and 7 below,

    1.1   loss of or damage to the subject-matter insured reasonably attributable to

    1.1.1   fire or explosion

    1.1.2   vessel or craft being stranded grounded sunk or capsized

    1.1.3   overturning or derailment of land conveyance

    1.1.4   collision or contact of vessel craft or conveyance with any external object other than water

    1.1.5   discharge of cargo at a port of distress

    1.1.6   earthquake volcanic eruption or lightning,

    1.2   loss of or damage to the subject-matter insured caused by

    1.2.1   general average sacrifice

    1.2.2   jettison or washing overboard

    1.2.3   entry of sea lake or river water into vessel craft hold conveyance container liftvan or place of storage,

    1.3   total loss of any package lost overboard or dropped whilst loading on to, or unloading from, vessel or craft.

General Average Clause

2   This insurance covers general average and salvage charges, adjusted or determined according to the contract of affreightment and/or the governing law and practice, induced to avoid or in connection with the avoidance of loss from any cause except those excluded in Clauses 4, 5, 6 and 7 or elsewhere in this insurance.

"Both to Blame Collision" Clause

3   This insurance is extended to indemnify the Assured against such proportion of liability under the contract of affreightment "Both to Blame Collision" Clause as is in respect of a loss recoverable hereunder. In the event of any claim by shipowners under the said Clause the Assured agree to notify the Underwriters who shall have the right, at their own cost and expense, to defend the Assured against such claim.

Exclusions

General Exclusions Clause

4   In no case shall this insurance cover
    4.1   loss damage or expense attributable to wilful misconduct of the Assured
    4.2   ordinary leakage, ordinary loss in weight or volume, or ordinary wear and tear of the subject-matter insured
    4.3   loss damage or expense caused by insufficiency or unsuitability of packing or preparation of the subject-matter insured (for the purpose of this Clause 4.3 "packing" shall be deemed to include stowage in a container or liftvan but only when such stowage is carried out prior to attachment of this insurance or by the Assured or their servants)
    4.4   loss damage or expense caused by inherent vice or nature of the subject-matter insured
    4.5   loss damage or expense proximately caused by delay, even though the delay be caused by a risk insured against (except expenses payable under Clause 2 above)
    4.6   loss damage or expense arising from insolvency or financial default of the owners managers charterers or operators of the vessel
    4.7   deliberate damage to or deliberate destruction of the subject-matter insured or any part thereof by the wrongful act of any person or persons
    4.8   loss damage or expense arising from the use of any weapon of war employing atomic or nuclear fission and/or fusion or other like reaction or radioactive force or matter.

Unseaworthiness and Unfitness Exclusion Clause

5   **5.1**   In no case shall this insurance cover loss damage or expense arising from unseaworthiness of vessel or craft,
              unfitness of vessel craft conveyance container or liftvan for the safe carriage of the subject-matter insured,
              where the Assured or their servants are privy to such unseaworthiness or unfitness, at the time the subject-matter insured is loaded therein.
    5.2   The Underwriters waive any breach of the implied warranties of seaworthiness of the ship and fitness of the ship to carry the subject-matter insured to destination, unless the Assured or their servants are privy to such unseaworthiness or unfitness.

War Exclusion Clause

6   In no case shall this insurance cover loss damage or expense caused by
    6.1   war civil war revolution rebellion insurrection, or civil strife arising therefrom, or any hostile act by or against a belligerent power
    6.2   capture seizure arrest restraint or detainment, and the consequences thereof or any attempt thereat
    6.3   derelict mines torpedoes bombs or other derelict weapons of war.

Strikes Exclusion Clause

7   In no case shall this insurance cover loss damage or expense
    7.1   caused by strikers, locked-out workmen, or persons taking part in labour disturbances, riots or civil commotions

7.2		resulting from strikes, lock-outs, labour disturbances, riots or civil commotions
7.3		caused by any terrorist or any person acting from a political motive.

Duration

Transit Clause

8	8.1	This insurance attaches from the time the goods leave the warehouse or place of storage at the place named herein for the commencement of the transit, continues during the ordinary course of transit and terminates either
	8.1.1	on delivery to the Consignees' or other final warehouse or place of storage at the destination named herein,
	8.1.2	on delivery to any other warehouse or place of storage, whether prior to or at the destination named herein, which the Assured elect to use either
	8.1.2.1	for storage other than in the ordinary course of transit or
	8.1.2.2	for allocation or distribution, or
	8.1.3	on the expiry of 60 days after completion of discharge overside of the goods hereby insured from the overseas vessel at the final port of discharge, whichever shall first occur.
	8.2	If, after discharge overside from the oversea vessel at the final port of discharge, but prior to termination of this insurance, the goods are to be forwarded to a destination other than that to which they are insured hereunder, this insurance, whilst remaining subject to termination as provided for above, shall not extend beyond the commencement of transit to such other destination.
	8.3	This insurance shall remain in force (subject to termination as provided for above and to the provisions of Clause 9 below) during delay beyond the control of the Assured, any deviation, forced discharge, reshipment or transhipment and during any variation of the adventure arising from the exercise of a liberty granted to shipowners or charterers under the contract of affreightment.

Termination of Contract of Carriage Clause

9	If owing to circumstances beyond the control of the Assured either the contract of carriage is terminated at a port or place other than the destination named therein or the transit is otherwise terminated before delivery of the goods as provided for in Clause 8 above, then this insurance shall also terminate *unless prompt notice is given to the Underwriters and continuation of cover is requested when the insurance shall remain in force, subject to an additional premium if required by the Underwriters,* either

	9.1	until the goods are sold and delivered at such port or place, or, unless otherwise specially agreed, until the expiry of 60 days after arrival of the goods hereby insured at such port or place, whichever shall first occur, or
	9.2	if the goods are forwarded within the said period of 60 days (or any agreed extension thereof) to the destination named herein or to any other destination, until terminated in accordance with the provisions of Clause 8 above.

Change of Voyage Clause

10 Where, after attachment of this insurance, the destination is changed by the Assured, *held covered at a premium and on conditions to be arranged subject to prompt notice being given to the Underwriters.*

Claims

Insurable Interest Clause

11 11.1   In order to recover under this insurance the Assured must have an insurable interest in the subject-matter insured at the time of the loss.

11.2   Subject to 11.1 above, the Assured shall be entitled to recover for insured loss occurring during the period covered by this insurance, notwithstanding that the loss occurred before the contract of insurance was concluded, unless the Assured were aware of the loss and the Underwriters were not.

Forwarding Charges Clause

12 Where, as a result of the operation a risk covered by this insurance, the insured transit is terminated at a port or place other than that to which the subject-matter is covered under this insurance, the Underwriters will reimburse the Assured for any extra charges properly and reasonably incurred in unloading storing and forwarding the subject-matter to the destination to which it is insured hereunder. This Clause 12, which does not apply to general average or salvage charges, shall be subject to the exclusions contained in Clauses 4, 5, 6 and 7 above, and shall not include charges arising from the fault negligence insolvency or financial default of the Assured or their servants.

Constructive Total Loss Clause

13 No claim for Constructive Total Loss shall be recoverable hereunder unless the subject-matter insured is reasonably abandoned either on account of its actual total loss appearing to be unavoidable or because the cost of recovering, reconditioning and forwarding the subject-matter to the destination to which it is insured would exceed its value on arrival.

Increased Value Clause

14 14.1   If any Increased Value insurance is effected by the Assured on the cargo insured herein the agreed value of the cargo shall be deemed to be increased to the total amount insured under this insurance and all Increased Value insurances covering the loss, and liability under this insurance shall be in such proportion as the sum insured herein bears to such total amount insured.

In the event of the claim the Assured shall provide the Underwriters with evidence of the amounts insured under all other insurances.

14.2   **Where this insurance is on Increased Value the following clause shall apply:**

The agreed value of the cargo shall be deemed to be equal to the total amount insured under the primary insurance and all Increased Value insurances covering the loss and effected on the cargo by the Assured, and liability under this insurance shall be in such proportion as the sum insured herein bears to such total amount insured.

In the event of claim the Assured shall provide the Underwriters with evidence of the amounts insured under all other insurances.

Benefit of Insurance

Not to Inure Clause

15   This insurance shall not inure to the benefit of the carrier or other bailee.

Minimising Losses

Duty of Assured Clause

16   It is the duty of the Assured and their servants and agents in respect of loss recoverable hereunder
    16.1   to take such measures as may be reasonable for the purpose of averting or minimising such loss, and
    16.2   to ensure that all rights against carriers, bailees or other third parties are properly preserved and exercised
and the Underwriters will, in addition to any loss recoverable hereunder, reimburse the Assured for any charges properly and reasonably incurred in pursuance of these duties.

Waiver Clause

17   Measures taken by the Assured or the Underwriters with the object of saving, protecting or recovering the subject-matter insured shall not be considered as a waiver of acceptance of abandonment or otherwise prejudice the rights of either party.

Avoidance of Delay

Reasonable Despatch Clause

18   It is a condition of this insurance that the Assured shall act with reasonable despatch in all circumstances within their control.

Law and Practice

English Law and Practice Clause

19   This insurance is subject to English law and practice.

NOTE:

—It is necessary for the Assured when they become aware of an event which is "held covered" under this insurance to give prompt notice to the Underwriters and the right to such cover is dependent upon compliance with this obligation.

Institute Cargo Clauses (C)

1/1/82—(FOR USE ONLY WITH THE NEW MARINE POLICY FORM)

Risks Covered

Risks Clause

1   This insurance covers, except as provided in Clauses 4, 5, 6 and 7 below,

     1.1   loss of or damage to the subject-matter insured reasonably attributable to

     1.1.1   fire or explosion

     1.1.2   vessel or craft being stranded grounded sunk or capsized

     1.1.3   overturning or derailment of land conveyance

     1.1.4   collision or contact of vessel craft or conveyance with any external object other than water

     1.1.5   discharge of cargo at a port of distress

     1.2   loss of or damage to the subject-matter insured caused by

     1.2.1   general average sacrifice

     1.2.2   jettison.

General Average Clause

2   This insurance covers general average and salvage charges, adjusted or determined according to the contract of affreightment and/or the governing law and practice, incurred to avoid or in connection with the avoidance of loss from any cause except those excluded in Clauses 4, 5, 6 and 7 or elsewhere in this insurance.

"Both to Blame Collision" Clause

3   This insurance is extended to indemnify the Assured against such proportion of liability under the contract of affreightment "Both to Blame Collision" Clause as is in respect of a loss recoverable hereunder. In the event of any claim by shipowners under the said Clause the Assured agree to notify the Underwriters who shall have the right, at their own cost and expense, to defend the Assured against such claim.

141

Exclusions

General Exclusions Clause

4   In no case shall this insurance cover
4.1   loss damage or expense attributable to wilful misconduct of the Assured
4.2   ordinary leakage, ordinary loss in weight or volume, or ordinary wear and tear of the subject-matter insured
4.3   loss damage or expense caused by insufficiency or unsuitability of packing or preparation of the subject-matter insured (for the purpose of this Clause 4.3 "packing" shall be deemed to include stowage in a container or liftvan but only when such stowage is carried out prior to attachment of this insurance or by the Assured or their servants)
4.4   loss damage or expense caused by inherent vice or nature of the subject-matter insured
4.5   loss damage or expense proximately caused by delay, even though the delay be caused by a risk insured against (except expenses payable under Clause 2 above)
4.6   loss damage or expense arising from insolvency or financial default of the owners managers charterers or operators of the vessel
4.7   deliberate damage to or deliberate destruction of the subject-matter insured or any part thereof by the wrongful act of any person or persons
4.8   loss damage or expense arising from the use of any weapon of war employing atomic or nuclear fission and/or fusion or other like reaction or radioactive force or matter

Unseaworthiness and Unfitness Exclusion Clause

5   5.1   In no case shall this insurance cover loss damage or expense arising from unseaworthiness of vessel or craft,
unfitness of vessel craft conveyance container or liftvan for the safe carriage of the subject-matter insured,
where the Assured or their servants are privy to such unseaworthiness or unfitness, at the time the subject-matter insured is loaded therein.
5.2   The Underwriters waive any breach of the implied warranties of seaworthiness of the ship and fitness of the ship to carry the subject-matter insured to destination, unless the Assured or their servants are privy to such unseaworthiness or unfitness.

War Exclusion Clause

6   In no case shall this insurance cover loss damage or expense caused by
6.1   war civil war revolution rebellion insurrection, or civil strife arising therefrom, or any hostile act by or against a belligerent power
6.2   capture seizure arrest restraint or detainment, and the consequences thereof or any attempt thereat
6.3   derelict mines torpedoes bombs or other derelict weapons of war.

Strikes Exclusion Clause

7   In no case shall this insurance cover loss damage or expense
7.1   caused by strikers, locked-out workmen, or persons taking part in labour disturbances, riots or civil commotions

7.2	resulting from strikes, lock-outs, labour disturbances, riots or civil commotions
7.3	caused by any terrorist or any person acting from a political motive.

Duration

Transit Clause

8	8.1	This insurance attaches from the time the goods leave the warehouse or place of storage at the place named herein for the commencement of the transit, continues during the ordinary course of transit and terminates either
	8.1.1	on delivery to the Consignees' or other final warehouse or place of storage at the destination named herein,
	8.1.2	on delivery to any other warehouse or place of storage, whether prior to or at the destination named herein, which the Assured elect to use either
	8.1.2.1	for storage other than in the ordinary course of transit or
	8.1.2.2	for allocation or distribution, or
	8.1.3	on the expiry of 60 days after completion of discharge overside of the goods hereby insured from the overseas vessel at the final port of discharge, whichever shall first occur.
	8.2	If, after discharge overside from the oversea vessel at the final port of discharge, but prior to termination of this insurance, the goods are to be forwarded to a destination other than that to which they are insured hereunder, this insurance, whilst remaining subject to termination as provided for above, shall not extend beyond the commencement of transit to such other destination.
	8.3	This insurance shall remain in force (subject to termination as provided for above and to the provisions of Clause 9 below) during delay beyond the control of the Assured, any deviation, forced discharge, reshipment or transhipment and during any variation of the adventure arising from the exercise of a liberty granted to shipowners or charterers under the contact of affreightment.

Termination of Contract of Carriage Clause

9	If owing to circumstances beyond the control of the Assured either the contract of carriage is terminated at a port or place other than the destination named therein or the transit is otherwise terminated before delivery of the goods as provided for in Clause 8 above, then this insurance shall also terminate *unless prompt notice is given to the Underwriters and continuation of cover is requested when the insurance shall remain in force, subject to an additional premium if required by the Underwriters,* either
9.1	until the goods are sold and delivered at such port or place, or, unless otherwise specially agreed, until the expiry of 60 days after arrival of the goods hereby insured at such port or place, whichever shall first occur, or

9.2   if the goods are forwarded within the said period of 60 days (or any agreed extension thereof) to the destination named herein or to any other destination, until terminated in accordance with the provisions of Clause 8 above.

Change of Voyage Clause

10   Where, after attachment of this insurance, the destination is changed by the Assured, *held covered at a premium and on conditions to be arranged subject to prompt notice being given to the Underwriters.*

Claims

Insurable Interest Clause

11   11.1   In order to recover under this insurance the Assured must have an insurable interest in the subject-matter insured at the time of the loss.

       11.2   Subject to 11.1 above, the Assured shall be entitled to recover for insured loss occurring during the period covered by this insurance, notwithstanding that the loss occurred before the contract of insurance was concluded, unless the Assured were aware of the loss and the Underwriters were not.

Forwarding Charges Clause

12   Where, as a result of the operation a risk covered by this insurance, the insured transit is terminated at a port or place other than that to which the subject-matter is covered under this insurance, the Underwriters will reimburse the Assured for any extra charges properly and reasonably incurred in unloading storing and forwarding the subject-matter to the destination to which it is insured hereunder. This Clause 12, which does not apply to general average or salvage charges, shall be subject to the exclusions contained in Clauses 4, 5, 6 and 7 above, and shall not include charges arising from the fault negligence insolvency or financial default of the Assured or their servants.

Constructive Total Loss Clause

13   No claim for Constructive Total Loss shall be recoverable hereunder unless the subject-matter insured is reasonably abandoned either on account of its actual total loss appearing to be unavoidable or because the cost of recovering, reconditioning and forwarding the subject-matter to the destination to which it is insured would exceed its value on arrival.

Increased Value Clause

14   14.1   If any Increased Value insurance is effected by the Assured on the cargo insured herein the agreed value of the cargo shall be deemed to be increased to the total amount insured under this insurance and all Increased Value insurances covering the loss, and liability under this insurance shall be in such proportion as the sum insured herein bears to such total amount insured.

            In the event of the claim the Assured shall provide the Underwriters with evidence of the amounts insured under all other insurances.

14.2   **Where this insurance is on Increased Value the following clause shall apply:**

The agreed value of the cargo shall be deemed to be equal to the total amount insured under the primary insurance and all Increased Value insurances covering the loss and effected on the cargo by the Assured, and liability under this insurance shall be in such proportion as the sum insured herein bears to such total amount insured.

In the event of claim the Assured shall provide the Underwriters with evidence of the amounts insured under all other insurances.

Benefit of Insurance

Not to Inure Clause

15   This insurance shall not inure to the benefit of the carrier or other bailee.

Minimising Losses

Duty of Assured Clause

16   It is the duty of the Assured and their servants and agents in respect of loss recoverable hereunder

    16.1   to take such measures as may be reasonable for the purpose of averting or minimising such loss, and

    16.2   to ensure that all rights against carriers, bailees or other third parties are properly preserved and exercised

and the Underwriters will, in addition to any loss recoverable hereunder, reimburse the Assured for any charges properly and reasonably incurred in pursuance of these duties.

Waiver Clause

17   Measures taken by the Assured or the Underwriters with the object of saving, protecting or recovering the subject-matter insured shall not be considered as a waiver of acceptance of abandonment or otherwise prejudice the rights of either party.

Avoidance of Delay

Reasonable Despatch Clause

18   It is a condition of this insurance that the Assured shall act with reasonable despatch in all circumstances within their control.

Law and Practice

English Law and Practice Clause

19   This insurance is subject to English law and practice.

NOTE:

—It is necessary for the Assured when they become aware of an event which is "held covered" under this insurance to give prompt notice to the Underwriters and the right to such cover is dependent upon compliance with this obligation.

Institute Classification Clause

1/8/97

THE MARINE TRANSIT RATES AGREED FOR THIS INSURANCE APPLY ONLY TO CARGOES AND/OR INTERESTS CARRIED BY MECHANICALLY SELF-PROPELLED VESSELS OF STEEL CONSTRUCTION, CLASSED AS BELOW BY ONE OF THE FOLLOWING CLASSIFICATION SOCIETIES,

Lloyd's Register	**100A1** or **B.S.**	
American Bureau of Shipping ..	**⚓A1**	
Bureau Veritas	**1 3/3 E⚓**	
China Classification Society ..	**★CSA**	
Germanischer Lloyd	**⚓100 A5**	Class
Korean Register of Shipping ..	**⚓KRS 1**	without any
Maritime Register of Shipping ..	**KM★**	modification
Nippon Kaiji Kyokai	**NS***	
Norske Veritas	**⚓1A1**	
Registro Italiano	**★100–A–1.1.**	

PROVIDED SUCH VESSELS ARE

a) (i) not bulk and/or combination carriers over 10 years of age.
    (ii) not mineral oil tankers exceeding 50,000 GRT which are over 10 years of age.

b) (i) not over 15 years of age, <u>OR</u>
    (ii) over 15 years of age but not over 25 years of age and have established and maintained a regular pattern of trading on an advertised schedule to load and unload at specified ports.

CHARTERED VESSELS AND ALSO VESSELS UNDER 1000 G.R.T. WHICH ARE MECHANICALLY SELF-PROPELLED AND OF STEEL CONSTRUCTION MUST BE CLASSED AS ABOVE AND NOT OVER THE AGE LIMITATIONS SPECIFIED ABOVE.

APPENDICES

THE REQUIREMENTS OF THE INSTITUTE CLASSIFICATION CLAUSE DO NOT APPLY TO ANY CRAFT, RAFT OR LIGHTER, USED TO LOAD OR UNLOAD THE VESSEL, WHILST THEY ARE WITHIN THE PORT AREA.

CARGOES AND/OR INTERESTS CARRIED BY MECHANICALLY SELF-PROPELLED VESSELS NOT FALLING WITHIN THE SCOPE OF THE ABOVE ARE HELD COVERED SUBJECT TO A PREMIUM AND ON CONDITIONS TO BE AGREED.

Institute Machinery Damage Additional Deductible Clause (for use only with the Institute Time Clauses—Hulls 1/11/95)

Notwithstanding any provision to the contrary in this insurance a claim for loss of or damage to any machinery, shaft, electrical equipment or wiring, boiler condenser heating coil or associated pipework, arising from any of the perils enumerated in Clauses 6.2.1 to 6.2.4 inclusive of the Institute Time Clauses—Hulls 1/11/95 or from fire or explosion when either has originated in a machinery space, shall be subject to a deductible amount agreed. Any balance remaining, after application of this deductible, with any other claim arising from the same accident or occurrence, shall then be subject to the deductible referred to in Clause 12.1 of the Institute Time Clauses—Hulls 1/11/95.

The provisions of Clauses 12.3 and 12.4 of the Institute Time Clauses—Hulls 1/11/95 shall apply to recoveries and interest comprised in recoveries against any claim which is subject to this Clause.

This Clause shall not apply to a claim for total or constructive total loss of the Vessel.

Institute Machinery Damage Additional Deductible Clause (for use only with Institute Voyage Clauses—Hulls 1/11/95)

Notwithstanding any provision to the contrary in this insurance a claim for loss of or damage to any machinery, shaft, electrical equipment or wiring, boiler condenser heating coil or associated pipework, arising from any of the perils enumerated in Clauses 4.2.1 to 4.2.4 inclusive of the Institute Voyage Clauses—Hulls 1/11/95 or from fire or explosion when either has originated in a machinery space, shall be subject to a deductible amount agreed. Any balance remaining, after application of this deductible, with any other claim arising from the same accident or occurrence, shall then be subject to the deductible referred to in Clause 10.1 of the Institute Voyage Clauses—Hulls 1/11/95.

The provisions of Clauses 10.3 and 10.4 of the Institute Voyage Clauses—Hulls 1/11/95 shall apply to recoveries and interest comprised in recoveries against any claim which is subject to this Clause.

This Clause shall not apply to a claim for total or constructive total loss of the Vessel.

Institute Malicious Damage Clause

1/8/82—(FOR USE ONLY WITH THE NEW MARINE POLICY FORM)

In consideration of an additional premium, it is hereby agreed that the exclusion "deliberate damage to or deliberate destruction of the subject-matter insured or any part thereof by the wrongful act of any person or persons" is deemed to be deleted and further that this insurance covers loss of or damage to the subject-matter insured caused by malicious acts vandalism or sabotage, subject always to the other exclusions contained in this insurance.

Institute Mortgagees' Interest
Clauses Hulls

1/3/97

This insurance is subject to English law and practice

A. Recital

Whereas the Assured has entered into a loan agreement commensurate with which the Assured holds certain collateral security including a first mortgage on the Mortgaged Vessel and endorsements of its interests on the Owners' Policies and Club Entries.
Now it is agreed as follows:

1   Insuring clause

1.1   This insurance will indemnify the Assured for loss resulting from loss of or damage to or liability of the Mortgaged Vessel which, in the absence of an Insured Peril set out in Clause 2.1 below, would prima facie be covered by the Owners' Policies and Club Entries, and not excluded therein, but in respect of which there is subsequent non-payment (or reduced payment which is approved in advance by the Underwriters hereon) by any of the underwriters of Owners' Policies and Club Entries as a result of any Insured Peril, **provided always that such Insured Peril occurs or exists without the privity of the Assured**.

1.2   The indemnity payable hereunder shall be

1.2.1   the amount of the Assured's Net Loss and any amounts recoverable under Clause 6 herein, collectively not exceeding the Sum Insured on the Mortgaged Vessel, or

1.2.2   the amount of the unrecoverable claim or part thereof under any of the Owners' Policies and Club Entries
whichever is the lesser amount.

1.3   All the above is subject to the Definitions, Exclusions, Warranties and Conditions below.

2   Definitions

2.1   INSURED PERILS

2.1.1   Avoidance of the Owners' Policies and Club Entries or any of them by the underwriters thereof on the grounds of a misrepresentation or non-disclosure of any material circumstance, whether such misrepresentation or non-disclosure arises from the assured thereunder or any of such assured's insurance agents or insurance brokers,

152

2.1.2   breach of any statutory provision or any express or implied promissory warranty or condition, including without limitation

2.1.2.1   breach of any implied warranty of seaworthiness or legality,

2.1.2.2   breach of Section 39(5) of the Marine Insurance Act of 1906,

2.1.2.3   breach of trading warranties contained in any of the Owners' Policies and Club Entries,

2.1.2.4   breach of any warranty or condition in any of the Owners' Policies and Club Entries in respect of the classification of the Mortgaged Vessel by a Classification Society or any failure to comply with the recommendations of such Society to the extent required by such warranty or condition,

2.1.2.5   breach of any warranty or condition in any of the Owners' Policies and Club Entries which requires compliance with any condition survey, structural survey or P&I Club survey requirements and pursuant to which clauses underwriters deny a claim,

2.1.2.6   breach of any warranty or condition in any of the Owners' Policies and Club Entries in respect of the ownership, flag, management or charter on a bareboat basis of the Mortgaged Vessel,

2.1.3   failure of the assured under the hull and machinery policy or the owners, manager or superintendents of the vessel or any of their onshore management to exercise due diligence in respect of any loss or damage to the Mortgaged Vessel where such failure to exercise due diligence entitles the underwriters of the owner's hull and machinery policy to deny a claim otherwise recoverable thereunder,

2.1.4   any deliberate or fraudulent casting away of or damage to the Mortgaged Vessel,

2.1.5   avoidance of a claim under any of the Owners' Policies and Club Entries or of any of the Owners' Policies and Club Entries by reason of breach of the duty of good faith in respect of such claim, or

2.1.6   the operation of any applicable provision in any of the Owners' Policies and Club Entries which provides for a time limitation on the presentation of claims,

2.1.7   in the event of the total loss of the Mortgaged Vessel, the final judgment or award of the courts or arbitration tribunal agreed to have jurisdiction under the express terms of Owners' Policies and Club Entries (or in the event of their being no such express terms, a competent court) following a contested hearing whereby the Owners' claim is not recoverable under either Owners' hull and machinery or war risks policies on the grounds that the loss has not been proved to have been proximately caused by a peril insured under those policies and is not otherwise excluded from payment by any exclusion or other provision therein.

2.2   **Owners' Policies and Club Entries**—means hull and machinery policies on terms equivalent to or wider than the current Institute Time Clauses Hulls or American Institute Hull Clauses, (if taken, increased value policies on terms equivalent to Institute Time Clauses—Hull Disbursements and Increased Value (Total Loss Only and Excess Liabilities) or American Institute Increased Value and Excess Liabilities Clauses), war risks on terms equivalent to current Institute War and Strikes Clauses Hulls—Time and full protection and indemnity risks on conditions equivalent to the rules of a P&I Club that is a member of the International Group of P&I Associations.

2.3 **Net Loss**—means the Assured's loss under the loan agreement to the extent secured by mortgage on the Mortgaged Vessel net of any amounts recovered or recoverable under all security arrangements contained in or collateral to the loan including but not limited to all mortgages (whether on vessels insured hereunder or on other vessels), liens, any floating and fixed charges, security interests, guarantees, insurance policies and pledges.

2.4 **Mortgaged Vessel**—means the vessel mortgaged to the Assured which is listed on the schedule attached hereto.

3   Exclusions

In no case shall this policy cover:

3.1 any loss or expense arising from or as a result of

3.1.1 the relevant Owners' Policies and Club Entries having been terminated or cancelled or cover suspended or non-payment of claims by the underwriters or insurance brokers thereof due to non-payment of premium or call,

3.1.2 insolvency or financial default of any of the underwriters of the Owners' Policies and Club Entries,

3.1.3 inability of any party to transmit funds,

3.1.4 any fluctuation in exchange rates,

3.1.5 the operation of any franchise deductible or provision for self-insurance,

3.2 loss or damage directly or indirectly caused by or contributed to by or arising from:

3.2.1 ionising radiation from or contamination by radioactivity from any nuclear fuel or from any nuclear waste or from combustion of nuclear fuel,

3.2.2 the radioactive, toxic, explosive or other hazardous or contaminating properties of any nuclear installation, reactor or other nuclear assembly or nuclear component thereof,

3.2.3 any weapon of war employing atomic or nuclear fission and/or fusion or other like reaction or radioactive force or matter.

4   Warranties

It is warranted in respect of the Mortgaged Vessel that:

4.1 Owners' Policies and Club Entries have been taken out and except as a result of the occurrence or existence of an Insured Peril without the privity of the Assured, shall be maintained throughout the currency of this insurance for an insured value and limit of liability not less than the amount insured hereunder or the amount of the outstanding loan to the extent secured by the Mortgaged Vessel.

4.2 each of the Owners' Policies and Club Entries is endorsed to the extent of the Assured's interest, and

4.3 the Assured has procured and registered a valid first mortgage.

5   Change of ownership or control

This insurance will terminate automatically at the time the Assured becomes or is aware of or privy to any change of:

5.1 Classification Society or of change, suspension, discontinuance, withdrawal or expiry of the Mortgaged Vessel's class within that Society,

5.2 ownership, flag, management or control of the Mortgaged Vessel.

unless the Assured gives prompt notice of such change in writing, and agrees to pay an additional premium, if required, and Owners' Policies and Club Entries are maintained.

6 Duty of Assured (Sue and Labour)

6.1 The Assured shall report in writing to the Underwriters any circumstances which may give rise to a claim under this insurance within 30 days of the Assured's knowledge of such circumstances and shall thereafter keep the Underwriters fully informed of all developments.

6.2 It is the duty of the Assured and their servants and agents to take such measures as may be reasonable for the purpose of averting or minimising a loss which would be recoverable under this insurance.

6.3 The Underwriters will reimburse charges properly and reasonably incurred by the Assured their servants or agents for such measures except for legal costs and expenses incurred by the Assured in relation to any claim under Owners' Policies and Club Entries which shall only be reimbursed in accordance with clause 6.4 herein.

6.4 Subject to the condition precedent that the Mortgaged Vessel is entered in a Freight, Demurrage and Defence Club covering the cost of the owner proceeding against the Owners' Policies and Club Entries, the Underwriters will reimburse those legal costs and expenses incurred by the Assured in pursuing the non-paying Owners' Policies and Club Entries not otherwise recoverable as part of the Net Loss but only where the Assured can demonstrate to the satisfaction of the Underwriters that it has made every reasonable effort to compel the owner to pursue the non-paying Owners' Policies and Club Entries. This policy shall not pay for legal costs and expenses incurred by the Assured in monitoring the claim against the Owners' Policies and Club Entries.

6.5 Any amounts payable under this clause shall be included within and shall not be additional to the Sum Insured.

6.6 Measures taken by the Assured or the Underwriters with the object of averting or minimising a loss which would be recoverable under this insurance shall not be considered as a waiver or acceptance of a claim or otherwise prejudice the rights of either party.

7 Claims

7.1 The Assured shall prove a claim under this insurance by:

7.1.1 demonstrating to the satisfaction of the Underwriters, that by reason of the perils insured under clause 2.1 there is no reasonable prospect of the Owners and/or Assured succeeding in the claim against the Underwriters of the Owners' Policies and Club Entries or

7.1.2 in the event of disagreement between the Underwriters and the Assured by either referring the issue to a sole arbitrator in London to be agreed upon between the Underwriters and the Assured or on final court judgement or arbitration award delivered in favour of the underwriters of Owners' Policies and Club Entries.

7.2 The Underwriters shall pay any claim hereunder within 3 months of the date that both the claim is proved in accordance with Clause 7.1 and Net Loss is established.

8 Subrogation

8.1 Upon payment to the Assured of a claim hereunder, the Underwriters shall be subrogated to all the rights and remedies of the Assured in respect of such payment.

8.2 It is a condition of this insurance that any payments by the Underwriters shall not be applied by the Assured in or towards discharge or satisfaction of the amount of the outstanding indebtedness.

9 Effect of under insurance

If the loan amounts are not fully insured hereunder at the time of loss then the indemnity payable hereunder including any sue and labour amounts shall be reduced in proportion to the under insurance.

10 Automatic termination

10.1 Cover hereunder for loss of or damage to or liability of a Mortgaged Vessel shall terminate in respect of those risks covered by the War and Strikes Clauses of the Mortgaged Vessel

10.1.1 AUTOMATICALLY upon the outbreak of war (whether there be a declaration of war or not) between any of the following:
United Kingdom, United States of America, France, the Russian Federation, the People's Republic of China

10.1.2 AUTOMATICALLY in respect of a Mortgaged Vessel in the event of that Mortgaged Vessel being requisitioned either for title or use

10.1.3 7 days after the Underwriters of the Owner's War Risks Insurances or any of them have given notice of cancellation unless such War Risks Insurances have been reinstated prior to or from the expiry of such notice and any new rate of premium and amendments to terms, conditions or warranties, if any, have been agreed, or

10.1.4 7 days after the Underwriters hereon have given notice of cancellation in respect of such risks.

10.2 Cancellation in accordance with Clauses 10.1.3 and 10.1.4 shall become effective on the expiry of 7 days from midnight on the day on which the notice of cancellation is given. The Underwriters agree however to reinstate this insurance subject to agreement between the Underwriters and the Assured prior to the expiry of such notice of cancellation as to new rate of premium and/or conditions and/or warranties.

Institute Notice of Cancellation, Automatic Termination of Cover and War and Nuclear Exclusions Clause—Hulls, etc

1/1/95

This clause shall be paramount and shall override anything contained in this insurance inconsistent therewith

1 Cancellation

Cover hereunder in respect of the risks of war, etc may be cancelled by either the Underwriters or the Assured giving 7 days notice (such cancellation becoming effective on the expiry of 7 days from midnight of the day on which notice of cancellation is issued by or to the Underwriters). The Underwriters agree however to reinstate cover subject to agreement between the Underwriters and the Assured prior to the expiry of such notice of cancellation as to new rate of premium and/or conditions and/or warranties.

2 Automatic Termination of Cover

Whether or not such notice of cancellation has been given cover hereunder in respect of the risks of war, etc, shall TERMINATE AUTOMATICALLY

2.1   upon the outbreak of war (whether there be a declaration of war or not) between any of the following:

United Kingdom, United States of America, France, the Russian Federation, the People's Republic of China;

2.2   in respect of any vessel, in connection with which cover is granted hereunder, in the event of such vessel being requisitioned either for title or use.

3 Five Powers War and Nuclear Exclusions

This insurance excludes

3.1   loss damage liability or expense arising from

3.1.1   the outbreak of war (whether there be a declaration of war or not) between any of the following:

United Kingdom, United States of America, France, the Russian Federation, the People's Republic of China;

3.1.2   requisition either for title or use.

3.2   loss damage liability or expense directly or indirectly caused by or arising from

157

3.2.1	ionising radiations from or contamination by radioactivity from any nuclear fuel or from any nuclear waste or from the combustion of nuclear fuel
3.2.2	the radioactive, toxic, explosive or other hazardous or contaminating properties of any nuclear installation, reactor or other nuclear assembly or nuclear component thereof
3.2.3	any weapon of war employing atomic or nuclear fission and/or fusion or other like reaction or radioactive force or matter.

4 Law and Practice

This clause is subject to English law and practice.

Cover in respect of the risks of war, etc shall not become effective if, subsequent to acceptance by the Underwriters and prior to the intended time of attachment of risk, there has occurred any event which would have automatically terminated cover under the provisions of this clause.

Institute Standard Conditions for Cargo Contracts

1/4/82—(FOR USE ONLY WITH THE NEW MARINE POLICY FORM)

1   This contract is to insure the subject-matter specified for the transits and on the conditions named shipped by or for account of...

....

or the insurance of which is under their control as selling or purchasing agent unless insured elsewhere prior to inception of this contract or to insurable interest being acquired.

This contract does not cover the interest of any other person, but this shall not prevent a transfer of the insurance by the Assured or Assignee.

2   It is a condition of this contract that the Assured are bound to declare hereunder every consignment without exception, Underwriters being bound to accept up to but not exceeding the amount specified in clause 3 below.

3   3.1   This contract is for an open amount but the amount declarable may not exceed the sum of...............in respect of any one vessel, aircraft or conveyance.

    3.2   Should this contract be expressed in the form of a floating policy the total amount declarable hereunder may not exceed ....subject always to the provisions of clause 3.1 above.

4   Notwithstanding anything to the contrary contained in this contract Underwriters' liability in respect of any one accident or series of accidents arising from the same event in any one location shall not exceed the sum of ....

....

5   In the event of loss accident or arrival before declaration of value it is agreed that the basis of valuation shall be the prime cost of the goods or merchandise plus the expenses of and incidental to shipping, the freight for which the Assured are liable, the charges of insurance and .....%.

6   This contract is subject to the Institute Classification Clause.

7   Should the risks of war, strikes, riots and civil commotions be included in the cover granted by this contract the relevant Institute War Clauses and Institute Strikes Clauses shall apply.

8   The Institute Clauses referred to herein are those current at the inception of this contract but should such clauses be revised during the period of this contract, and provided that Underwriters shall have given at least 30 days notice thereof, then the revised Institute Clauses shall apply to risks attaching subsequent to the date of expiry of the said notice.

9   This contract may be cancelled by either Underwriters or the Assured giving ....
days notice in writing to take effect from .... but risks covered by Institute War
Clauses may be cancelled at seven days notice and risks covered by the Institute Strikes
Clauses may be cancelled at seven days notice, or at forty-eight hours notice in respect
of shipments to or from the United States of America. Notice shall commence from
midnight of the day when it is issued but cancellation shall not apply to any risks which
have attached in accordance with the cover granted hereunder before the cancellation
becomes effective.

NOTE

**—The Assured are required to give the earliest provisional notice of intended
shipments advising in each case the name of the vessel and approximate value of the
shipments.**

Institute Strikes Clauses Builders' Risks

1/6/88—(FOR USE ONLY WITH THE NEW MARINE POLICY FORM)

(This insurance is subject to English law and practice)

1   Perils

Subject always to the exclusions hereinafter referred to, this insurance covers loss of or damage to the subject-matter insured caused by

1.1   strikers, locked-out workmen, or persons taking part in labour disturbances, riots or civil commotions

1.2   any terrorist or any person acting maliciously or from a political motive.

2   Protection and indemnity

This insurance also covers, subject to the limitation of liability provided for in Clauses 19.5 and 19.6 of the Institute Clauses for Builders' Risks 1/6/88, the liability under Clause 19 of the Institute Clauses for Builders' Risks 1/6/88 which is excluded by Clause 22.1.

3   Incorporation

The Institute Clauses for Builders' Risks 1/6/88 are deemed to be incorporated in this insurance, in so far as they do not conflict with the provisions of these clauses, but this insurance excludes any claim which would be recoverable under the said clauses.

4   Returns of premium

No return of premium hereunder unless specially agreed.

5   Exclusions

This insurance excludes

5.1   any loss of or damage to the subject-matter insured covered by the Institute War Clauses Builders' Risks 1/6/88

5.2   any claim for expenses arising from delay except such expenses as would be recoverable in principle in English law and practice under the York-Antwerp Rules 1974

161

5.3 piracy (but this exclusion shall not affect cover under Clause 1.1)

5.4 any claim based upon loss of or frustration of any voyage or contract for sale or other adventure.

The following clauses shall be paramount and shall override anything contained in this insurance inconsistent therewith.

6 War exclusion

In no case shall this insurance cover loss damage or expense caused by war civil war revolution rebellion insurrection, or civil strife arising therefrom, or any hostile act by or against a belligerent power.

7 Nuclear exclusion

In no case shall this insurance cover loss damage liability or expense directly or indirectly caused by or contributed to by or arising from

7.1 ionising radiations from or contamination by radioactivity from any nuclear fuel or from any nuclear waste from the combustion of nuclear fuel

7.2 the radioactive, toxic, explosive or other hazardous properties of any explosive nuclear assembly or nuclear component thereof

7.3 any weapon of war employing atomic or nuclear fission and/or fusion or other like reaction or radioactive force or matter.

Institute Strikes Clauses (Cargo)

1/1/82—(FOR USE ONLY WITH THE NEW MARINE POLICY FORM)

Risks Covered

Risks Clause

1 This insurance covers, except as provided in Clauses 3 and 4 below, loss of or damage to the subject-matter insured caused by
    1.1   strikers, locked-out workmen, or persons taking part in labour disturbances, riots or civil commotions
    1.2   any terrorist or any person acting from a political motive.

General Average Clause

2 This insurance covers general average and salvage charges, adjusted or determined according to the contract of affreightment and/or the governing law and practice, incurred to avoid or in connection with the avoidance of loss from a risk covered under these clauses.

Exclusions

General Exclusions Clause

3 In no case shall this insurance cover
    3.1   loss damage or expense attributable to wilful misconduct of the Assured
    3.2   ordinary leakage, ordinary loss in weight or volume, or ordinary wear and tear of the subject-matter insured
    3.3   loss damage or expense caused by insufficiency or unsuitability of packing or preparation of the subject-matter insured (for the purpose of this Clause 3.3 "packing" shall be deemed to include stowage in a container or liftvan but only when such stowage is carried out prior to attachment of this insurance or by the Assured or their servants)
    3.4   loss damage or expense caused by inherent vice or nature of the subject-matter insured
    3.5   loss damage or expense proximately caused by delay, even though the delay be caused by a risk insured against (except expenses payable under Clause 2 above)

163

3.6   loss damage or expense arising from insolvency or financial default of the owners managers charterers or operators of the vessel

3.7   loss damage or expense arising from the absence shortage or withholding of labour of any description whatsoever resulting from any strike, lockout, labour disturbance, riot or civil commotion

3.8   any claim based upon loss of or frustration of the voyage or adventure

3.9   loss damage or expense arising from the use of any weapon of war employing atomic or nuclear fission and/or fusion or other like reaction or radioactive force or matter

3.10   loss damage or expense caused by war civil war revolution rebellion insurrection, or civil strife arising therefrom, or any hostile act by or against a belligerent power.

Unseaworthiness and Unfitness Exclusion Clause

4   4.1   In no case shall this insurance cover loss damage or expense arising from unseaworthiness of vessel or craft,
unfitness of vessel craft conveyance container or liftvan for the safe carriage of the subject-matter insured,
where the Assured or their servants are privy to such unseaworthiness or unfitness, at the time the subject-matter insured is loaded therein.

     4.2   The Underwriters waive any breach of the implied warranties of seaworthiness of the ship and fitness of the ship to carry the subject-matter insured to destination, unless the Assured or their servants are privy to such unseaworthiness or unfitness.

Duration

Transit Clause

5   5.1   This insurance attaches from the time the goods leave the warehouse or place of storage at the place named herein for the commencement of the transit, continues during the ordinary course of transit and terminates either

     5.1.1   on delivery to the Consignees' or other final warehouse or place of storage at the destination named herein,

     5.1.2   on delivery to any other warehouse or place of storage, whether prior to or at the destination named herein, which the Assured elect to use either

     5.1.2.1   for storage other than in the ordinary course of transit or

     5.1.2.2   for allocation or distribution,
or

     5.1.3   on the expiry of 60 days after completion of discharge overside of the goods hereby insured from the overseas vessel at the final port of discharge, whichever shall first occur.

     5.2   If, after discharge overside from the oversea vessel at the final port of discharge, but prior to termination of this insurance, the goods are to be forwarded to a destination other than that to which they are insured hereunder, this insurance, whilst remaining subject to termination as provided for above, shall not extend beyond the commencement of transit to such other destination.

   5.3   This insurance shall remain in force (subject to termination as provided for above and to the provisions of Clause 6 below) during delay beyond the control of the Assured, any deviation, forced discharge, reshipment or transhipment and during any variation of the adventure arising from the exercise of a liberty granted to shipowners or charterers under the contract of affreightment.

Termination of Contract of Carriage Clause

6   If owing to circumstances beyond the control of the Assured either the contract of carriage is terminated at a port or place other than the destination named therein or the transit is otherwise terminated before delivery of the goods as provided for in Clause 5 above, then this insurance shall also terminate *unless prompt notice is given to the Underwriters and continuation of cover is requested when the insurance shall remain in force, subject to an additional premium if required by the Underwriters, either*

   6.1   until the goods are sold and delivered at such port or place, or, unless otherwise specially agreed, until the expiry of 60 days after arrival of the goods hereby insured at such port or place, whichever shall first occur, or

   6.2   if the goods are forwarded within the said period of 60 days (or any agreed extension thereof) to the destination named herein or to any other destination, until terminated in accordance with the provisions of Clause 5 above.

Change of Voyage Clause

7   Where, after attachment of this insurance, the destination is changed by the Assured, *held covered at a premium and on conditions to be arranged subject to prompt notice being given to the Underwriters.*

Insurable Interest Clause

8 **8.1**   In order to recover under this insurance the Assured must have an insurable interest in the subject-matter insured at the time of the loss.

   8.2   Subject to 8.1 above, the Assured shall be entitled to recover for insured loss occurring during the period covered by this insurance, notwithstanding that the loss occurred before the contract of insurance was concluded, unless the Assured were aware of the loss and the Underwriters were not.

Increased Value Clause

9 **9.1**   If any Increased Value insurance is effected by the Assured on the cargo insured herein the agreed value of the cargo shall be deemed to be increased to the total amount insured under this insurance and all Increased Value insurances covering the loss, and liability under this insurance shall be in such proportion as the sum insured herein bears to such total amount insured.

                In the event of claim the Assured shall provide the Underwriters with evidence of the amounts insured under all other insurances.

   9.2   **Where this insurance is on Increased Value the following clause shall apply:**

The agreed value of the cargo shall be deemed to be equal to the total amount insured under the primary insurance and all Increased Value insurances covering the loss and effected on the cargo by the Assured, and liability under this insurance shall be in such proportion as the sum insured herein bears to such total amount insured.

In the event of claim the Assured shall provide the Underwriters with evidence of the amounts insured under all other insurances.

Benefit of Insurance

Not to Inure Clause

10 This insurance shall not inure to the benefit of the carrier or other bailee.

Minimising Losses

Duty of Assured Clause

11 It is the duty of the Assured and their servants and agents in respect of loss recoverable hereunder

    11.1   to take such measures as may be reasonable for the purpose of averting or minimising such loss,

          and

    11.2   to ensure that all rights against carriers, bailees or other third parties are properly preserved and exercised

and the Underwriters will, in addition to any loss recoverable hereunder, reimburse the Assured for any charges properly and reasonably incurred in pursuance of these duties.

Waiver Clause

12 Measures taken by the Assured or the Underwriters with the object of saving, protecting or recovering the subject-matter insured shall not be considered as a waiver or acceptance of abandonment or otherwise prejudice the rights of either party.

Avoidance of Delay

Reasonable Despatch Clause

13 It is a condition of this insurance that the Assured shall act with reasonable despatch in all circumstances within their control.

Law and Practice

English Law and Practice Clause

14 This insurance is subject to English law and practice.

NOTE:

—It is necessary for the Assured when they become aware of an event which is "held covered" under this insurance to give prompt notice to the Underwriters and the right to such cover is dependent upon compliance with this obligation.

Institute Time Clauses—Hulls: Excess Liabilities

1/11/95—(FOR USE ONLY WITH THE CURRENT MAR POLICY FORM)

This insurance is subject to English law and practice

1   1.1   This insurance covers only:

1.1.1   **General Average, Salvage and Salvage Charges** recoverable under the insurances on hull and machinery but not recoverable in full by reason of the difference between the insured value of the Vessel as stated therein (or any reduced value arising from the deduction therefrom in process of adjustment of any claim which law or practice or the terms of the insurances covering hull and machinery may have required) and the value of the Vessel adopted for the purpose of contribution to general average, salvage or salvage charges, the liability under this insurance being for such proportion of the amount not recoverable as the amount insured hereunder bears to the said difference or to the total sum insured against excess liabilities if it exceed such difference.

1.1.2   **Sue and Labour Charges** recoverable under the insurances on hull and machinery but not recoverable in full by reason of the difference between the insured value of the Vessel as stated therein and the value of the Vessel adopted for the purpose of ascertaining the amount recoverable under the insurances on hull and machinery, the liability under this insurance being for such proportion of the amount not recoverable as the amount insured hereunder bears to the said difference or to the total sum insured against excess liabilities if it exceed such difference.

1.1.3   **Collision Liability (three-fourths)** recoverable under the Institute 3/4ths Collision Liability and Sistership Clauses in the insurances on hull and machinery but not recoverable in full by reason of such three-fourths liability exceeding three-fourths of the insured value of the Vessel as stated therein, in which case the amount recoverable under this insurance shall be such proportion of the difference so arising as the amount insured hereunder bears to the total sum insured against excess liabilities.

1.2   The Underwriter's liability under 1.1.1, 1.1.2 and 1.1.3 separately, in respect of any one claim, shall not exceed the amount insured hereunder.

167

2 Returns

To return pro rata monthly net for each uncommenced month if this insurance be cancelled by agreement.

The following clauses shall be paramount and shall override anything contained in this insurance inconsistent therewith.

3 War Exclusion

In no case shall this insurance cover loss damage liability or expense caused by

3.1 war civil war revolution rebellion insurrection, or civil strife arising therefrom, or any hostile act by or against a belligerent power

3.2 capture seizure arrest restraint or detainment (barratry and piracy excepted), and the consequences thereof or any attempt thereat

3.3 derelict mines torpedoes bombs or other derelict weapons of war.

4 Strikes Exclusion

In no case shall this insurance cover loss damage liability or expense caused by

4.1 strikers, locked-out workmen, or persons taking part in labour disturbances, riots or civil commotions

4.2 any terrorist or any person acting from a political motive.

5 Malicious Acts Exclusion

In no case shall this insurance cover loss damage liability or expense arising from

5.1 the detonation of an explosive

5.2 any weapon of war

and caused by any person acting maliciously or from a political motive.

6 Radioactive Contamination Exclusion Clause

In no case shall this insurance cover loss damage liability or expense directly or indirectly caused by or contributed to by or arising from

6.1 ionising radiations from or contamination by radioactivity from any nuclear fuel or from any nuclear waste or from the combustion of nuclear fuel

6.2 the radioactive, toxic, explosive or other hazardous or contaminating properties of any nuclear installation, reactor or other nuclear assembly or nuclear component thereof

6.3 any weapon of war employing atomic or nuclear fission and/or fusion or other like reaction or radioactive force of matter.

Institute Time Clauses Freight

1/11/95—(FOR USE ONLY WITH THE CURRENT MAR POLICY FORM)

This insurance is subject to English law and practice

1 Navigation

1.1   The Vessel has leave to dock and undock, to go into graving dock, to sail or navigate with or without pilots, to go on trial trips and to assist and tow vessels or craft in distress, but it is warranted that the Vessel shall not be towed, except as is customary or to the first safe port or place when in need of assistance, or undertake towage or salvage services under a contract previously arranged by the Assured and/or Owners and/or Managers and/or Charterers. This Clause 1 shall not exclude customary towage in connection with loading and discharging.

1.2   This insurance shall not be prejudiced by reason of the Assured entering into any contract with pilots or for customary towage which limits or exempts the liability of the pilots and/or tugs and/or towboats and/or their owners when the Assured or their agents accept or are compelled to accept such contracts in accordance with established local law or practice.

1.3   The practice of engaging helicopters for the transportation of personnel, supplies and equipment to and/or from the Vessel shall not prejudice this insurance.

2 Craft Risk

Including risk of craft and/or lighter to and from the Vessel.

3 Continuation

Should the Vessel at the expiration of this insurance be at sea and in distress or missing, the subject-matter insured shall, provided notice be given to the Underwriters prior to the expiration of this insurance, be held covered until arrival of the Vessel at the next port in good safety, or if in port and in distress until the Vessel is made safe, at a pro rata monthly premium.

169

4 Breach of Warranty

Held covered in case of any breach of warranty as to cargo, trade, locality, towage, salvage services or date of sailing, provided notice be given to the Underwriters immediately after receipt of advices and any amended terms of cover and any additional premium required by them be agreed.

5 Classification

5.1	It is the duty of the Assured, Owners and Managers at the inception of and throughout the period of this insurance to ensure that
5.1.1	the Vessel is classed with a Classification Society agreed by the Underwriters and that her class within that Society is maintained
5.1.2	any recommendations requirements or restrictions imposed by the Vessel's Classification Society which relate to the Vessel's seaworthiness or to her maintenance in a seaworthy condition are complied with by the date required by that Society.
5.2	In the event of any breach of the duties set out in Clause 5.1 above, unless the Underwriters agree to the contrary in writing, they will be discharged from liability under this insurance as from the date of the breach, provided that if the Vessel is at sea at such date the Underwriters' discharge from liability is deferred until arrival at her next port.
5.3	Any incident condition or damage in respect of which the Vessel's Classification Society might make recommendations as to repairs or other action to be taken by the Assured, Owners or Managers must be promptly reported to the Classification Society.
5.4	Should the Underwriters wish to approach the Classification Society directly for information and/or documents, the Assured will provide the necessary authorization.

6 Termination

The Clause 6 shall prevail notwithstanding any provision whether written typed or printed in this insurance inconsistent therewith.

Unless the Underwriters agree to the contrary in writing, this insurance shall terminate automatically at the time of

6.1	change of the Classification Society of the Vessel, or change, suspension, discontinuance, withdrawal or expiry of her Class therein, or any of the Classification Society's periodic surveys becoming overdue unless an extension of time for such survey be agreed by the Classification Society, provided that if the Vessel is at sea such automatic termination shall be deferred until arrival at her next port. However where such change, suspension, discontinuance or withdrawal of her Class or where a periodic survey becoming overdue has resulted from loss or damage covered by Clause 7 of this insurance or which would be covered by an insurance of the Vessel subject to current Institute Time Clauses Hulls or Institute War and Strikes Clauses Hulls-Time such automatic termination shall only operate should the Vessel sail from her next port without the prior approval of the Classification Society or in the case of a periodic survey becoming overdue without the Classification Society having agreed an extension of time for such survey,
6.2	any change, voluntary or otherwise, in the ownership or flag, transfer to new management, or charter on a bareboat basis, or requisition for title or use of

the Vessel, provided that, if the Vessel has cargo on board and has already sailed from her loading port or is at sea in ballast, such automatic termination shall if required be deferred, whilst the Vessel continues her planned voyage, until arrival at final port of discharge if with cargo or at port of destination if in ballast. However, in the event of requisition for title or use without the prior execution of a written agreement by the Assured, such automatic termination shall occur fifteen days after such requisition whether the Vessel is at sea or in port.

A pro rata daily net return of premium shall be made provided that a total loss of the Vessel, whether by insured perils or otherwise, has not occurred during the period covered by this insurance or any extension thereof.

7 Perils

7.1	This insurance covers loss of the subject-matter insured caused by
7.1.1	perils of the seas rivers lakes or other navigable waters
7.1.2	fire, explosion
7.1.3	violent theft by persons from outside the Vessel
7.1.4	jettison
7.1.5	piracy
7.1.6	contact with land conveyance, dock or harbour equipment or installation
7.1.7	earthquake volcanic eruption or lightning
7.1.8	accidents in loading, discharging or shifting cargo or fuel.
7.2	This insurance covers loss of the subject-matter insured caused by
7.2.1	bursting of boilers breakage of shafts or any latent defect in the machinery or hull
7.2.2	negligence of Master Officers Crew or Pilots
7.2.3	negligence of repairers or charterers provided such repairers or charterers are not an Assured hereunder
7.2.4	barratry of Master Officers or Crew
7.2.5	contact with aircraft, helicopters or similar objects or objects falling therefrom
	provided that such loss has not resulted from want of due diligence by the Assured, Owners, Managers or Superintendents or any of their onshore management.
7.3	Masters Officers Crew or Pilots not to be considered Owners within the meaning of this Clause 7 should they hold shares in the Vessel.

8 Pollution Hazard

This insurance covers loss of the subject matter insured caused by any governmental authority acting under the powers vested in it to prevent or mitigate a pollution hazard or damage to the environment, or threat thereof, resulting directly from a peril covered by this insurance, provided that such act of governmental authority has not resulted from want of due diligence by the Assured, Owners or Managers to prevent or mitigate such hazard or damage, or threat thereof. Masters Officers Crew or Pilots not to be considered Owners within the meaning of this Clause 8 should they hold shares in the Vessel.

9 Freight Collision

9.1   It is further agreed that if the Vessel shall come into collision with any other vessel and the Assured shall in consequence thereof become liable to pay and shall pay by way of damages to any other person or persons any sum or sums in respect of the amount of freight taken into account in calculating the measure of the liability of the Assured for

9.1.1   loss of or damage to any other vessel or property on any other vessel

9.1.2   delay to or loss of use of any such other vessel or property thereon

9.1.3   general average of, salvage of, or salvage under contract of, any such other vessel or property thereon,

the Underwriters will pay the Assured such proportion of three-fourths of such sum or sums so paid applying to freight as their respective subscriptions hereto bear to the total amount insured on freight, or to the gross freight earned on the voyage during which the collision occurred if this be greater.

9.2   Provided always that:

9.2.1   liability of the Underwriters in respect of any one such collision shall not exceed their proportionate part of three-fourths of the total amount insured hereon on freight, and in cases in which, with the prior consent in writing of the Underwriters, the liability of the vessel has been contested or proceedings have been taken to limit liability, they will also pay a like proportion of three-fourths of the costs, appertaining proportionately to the freight portion of damages, which the Assured shall thereby incur or be compelled to pay;

9.2.2   no claim shall attach to this insurance:

9.2.2.1   which attaches to any other insurances covering collision liabilities

9.2.2.2   which is, or would be, recoverable in the terms of the Institute 3/4ths Collision Liability Clause if the Vessel were insured in the terms of such Institute 3/4ths Collision Liability Clause for a value not less than the equivalent in pounds sterling, at the time of commencement of this insurance, of the Vessel's limit of liability calculated in accordance with Article 6.1(b) of the 1976 Limitation Convention,

9.2.3   this Clause 9 shall in no case extend or be deemed to extend to any sum which the Assured may become liable to pay or shall pay for or in respect of:

9.2.3.1   removal or disposal, under statutory powers or otherwise, of obstructions, wrecks, cargoes or any other thing whatsoever

9.2.3.2   any real or personal property or thing whatsoever except other vessels or property on other vessels

9.2.3.3   pollution or contamination, or threat thereof, of any real or personal property or thing whatsoever (except other vessels with which the insured Vessel is in collision or property on such other vessels) or damage to the environment or threat thereof, save that this exclusion shall not extend to any sum which the insured shall pay for or in respect of salvage remuneration in which the skill and efforts of the salvors in preventing or minimising damage to the environment as is referred to in Article 13 paragraph 1(b) of the

	International Convention on Salvage, 1989 have been taken into account
9.2.3.4	the cargo or other property in or the engagements of the Vessel
9.2.3.5	loss of life, personal injury or illness.

10 Sistership

Should the Vessel named herein come into collision with or receive salvage services from another vessel belonging wholly or in part to the same Owners, or under the same management, the Assured shall have the same rights under this insurance as they would have were the other vessel entirely the property of Owners not interested in the Vessel named herein; but in such cases the liability for the collision or the amount payable for the services rendered shall be referred to a sole arbitrator to be agreed upon between the Underwriters and the Assured.

11 General Average and Salvage

11.1	This insurance covers the proportion of general average, salvage and/or salvage charges attaching to freight at risk of the Assured, reduced in respect of any under-insurance.
11.2	Adjustment to be according to the law and practice obtaining at the place where the adventure ends, as if the contract of affreightment contained no special terms upon the subject; but where the contract of affreightment so provides the adjustment shall be according to the York-Antwerp Rules.
11.3	No claim under this Clause 11 shall in any case be allowed where the loss was not incurred to avoid or in connection with the avoidance of a peril insured against.
11.4	No claim under this Clause 11 shall in any case be allowed for or in respect of
11.4.1	special compensation payable to a salvor under Article 14 of the International Convention on Salvage, 1989 or under any other provision in any statute, rule, law or contract which is similar in substance
11.4.2	expenses or liabilities incurred in respect of damage to the environment, or the threat of such damage, or as a consequence of the escape or release of pollutant substances from the Vessel, or the threat of such escape or release.
11.5	Clause 11.4 shall not however exclude any sum which the Assured shall pay to salvors for or in respect of salvage remuneration in which the skill and efforts of the salvors in preventing or minimising damage to the environment as is referred to in Article 13 paragraph 1(b) of the International Convention on Salvage, 1989 have been taken into account.

12 Franchise

This insurance does not cover partial loss, other than general average loss, under 3% unless caused by fire, sinking, stranding or collision with another vessel. Each craft and/or lighter to be deemed a separate insurance if required by the Assured.

13 Assignment

No assignment of or interest in this insurance or in any moneys which may be or become payable thereunder is to be binding on or recognised by the Underwriters unless a dated notice of such assignment or interest signed by the Assured, and by the assignor in the case of subsequent assignment, is endorsed on the Policy and the Policy with such endorsement is produced before payment of any claim or return of premium thereunder.

14 Measure of Indemnity

14.1 The amount recoverable under this insurance for any claim for loss of freight shall not exceed the gross freight actually lost.

14.2 Where insurances on freight other than this insurance are current at the time of the loss, all such insurances shall be taken into consideration in calculating the liability under this insurance and the amount recoverable hereunder shall not exceed the rateable proportion of the gross freight lost, notwithstanding any valuation in this or any other insurance.

14.3 In calculating the liability under Clause 11 all insurances on freight shall likewise be taken into consideration.

14.4 Nothing in this Clause 14 shall apply to any claim arising under Clause 16.

15 Loss of Time

This insurance does not cover any claims consequent on loss of time whether arising from a peril of the sea or otherwise.

16 Total Loss

16.1 In the event of the total loss (actual or constructive) of the Vessel named herein the amount insured shall be paid in full, whether the Vessel be fully or partly loaded or in ballast, chartered or unchartered.

16.2 In ascertaining whether the Vessel is a constructive total loss, the insured value in the insurances on hull and machinery shall be taken as the repaired value and nothing in respect of the damaged or break-up value of the Vessel or wreck shall be taken into account.

16.3 Should the Vessel be a constructive total loss but the claim on the insurances on hull and machinery be settled as a claim for partial loss, no payment shall be due under this Clause 16.

17 Returns for Lay-up and Cancellation

17.1 To return as follows:

17.1.1 pro rata monthly net for each uncommenced month if this insurance be cancelled by agreement,

17.1.2 for each period of 30 consecutive days the Vessel may be laid up in a port or in a lay-up area provided such port or lay-up area is approved by the Underwriters

(a) .... per cent net not under repair

(b) .... per cent net under repair.

17.1.3 The Vessel shall not be considered to be under repair when work is undertaken in respect of ordinary wear and tear of the Vessel and/or following recommendations in the Vessel's Classification Society survey, but any repairs following loss of or damage to the Vessel or involving structural alterations, whether covered by this insurance or otherwise shall be considered as under repair.

17.1.4   If the Vessel is under repair during part only of a period for which a return is claimable, the return shall be calculated pro rata to the number of days under 17.1.2(a) and (b) respectively.

17.2   PROVIDED ALWAYS THAT

17.2.1   a total loss of the Vessel, whether by insured perils or otherwise, has not occurred during the period covered by this insurance or any extension therein

17.2.2   in no case shall a return be allowed when the vessel is lying in exposed or unprotected waters, or in a port or lay-up area not approved by the Underwriters

17.2.3   loading or discharging operations or the presence of cargo on board shall not debar returns but no return shall be allowed for any period during which the Vessel is being used for the storage of cargo or for lightering purposes

17.2.4   in the event of any amendment of the annual rate, the above rates of return shall be adjusted accordingly

17.2.5   in the event of any return recoverable under this Clause 17 being based on 30 consecutive days which fall on successive insurances effected for the same Assured, this insurance shall only be liable for an amount calculated at pro rata of the period rates 17.1.2(a) and/or (b) above for the number of days which come within the period of this insurance and to which a return is actually applicable. Such overlapping period shall run, at the option of the Assured, either from the first day on which the Vessel is laid up or the first day of a period of 30 consecutive days as provided under 17.1.2(a) or (b) above.

Institute Time Clauses Hulls

1/11/95—(FOR USE ONLY WITH THE CURRENT MAR POLICY FORM)

This insurance is subject to English law and practice

1 Navigation

1.1 The Vessel is covered subject to the provisions of this insurance at all times and has leave to sail or navigate with or without pilots, to go on trial trips and to assist and tow vessels or craft in distress, but it is warranted that the Vessel shall not be towed, except as is customary or to the first safe port or place when in need of assistance, or undertake towage or salvage services under a contract previously arranged by the Assured and/or Owners and/or Manager and/or Charterers. This Clause 1.1 shall not exclude customary towage in connection with loading and discharging.

1.2 This insurance shall not be prejudiced by reason of the Assured entering into any contract with pilots or for customary towage which limits or exempts the liability of the pilots and/or tugs and/or towboats and/or their owners when the Assured or their agents accept or are compelled to accept such contracts in accordance with established local law or practice.

1.3 The practice of engaging helicopters for the transportation of personnel, supplies and equipment to and/or from the Vessel shall not prejudice this insurance.

1.4 In the event of the Vessel being employed in trading operations which entail cargo loading or discharging at sea from or into another vessel (not being a harbour or inshore craft) no claim shall be recoverable under this insurance for loss of or damage to the Vessel or liability to any other vessel arising from such loading or discharging operations, including whilst approaching, lying alongside and leaving, unless previous notice that the Vessel is to be employed in such operations has been given to the Underwriters and any amended terms of cover and any additional premium required by them have been agreed.

1.5 In the event of the Vessel sailing (with or without cargo) with an intention of being (a) broken up, or (b) sold for breaking up, any claim for loss of or damage to the Vessel occurring subsequent to such sailing shall be limited to the market value of the Vessel as scrap at the time when the loss or damage is sustained, unless previous notice has been given to the Underwriters and

176

any amendments to the terms of cover, insured value and premium required by them having been agreed. Nothing in this Clause 1.5 shall affect claims under Clauses 8 and/or 10.

2 Continuation

Should the Vessel at the expiration of this insurance be at sea and in distress or missing, she shall, provided notice be given to the Underwriters prior to the expiration of this insurance, be held covered until arrival at the next port in good safety, or if in port and in distress until the Vessel is made safe, at a pro rata monthly premium.

3 Breach of warranty

Held covered in case of any breach of warranty as to cargo, trade, locality, towage, salvage services or date of sailing, provided notice be given to the Underwriters immediately after receipt of advices and any amended terms of cover and any additional premium required by them be agreed.

4 Classification

4.1	It is the duty of the Assured, Owners and Managers at the inception of and throughout the period of this insurance to ensure that
4.1.1	the Vessel is classed with a Classification Society agreed by the Underwriters and that her class within that Society is maintained,
4.1.2	any recommendations requirements or restrictions imposed by the Vessel's Classification Society which relate to the Vessel's seaworthiness or to her maintenance in a seaworthy condition are complied with by the dates required by that Society.
4.2	In the event of any breach of the duties set out in Clause 4.1 above, unless the Underwriters agree to the contrary in writing, they will be discharged from liability under this insurance as from the date of the breach provided that if the Vessel is at sea at such date the Underwriters' discharge from liability is deferred until arrival at her next port.
4.3	Any incident condition or damage in respect of which the Vessel's Classification Society might make recommendations as to repairs or other action to be taken by the Assured, Owners or Managers must be promptly reported to the Classification Society.
4.4	Should the Underwriters wish to approach the Classification Society directly for information and/or documents, the Assured will provide the necessary authorization.

5 Termination

This Clause 5 shall prevail notwithstanding any provision whether written typed or printed in this insurance inconsistent therewith.
Unless the Underwriters agree to the contrary in writing, this insurance shall terminate automatically at the time of

5.1	change of the Classification Society of the Vessel, or change, suspension, discontinuance, withdrawal or expiry of her Class therein, or any of the Classification Society's periodic surveys becoming overdue unless an extension of time for such survey be agreed by the Classification Society, provided

that if the Vessel is at sea such automatic termination shall be deferred until arrival at her next port. However where such change, suspension, discontinuance or withdrawal of her Class or where a periodic survey becoming overdue has resulted from loss or damage covered by Clause 6 of this insurance or which would be covered by an insurance of the Vessel subject to current Institute War and Strikes Clauses Hulls—Time such automatic termination shall only operate should the Vessel sail from her next port without the prior approval of the Classification Society or in the case of a periodic survey becoming overdue without the Classification Society having agreed an extension of time for such survey,

5.2   any change, voluntary or otherwise, in the ownership or flag, transfer to new management, or charter on a bareboat basis, or requisition for title or use of the Vessel, provided that, if the Vessel has cargo on board and has already sailed from her loading port or is at sea in ballast, such automatic termination shall if required be deferred, whilst the Vessel continues her planned voyage, until arrival at final port of discharge if with cargo or at port of destination if in ballast. However, in the event of requisition for title or use without the prior execution of a written agreement by the Assured, such automatic termination shall occur fifteen days after such requisition whether the Vessel is at sea or in port.

A pro rata daily net return of premium shall be made provided that a total loss of the Vessel, whether by insured perils or otherwise, has not occurred during the period covered by this insurance or any extension thereof.

6   Perils

6.1   This insurance covers loss of or damage to the subject-matter insured caused by

6.1.1   perils of the seas rivers lakes or other navigable waters

6.1.2   fire, explosion

6.1.3   violent theft by persons from outside the Vessel

6.1.4   jettison

6.1.5   piracy

6.1.6   contact with land conveyance, dock or harbour equipment or installation

6.1.7   earthquake volcanic eruption or lightning

6.1.8   accidents in loading discharging or shifting cargo or fuel.

6.2   This insurance covers loss of or damage to the subject-matter insured caused by

6.2.1   bursting of boilers breakage of shafts or any latent defect in the machinery or hull

6.2.2   negligence of Master Officers Crew or Pilots

6.2.3   negligence of repairers or charterers provided such repairers or charterers are not an Assured hereunder

6.2.4   barratry of Master Officers or Crew

6.2.5   contact with aircraft, helicopters or similar objects, or objects falling therefrom

provided that such loss or damage has not resulted from want of due diligence by the Assured, Owners, Managers or Superintendents or any of their onshore management.

6.3   Masters Officers Crew or Pilots not to be considered Owners within the meaning of this Clause 6 should they hold shares in the Vessel.

7   Pollution hazard

This insurance covers loss of or damage to the Vessel caused by any governmental authority acting under the powers vested in it to prevent or mitigate a pollution hazard or damage to the environment, or threat thereof, resulting directly from damage to the Vessel for which the Underwriters are liable under this insurance, provided that such act of governmental authority has not resulted from want of due diligence by the Assured, Owners or Managers to prevent or mitigate such hazard or damage, or threat thereof. Master Officers Crew or Pilots not to be considered Owners within the meaning of this Clause 7 should they hold shares in the Vessel.

8   3/4ths collision liability

8.1   The Underwriters agree to indemnify the Assured for three-fourths of any sum or sums paid by the Assured to any other person or persons by reason of the Assured becoming legally liable by way of damages for

8.1.1   loss of or damage to any other vessel or property on any other vessel

8.1.2   delay to or loss of use of any such other vessel or property thereon

8.1.3   general average of, salvage of, or salvage under contract of, any such other vessel or property thereon,

where such payment by the Assured is in consequence of the Vessel hereby insured coming into collision with any other vessel.

8.2   The indemnity provided by this Clause 8 shall be in addition to the indemnity provided by the other terms and conditions of this insurance and shall be subject to the following provisions:

8.2.1   where the insured Vessel is in collision with another vessel and both vessels are to blame then, unless the liability of one or both vessels becomes limited by law, the indemnity under this Clause 8 shall be calculated on the principle of cross-liabilities as if the respective Owners had been compelled to pay to each other such proportion of each other's damages as may have been properly allowed in ascertaining the balance or sum payable by or to the Assured in consequence of the collision,

8.2.2   in no case shall the Underwriters' total liability under Clauses 8.1 and 8.2 exceed their proportionate part of three-fourths of the insured value of the Vessel hereby insured in respect of any one collision.

8.3   The Underwriters will also pay three-fourths of the legal costs incurred by the Assured or which the Assured may be compelled to pay in contesting liability or taking proceedings to limit liability, with the prior written consent of the Underwriters.

EXCLUSIONS

8.4   Provided always that this Clause 8 shall in no case extend to any sum which the Assured shall pay for or in respect of

8.4.1   removal or disposal of obstructions, wrecks, cargoes or any other thing whatsoever

8.4.2   any real or personal property or thing whatsoever except other vessels or property on other vessels

8.4.3   the cargo or other property on, or the engagements of, the insured Vessel

8.4.4   loss of life, personal injury or illness

8.4.5   pollution or contamination, or threat thereof, of any real or personal property or thing whatsoever (except other vessels with which the insured Vessel is in collision or property on such other vessels) or damage to the environment, or threat thereof, save that this exclusion shall not extend to any sum which the Assured shall pay for or in respect of salvage remuneration in which the skill and efforts of the salvors in preventing or minimising damage to the environment as is referred to in Article 13 paragraph 1(b) of the International Convention on Salvage, 1989 have been taken into account.

9   Sistership

Should the Vessel hereby insured come into collision with or receive salvage services from another vessel belonging wholly or in part to the same Owners or under the same management, the Assured shall have the same rights under this insurance as they would have were the other vessel entirely the property of Owners not interested in the Vessel hereby insured; but in such cases the liability for the collision or the amount payable for the services rendered shall be referred to a sole arbitrator to be agreed upon between the Underwriters and the Assured.

10   General average and salvage

10.1   This insurance covers the Vessel's proportion of salvage, salvage charges and/or general average, reduced in respect of any under-insurance, but in case of general average sacrifice of the Vessel the Assured may recover in respect of the whole loss without first enforcing their right of contribution from other parties.

10.2   Adjustment to be according to the law and practice obtaining at the place where the adventure ends, as if the contract of affreightment contained no special terms upon the subject; but where the contract of affreightment so provides the adjustment shall be according to the York-Antwerp Rules.

10.3   When the Vessel sails in ballast, not under charter, the provisions of the York-Antwerp Rules, 1994 (excluding Rules XI(d), XX and XXI) shall be applicable, and the voyage for this purpose shall be deemed to continue from the port or place of departure until the arrival of the Vessel at the first port or place thereafter other than a port or place of refuge or a port or place of call for bunkering only. If at any such intermediate port or place there is an abandonment of the adventure originally contemplated the voyage shall thereupon be deemed to be terminated.

10.4   No claim under this Clause 10 shall in any case be allowed where the loss was not incurred to avoid or in connection with the avoidance of a peril insured against.

10.5   No claim under this Clause 10 shall in any case be allowed for or in respect of

10.5.1   special compensation payable to a salvor under Article 14 of the International Convention on Salvage, 1989 or under any other provision in any statute, rule, or contract which is similar in substance

10.5.2   expenses or liabilities incurred in respect of damage to the environment, or the threat of such damage, or as a consequence of the escape or release of pollutant substances from the Vessel, or the threat of such escape or release.

10.6   Clause 10.5 shall not however exclude any sum which the Assured shall pay to salvors for or in respect of salvage remuneration in which the skill and efforts of the salvors in preventing or minimising damage to the environment as is referred to in Article 13 paragraph 1(b) of the International Convention on Salvage, 1989 have been taken into account.

11   Duty of assured (Sue and Labour)

11.1   In case of any loss or misfortune it is the duty of the Assured and their servants and agents to take such measures as may be reasonable for the purpose of averting or minimising a loss which would be recoverable under this insurance.

11.2   Subject to the provisions below and to Clause 12 the Underwriters will contribute to charges properly and reasonably incurred by the Assured their servants or agents for such measures. General average, salvage charges (except as provided for in Clause 11.5), special compensation and expenses as referred to in Clause 10.5 and collision defence or attack costs are not recoverable under this Clause 11.

11.3   Measures taken by the Assured or the Underwriters with the object of saving, protecting or recovering the subject-matter insured shall not be considered as a waiver or acceptance of abandonment or otherwise prejudice the rights of either party.

11.4   When expenses are incurred pursuant to this Clause 11 the liability under this insurance shall not exceed the proportion of such expenses that the amount insured hereunder bears to the value of the Vessel as stated herein, or to the sound value of the Vessel at the time of the occurrence giving rise to the expenditure if the sound value exceeds that value. Where the Underwriters have admitted a claim for total loss and property insured by this insurance is saved, the foregoing provisions shall not apply unless the expenses of suing and labouring exceed the value of such property saved and then shall apply only to the amount of the expenses which is in excess of such value.

11.5   When a claim for total loss of the Vessel is admitted under this insurance and expenses have been reasonably incurred in saving or attempting to save the Vessel and other property and there are no proceeds, or the expenses exceed the proceeds, then this insurance shall bear its pro rata share of such proportion of the expenses, or of the expenses in excess of the proceeds, as the case may be, as may reasonably be regarded as having been incurred in respect of the Vessel, excluding all special compensation and expenses as referred to in Clause 10.5; but if the Vessel be insured for less than its sound value at the time of the occurrence giving rise to the expenditure, the amount recoverable under this clause shall be reduced in proportion to the under-insurance.

11.6   The sum recoverable under this Clause 11 shall be in addition to the loss otherwise recoverable under this insurance but shall in no circumstances exceed the amount insured under this insurance in respect of the Vessel.

12 Deductible

12.1   No claim arising from a peril insured against shall be payable under this insurance unless the aggregate of all such claims arising out of each separate accident or occurrence (including claims under Clauses 8, 10 and 11) exceeds the deductible amount agreed in which case this sum shall be deducted. Nevertheless the expense of sighting the bottom after stranding, if reasonably incurred specially for that purpose, shall be paid even if no damage be found. This Clause 12.1 shall not apply to a claim for total or constructive total loss of the Vessel or, in the event of such a claim, to any associated claim under Clause 11 arising from the same accident or occurrence.

12.2   Claims for damage by heavy weather occurring during a single sea passage between two successive ports shall be treated as being due to one accident. In the case of such heavy weather extending over a period not wholly covered by this insurance the deductible to be applied to the claim recoverable hereunder shall be the proportion of the above deductible that the number of days of such heavy weather falling within the period of this insurance bears to the number of days of heavy weather during the single sea passage. The expression "heavy weather" in this Clause 12.2 shall be deemed to include contact with floating ice.

12.3   Excluding any interest comprised therein, recoveries against any claim which is subject to the above deductible shall be credited to the Underwriters in full to the extent of the sum by which the aggregate of the claim unreduced by any recoveries exceeds the above deductible.

12.4   Interest comprised in recoveries shall be apportioned between the Assured and the Underwriters, taking into account the sums paid by the Underwriters and the dates when such payments were made, notwithstanding that by the addition of interest the Underwriters may receive a larger sum than they have paid.

13 Notice of claim and tenders

13.1   In the event of accident whereby loss or damage may result in a claim under this insurance, notice must be given to the Underwriters promptly after the date on which the Assured, Owners or Managers become or should have become aware of the loss or damage and prior to survey so that a surveyor may be appointed if the Underwriters so desire.

If notice is not given to the Underwriters within twelve months of that date unless the Underwriters agree to the contrary in writing, the Underwriters will be automatically discharged from liability for any claim under this insurance in respect of or arising out of such accident or the loss or damage.

13.2   The Underwriters shall be entitled to decide the port to which the Vessel shall proceed for docking or repair (the actual additional expense of the voyage arising from compliance with the Underwriters' requirements being refunded to the Assured) and shall have a right of veto concerning a place of repair or a repairing firm.

13.3   The Underwriters may also take tenders or may require further tenders to be taken for the repair of the Vessel. Where such a tender has been taken and a tender is accepted with the approval of the Underwriters, an allowance shall be made at the rate of 30% per annum on the insured value for time lost between the despatch of the invitations to tender required by the Underwriters and the acceptance of a tender to the extent that such time is lost solely as the result of tenders having been taken and provided that the tender is accepted without delay after receipt of the Underwriters' approval.

Due credit shall be given against the allowance as above for any amounts recovered in respect of fuel and stores and wages and maintenance of the Master Officers and Crew or any member thereof, including amounts allowed in general average, and for any amounts recovered from third parties in respect of damages for detention and/or loss of profit and/or running expenses, for the period covered by the tender allowance or any part thereof.

Where a part of the cost of the repair of damage other than a fixed deductible is not recoverable from the Underwriters the allowance shall be reduced by a similar proportion.

13.4 In the event of failure by the Assured to comply with the conditions of Clauses 13.2 and/or 13.3 a deduction of 15% shall be made from the amount of the ascertained claim.

14 New for old

Claims payable without deduction new for old.

15 Bottom treatment

In no case shall a claim be allowed in respect of scraping gritblasting and/or other surface preparation or painting of the Vessel's bottom except that

15.1 gritblasting and/or other surface preparation of new bottom plates ashore and supplying and applying any "shop" primer thereto,

15.2 gritblasting and/or other surface preparation of:
the butts or area of plating immediately adjacent to any renewed or refitted plating damaged during the course of welding and/or repairs,
areas of plating damaged during the course of fairing, either in place or ashore,

15.3 supplying and applying the first coat of primer/anti-corrosive to those particular areas mentioned in 15.1 and 15.2 above,

shall be allowed as part of the reasonable cost of repairs in respect of bottom plating damaged by an insured peril.

16 Wages and maintenance

No claim shall be allowed, other than in general average, for wages and maintenance of the Master Officers and Crew or any member thereof, except when incurred solely for the necessary removal of the Vessel from one port to another for the repair of damage covered by the Underwriters, or for trial trips for such repairs, and then only for such wages and maintenance as are incurred whilst the Vessel is under way.

17 Agency commission

In no case shall any sum be allowed under this insurance either by way of remuneration of the Assured for time and trouble taken to obtain and supply information or documents or in respect of the commission or charges of any manager, agent, managing or agency company or the like, appointed by or on behalf of the Assured to perform such services.

18 Unrepaired damage

18.1 The measure of indemnity in respect of claims for unrepaired damage shall be the reasonable depreciation in the market value of the Vessel at the time this insurance terminates arising from such unrepaired damage, but not exceeding the reasonable cost of repairs.

18.2 In no case shall the Underwriters be liable for unrepaired damage in the event of a subsequent total loss (whether or not covered under this insurance) sustained during the period covered by this insurance or any extension thereof.

18.3 The Underwriters shall not be liable in respect of unrepaired damage for more than the insured value at the time this insurance terminates.

19 Constructive total loss

19.1 In ascertaining whether the Vessel is a constructive total loss, the insured value shall be taken as the repaired value and nothing in respect of the damaged or break-up value of the Vessel or wreck shall be taken into account.

19.2 No claim for constructive total loss based upon the cost of recovery and/or repair of the Vessel shall be recoverable hereunder unless such cost would exceed the insured value. In making this determination, only the cost relating to a single accident or sequence of damages arising from the same accident shall be taken into account.

20 Freight waiver

In the event of total or constructive total loss no claim to be made by the Underwriters for freight whether notice of abandonment has been given or not.

21 Assignment

No assignment of or interest in this insurance or in any moneys which may be or become payable thereunder is to be binding on or recognised by the Underwriters unless a dated notice of such assignment or interest signed by the Assured, and by the assignor in the case of subsequent assignment, is endorsed on the Policy and the Policy with such endorsement is produced before payment of any claim or return of premium thereunder.

22 Disbursements warranty

22.1 Additional insurances as follows are permitted:

22.1.1 *Disbursements, Managers' Commissions, Profits or Excess or Increased Value of Hull and Machinery.* A sum not exceeding 25% of the value stated herein.

22.1.2 *Freight, Chartered Freight or Anticipated Freight, insured for time.* A sum not exceeding 25% of the value as stated herein less any sum insured, however described, under 22.1.1.

22.1.3 *Freight or Hire, under contracts for voyage.* A sum not exceeding the gross freight or hire for the current cargo passage and next succeeding cargo passage (such insurance to include, if required, a preliminary and an intermediate ballast passage) plus the charges of insurance. In the case of a voyage charter where payment is made on a time basis, the sum permitted for insurance shall be calculated on the estimated duration of the voyage, subject to the limitation of two cargo passages as laid down herein. Any sum insured under 22.1.2 to be taken into account and only the excess thereof may be insured, which excess shall be reduced as the freight or hire is advanced or earned by the gross amount so advanced or earned.

22.1.4   *Anticipated Freight if the Vessel sails in ballast and not under Charter.* A sum not exceeding the anticipated gross freight on next cargo passage, such sum to be reasonably estimated on the basis of the current rate of freight at time of insurance plus the charges of insurance. Any sum insured under 22.1.2 to be taken into account and only the excess thereof may be insured.

22.1.5   *Time Charter Hire or Charter Hire for Series of Voyages.* A sum not exceed-ing 50% of the gross hire which is to be earned under the charter in a period not exceeding 18 months. Any sum insured under 22.1.2 to be taken into account and only the excess thereof may be insured, which excess shall be reduced as the hire is advanced or earned under the charter by 50% of the gross amount so advanced or earned but the sum insured need not be reduced while the total of the sums insured under 22.1.2 and 22.1.5 does not exceed 50% of the gross hire still to be earned under the charter. An insurance under this Section may begin on the signing of the charter.

22.1.6   *Premiums.* A sum not exceeding the actual premiums of all interests insured for a period not exceeding 12 months (excluding premiums insured under the foregoing sections but including, if required, the premium or estimated calls on any Club or War etc. Risk insurance) reducing pro rata monthly.

22.1.7   *Returns of Premium.* A sum not exceeding the actual returns which are allowable under any insurance but which would not be recoverable thereunder in the event of a total loss of the Vessel whether by insured perils or otherwise.

22.1.8   *Insurance irrespective of amount against:*
Any risks excluded by Clauses 24, 25, 26 and 27 below.

22.2   Warranted that no insurance on any interest enumerated in the foregoing 22.1.1 to 22.1.7 in excess of the amounts permitted therein and no other insurance which includes total loss of the Vessel P.P.I., F.I.A., or subject to any other like term, is or shall be effected to operate during the currency of this insurance by or for account of the Assured, Owners, Managers or Mortgagees. Provided always that a breach of this warranty shall not afford the Underwriters any defence to a claim by a Mortgagee who has accepted this insurance without knowledge of such breach.

23   Returns for lay-up and cancellation

23.1   To return as follows:

23.1.1   pro rata monthly net for each uncommenced month if this insurance be cancelled by agreement,

23.1.2   for each period of 30 consecutive days the Vessel may be laid up in a port or in a lay-up area provided such port or lay-up area is approved by the Underwriters

(a)   . . . . per cent net not under repair

(b)   . . . . per cent net under repair.

23.1.3   The Vessel shall not be considered to be under repair when work is undertaken in respect of ordinary wear and tear of the Vessel and/or following recommendations in the Vessel's Classification Society survey, but any repairs following loss of or damage to the Vessel or involving structural alterations, whether covered by this insurance or otherwise shall be considered as under repair.

23.1.4   If the Vessel is under repair during part only of a period for which a return is claimable, the return shall be calculated pro rata to the number of days under 23.1.2 (a) and (b) respectively.

23.2   PROVIDED ALWAYS THAT

23.2.1   a total loss of the Vessel, whether by insured perils or otherwise, has not occurred during the period covered by this insurance or any extension thereof

23.2.2   in no case shall a return be allowed when the Vessel is lying in exposed or unprotected waters, or in a port or lay-up area not approved by the Underwriters

23.2.3   loading or discharging operations or the presence of cargo on board shall not debar returns but no return shall be allowed for any period during which the Vessel is being used for the storage of cargo or for lightering purposes

23.2.4   in the event of any amendment of the annual rate, the above rates of return shall be adjusted accordingly

23.2.5   in the event of any return recoverable under this Clause 23 being based on 30 consecutive days which fall on successive insurances effected for the same Assured, this insurance shall only be liable for an amount calculated at pro rata of the period rates 23.1.2(a) and/or (b) above for the number of days which come within the period of this insurance and to which a return is actually applicable. Such overlapping period shall run, at the option of the Assured, either from the first day on which the Vessel is laid up or the first day of a period of 30 consecutive days as provided under 23.1.2(a) or (b) above.

The following clauses shall be paramount and shall override anything contained in this insurance inconsistent therewith.

24 War exclusion

In no case shall this insurance cover loss damage liability or expense caused by

24.1   war civil war revolution rebellion insurrection, or civil strife arising therefrom, or any hostile act by or against a belligerent power

24.2   capture seizure arrest restraint or detainment (barratry and piracy excepted), and the consequences thereof or any attempt thereat

24.3   derelict mines torpedoes bombs or other derelict weapons of war.

25 Strikes exclusion

In no case shall this insurance cover loss damage liability or expense caused by

25.1   strikers, locked-out workmen, or persons taking part in labour disturbances, riots or civil commotions

25.2   any terrorist or any person acting from a political motive.

26 Malicious acts exclusion

In no case shall this insurance cover loss damage liability or expense arising from

26.1   the detonation of an explosive

26.2   any weapon of war

and caused by any person acting maliciously or from a political motive.

27 Radioactive contamination exclusion clause

In no case shall this insurance cover loss damage liability or expense directly or indirectly caused by or contributed to by or arising from

27.1   ionising radiations from or contamination by radioactivity from any nuclear fuel or from any nuclear waste or from the combustion of nuclear fuel

27.2   the radioactive, toxic, explosive or other hazardous or contaminating properties of any nuclear installation, reactor or other nuclear assembly or nuclear component thereof

27.3   any weapon of war employing atomic or nuclear fission and/or fusion or other like reaction or radioactive force or matter.

Institute Time Clauses—Hulls: Disbursements and Increased Value (Total Loss only, including Excess Liabilities)

1/11/95—(FOR USE ONLY WITH THE CURRENT MAR POLICY FORM)

This insurance is subject to English law and practice

1 Navigation

1.1 The subject-matter insured is covered subject to the provisions of this insurance at all times and the Vessel has leave to sail or navigate with or without pilots, to go on trial trips and to assist and tow vessels or craft in distress, but it is warranted that the Vessel shall not be towed, except as is customary or to the first safe port or place when in need of assistance, or undertake towage or salvage services under a contract previously arranged by the Assured and/or Owners and/or Managers and/or Charterers. This Clause 1.1 shall not exclude customary towage in connection with loading and discharging.

1.2 This insurance shall not be prejudiced by reason of the Assured entering into any contract with pilots or for customary towage which limits or exempts the liability of the pilots and/or tugs and/or towboats and/or their owners when the Assured or their agents accept or are compelled to accept such contracts in accordance with established local law or practice.

1.3 The practice of engaging helicopters for the transportation of personnel, supplies and equipment to and/or from the Vessel shall not prejudice this insurance.

1.4 In the event of the Vessel being employed in trading operations which entail cargo loading or discharging at sea from or into another vessel (not being a harbour or inshore craft) no claim shall be recoverable under this insurance in respect of loss of or damage to the subject-matter insured or for liability to any other vessel arising from such loading or discharging operations, including whilst approaching, lying alongside and leaving, unless previous notice that the Vessel is to be employed in such operations has been given to the Underwriters and any amended terms of cover and any additional premium required by them have been agreed.

1.5 In the event of the Vessel sailing (with or without cargo) with an intention of being (a) broken up, or (b) sold for breaking up, no claim shall be recoverable under this insurance in respect of loss or damage to the Vessel occurring subsequent to such sailing unless previous notice has been given to the Underwriters and any amendments to the terms of cover, amount insured and premium required by them have been agreed.

2   Continuation

Should the Vessel at the expiration of this insurance be at sea and in distress or missing, she shall, provided notice be given to the Underwriters prior to the expiration of this insurance, be held covered until arrival at the next port in good safety, or if in port and in distress until the Vessel is made safe, at a pro rata monthly premium.

3   Breach of Warranty

Held covered in case of any breach of warranty as to cargo, locality, trade, towage, salvage services or date of sailing, provided notice be given to the Underwriters immediately after receipt of advices and any amended terms of cover and any additional premium required by them be agreed.

4   Classification

4.1	It is the duty of the Assured, Owners and Managers at the inception of and throughout the period of this insurance to ensure that
4.1.1	the Vessel is classed with a Classification Society agreed by the Underwriters and that her class within that Society is maintained,
4.1.2	any recommendations requirements or restrictions imposed by the Vessel's Classification Society which relate to the Vessel's seaworthiness or to her maintenance in a seaworthy condition are complied with by the dates required by that Society.
4.2	In the event of any breach of the duties set out in Clause 4.1 above, unless the Underwriters agree to the contrary in writing, they will be discharged from liability under this insurance as from the date of the breach provided that if the Vessel is at sea at such date the Underwriters discharge from liability is deferred until arrival at her next port.
4.3	Any incident condition or damage in respect of which the Vessel's Classification Society might make recommendations as to repairs or other action to be taken by the Assured, Owners or Managers must be promptly reported to the Classification Society.
4.4	Should the Underwriters wish to approach the Classification Society directly for information and/or documents, the Assured will provide the necessary authorization.

5   Termination

This Clause 5 shall prevail notwithstanding any provision whether written typed or printed in this insurance inconsistent therewith.
Unless the Underwriters agree to the contrary in writing, this insurance shall terminate automatically at the time of

5.1	change of the Classification Society of the Vessel, or change, suspension, discontinuance, withdrawal or expiry of her Class therein, or any of the Classification Society's periodic surveys becoming overdue unless an extension of time for such survey be agreed by the Classification Society, provided that if the Vessel is at sea such automatic termination shall be deferred until arrival at her next port. However where such change, suspension, discontinuance or withdrawal of her Class or where a periodic survey becoming overdue has resulted from loss or damage covered by Clause 6 of this insurance or which would be covered by an insurance of the Vessel subject to current

Institute Time Clauses—Hulls or Institute War and Strikes Clauses Hulls —Time such automatic termination shall only operate should the Vessel sail from her next port without the prior approval of the Classification Society or in the case of a periodic survey becoming overdue without the Classification Society having agreed an extension of time for such survey,

5.2   any change, voluntary or otherwise, in the ownership or flag, transfer to new management, or charter on a bareboat basis, or requisition for title or use of the Vessel, provided that, if the Vessel has cargo on board and has already sailed from her loading port or is at sea in ballast, such automatic termination shall if required be deferred, whilst the Vessel continues her planned voyage, until arrival at final port of discharge if with cargo or at port of destination if in ballast. However, in the event of requisition for title or use without the prior execution of a written agreement by the Assured, such automatic termination shall occur fifteen days after such requisition whether the Vessel is at sea or in port.

A pro rata daily net return of premium shall be made provided that a total loss of the Vessel, whether by insured perils or otherwise, has not occurred during the period covered by this insurance or any extension thereof.

6 Perils

6.1   This insurance covers total loss (actual or constructive) of the subject-matter insured caused by

6.1.1   perils of the seas rivers lakes or other navigable waters

6.1.2   fire, explosion

6.1.3   violent theft by persons from outside the Vessel

6.1.4   jettison

6.1.5   piracy

6.1.6   contact with land conveyance, dock or harbour equipment or installation

6.1.7   earthquake volcanic eruption or lightning

6.1.8   accidents in loading discharging or shifting cargo or fuel.

6.2   This insurance covers total loss (actual or constructive) of the subject-matter insured caused by

6.2.1   bursting of boilers breakage of shafts or any latent defect in the machinery or hull

6.2.2   negligence of Master Officers Crew or Pilots

6.2.3   negligence of repairers or charterers provided such repairers or charterers are not an Assured hereunder

6.2.4   barratry of Master Officers or Crew

6.2.5   contact with aircraft, helicopters or similar objects, or objects falling therefrom

provided such loss or damage has not resulted from want of due diligence by the Assured, Owners, Managers or Superintendents or any of their onshore management.

6.3   Masters Officers Crew or Pilots not to be considered Owners within the meaning of this Clause 6 should they hold shares in the Vessel.

6.4   This insurance covers:

6.4.1   **General Average, Salvage and Salvage Charges** recoverable under the insurances on hull and machinery but not recoverable in full by reason of the difference between the insured value of the Vessel as stated therein (or any reduced value arising from the deduction therefrom in process of adjustment of any claim which law or practice or the terms of the insurances covering hull and machinery may have required) and the value of the Vessel adopted for the purpose of contribution to general average, salvage or salvage charges, the liability under this insurance being for such proportion of the amount not recoverable as the amount insured hereunder bears to the said difference or to the total sum insured against excess liabilities if it exceed such difference.

6.4.2   **Sue and Labour Charges** recoverable under the insurances on hull and machinery but not recoverable in full by reason of the difference between the insured value of the Vessel as stated therein and the value of the Vessel adopted for the purpose of ascertaining the amount recoverable under the insurances on hull and machinery, the liability under this insurance being for such proportion of the amount not recoverable as the amount insured hereunder bears to the said difference or to the total sum insured against excess liabilities if it exceed such difference.

6.4.3   **Collision Liability (three-fourths)** recoverable under the Institute $\frac{3}{4}$ths Collision Liability and Sistership Clauses in the insurances on hull and machinery but not recoverable in full by reason of such three-fourths liability exceeding three-fourths of the insured value of the Vessel as stated therein, in which case the amount recoverable under this insurance shall be such proportion of the difference so arising as the amount insured hereunder bears to the total sum insured against excess liabilities.

6.5   The Underwriters' liability under 6.4.1, 6.4.2 and 6.4.3 separately, in respect of any one claim, shall not exceed the amount insured hereunder.

7   Pollution Hazard

This insurance covers total loss (actual or constructive) of the Vessel caused by any governmental authority acting under the powers vested in it to prevent or mitigate a pollution hazard or damage to the environment, or threat thereof, resulting directly from damage to the Vessel caused by a peril covered by this insurance, provided that such act of governmental authority has not resulted from want of due diligence by the Assured, Owners or Managers to prevent or mitigate such hazard or damage, or threat thereof. Master Officers Crew or Pilots not to be considered Owners within the meaning of this Clause 7 should they hold shares in the Vessel.

8   Notice of Claim

In the event of accident whereby loss or damage may result in a claim under this insurance, notice must be given to the Underwriters promptly after the date on which the Assured, Owners or Managers become or should have become aware of the loss or damage and prior to survey so that a surveyor may be appointed if the Underwriters so desire.

If notice is not given to the Underwriters within twelve months of that date unless the Underwriters agree to the contrary in writing, the Underwriters will be automatically discharged from liability for any claim under this insurance in respect of or arising out of such loss or damage.

9 Constructive total loss

9.1   In ascertaining whether the Vessel is a constructive total loss, the insured value in the insurances on hull and machinery shall be taken as the repaired value and nothing in respect of the damaged or break-up value of the Vessel or wreck shall be taken into account.

9.2   No claim for constructive total loss based upon the cost of recovery and/or repair of the Vessel shall be recoverable hereunder unless such cost would exceed the insured value in the insurances on hull and machinery. In making this determination, only the cost relating to a single accident or sequence of damages arising from the same accident shall be taken into account.

9.3   Provided that the Constructive Total Loss Clause in the current Institute Time Clauses Hulls or a clause having a similar effect is contained in the insurances on hull and machinery, the settlement of a claim for constructive total loss thereunder shall be accepted as proof of the constructive total loss of the Vessel.

9.4   Should the Vessel be a constructive total loss but the claim on the insurances on hull and machinery be settled as a claim for partial loss, no payment shall be due under this Clause 9.

10 Compromised Total Loss

In the event of a claim for total loss or constructive total loss being settled on the insurances on hull and machinery as a compromised total loss the amount payable hereunder shall be the same percentage of the amount insured as is paid on the said insurances.

11 Assignment

No assignment of or interest in this insurance or in any moneys which may be or become payable thereunder is to be binding on or recognised by the Underwriters unless a dated notice of such assignment or interest signed by the Assured and by the assignor in the case of subsequent assignment, is endorsed on the Policy and the Policy with such endorsement is produced before payment of any claim or return of premium thereunder.

12 Returns for Lay-up and Cancellation

12.1   To return as follows:

12.1.1   pro rata monthly net for each uncommenced month if this insurance be cancelled by agreement,

12.1.2   for each period of 30 consecutive days the Vessel may be laid up in a port or in a lay-up area provided such port or lay-up area is approved by the Underwriters

(a) . . . . per cent net not under repair

(b) . . . . per cent net under repair.

12.1.3   The Vessel shall not be considered to be under repair when work is undertaken in respect of ordinary wear and tear of the Vessel and/or following recommendations in the Vessel's Classification Society survey, but any repairs following loss of or damage to the Vessel or involving structural alterations, whether covered by this insurance or otherwise shall be considered as under repair.

12.1.4	If the Vessel is under repair during part only of a period for which a return is claimable, the return shall be calculated pro rata to the number of days under 12.1.2(a) and (b) respectively.
12.2	PROVIDED ALWAYS THAT
12.2.1	a total loss of the Vessel, whether by insured perils or otherwise, has not occurred during the period covered by this insurance or any extension thereof
12.2.2	in no case shall a return be allowed when the Vessel is lying in exposed or unprotected waters, or in a port or lay-up area not approved by the Underwriters
12.2.3	loading or discharging operations or the presence of cargo on board shall not debar returns but no return shall be allowed for any period during which the Vessel is being used for the storage of cargo or for lightering purposes
12.2.4	in the event of any amendment of the annual rate, the above rates of return shall be adjusted accordingly
12.2.5	in the event of any return recoverable under this Clause 12 being based on 30 consecutive days which fall on successive insurances effected for the same Assured, this insurance shall only be liable for an amount calculated at pro rata of the period rates 12.1.2(a) and/or (b) above for the number of days which come within the period of this insurance and to which a return is actually applicable. Such overlapping period shall run, at the option of the Assured, either from the first day on which the Vessel is laid up or the first day of a period of 30 consecutive days as provided under 12.1.2(a) or (b) above.

The following clauses shall be paramount and shall override anything contained in this insurance inconsistent therewith.

13 War Exclusion

In no case shall this insurance cover loss damage liability or expense caused by

13.1	war civil war revolution rebellion insurrection, or civil strife arising therefrom, or any hostile act by or against a belligerent power
13.2	capture seizure arrest restraint or detainment (barratry and piracy excepted), and the consequences thereof or any attempt thereat
13.3	derelict mines torpedoes bombs or other derelict weapons of war.

14 Strikes Exclusion

In no case shall this insurance cover loss damage liability or expense caused by

14.1	strikers, locked-out workmen, or persons taking part in labour disturbances, riots or civil commotions
14.2	any terrorist or any person acting from a political motive.

15 Malicious Acts Exclusion

In no case shall this insurance cover loss damage liability or expense arising from

15.1	the detonation of an explosive
15.2	any weapon of war

and caused by any person acting maliciously or from a political motive.

16 Radioactive Contamination Exclusion Clause

In no case shall this insurance cover loss damage liability or expense directly or indirectly caused by or contributed to by or arising from

16.1   ionising radiations from or contaminations by radioactivity from any nuclear fuel or from any nuclear waste or from the combustion of nuclear fuel

16.2   the radioactive, toxic, explosive or other hazardous or contaminating properties of any nuclear installation, reactor or other nuclear assembly or nuclear component thereof

16.3   any weapon of war employing atomic or nuclear fission and/fusion [*sic*] or other like reaction or radioactive force or matter.

Institute Time Clauses Hulls—Port Risks

20/7/87—(FOR USE ONLY WITH THE NEW MARINE POLICY FORM)

This insurance is subject to English law and practice

1 Navigation

The Vessel has leave to proceed to and from any wet or dry docks harbours ways cradles and pontoons, within the limits specified in this insurance.

2 Termination

This Clause 2 shall prevail notwithstanding any provision whether written typed or printed in this insurance inconsistent therewith.
Unless Underwriters agree to the contrary in writing, this insurance shall terminate automatically at the time of

    2.1   change of the Classification Society of the Vessel, or change, suspension, discontinuance, withdrawal or expiry of her Class therein. However where such change, suspension, discontinuance or withdrawal of her Class has resulted from loss or damage covered by Clause 4 of this insurance or which would be covered by an insurance of the Vessel subject to current Institute War and Strikes Clauses Hulls—Time such automatic termination shall not operate.

    2.2   any change, voluntary or otherwise, in the ownership or flag, transfer to new management, or charter on a bareboat basis, or requisition for title or use of the Vessel. However, in the event of requisition for title or use without the prior execution of a written agreement by the Assured, such automatic termination shall occur fifteen days after such requisition whether the Vessel is in port or at sea.

3 Assignment

No assignment of or interest in this insurance or in any moneys which may be or become payable thereunder is to be binding on or recognised by the Underwriters unless a dated notice of such assignment or interest signed by the Assured, and by the assignor in the case of subsequent assignment, is endorsed on the Policy and the Policy with such endorsement is produced before payment of any claim or return or premium thereunder.

4 Perils

4.1 This insurance covers loss of or damage to the subject-matter insured caused by

4.1.1 perils of the seas rivers lakes or other navigable waters

4.1.2 fire lightning explosion

4.1.3 violent theft by persons from outside the Vessel

4.1.4 jettison

4.1.5 piracy

4.1.6 breakdown of or accident to nuclear installations or reactors

4.1.7 contact with aircraft or similar objects, or objects falling therefrom, land conveyance, dock or harbour equipment or installation.

4.2 This insurance covers loss of or damage to the subject-matter insured caused by

4.2.1 accidents in loading discharging or shifting cargo or fuel

4.2.2 bursting of boilers breakage of shafts or any latent defect in the machinery or hull

4.2.3 negligence of Master Officers Crew or Pilots

4.2.4 negligence of repairers or charterers provided such repairers or charterers are not an Assured hereunder

4.2.5 barratry of Master Officers or Crew,

provided such loss or damage has not resulted from want of due diligence by the Assured, Owners or Managers.

4.3 Master Officers Crew or Pilots not to be considered Owners within the meaning of this Clause 4 should they hold shares in the Vessel.

5 Earthquake and Volcanic Eruption Exclusion

In no case shall this insurance cover loss damage liability or expense caused by earthquake or volcanic eruption. This exclusion applies to all claims including claims under Clauses 7, 9, 11 and 13.

6 Pollution Hazard

This insurance covers loss of or damage to the Vessel caused by any governmental authority acting under the powers vested in it to prevent or mitigate a pollution hazard, or threat thereof, resulting directly from damage to the Vessel for which the Underwriters are liable under this insurance, provided such act of governmental authority has not resulted from want of due diligence by the Assured, the Owners, or Managers of the Vessel or any of them to prevent or mitigate such hazard or threat. Master, Officers, Crew or Pilots not to be considered Owners within the meaning of this Clause 6 should they hold shares in the Vessel.

7 Collision Liability

7.1 The Underwriters agree to indemnify the Assured for any sum or sums paid by the Assured to any other person or persons by reason of the Assured becoming legally liable by way of damages for

7.1.1 loss of or damage to any other vessel or property on any other vessel

7.1.2 delay to or loss of use of any such other vessel or property thereon

7.1.3 general average of, salvage of, or salvage under contract of, any such other vessel or property thereon, where such payment by the Assured is in consequence of the Vessel hereby insured coming into collision with any other vessel.

7.2 The indemnity provided by this Clause 7 shall be in addition to the indemnity provided by the other terms and conditions of this insurance and shall be subject to the following provisions:

7.2.1 Where the insured Vessel is in collision with another vessel and both vessels are to blame then, unless the liability of one or both vessels becomes limited by law, the indemnity under this Clause 7 shall be calculated on the principle of cross-liabilities as if the respective Owners had been compelled to pay to each other such proportion of each other's damages as may have been properly allowed in ascertaining the balance or sum payable by or to the Assured in consequence of the collision.

7.2.2 In no case shall the Underwriters' total liability under Clauses 7.1 and 7.2 exceed their proportionate part of the insured value of the Vessel hereby insured in respect of any one such collision.

7.3 The Underwriters will also pay the legal costs incurred by the Assured or which the Assured may be compelled to pay in contesting liability or taking proceedings to limit liability, with the prior written consent of the Underwriters.

EXCLUSIONS

7.4 Provided always that this Clause 7 shall in no case extend to any sum which the Assured shall pay for or in respect of

7.4.1 removal or disposal of obstructions, wrecks, cargoes or any other thing whatsoever

7.4.2 any real or personal property or thing whatsoever except other vessels or property on other vessels

7.4.3 the cargo or other property on, or the engagements of, the insured Vessel

7.4.4 loss of life, personal injury or illness

7.4.5 pollution or contamination of any real or personal property or thing whatsoever (except other vessels with which the insured Vessel is in collision or property on such other vessels).

8 Sistership

Should the Vessel hereby insured come into collision with or receive salvage services from another vessel belonging wholly or in part to the same Owners or under the same management, the Assured shall have the same rights under this insurance as they would have were the other vessel entirely the property of Owners not interested in the Vessel hereby insured; but in such cases the liability for the collision or the amount payable for the services rendered shall be referred to a sole arbitrator to be agreed upon between the Underwriters and the Assured.

9 Protection and Indemnity

9.1 The Underwriters agree to indemnify the Assured for any sum or sums paid by the Assured to any other person or persons by reason of the Assured becoming legally liable, as owner of the Vessel, for any claim, demand, damages and/or expenses, where such liability is in consequence of any of the

197

following matters or things and arises from an accident or occurrence during the period of this insurance:

9.1.1   loss of or damage to any fixed or movable object or property or other thing or interest whatsoever, other than the Vessel, arising from any cause whatsoever in so far as such loss or damage is not covered by Clause 7

9.1.2   any attempted or actual raising, removal or destruction of any fixed or movable object or property or other thing, including the wreck of the Vessel, or any neglect or failure to raise, remove, or destroy the same

9.1.3   liability assumed by the Assured under contracts of customary towage for the purpose of entering or leaving port or manoeuvring within the port during the ordinary course of trading

9.1.4   loss of life, personal injury, illness or payments made for life salvage

9.1.5   liability under Clause 1(a) of the current Lloyd's Standard Form of Salvage Agreement in respect of unsuccessful, partially successful, or uncompleted services if and to the extent that the salvor's expenses plus the increment exceed any amount otherwise recoverable under the Agreement.

9.2   The Underwriters agree to indemnify the Assured for any of the following arising from an accident or occurrence during the period of this insurance:

9.2.1   the additional cost of fuel, insurance, wages, stores, provisions and port charges reasonably incurred solely for the purpose of landing from the Vessel sick or injured persons or stowaways, refugees, or persons saved at sea

9.2.2   additional expenses brought about by the outbreak of infectious disease on board the Vessel or ashore

9.2.3   fines imposed on the Vessel, on the Assured, or on any Master Officer crew member or agent of the Vessel who is reimbursed by the Assured, for any act or neglect or breach of any statute or regulation relating to the operation of the Vessel, provided that the Underwriters shall not be liable to indemnify the Assured for any fines which result from any act neglect failure or default of the Assured their agents or servants other than Master Officer or crew member

9.2.4   the expenses of the removal of the wreck of the Vessel from any place owned, leased or occupied by the Assured

9.2.5   legal costs incurred by the Assured, or which the Assured may be compelled to pay, in avoiding, minimising or contesting liability with the prior written consent of the Underwriters.

EXCLUSIONS

9.3   Notwithstanding the provisions of Clauses 9.1 and 9.2 this Clause 9 does not cover any liability cost or expense arising in respect of:

9.3.1   any direct or indirect payment by the Assured under workmen's compensation or employers' liability acts and any other statutory or common law, general maritime law or other liability whatsoever in respect of accidents to or illness of workmen or any other persons employed in any capacity whatsoever by the Assured or others in on or about or in connection with the Vessel or her cargo, materials or repairs

9.3.2   liability assumed by the Assured under agreement expressed or implied in respect of death or illness of or injury to any person employed under

	a contract of service or apprenticeship by the other party to such agreement
9.3.3	punitive or exemplary damages, however described
9.3.4	cargo or other property carried, to be carried or which has been carried on board the Vessel but this Clause 9.3.4 shall not exclude any claim in respect of the extra cost of removing cargo from the wreck of the Vessel
9.3.5	property, owned by builders or repairers or for which they are responsible, which is on board the Vessel
9.3.6	liability arising under a contract or indemnity in respect of containers, equipment, fuel or other property on board the Vessel and which is owned or leased by the Assured
9.3.7	cash, negotiable instruments, precious metals or stones, valuables or objects of a rare or precious nature, belonging to persons on board the Vessel, or non-essential personal effects of any Master, Officer or crew member
9.3.8	fuel, insurance, wages, stores, provisions and port charges arising from delay to the Vessel while awaiting a substitute for any Master, Officer or crew member
9.3.9	fines or penalties arising from overloading or illegal fishing
9.3.10	pollution or contamination of any real or personal property or thing whatsoever (this Clause 9.3.10 shall not exclude any amount recoverable under Clause 9.1.5)
9.3.11	general average, sue and labour and salvage charges, salvage, and/or collision liability to any extent that they are not recoverable under Clauses 7, 11 and 13 by reason of the agreed value and/or the amount insured in respect of the Vessel being inadequate.
9.4	The indemnity provided by this Clause 9 shall be in addition to the indemnity provided by the other terms and conditions of this insurance.
9.5	Where the Assured or the Underwriters may or could have limited their liability the indemnity under this Clause 9 in respect of such liability shall not exceed Underwriters' proportionate part of the amount of such limitation.
9.6	In no case shall the Underwriters' liability under this Clause 9 in respect of each separate accident or occurrence or series of accidents arising out of the same event, exceed their proportionate part of the insured value of the Vessel.
9.7	PROVIDED ALWAYS THAT
9.7.1	prompt notice must be given to the Underwriters of every casualty event or claim upon the Assured which may give rise to a claim under this Clause 9 and of every event or matter which may cause the Assured to incur liability costs or expense for which he may be insured under this Clause 9
9.7.2	the Assured shall not admit liability for or settle any claim for which he may be insured under this Clause 9 without the prior written consent of the Underwriters.

10 Notice of Claim and Tenders

10.1	In the event of accident whereby loss or damage may result in a claim under this insurance, notice shall be given to the Underwriters prior to

survey and also, if the Vessel is abroad, to the nearest Lloyd's Agent so that a surveyor may be appointed to represent the Underwriters should they so desire.

10.2   The Underwriters shall be entitled to decide the port to which the Vessel shall proceed for docking or repair (the actual additional expense of the voyage arising from compliance with the Underwriters' requirements being refunded to the Assured) and shall have a right of veto concerning a place of repair or a repairing firm.

10.3   The Underwriters may also take tenders or may require further tenders to be taken for the repair of the Vessel. Where such a tender has been taken and a tender is accepted with the approval of the Underwriters, an allowance shall be made at the rate of 30% per annum on the insured value for time lost between the despatch of the invitations to tender required by Underwriters and the acceptance of a tender to the extent that such time is lost solely as the result of tenders having been taken and provided that the tender is accepted without delay after receipt of the Underwriters' approval.

Due credit shall be given against the allowance as above for any amounts recovered in respect of fuel and stores and wages and maintenance of the Master Officers and Crew or any member thereof, including amounts allowed in general average, and for any amounts recovered from third parties in respect of damages for detention and/or loss of profit and/or running expenses, for the period covered by the tender allowance or any part thereof.

Where a part of the cost of the repair of damage other than a fixed deductible is not recoverable from the Underwriters the allowance shall be reduced by a similar proportion.

10.4   In the event of failure to comply with the conditions of this Clause 10, a deduction of 15% shall be made from the amount of the ascertained claim.

11   General Average and Salvage

11.1   This insurance covers the Vessel's proportion of salvage, salvage charges and/or general average, reduced in respect of any under-insurance, but in case of general average sacrifice of the Vessel the Assured may recover in respect of the whole loss without first enforcing their right of contribution from other parties.

11.2   Adjustment to be according to the law and practice obtaining at the place where the adventure ends, as if the contract of affreightment contained no special terms upon the subject; but where the contract of affreightment so provides the adjustment shall be according to the York-Antwerp Rules.

11.3   No claim under this Clause 11 shall in any case be allowed where the loss was not incurred to avoid or in connection with the avoidance of a peril insured against.

12   Deductible

12.1   No claim arising from a peril insured against shall be payable under this insurance unless the aggregate of all such claims arising out of each separate accident or occurrence (including claims under Clauses 7, 9, 11 and 13) exceeds .... in which case this sum shall be deducted. Nevertheless the expense of sighting the bottom after stranding, if reasonably incurred specially for that purpose, shall be paid even if no damage be found. This Clause 12.1 shall not apply to a claim for total or constructive total loss of the Vessel or, in the event of such a claim, to any associated claim under Clause 13 arising from the same accident or occurrence.

12.2   Excluding any interest comprised therein, recoveries against any claim which is subject to the above deductible shall be credited to the Underwriters in full to the extent of the sum by which the aggregate of the claim unreduced by any recoveries exceeds the above deductible.

12.3   Interest comprised in recoveries shall be apportioned between the Assured and the Underwriters, taking into account the sums paid by the Under-writers and the dates when such payments were made, notwithstanding that by the addition of interest the Underwriters may receive a larger sum than they have paid.

13   Duty of Assured (Sue and Labour)

13.1   In case of any loss or misfortune it is the duty of the Assured and their servants and agents to take such measures as may be reasonable for the purpose of averting or minimising a loss which would be recoverable under this insurance.

13.2   Subject to the provisions below and to Clause 12 the Underwriters will contribute to charges properly and reasonably incurred by the Assured their servants or agents for such measures. General average, salvage charges (except as provided for in Clause 13.5) collision defence or attack costs and costs incurred by the Assured in avoiding, minimising or contesting liability covered by Clause 9 are not recoverable under this Clause 13.

13.3   Measures taken by the Assured or the Underwriters with the object of saving, protecting or recovering the subject-matter insured shall not be considered as a waiver or acceptance of abandonment or otherwise prejudice the rights of either party.

13.4   When expenses are incurred pursuant to this Clause 13 the liability under this insurance shall not exceed the proportion of such expenses that the amount insured hereunder bears to the value of the Vessel as stated herein, or to the sound value of the Vessel at the time of the occurrence giving rise to the expenditure if the sound value exceeds that value. Where the Underwriters have admitted a claim for total loss and property insured by this insurance is saved, the foregoing provisions shall not apply unless the expenses of suing and labouring exceed the value of such property saved and then shall apply only to the amount of the expenses which is in excess of such value.

13.5   When a claim for total loss of the Vessel is admitted under this insurance and expenses have been reasonably incurred in a saving or attempting to save the Vessel and other property and there are no proceeds, or the expenses exceed the proceeds, then this insurance shall bear its pro rata share of such proportion of the expenses, or of the expenses in excess of the proceeds, as the case may be, as may reasonably be regarded as having been incurred in respect of the Vessel; but if the Vessel be insured for less than its sound value at the time of the occurrence giving rise to the expenditure, the amount recoverable under this clause shall be reduced in proportion to the under-insurance.

201

13.6 The sum recoverable under this Clause 13 shall be in addition to the loss otherwise recoverable under this insurance but shall in no circumstances exceed the amount insured under this insurance in respect of the Vessel.

14 New for Old

Claims payable without deduction new for old.

15 Bottom Treatment

In no case shall a claim be allowed in respect of scraping gritblasting and/or other surface preparation or painting of the Vessel's bottom except that

15.1 gritblasting and/or other surface preparation of new bottom plates ashore and supplying and applying any "shop" primer thereto,

15.2 gritblasting and/or other surface preparation of:
the butts or area of plating immediately adjacent to any renewed or refitted plating damaged during the course of welding and/or repairs,
areas of plating damaged during the course of fairing, either in place or ashore,

15.3 supplying and applying the first coat of primer/anti-corrosive to those particular areas mentioned in 15.1 and 15.2 above,

shall be allowed as part of the reasonable cost of repairs in respect of bottom plating damaged by an insured peril.

16 Wages and Maintenance

No claim shall be allowed, other than in general average, for wages and maintenance of the Master, Officers and Crew, or any member thereof, except when incurred solely for the necessary removal of the Vessel, with the agreement of the Underwriters, from one port to another for the repair of damage covered by the Underwriters, or for trial trips for such repairs, and then only for such wages and maintenance as are incurred whilst the Vessel is under way.

17 Agency Commission

In no case shall any sum be allowed under this insurance either by way of remuneration of the Assured for time and trouble taken to obtain and supply information or documents or in respect of the commission or charges of any manager, agent, managing or agency company or the like, appointed by or on behalf of the Assured to perform such services.

18 Unrepaired Damage

18.1 The measure of indemnity in respect of claims for unrepaired damage shall be the reasonable depreciation in the market value of the Vessel at the time this insurance terminates arising from such unrepaired damage, but not exceeding the reasonable cost of repairs.

18.2 In no case shall the Underwriters be liable for unrepaired damage in the event of a subsequent total loss (whether or not covered under this insurance) sustained during the period covered by this insurance or any extension thereof.

18.3 The Underwriters shall not be liable in respect of unrepaired damage for more than the insured value at the time this insurance terminates.

19 Constructive Total Loss

19.1   In ascertaining whether the Vessel is a constructive total loss, the insured value shall be taken as the repaired value and nothing in respect of the damaged or break-up value of the Vessel or wreck shall be taken into account.

19.2   No claim for constructive total loss based upon the cost of recovery and/or repair of the Vessel shall be recoverable hereunder unless such cost would exceed the insured value. In making this determination only the cost relating to a single accident or sequence of damages arising from the same accident shall be taken into account.

20 Disbursements Warranty

20.1   Additional insurances as follows are permitted:

20.1.1   *Disbursements, Managers' Commissions, Profits or Excess or Increased Value of Hull and Machinery.* A sum not exceeding 25% of the value stated herein.

20.1.2   *Earnings or Anticipated Freight, insured for time.* A sum not exceeding 25% of the value as stated herein less any sum insured, however described, under 20.1.1.

20.1.3   *Freight or Hire, under contracts for voyage.* A sum not exceeding the gross freight or hire for the first passage and next succeeding cargo passage plus the charges of insurance. In the case of a voyage charter where payment is made on a time basis, the sum permitted for insurance shall be calculated on the estimated duration of the voyage, subject to the limitation of two cargo passages as laid down herein. Any sum insured under 20.1.2 to be taken into account and only the excess thereof may be insured.

20.1.4   *Time Charter Hire or Charter Hire for Series of Voyages.* A sum not exceeding 50% of the gross hire which is to be earned under the charter in a period not exceeding 18 months. Any sum insured under 20.1.2 to be taken into account and only the excess thereof may be insured. An insurance under this Section may begin on the signing of the charter.

20.1.5   *Premiums.* A sum not exceeding the actual premiums of all interests insured for a period not exceeding 12 months (excluding premiums insured under the foregoing sections but including, if required, the premium or estimated calls on any Club or War etc. Risk Insurance) reducing pro rata monthly.

20.1.6   *Returns of Premium.* A sum not exceeding the actual returns which are allowable under any insurance but which would not be recoverable thereunder in the event of a total loss of the Vessel whether by insured perils or otherwise.

20.1.7   *Insurance irrespective of amount against:*
Any risks excluded by Clauses 5, 22, 23, 24 and 25.

20.2   Warranted that no insurance on any interest enumerated in the foregoing 20.1.1 to 20.1.6 in excess of the amounts permitted therein and no other insurance which includes total loss of the Vessel P.P.I., F.I.A., or subject to any other like term, is or shall be effected to operate during the currency of this insurance by or for account of the Assured, Owners, Managers or Mortgagees. Provided always that a breach of this warranty shall not afford the Underwriters any defence to a claim by a Mortgagee who has accepted this insurance without knowledge of such breach.

21 Returns for Cancellation

To return pro rata monthly net for each uncommenced month if this insurance be cancelled either by agreement or by the operation of Clause 2 provided that a total loss of the Vessel, whether by insured perils or otherwise, has not occurred during the period of this insurance or any extension thereof.

The following clauses shall be paramount and shall override anything contained in this insurance inconsistent therewith.

22 War Exclusion

In no case shall this insurance cover loss damage liability or expense caused by

22.1	war civil war revolution rebellion insurrection, or civil strife arising there-from, or any hostile act by or against a belligerent power
22.2	capture seizure arrest restraint or detainment (barratry and piracy excepted), and the consequences thereof or any attempt thereat.
22.3	derelict mines torpedoes bombs or other derelict weapons of war.

23 Strikes Exclusion

In no case shall this insurance cover loss damage liability or expense caused by

23.1	strikers, locked-out workmen, or persons taking part in labour disturbances, riots or civil commotions
23.2	any terrorist or any person acting from a political motive.

24 Malicious Acts Exclusion

In no case shall this insurance cover loss damage liability or expense arising from

24.1	the detonation of an explosive
24.2	any weapon of war

and caused by any person acting maliciously or from a political motive.

25 Nuclear Exclusion

In no case shall this insurance cover loss damage liability or expense arising from any weapon of war employing atomic or nuclear fission and/or fusion or other like reaction or radioactive force or matter.

Institute Time Clauses Hulls—Port Risks including Limited Navigation

20/7/87—(FOR USE ONLY WITH THE NEW MARINE POLICY FORM)

This insurance is subject to English law and practice

1   Navigation

1.1   The Vessel has leave to proceed to and from any wet or dry docks harbours ways cradles and pontoons, within the limits specified in this insurance.

1.2   The Vessel is held covered in case of deviation or change of voyage, provided notice be given immediately after receipt of advices and any amended terms of cover and any additional premium required be agreed.

2   Continuation

Should the Vessel at the expiration of this insurance be at sea or in distress or at a port of a refuge or of call, she shall, provided previous notice be given to the Underwriters, be held covered at a pro rata monthly premium to her port of destination.

3   Termination

This Clause 3 shall prevail notwithstanding any provision whether written typed or printed in this insurance inconsistent therewith.
Unless the Underwriters agree to the contrary in writing, this insurance shall terminate automatically at the time of

3.1   change of the Classification Society of the Vessel, or change, suspension, discontinuance, withdrawal or expiry of her Class therein, provided that if the Vessel is at sea such automatic termination shall be deferred until arrival at her next port. However where such change, suspension, discontinuance or withdrawal of her Class has resulted from loss or damage covered by Clause 5 of this insurance or which would be covered by an insurance of the Vessel subject to current Institute War and Strikes Clauses Hulls—Time such automatic termination shall only operate should the Vessel sail from her next port without the prior approval of the Classification Society,

3.2   any change, voluntary or otherwise, in the ownership or flag, transfer to new management, or charter on a bareboat basis, or requisition for title or use of the Vessel. However, in the event of requisition for title or use without the prior execution of a written agreement by the Assured, such automatic termination shall occur fifteen days after such requisition whether the Vessel is in port or at sea.

4   Assignment

No assignment of or interest in this insurance or in any moneys which may be or become payable thereunder is to be binding on or recognised by the Underwriters unless a dated notice of such assignment or interest signed by the Assured, and by the assignor in the case of subsequent assignment, is endorsed on the Policy and the Policy with such endorsement is produced before payment of any claim or return of premium thereunder.

5   Perils

5.1	This insurance covers loss of or damage to the subject-matter insured caused by
5.1.1	perils of the seas rivers lakes or other navigable waters
5.1.2	fire lightning explosion
5.1.3	violent theft by persons from outside the Vessel
5.1.4	jettison
5.1.5	piracy
5.1.6	breakdown of or accident to nuclear installations or reactors
5.1.7	contact with aircraft or similar objects, or objects falling therefrom, land conveyance, dock or harbour equipment or installation.
5.2	This insurance covers loss of or damage to the subject-matter insured caused by
5.2.1	accidents in loading discharging or shifting cargo or fuel
5.2.2	bursting of boilers breakage of shafts or any latent defect in the machinery or hull
5.2.3	negligence of Master Officers Crew or Pilots
5.2.4	negligence of repairers or charterers provided such repairers or charterers are not an Assured hereunder
5.2.5	barratry of Master Officers or Crew,

provided such loss or damage has not resulted from want of due diligence by the Assured, Owners or Managers.

5.3	Master Officers Crew or Pilots not to be considered Owners within the meaning of this Clause 5 should they hold shares in the Vessel.

6   Earthquake and volcanic eruption exclusion

In no case shall this insurance cover loss damage liability or expense caused by earthquake or volcanic eruption. This exclusion applies to all claims including claims under Clauses 8, 10, 12 and 14.

7   Pollution hazard

This insurance covers loss of or damage to the Vessel caused by any governmental authority acting under the powers vested in it to prevent or mitigate a pollution hazard, or threat thereof, resulting directly from damage to the Vessel for which the Underwriters are liable under this insurance, provided such act of governmental authority has not resulted from want of due diligence by the Assured, the Owners, or Managers of the Vessel or any of them to prevent or mitigate such hazard or threat. Master, Officers, Crew or Pilots not to be considered Owners within the meaning of this Clause 7 should they hold shares in the Vessel.

8 Collision liability

8.1 The Underwriters agree to indemnify the Assured for any sum or sums paid by the Assured to any other person or persons by reason of the Assured becoming legally liable by way of damages for

8.1.1 loss of or damage to any other vessel or property on any other vessel

8.1.2 delay to or loss of use of any such other vessel or property thereon

8.1.3 general average of, salvage of, or salvage under contract of, any such other vessel or property thereon,

where such payment by the Assured is in consequence of the Vessel hereby insured coming into collision with any other vessel.

8.2 The indemnity provided by this Clause 8 shall be in addition to the indemnity provided by the other terms and conditions of this insurance and shall be subject to the following provisions:

8.2.1 Where the insured Vessel is in collision with another vessel and both vessels are to blame then, unless the liability of one or both vessels becomes limited by law, the indemnity under this Clause 8 shall be calculated on the principle of cross-liabilities as if the respective Owners had been compelled to pay to each other such proportion of each other's damages as may have been properly allowed in ascertaining the balance or sum payable by or to the Assured in consequence of the collision.

8.2.2 In no case shall the Underwriters' total liability under Clauses 8.1 and 8.2 exceed their proportionate part of the insured value of the Vessel hereby insured in respect of any one such collision.

8.3 The Underwriters will also pay the legal costs incurred by the Assured or which the Assured may be compelled to pay in contesting liability or taking proceedings to limit liability, with the prior written consent of the Underwriters.

EXCLUSIONS

8.4 Provided always that this Clause 8 shall in no case extend to any sum which the Assured shall pay for or in respect of

8.4.1 removal or disposal of obstructions, wrecks, cargoes or any other thing whatsoever

8.4.2 any real or personal property or thing whatsoever except other vessels or property on other vessels

8.4.3 the cargo or other property on, or the engagements of, the insured Vessel

8.4.4 loss of life, personal injury or illness

8.4.5 pollution or contamination of any real or personal property or thing whatsoever (except other vessels with which the insured Vessel is in collision or property on such other vessels).

9 Sistership

Should the Vessel hereby insured come into collision with or receive salvage services from another vessel belonging wholly or in part to the same Owners or under the same management, the Assured shall have the same rights under this insurance as they would have were the other vessel entirely the property of Owners not interested in the Vessel hereby insured; but in such cases the liability for the collision or the amount payable for the services rendered shall be referred to a sole arbitrator to be agreed upon between the Underwriters and the Assured.

10   Protection and indemnity

10.1   The Underwriters agree to indemnify the Assured for any sum or sums paid by the Assured to any other person or persons by reason of the Assured becoming legally liable, as owner of the Vessel, for any claim, demand, damages and/or expenses, where such liability is in consequence of any of the following matters or things and arises from an accident or occurrence during the period of this insurance:

10.1.1   loss of or damage to any fixed or movable object or property or other thing or interest whatsoever, other than the Vessel, arising from any cause whatsoever in so far as such loss or damage is not covered by Clause 8

10.1.2   any attempted or actual raising, removal or destruction of any fixed or movable object or property or other thing, including the wreck of the Vessel, or any neglect or failure to raise, remove, or destroy the same

10.1.3   liability assumed by the Assured under contracts of customary towage for the purpose of entering or leaving port or manoeuvring within the port during the ordinary course of trading

10.1.4   loss of life, personal injury, illness or payments made for life salvage

10.1.5   liability under Clause 1(a) of the current Lloyd's Standard Form of Salvage Agreement in respect of unsuccessful, partially successful, or uncompleted services if and to the extent that the salvor's expenses plus the increment exceed any amount otherwise recoverable under the Agreement.

10.2   The Underwriters agree to indemnify the Assured for any of the following arising from an accident or occurrence during the period of this insurance:

10.2.1   the additional cost of fuel, insurance, wages, stores, provisions and port charges reasonably incurred solely for the purpose of landing from the Vessel sick or injured persons or stowaways, refugees, or persons saved at sea

10.2.2   additional expenses brought about by the outbreak of infectious disease on board the Vessel or ashore

10.2.3   fines imposed on the Vessel, on the Assured, or on any Master Officer crew member or agent of the Vessel who is reimbursed by the Assured, for any act or neglect or breach of any statute or regulation relating to the operation of the Vessel, provided that the Underwriters shall not be liable to indemnify the Assured for any fines which result from any act neglect failure or default of the Assured their agents or servants other than Master Officer or crew member

10.2.4   the expenses of the removal of the wreck of the Vessel from any place owned, leased or occupied by the Assured

10.2.5   legal costs incurred by the Assured, or which the Assured may be compelled to pay, in avoiding, minimising or contesting liability with the prior written consent of the Underwriters.

EXCLUSIONS

10.3   Notwithstanding the provisions of Clause 10.1 and 10.2 this Clause 10 does not cover any liability cost or expense arising in respect of:

10.3.1   any direct or indirect payment by the Assured under workmen's compensation or employers' liability acts and any other statutory or common law, general maritime law or other liability whatsoever in respect of accidents to or illness of workmen or any other persons employed in any capacity whatsoever by the Assured or others in on or about or in connection with the Vessel or her cargo, materials or repairs

10.3.2   liability assumed by the Assured under agreement expressed or implied in respect of death or illness of or injury to any person employed under a contract of service or apprenticeship by the other party to such agreement

10.3.3   punitive or exemplary damages, however described

10.3.4   cargo or other property carried, to be carried or which has been carried on board the Vessel but this Clause 10.3.4 shall not exclude any claim in respect of the extra cost of removing cargo from the wreck of the Vessel

10.3.5   property, owned by builders or repairers or for which they are responsible, which is on board the Vessel

10.3.6   liability arising under a contract of indemnity in respect of containers, equipment, fuel or other property on board the Vessel and which is owned or leased by the Assured

10.3.7   cash, negotiable instruments, precious metals or stones, valuables or objects of a rare or precious nature, belonging to persons on board the Vessel, or non-essential personal effects of any Master, Officer or crew member

10.3.8   fuel, insurance, wages, stores, provisions and port charges arising from delay to the Vessel while awaiting a substitute for any Master, Officer or crew member

10.3.9   fines or penalties arising from overloading or illegal fishing

10.3.10   pollution or contamination of any real or personal property or thing whatsoever (This Clause 10.3.10 shall not exclude any amount recoverable under Clause 10.1.5).

10.3.11   general average, sue and labour and salvage charges, salvage, and/or collision liability to any extent that they are not recoverable under Clauses 8, 12 and 14 by reason of the agreed value and/or the amount insured in respect of the Vessel being inadequate.

10.4   The indemnity provided by this Clause 10 shall be in addition to the indemnity provided by the other terms and conditions of this insurance.

10.5   Where the Assured or the Underwriters may or could have limited their liability the indemnity under this Clause 10 in respect of such liability shall not exceed Underwriters' proportionate part of the amount of such limitation.

10.6   In no case shall the Underwriters' liability under this Clause 10 in respect of each separate accident or occurrence or series of accidents arising out of the same event, exceed their proportionate part of the insured value of the Vessel.

10.7   PROVIDED ALWAYS THAT

10.7.1   prompt notice must be given to the Underwriters of every casualty event or claim upon the Assured which may give rise to a claim under this Clause 10 and of every event or matter which may cause the Assured to incur liability costs or expense for which he may be insured under this Clause 10

10.7.2   the Assured shall not admit liability for or settle any claim for which he may be insured under this Clause 10 without the prior written consent of the Underwriters.

11   Notice of claim and tenders

11.1   In the event of accident whereby loss or damage may result in a claim under this insurance, notice shall be given to the Underwriters prior to survey and also, if the Vessel is abroad, to the nearest Lloyd's Agent so that a surveyor may be appointed to represent the Underwriters should they so desire.

11.2   The Underwriters shall be entitled to decide the port to which the Vessel shall proceed for docking or repair (the actual additional expense of the voyage arising from compliance with the Underwriters' requirements being refunded to the Assured) and shall have a right of veto concerning a place of repair or a repairing firm.

11.3   The Underwriters may also take tenders or may require further tenders to be taken for the repair of the Vessel. Where such a tender has been taken and a tender is accepted with the approval of the Underwriters, an allowance shall be made at the rate of 30% per annum on the insured value for time lost between the despatch of the invitations to tender required by Underwriters and the acceptance of a tender to the extent that such time is lost solely as the result of tenders having been taken and provided that the tender is accepted without delay after receipt of the Underwriters' approval.

Due credit shall be given against the allowance as above for any amounts recovered in respect of fuel and stores and wages and maintenance of the Master Officers and Crew or any member thereof, including amounts allowed in general average, and for any amounts recovered from third parties in respect of damages for detention and/or loss of profit and/or running expenses, for the period covered by the tender allowance or any part thereof.

Where a part of the cost of the repair of damage other than a fixed deductible is not recoverable from the Underwriters the allowance shall be reduced by a similar proportion.

11.4   In the event of failure to comply with the conditions of this Clause 11, a deduction of 15% shall be made from the amount of the ascertained claim.

12   General average and salvage

12.1   This insurance covers the Vessel's proportion of salvage, salvage charges and/or general average, reduced in respect of any under-insurance, but in case of general average sacrifice of the Vessel the Assured may recover in respect of the whole loss without first enforcing their right of contribution from other parties.

12.2   Adjustment to be according to the law and practice obtaining at the place where the adventure ends, as if the contract of affreightment contained no special terms upon the subject; but where the contract of affreightment so provides the adjustment shall be according to the York-Antwerp Rules.

12.3   When the Vessel sails in ballast, not under charter, the provisions of the York-Antwerp Rules, 1974 (excluding Rules XX and XXI) shall be applicable, and the voyage for this purpose shall be deemed to continue from the port or place of departure until the arrival of the Vessel at the first port or place thereafter other than a port or place of refuge or a port or place of call for bunkering only. If at any such intermediate port or place there is an abandonment of the adventure originally contemplated the voyage shall thereupon be deemed to be terminated.

12.4   No claim under this Clause 12 shall in any case be allowed where the loss was not incurred to avoid or in connection with the avoidance of a peril insured against.

13 Deductible

13.1   No claim arising from a peril insured against shall be payable under this insurance unless the aggregate of all such claims arising out of each separate accident or occurrence (including claims under Clauses 8, 10, 12 and 14) exceeds ....in which case this sum shall be deducted. Nevertheless the expense of sighting the bottom after stranding, if reasonably incurred specially for that purpose, shall be paid even if no damage be found. This Clause 13.1 shall not apply to a claim for total or constructive total loss of the Vessel or, in the event of such a claim, to any associated claim under Clause 14 arising from the same accident or occurrence.

13.2   Excluding any interest comprised therein, recoveries against any claim which is subject to the above deductible shall be credited to the Underwriters in full to the extent of the sum by which the aggregate of the claim unreduced by any recoveries exceeds the above deductible.

13.3   Interest comprised in recoveries shall be apportioned between the Assured and the Underwriters, taking into account the sums paid by the Underwriters and the dates when such payments were made, notwithstanding that by the addition of interest the Underwriters may receive a larger sum than they have paid.

14 Duty of assured (Sue and Labour)

14.1   In case of any loss or misfortune it is the duty of the Assured and their servants and agents to take such measures as may be reasonable for the purpose of averting or minimising a loss which would be recoverable under this insurance.

14.2   Subject to the provisions below and to Clause 13 the Underwriters will contribute to charges properly and reasonably incurred by the Assured their servants or agents for such measures. General average, salvage charges (except as provided for in Clause 14.5) collision defence or attack costs and costs incurred by the Assured in avoiding, minimising or contesting liability covered by Clause 10 are not recoverable under this Clause 14.

14.3   Measures taken by the Assured or the Underwriters with the object of saving, protecting or recovering the subject-matter insured shall not be considered as a waiver or acceptance of abandonment or otherwise prejudice the rights of either party.

14.4   When expenses are incurred pursuant to this Clause 14 the liability under this insurance shall not exceed the proportion of such expenses that the amount insured hereunder bears to the value of the Vessel as stated herein, or to the sound value of the Vessel at the time of the occurrence giving rise to the expenditure if the sound value exceeds that value. Where the Underwriters have admitted a claim for total loss and property insured by this insurance is saved, the foregoing provisions shall not apply unless the expenses of suing and labouring exceed the value of such property saved and then shall apply only to the amount of the expenses which is in excess of such value.

14.5   When a claim for total loss of the Vessel is admitted under this insurance and expenses have been reasonably incurred in saving or attempting to save the Vessel and other property and there are no proceeds, or the expenses exceed the proceeds, then this insurance shall bear its pro rata share of such proportion of the expenses, or of the expenses in excess of the proceeds, as the case may be, as may reasonably be regarded as having been incurred in respect of the Vessel; but if the Vessel be insured for less than its sound value at the time of the occurrence giving rise to the expenditure, the amount recoverable under this clause shall be reduced in proportion to the under-insurance.

14.6   The sum recoverable under this Clause 14 shall be in addition to the loss otherwise recoverable under this insurance but shall in no circumstances exceed the amount insured under this insurance in respect of the Vessel.

15   New for old

Claims payable without deduction new for old.

16   Bottom treatment

In no case shall a claim be allowed in respect of scraping gritblasting and/or other surface preparation or painting of the Vessel's bottom except that

16.1   gritblasting and/or other surface preparation of new bottom plates ashore and supplying and applying any "shop" primer thereto,

16.2   gritblasting and/or other surface preparation of:
the butts or area of plating immediately adjacent to any renewed or refitted plating damaged during the course of welding and/or repairs,
areas of plating damaged during the course of fairing, either in place or ashore,

16.3   supplying and applying the first coat of primer/anti-corrosive to those particular areas mentioned in 16.1 and 16.2 above,

shall be allowed as part of the reasonable cost of repairs in respect of bottom plating damaged by an insured peril.

17   Wages and maintenance

No claim shall be allowed, other than in general average, for wages and maintenance of the Master, Officers and Crew, or any member thereof, except when incurred solely for the necessary removal of the Vessel, with the agreement of the Underwriters, from one port to another for the repair of damage covered by the Underwriters, or for trial trips for such repairs, and then only for such wages and maintenance as are incurred whilst the Vessel is under way.

18   Agency commission

In no case shall any sum be allowed under this insurance either by way of remuneration of the Assured for time and trouble taken to obtain and supply information or documents or in respect of the commission or charges of any manager, agent, managing or agency company or the like, appointed by or on behalf of the Assured to perform such services.

19   Unrepaired damage

19.1   The measure of indemnity in respect of claims for unrepaired damage shall be the reasonable depreciation in the market value of the Vessel at the time this insurance terminates arising from such unrepaired damage, but not exceeding the reasonable cost of repairs,

19.2   In no case shall the Underwriters be liable for unrepaired damage in the event of a subsequent total loss (whether or not covered under this insurance) sustained during the period covered by this insurance or any extension thereof,

19.3   The Underwriters shall not be liable in respect of unrepaired damage for more than the insured value at the time this insurance terminates.

20   Constructive total loss

20.1   In ascertaining whether the Vessel is a constructive total loss, the insured value shall be taken as the repaired value and nothing in respect of the damaged or break-up value of the Vessel or wreck shall be taken into account.

20.2   No claim for constructive total loss based upon the cost of recovery and/or repair of the Vessel shall be recoverable hereunder unless such cost would exceed the insured value. In making this determination only the cost relating to a single accident or sequence of damages arising from the same accident shall be taken into account.

21   Freight waiver

In the event of total or constructive total loss no claim to be made by the Underwriters for freight whether notice of abandonment has been given or not.

22   Disbursements warranty

22.1   Additional insurances as follows are permitted

22.1.1   *Disbursements, Managers' Commissions, Profits or Excess or Increased Value of Hull and Machinery.* A sum not exceeding 25% of the value stated herein.

22.1.2   *Freight, Chartered Freight or Anticipated Freight, insured for time.* A sum not exceeding 25% of the value as stated herein less any sum insured, however described, under 22.1.1.

22.1.3 *Freight or Hire, under contracts for voyage.* A sum not exceeding the gross freight or hire for the current cargo passage and next succeeding cargo passage (such insurance to include, if required, a preliminary and an intermediate ballast passage) plus the charges of insurance. In the case of a voyage charter where payment is made on a time basis, the sum permitted for insurance shall be calculated on the estimated duration of the voyage, subject to the limitation of two cargo passages as laid down herein. Any sum insured under 22.1.2 to be taken into account and only the excess thereof may be insured, which excess shall be reduced as the freight or hire is advanced or earned by the gross amount so advanced or earned.

22.1.4 *Anticipated Freight if the Vessel sails in ballast and not under Charter.* A sum not exceeding the anticipated gross freight on next cargo passage, such sum to be reasonably estimated on the basis of the current rate of freight at time of insurance plus the charges of insurance. Any sum insured under 22.1.2 to be taken into account and only the excess thereof may be insured.

22.1.5 *Time Charter Hire or Charter Hire for Series of Voyages.* A sum not exceeding 50% of the gross hire which is to be earned under the charter in a period not exceeding 18 months. Any sum insured under 22.1.2 to be taken into account and only the excess thereof may be insured, which excess shall be reduced as the hire is advanced or earned under the charter by 50% of the gross amount so advanced or earned but the sum insured need not be reduced while the total of the sums insured under 22.1.2 and 22.1.5 does not exceed 50% of the gross hire still to be earned under the charter. An insurance under this Section may begin on the signing of the charter.

22.1.6 *Premiums.* A sum not exceeding the actual premiums of all interests insured for a period not exceeding 12 months (excluding premiums insured under the foregoing sections but including, if required, the premium or estimated calls on any Club or War etc. Risk insurance) reducing pro rata monthly.

22.1.7 *Returns of Premium.* A sum not exceeding the actual returns which are allowable under any insurance but which would not be recoverable thereunder in the event of a total loss of the Vessel whether by insured perils or otherwise.

22.1.8 *Insurance irrespective of amount against:*
Any risks excluded by Clauses 6, 24, 25, 26 and 27.

22.2 Warranted that no insurance on any interests enumerated in the foregoing 22.1.1 to 22.1.7 in excess of the amounts permitted therein and no other insurance which includes total loss of the Vessel P.P.I., F.I.A., or subject to any other like term, is or shall be effected to operate during the currency of this insurance by or for account of the Assured, Owners, Managers or Mortgagees. Provided always that a breach of this warranty shall not afford the Underwriters any defence to a claim by a Mortgagee who has accepted this insurance without knowledge of such breach.

23 Returns for cancellation

To return pro rata monthly net for each uncommenced month if this insurance be cancelled either by agreement or by the operation of Clause 3 provided that a total loss of the Vessel, whether by insured perils or otherwise, has not occurred during the period of this insurance or any extension thereof.

The following clauses shall be paramount and shall override anything contained in this insurance inconsistent therewith.

24 War exclusion

In no case shall this insurance cover loss damage liability or expense caused by

24.1   war civil war revolution rebellion insurrection, or civil strife arising therefrom, or any hostile act by or against a belligerent power

24.2   capture seizure arrest restraint or detainment (barratry and piracy excepted), and the consequences thereof or any attempt thereat

24.3   derelict mines torpedoes bombs or other derelict weapons of war.

25 Strikes exclusion

In no case shall this insurance cover loss damage liability or expense caused by

25.1   strikers, locked-out workmen, or persons taking part in labour disturbances, riots or civil commotions

25.2   any terrorist or any person acting from a political motive.

26 Malicious acts exclusion

In no case shall this insurance cover loss damage liability or expense arising from

26.1   the detonation of an explosive

26.2   any weapon of war

and caused by any person acting maliciously or from a political motive.

27 Nuclear exclusion

In no case shall this insurance cover loss damage liability or expense arising from any weapon of war employing atomic or nuclear fission and/or fusion or other like reaction or radioactive force or matter.

Institute Time Clauses Hulls—Restricted Perils

1/11/95—(FOR USE ONLY WITH THE NEW MARINE POLICY FORM)

This insurance is subject to English law and practice

1 Navigation

1.1 The Vessel is covered subject to the provisions of this insurance at all times and has leave to sail or navigate with or without pilots, to go on trial trips and to assist and tow vessels or craft in distress, but it is warranted that the Vessel shall not be towed, except as is customary or to the first safe port or place when in need of assistance, or undertake towage or salvage services under a contract previously arranged by the Assured and/or Owners and/or Managers and/or Charterers. This Clause 1.1 shall not exclude customary towage in connection with loading and discharging.

1.2 This insurance shall not be prejudiced by reason of the Assured entering into any contract with pilots or for customary towage which limits or exempts the liability of the pilots and/or tugs and/or towboats and/or their owners when the Assured or their agents accept or are compelled to accept such contracts in accordance with established local law or practice.

1.3 The practice of engaging helicopters for the transportation of personnel, supplies and equipment to and/or from the Vessel shall not prejudice this insurance.

1.4 In the event of the Vessel being employed in trading operations which entail cargo loading or discharging at sea from or into another vessel (not being a harbour or inshore craft) no claim shall be recoverable under this insurance for loss of or damage to the Vessel or liability to any other vessel arising from such loading or discharging operations, including whilst approaching, lying alongside and leaving, unless previous notice that the Vessel is to be employed in such operations has been given to the Underwriters and any amended terms of cover and any additional premium required by them have been agreed.

1.5 In the event of the Vessel sailing (with or without cargo) with an intention of being (a) broken up, or (b) sold for breaking up, any claim for loss of or damage to the Vessel occurring subsequent to such sailing shall be limited to the market value of the Vessel as scrap at the time when the loss or damage is sustained, unless previous notice has been given to the Underwriters and

216

any amendments to the terms of cover, insured value and premium required by them have been agreed. Nothing in this Clause 1.5 shall affect claims under Clauses 8 and/or 10.

2   Continuation

Should the Vessel at the expiration of this insurance be at sea or in distress or missing, she shall, provided notice be given to the Underwriters prior to the expiration of this insurance, be held covered until arrival at the next port in good safety, or if in port and in distress until the Vessel is made safe, at a pro rata monthly premium.

3   Breach of warranty

Held covered in case of any breach of warranty as to cargo, trade, locality, towage, salvage services or date of sailing, provided notice be given to the Underwriters immediately after receipt of advices and any amended terms of cover and any additional premium required by them be agreed.

4   Classification

4.1	It is the duty of the Assured, Owners and Managers at the inception of and throughout the period of this insurance to ensure that
4.1.1	the Vessel is classed with a Classification Society agreed by the Underwriters and that her class within that Society is maintained,
4.1.2	any recommendations requirements or restrictions imposed by the Vessel's Classification Society which relate to the Vessel's seaworthiness or to her maintenance in a seaworthy condition are complied with by the dates required by that Society.
4.2	In the event of any breach of the duties set out in Clause 4.1 above, unless the Underwriters agree to the contrary in writing, they will be discharged from liability under this insurance as from the date of the breach provided that if the Vessel is at sea at such date the Underwriters' discharge from liability is deferred until arrival at her next port.
4.3	Any incident condition or damage in respect of which the Vessel's Classification Society might make recommendations as to repairs or other action to be taken by the Assured, Owners or Managers must be promptly reported to the Classification Society.
4.4	Should the Underwriters wish to approach the Classification Society directly for information and/or documents, the Assured will provide the necessary authorisation.

5   Termination

This Clause 5 shall prevail notwithstanding any provision whether written typed or printed in this insurance inconsistent therewith.

Unless the Underwriters agree to the contrary in writing, this insurance shall terminate automatically at the time of

5.1	change of the Classification Society of the Vessel, or change, suspension, discontinuance, withdrawal or expiry of her Class therein, or any of the Classification Society's periodic surveys becoming overdue unless an extension of time for such survey be agreed by the Classification Society, provided

that if the Vessel is at sea such automatic termination shall be deferred until arrival at her next port. However where such change, suspension, discontinuance or withdrawal of her Class or where a periodic survey becoming overdue has resulted from loss or damage covered by Clause 6 of this insurance or which would be covered by an insurance of the Vessel subject to current Institute War and Strikes Clauses Hulls—Time such automatic termination shall only operate should the Vessel sail from her next port without the prior approval of the Classification Society or in the case of a periodic survey becoming overdue without the Classification Society having agreed an extension of time for such survey,

5.2   any change, voluntary or otherwise, in the ownership or flag, transfer to new management, or charter on a bareboat basis, or requisition for title or use of the Vessel, provided that, if the Vessel has cargo on board and has already sailed from her loading port or is at sea in ballast, such automatic termination shall if required be deferred, whilst the Vessel continues her planned voyage, until arrival at final port of discharge if with cargo or at port of destination if in ballast. However, in the event of requisition for title or use without the prior execution of a written agreement by the Assured, such automatic termination shall occur fifteen days after such requisition whether the Vessel is at sea or in port.

A pro rata daily net return of premium shall be made provided that a total loss of the Vessel, whether by insured perils or otherwise, has not occurred during the period covered by this insurance or any extension thereof.

6   Perils

6.1   This insurance covers loss of or damage to the subject-matter insured caused by

6.1.1   perils of the seas rivers lakes or other navigable waters

6.1.2   fire explosion

6.1.3   violent theft by persons from outside the Vessel

6.1.4   jettison

6.1.5   piracy

6.1.6   contact with land conveyance, dock or harbour equipment or installation

6.1.7   earthquake volcanic eruption or lightning

6.1.8   accidents in loading discharging or shifting cargo or fuel.

6.2   This insurance covers loss of or damage to the subject-matter insured caused by

6.2.1   any latent defect in the machinery or hull

6.2.2   negligence of Pilots provided such Pilots are not a Master, Officer or Member of the Crew of the Vessel

6.2.3   negligence of repairers or charterers provided such repairers or charterers are not an Assured hereunder

6.2.4   contact with aircraft, helicopters or similar objects, or objects falling therefrom provided that such loss or damage has not resulted from want of due diligence by the Assured, Owners, Managers or Superintendents or any of their onshore management.

6.3   Master Officers Crew or Pilots not to be considered Owners within the meaning of this Clause 6 should they hold shares in the Vessel.

7   Pollution hazard

This insurance covers loss of or damage to the Vessel caused by any governmental authority acting under the powers vested in it to prevent or mitigate a pollution hazard or damage to the environment, or threat thereof, resulting directly from damage to the Vessel for which the Underwriters are liable under this insurance, provided that such act of governmental authority has not resulted from want of due diligence by the Assured, Owners, or Managers to prevent or mitigate such hazard or damage, or threat thereof, Master, Officers, Crew or Pilots not to be considered Owners within the meaning of this Clause 7 should they hold shares in the Vessel.

8   3/4ths collision liability

8.1	The Underwriters agree to indemnify the Assured for three-fourths of any sum or sums paid by the Assured to any other person or persons by reason of the Assured becoming legally liable by way of damages for
8.1.1	loss of or damage to any other vessel or property on any other vessel
8.1.2	delay to or loss of use of any such other vessel or property thereon
8.1.3	general average of, salvage of, or salvage under contract of, any such other vessel or property thereon,
	where such payment by the Assured is in consequence of the Vessel hereby insured coming into collision with any other vessel.
8.2	The indemnity provided by this Clause 8 shall be in addition to the indemnity provided by the other terms and conditions of this insurance and shall be subject to the following provisions:
8.2.1	where the insured Vessel is in collision with another vessel and both vessels are to blame then, unless the liability of one or both vessels becomes limited by law, the indemnity under this Clause 8 shall be calculated on the principle of cross-liabilities as if the respective Owners had been compelled to pay to each other such proportion of each other's damages as may have been properly allowed in ascertaining the balance or sum payable by or to the Assured in consequence of the collision,
8.2.2	in no case shall the Underwriters' total liability under Clauses 8.1 and 8.2 exceed their proportionate part of three-fourths of the insured value of the Vessel hereby insured in respect of any one collision.
8.3	The Underwriters will also pay three-fourths of the legal costs incurred by the Assured or which the Assured may be compelled to pay in contesting liability or taking proceedings to limit liability, with the prior written consent of the Underwriters.

EXCLUSIONS

8.4	Provided always that this Clause 8 shall in no case extend to any sum which the Assured shall pay for or in respect of
8.4.1	removal or disposal of obstructions, wrecks, cargoes or any other thing whatsoever
8.4.2	any real or personal property or thing whatsoever except other vessels or property on other vessels
8.4.3	the cargo or other property on, or the engagements of, the insured Vessel
8.4.4	loss of life, personal injury or illness

8.4.5   pollution or contamination, or threat thereof, of any real or personal property or thing whatsoever (except other vessels with which the insured Vessel is in collision or property on such other vessels) or damage to the environment, or threat thereof, save that this exclusion shall not extend to any sum which the Assured shall pay for or in respect of salvage remuneration in which the skill and efforts of the salvors in preventing or minimising damage to the environment as is referred to in Article 13 paragraph 1(b) of the International Convention on Salvage, 1989 have been taken into account.

9   Sistership

Should the Vessel hereby insured come into collision with or receive salvage services from another vessel belonging wholly or in part to the same Owners or under the same management, the Assured shall have the same rights under this insurance as they would have were the other vessel entirely the property of Owners not interested in the Vessel hereby insured; but in such cases the liability for the collision or the amount payable for the services rendered shall be referred to a sole arbitrator to be agreed upon between the Underwriters and the Assured.

10   General average and salvage

10.1   This insurance covers the Vessel's proportion of salvage, salvage charges and/or general average, reduced in respect of any under-insurance, but in case of general average sacrifice of the Vessel the Assured may recover in respect of the whole loss without first enforcing their right of contribution from other parties.

10.2   Adjustment to be according to the law and practice obtaining at the place where the adventure ends, as if the contract of affreightment contained no special terms upon the subject; but where the contract of affreightment so provides the adjustment shall be according to the York-Antwerp Rules.

10.3   When the Vessel sails in ballast, not under charter, the provisions of the York-Antwerp Rules, 1994 (excluding Rules XI(d), XX and XXI) shall be applicable, and the voyage for this purpose shall be deemed to continue from the port or place of departure until the arrival of the Vessel at the first port or place thereafter other than a port or place of refuge or a port or place of call for bunkering only. If at any such intermediate port or place there is an abandonment of the adventure originally contemplated the voyage shall thereupon be deemed to be terminated.

10.4   No claim under this Clause 10 shall in any case be allowed where the loss was not incurred to avoid or in connection with the avoidance of a peril insured against.

10.5   No claim under this Clause 10 shall in any case be allowed for or in respect of

10.5.1   special compensation payable to a salvor under Article 14 of the International Convention on Salvage, 1989 or under any other provision in any statute, rule or contract which is similar in substance

10.5.2   expenses or liabilities incurred in respect of damage to the environment, or the threat of such damage, or as a consequence of the escape or release of pollutant substances from the Vessel, or the threat of such escape or release.

10.6 Clause 10.5 shall not however exclude any sum which the Assured shall pay to salvors for or in respect of salvage remuneration in which the skill and efforts of the salvors in preventing or minimising damage to the environment as is referred to in Article 13 paragraph 1(b) of the International Convention on Salvage, 1989 have been taken into account.

11 Duty of assured (Sue and Labour)

11.1 In case of any loss or misfortune it is the duty of the Assured and their servants and agents to take such measures as may be reasonable for the purpose of averting or minimising a loss which would be recoverable under this insurance.

11.2 Subject to the provisions below and to Clause 12 the Underwriters will contribute to charges properly and reasonably incurred by the Assured their servants or agents for such measures. General average, salvage charges (except as provided for in Clause 11.5), special compensation and expenses as referred to in Clause 10.5 and collision defence or attack costs are not recoverable under this Clause 11.

11.3 Measures taken by the Assured or the Underwriters with the object of saving, protecting or recovering the subject-matter insured shall not be considered as a waiver or acceptance of abandonment or otherwise prejudice the rights of either party.

11.4 When expenses are incurred pursuant to this Clause 11 the liability under this insurance shall not exceed the proportion of such expenses that the amount insured hereunder bears to the value of the Vessel as stated herein, or to the sound value of the Vessel at the time of the occurrence giving rise to the expenditure if the sound value exceeds that value. Where the Underwriters have admitted a claim for total loss and property insured by this insurance is saved, the foregoing provisions shall not apply unless the expenses of suing and labouring exceed the value of such property saved and then shall apply only to the amount of the expenses which is in excess of such value.

11.5 When a claim for total loss of the Vessel is admitted under this insurance and expenses have been reasonably incurred in saving or attempting to save the Vessel and other property and there are no proceeds, or the expenses exceed the proceeds, then this insurance shall bear its pro rata share of such proportion of the expenses, or of the expenses in excess of the proceeds, as the case may be, as may reasonably be regarded as having been incurred in respect of the Vessel, excluding all special compensation and expenses as referred to in Clause 10.5; but if the Vessel be insured for less than its sound value at the time of the occurrence giving rise to the expenditure, the amount recoverable under this clause shall be reduced in proportion to the under-insurance.

11.6 The sum recoverable under this Clause 11 shall be in addition to the loss otherwise recoverable under this insurance but shall in no circumstances exceed the amount insured under this insurance in respect of the Vessel.

12 Deductible

12.1 No claim arising from a peril insured against shall be payable under this insurance unless the aggregate of all such claims arising out of each separate accident or occurrence (including claims under Clauses 8, 10 and 11) exceeds the deductible amount agreed in which case this sum shall be deducted. Nevertheless the expense of sighting the bottom after stranding, if reasonably incurred specially for that purpose, shall be paid even if no damage be found. This Clause 12.1 shall not apply to a claim for total or constructive total loss of the Vessel or, in the event of such a claim, to any associated claim under Clause 11 arising from the same accident or occurrence.

12.2   Claims for damage by heavy weather occurring during a single sea passage between two successive ports shall be treated as being due to one accident. In the case of such heavy weather extending over a period not wholly covered by this insurance the deductible to be applied to the claim recoverable hereunder shall be the proportion of the above deductible that the number of days of such heavy weather falling within the period of this insurance bears to the number of days of heavy weather during the single sea passage. The expression "heavy weather" in this Clause 12.2 shall be deemed to include contact with floating ice.

12.3   Excluding any interest comprised therein, recoveries against any claim which is subject to the above deductible shall be credited to the Underwriters in full to the extent of the sum by which the aggregate of the claim unreduced by any recoveries exceeds the above deductible.

12.4   Interest comprised in recoveries shall be apportioned between the Assured and the Underwriters, taking into account the sums paid by the Underwriters and the dates when such payments were made, notwithstanding that by the addition of interest the Underwriters may receive a larger sum than they have paid.

13 Notice of claim and tenders

13.1   In the event of accident whereby loss or damage may result in a claim under this insurance, notice must be given to the Underwriters promptly after the date on which the Assured, Owners or Managers become or should have become aware of the loss or damage and prior to survey so that a surveyor may be appointed if the Underwriters so desire.

If notice is not given to the Underwriters within twelve months of that date unless Underwriters agree to the contrary in writing, the Underwriters will be automatically discharged from liability for any claim under this insurance in respect of or arising out of such accident or the loss or damage.

13.2   The Underwriters shall be entitled to decide the port to which the Vessel shall proceed for docking or repair (the actual additional expense of the voyage arising from compliance with the Underwriters' requirements being refunded to the Assured) and shall have a right of veto concerning a place of repair or a repairing firm.

13.3   The Underwriters may also take tenders or may require further tenders to be taken for the repair of the Vessel. Where such a tender has been taken and a tender is accepted with the approval of the Underwriters, an allowance shall be made at the rate of 30% per annum on the insured value for time lost between the despatch of the invitations to tender required by the Underwriters and the acceptance of a tender to the extent that such time is lost solely as the result of tenders having been taken and provided that the tender is accepted without delay after receipt of the Underwriters' approval.

Due credit shall be given against the allowance as above for any amounts recovered in respect of fuel and stores and wages and maintenance of the Master Officers and Crew or any member thereof, including amounts allowed in general average, and for any amounts recovered from third parties in respect of damages for detention and/or loss of profit and/or running expenses, for the period covered by the tender allowance or any part thereof.

Where a part of the cost of the repair of damage other than a fixed deductible is not recoverable from the Underwriters the allowance shall be reduced by a similar proportion.

13.4   In the event of failure by the Assured to comply with the conditions of Clauses 13.2 and/or 13.3 a deduction of 15% shall be made from the amount of the ascertained claim.

14 New for old

Claims payable without deduction new for old.

15 Bottom treatment

In no case shall a claim be allowed in respect of scraping gritblasting and/or other surface preparation or painting of the Vessel's bottom except that

15.1   gritblasting and/or other surface preparation of new bottom plates ashore and supplying and applying any "shop" primer thereto,

15.2   gritblasting and/or other surface preparation of:
the butts or area of plating immediately adjacent to any renewed or refitted plating damaged during the course of welding and/or repairs,
areas of plating damaged during the course of fairing, either in place or ashore,

15.3   supplying and applying the first coat of primer/anti-corrosive to those particular areas mentioned in 15.1 and 15.2 above,

shall be allowed as part of the reasonable cost of repairs in respect of bottom plating damaged by an insured peril.

16 Wages and maintenance

No claim shall be allowed, other than in general average, for wages and maintenance of the Master, Officers and Crew or any member thereof, except when incurred solely for the necessary removal of the Vessel from one port to another for the repair of damage covered by the Underwriters, or for trial trips for such repairs, and then only for such wages and maintenance as are incurred whilst the Vessel is under way.

17 Agency commission

In no case shall any sum be allowed under this insurance either by way of remuneration of the Assured for time and trouble taken to obtain and supply information or documents or in respect of the commission or charges of any manager, agent, managing or agency company or the like, appointed by or on behalf of the Assured to perform such services.

18 Unrepaired damage

18.1   The measure of indemnity in respect of claims for unrepaired damage shall be the reasonable depreciation in the market value of the Vessel at the time

223

	this insurance terminates arising from such unrepaired damage, but not exceeding the reasonable cost of repairs.
18.2	In no case shall the Underwriters be liable for unrepaired damage in the event of a subsequent total loss (whether or not covered under this insurance) sustained during the period covered by this insurance or any extension thereof.
18.3	The Underwriters shall not be liable in respect of unrepaired damage for more than the insured value at the time this insurance terminates.

19 Constructive total loss

19.1	In ascertaining whether the Vessel is a constructive total loss, the insured value shall be taken as the repaired value and nothing in respect of the damaged or break-up value of the Vessel or wreck shall be taken into account.
19.2	No claim for constructive total loss based upon the cost of recovery and/or repair of the Vessel shall be recoverable hereunder unless such cost would exceed the insured value. In making this determination only the cost relating to a single accident or sequence of damages arising from the same accident shall be taken into account.

20 Freight waiver

In the event of total or constructive total loss no claim to be made by the Underwriters for freight whether notice of abandonment has been given or not.

21 Assignment

No assignment of or interest in this insurance or in any moneys which may be or become payable thereunder is to be binding on or recognised by the Underwriters unless a dated notice of such assignment or interest signed by the Assured, and by the assignor in the case of subsequent assignment, is endorsed on the Policy and the Policy with such endorsement is produced before payment of any claim or return of premium thereunder.

22 Disbursements warranty

22.1	Additional insurances as follows are permitted:
22.1.1	*Disbursements, Managers' Commissions, Profits or Excess or Increased Value of Hull and Machinery.* A sum not exceeding 25% of the value stated herein.
22.1.2	*Freight, Chartered Freight or Anticipated Freight, insured for time.* A sum not exceeding 25% of the value as stated herein less any sum insured, however described, under 22.1.1.
22.1.3	*Freight or Hire, under contracts for voyage.* A sum not exceeding the gross freight or hire for the current cargo passage and next succeeding cargo passage (such insurance to include, if required, a preliminary and an intermediate ballast passage) plus the charges of insurance. In the case of a voyage charter where payment is made on a time basis, the sum permitted for insurance shall be calculated on the estimated duration of the voyage, subject to the limitation of two cargo passages as laid down herein. Any sum insured under 22.1.2 to be taken into account and only

the excess thereof may be insured, which excess shall be reduced as the freight or hire is advanced or earned by the gross amount so advanced or earned.

22.1.4   *Anticipated Freight if the Vessel sails in ballast and not under Charter.* A sum not exceeding the anticipated gross freight on next cargo passage, such sum to be reasonably estimated on the basis of the current rate of freight at time of insurance plus the charges of insurance. Any sum insured under 22.1.2 to be taken into account and only the excess thereof may be insured.

22.1.5   *Time Charter Hire or Charter Hire for Series of Voyages.* A sum not exceeding 50% of the gross hire which is to be earned under the charter in a period not exceeding 18 months. Any sum insured under 22.1.2 to be taken into account and only the excess thereof may be insured, which excess shall be reduced as the hire is advanced or earned under the charter by 50% of the gross amount so advanced or earned but the sum insured need not be reduced while the total of the sums insured under 22.1.2 and 22.1.5 does not exceed 50% of the gross hire still to be earned under the charter. An insurance under this Section may begin on the signing of the charter.

22.1.6   *Premiums.* A sum not exceeding the actual premiums of all interests insured for a period not exceeding 12 months (excluding premiums insured under the foregoing sections but including, if required, the premium or estimated calls on any Club or War etc. Risk insurance) reducing pro rata monthly.

22.1.7   *Returns of Premium.* A sum not exceeding the actual returns which are allowable under any insurance but which would not be recoverable thereunder in the event of a total loss of the Vessel whether by insured perils or otherwise.

22.1.8   *Insurance irrespective of amount against:*
Any risks excluded by Clauses 24, 25, 26 and 27 below.

22.2   Warranted that no insurance on any interests enumerated in the foregoing 22.1.1 to 22.1.7 in excess of the amounts permitted therein and no other insurance which includes total loss of the Vessel P.P.I., F.I.A., or subject to any other like term, is or shall be effected to operate during the currency of this insurance by or for account of the Assured, Owners, Managers or Mortgagees. Provided always that a breach of this warranty shall not afford the Underwriters any defence to a claim by a Mortgagee who has accepted this insurance without knowledge of such breach.

23   Returns for lay-up and cancellation

23.1   To return as follows:

23.1.1   pro rata monthly net for each uncommenced month if this insurance be cancelled by agreement,

23.1.2   for each period of 30 consecutive days the Vessel may be laid up in a port or in a lay-up area provided such port or lay-up area is approved by the Underwriters

(a) .... per cent net not under repair

(b) .... per cent net under repair.

23.1.3   The Vessel shall not be considered to be under repair when work is undertaken in respect of ordinary wear and tear of the Vessel and/or following recommendations in the Vessel's Classification Society survey, but any repairs following loss of or damage to the Vessel or involving structural alterations, whether covered by this insurance or otherwise shall be considered as under repair.

23.1.4 If the Vessel is under repair during part only of a period for which a return is claimable, the return shall be calculated pro rata to the number of days under 23.1.2(a) and (b) respectively.

23.2 PROVIDED ALWAYS THAT

23.2.1 a total loss of the Vessel, whether by insured perils or otherwise, has not occurred during the period covered by this insurance or any extension thereof

23.2.2 in no case shall a return be allowed when the Vessel is lying in exposed or unprotected waters, or in a port or lay-up area not approved by the Underwriters

23.2.3 loading or discharging operations or the presence of cargo on board shall not debar returns but no return shall be allowed for any period during which the Vessel is being used for the storage of cargo or for lightering purposes

23.2.4 in the event of any amendment of the annual rate, the above rates of return shall be adjusted accordingly

23.2.5 in the event of any return recoverable under this Clause 23 being based on 30 consecutive days which fall on successive insurances effected for the same Assured, this insurance shall only be liable for an amount calculated at pro rata of the period rates 23.1.2(a) and/or (b) above for the number of days which come within the period of this insurance and to which a return is actually applicable. Such overlapping period shall run, at the option of the Assured, either from the first day on which the Vessel is laid up or the first day of a period of 30 consecutive days as provided under 23.1.2(a) or (b) above.

The following clauses shall be paramount and shall override anything contained in this insurance inconsistent therewith.

24 War exclusion

In no case shall this insurance cover loss damage liability or expense caused by

24.1 war civil war revolution rebellion insurrection, or civil strife arising therefrom, or any hostile act by or against a belligerent power

24.2 capture seizure arrest restraint or detainment (piracy excepted), and the consequences thereof or any attempt thereat

24.3 derelict mines torpedoes bombs or other derelict weapons of war.

25 Strikes exclusion

In no case shall this insurance cover loss damage liability or expense caused by

25.1 strikers, locked-out workmen, or persons taking part in labour disturbances, riots or civil commotions

25.2 any terrorist or any person acting from a political motive.

26 Malicious acts exclusion

In no case shall this insurance cover loss damage liability or expense arising from

26.1 the detonation of an explosive

26.2   any weapon of war

and caused by any person acting maliciously or from a political motive.

27 Radioactive contamination exclusion clause

In no case shall this insurance cover loss damage liability or expense directly or indirectly caused by or contributed to by or arising from

27.1   ionising radiations from or contamination by radioactivity from any nuclear fuel or from any nuclear waste or from the combustion of nuclear fuel

27.2   the radioactive, toxic, explosive or other hazardous or contaminating properties of any nuclear installation, reactor or other nuclear assembly or nuclear component thereof

27.3   any weapon of war employing atomic or nuclear fission and/or fusion or other like reaction or radioactive force or matter.

Institute Time Clauses—Hulls—Total Loss, General Average and 3/4ths Collision Liability (Including Salvage, Salvage Charges and Sue and Labour)

1/11/95—(FOR USE ONLY WITH THE CURRENT MAR POLICY FORM)

This insurance is subject to English law and practice

1 Navigation

1.1 The Vessel is covered subject to the provisions of this insurance at all times and has leave to sail or navigate with or without pilots, to go on trial trips and to assist and tow vessels or craft in distress, but it is warranted that the Vessel shall not be towed, except as is customary or to the first safe port or place when in need of assistance, or undertake towage or salvage services under a contract previously arranged by the Assured and/or Owners and/or Managers and/or Charterers. This Clause 1.1 shall not exclude customary towage in connection with loading and discharging.

1.2 This insurance shall not be prejudiced by reason of the Assured entering into any contract with pilots or for customary towage which limits or exempts the liability of the pilots and/or tugs and/or towboats and/or their owners when the Assured or their agents accept or are compelled to accept such contracts in accordance with established local law or practice.

1.3 The practice of engaging helicopters for the transportation of personnel, supplies and equipment to and/or from the Vessel shall not prejudice this insurance.

1.4 In the event of the Vessel being employed in trading operations which entail cargo loading or discharging at sea from or into another vessel (not being a harbour or inshore craft) no claim shall be recoverable under this insurance for loss of or damage to the Vessel or liability to any other vessel arising from such loading or discharging operations, including whilst approaching, lying alongside and leaving, unless previous notice that the Vessel is to be employed in such operations has been given to the Underwriters and any amended terms of cover and any additional premium required by them have been agreed.

1.5 In the event of the Vessel sailing (with or without cargo) with an intention of being (a) broken up, or (b) sold for breaking up, any claim for loss of or damage to the Vessel occurring subsequent to such sailing shall be limited to the market value of the Vessel as scrap at the time when the loss or damage is sustained, unless previous notice has been given to the Underwriters and any amendments to the terms of cover, insured value and premium required by them have been agreed. Nothing in this Clause 1.5 shall affect claims under Clauses 8 and/or 10.

2   Continuation

Should the Vessel at the expiration of this insurance be at sea and in distress or missing, she shall, provided notice be given to the Underwriters prior to the expiration of this insurance, be held covered until arrival at the next port in good safety, or if in port and in distress until the Vessel is made safe, at a pro rata monthly premium.

3   Breach of Warranty

Held covered in case of any breach of warranty as to cargo, trade, locality, towage, salvage services or date of sailing, provided notice be given to the Underwriters immediately after receipt of advices and any amended terms of cover and any additional premium required by them be agreed.

4   Classification

4.1	It is the duty of the Assured, Owners and Managers at the inception of and throughout the period of this insurance to ensure that
4.1.1	the Vessel is classed with a Classification Society agreed by the Underwriters and that her class within that Society is maintained,
4.1.2	any recommendations requirements or restrictions imposed by the Vessel's Classification Society which relate to the Vessel's seaworthiness or to her maintenance in a seaworthy condition are complied with by the dates required by that Society.
4.2	In the event of any breach of the duties set out in Clause 4.1 above, unless the Underwriters agree to the contrary in writing, they will be discharged from liability under this insurance as from the date of the breach provided that if the Vessel is at sea at such date the Underwriters' discharge from liability is deferred until arrival at her next port.
4.3	Any incident condition or damage in respect of which the Vessel's Classification Society might make recommendations as to repairs or other action to be taken by the Assured, Owners or Managers must be promptly reported to the Classification Society.
4.4	Should the Underwriters wish to approach the Classification Society directly for information and/or documents, the Assured will provide the necessary authorization.

5   Termination

This Clause 5 shall prevail notwithstanding any provision whether written typed or printed in this insurance inconsistent therewith.

Unless the Underwriters agree to the contrary in writing, this insurance shall terminate automatically at the time of

5.1	change of the Classification Society of the Vessel, or change, suspension, discontinuance, withdrawal or expiry of her Class therein, or any of the Classification Society's periodic surveys becoming overdue unless an extension of time for such survey be agreed by the Classification Society, provided

that if the Vessel is at sea such automatic termination shall be deferred until arrival at her next port. However where such change, suspension, discontinuance or withdrawal of her Class or where a periodic survey becoming overdue has resulted from loss or damage covered by Clause 6 of this insurance or which would be covered by an insurance of the Vessel subject to current Institute Time Clauses—Hulls or Institute War and Strikes Clauses Hulls —Time such automatic termination shall only operate should the Vessel sail from her next port without the prior approval of the Classification Society or in the case of a periodic survey becoming overdue without the Classification Society having agreed an extension of time for such survey,

5.2   any change, voluntary or otherwise, in the ownership or flag, transfer to new management, or charter on a bareboat basis, or requisition for title or use of the Vessel, provided that, if the Vessel has cargo on board and has already sailed from her loading port or is at sea in ballast, such automatic termination shall if required be deferred, whilst the Vessel continues her planned voyage, until arrival at final port of discharge if with cargo or at port of destination if in ballast. However, in the event of requisition for title or use without the prior execution of a written agreement by the Assured, such automatic termination shall occur fifteen days after such requisition whether the Vessel is at sea or in port.

A pro rata daily net return of premium shall be made provided that a total loss of the Vessel, whether by insured perils or otherwise, has not occurred during the period covered by this insurance or any extension thereof.

6   Perils

6.1   This insurance covers total loss (actual or constructive) of the subject-matter insured caused by

6.1.1   perils of the seas rivers lakes or other navigable waters

6.1.2   fire, explosion

6.1.3   violent theft by persons from outside the Vessel

6.1.4   jettison

6.1.5   piracy

6.1.6   contact with land conveyance, dock or harbour equipment or installation

6.1.7   earthquake volcanic eruption or lightning

6.1.8   accidents in loading discharging or shifting cargo or fuel.

6.2   This insurance covers total loss (actual or constructive) of the subject-matter insured caused by

6.2.1   bursting of boilers breakage of shafts or any latent defect in the machinery or hull

6.2.2   negligence of Master Officers Crew or Pilots

6.2.3   negligence of repairers or charterers provided such repairers or charterers are not an Assured hereunder

6.2.4   barratry of Master Officers or Crew

6.2.5   contact with aircraft, helicopters or similar objects, or objects falling therefrom

provided that such loss or damage has not resulted from want of due diligence by the Assured, Owners or Managers or Superintendents or any of their onshore management.

6.3   Master Officers Crew or Pilots not to be considered Owners within the meaning of this Clause 6 should they hold shares in the Vessel.

7   Pollution Hazard

This insurance covers total loss (actual or constructive) of the Vessel caused by any governmental authority acting under the powers vested in it to prevent or mitigate a pollution hazard or damage to the environment, or threat thereof, resulting directly from damage to the Vessel for which the Underwriters are liable under this insurance, provided that such act of governmental authority has not resulted from want of due diligence by the Assured, the Owners, or Managers to prevent or mitigate such hazard or damage, or threat thereof. Master, Officers, Crew or Pilots not to be considered Owners within the meaning of this Clause 7 should they hold shares in the Vessel.

8   3/4ths Collision Liability

8.1   The Underwriters agree to indemnify the Assured for three-fourths of any sum or sums paid by the Assured to any other person or persons by reason of the Assured becoming legally liable by way of damages for

8.1.1   loss of or damage to any other vessel or property on any other vessel

8.1.2   delay to or loss of use of any such other vessel or property thereon

8.1.3   general average of, salvage of, or salvage under contract of, any such other vessel or property thereon,

where such payment by the Assured is in consequence of the Vessel hereby insured coming into collision with any other vessel.

8.2   The indemnity provided by this Clause 8 shall be in addition to the indemnity provided by the other terms and conditions of this insurance and shall be subject to the following provisions:

8.2.1   where the insured Vessel is in collision with another vessel and both vessels are to blame then, unless the liability of one or both vessels becomes limited by law, the indemnity under this Clause 8 shall be calculated on the principle of cross-liabilities as if the respective Owners had been compelled to pay to each other such proportion of each other's damages as may have been properly allowed in ascertaining the balance or sum payable by or to the Assured in consequence of the collision,

8.2.2   in no case shall the Underwriters' total liability under Clauses 8.1 and 8.2 exceed their proportionate part of three-fourths of the insured value of the Vessel hereby insured in respect of any one collision.

8.3   The Underwriters will also pay three-fourths of the legal costs incurred by the Assured or which the Assured may be compelled to pay in contesting liability or taking proceedings to limit liability, with the prior written consent of the Underwriters.

EXCLUSIONS

8.4   Provided always that this Clause 8 shall in no case extend to any sum which the Assured shall pay for or in respect of

8.4.1   removal or disposal of obstructions, wrecks, cargoes or any other thing whatsoever

8.4.2   any real or personal property or thing whatsoever except other vessels or property on other vessels

8.4.3   the cargo or other property on, or the engagements of, the insured Vessel

8.4.4   loss of life, personal injury or illness

8.4.5   pollution or contamination, or threat thereof, of any real or personal property or thing whatsoever (except other vessels with which the insured Vessel is in collision or property on such other vessels) or damage to the environment, or threat thereof, save that this exclusion shall not extend to any sum which the Assured shall pay for or in respect of salvage remuneration in which the skill and efforts of the salvors in preventing or minimising damage to the environment as is referred to in Article 13 paragraph 1(b) of the International Convention on Salvage, 1989 have been taken into account.

9   Sistership

Should the Vessel hereby insured come into collision with or receive salvage services from another vessel belonging wholly or in part to the same Owners or under the same management, the Assured shall have the same rights under this insurance as they would have were the other vessel entirely the property of Owners not interested in the Vessel hereby insured; but in such cases the liability for the collision or the amount payable for the services rendered shall be referred to a sole arbitrator to be agreed upon between the Underwriters and the Assured.

10   General Average and Salvage

10.1   This insurance covers the Vessel's proportion of salvage, salvage charges and/or general average, reduced in respect of any under-insurance.

10.2   **This insurance does not cover partial loss of and/or damage to the Vessel except for any proportion of general average loss or damage which may be recoverable under Clause 10.1 above.**

10.3   Adjustment to be according to the law and practice obtaining at the place where the adventure ends, as if the contract of affreightment contained no special terms upon the subject; but where the contract of affreightment so provides the adjustment shall be according to the York-Antwerp Rules.

10.4   When the Vessel sails in ballast, not under charter, the provisions of the York-Antwerp Rules, 1994 (excluding Rules XI(d), XX and XXI) shall be applicable, and the voyage for this purpose shall be deemed to continue from the port or place of departure until the arrival of the Vessel at the first port or place thereafter other than a port or place of refuge or a port or place of call for bunkering only. If at any such intermediate port or place there is an abandonment of the adventure originally contemplated the voyage shall thereupon be deemed to be terminated.

10.5   No claim under this Clause 10 shall in any case be allowed where the loss was not incurred to avoid or in connection with the avoidance of a peril insured against.

10.6   No claim under this Clause 10 shall in any case be allowed for or in respect of

10.6.1   special compensation payable to a salvor under Article 14 of the International Convention on Salvage, 1989 or under any other provision in any statute, rule, law or contract which is similar in substance

10.6.2   expenses or liabilities incurred in respect of damage to the environment, or the threat of such damage, or as a consequence of the escape or release of pollutant substances from the Vessel, or the threat of such escape or release.

10.7   Clause 10.6 shall not however exclude any sum which the Assured shall pay to salvors for or in respect of salvage remuneration in which the skill and efforts of the salvors in preventing or minimising damage to the environment as is referred to in Article 13 paragraph 1(b) of the International Convention on Salvage, 1989 have been taken into account.

11   Duty of Assured (Sue and Labour)

11.1   In case of any loss or misfortune it is the duty of the Assured and their servants and agents to take such measures as may be reasonable for the purpose of averting or minimising a loss which would be recoverable under this insurance.

11.2   Subject to the provisions below and to Clause 12 the Underwriters will contribute to charges properly and reasonably incurred by the Assured their servants or agents for such measures. General average, salvage charges (except as provided for in Clause 11.5), special compensation and expenses as referred to in Clause 10.6 and collision defence or attack costs are not recoverable under this Clause 11.

11.3   Measures taken by the Assured or the Underwriters with the object of saving, protecting or recovering the subject-matter insured shall not be considered as a waiver or acceptance of abandonment or otherwise prejudice the rights of either party.

11.4   When expenses are incurred pursuant to this Clause 11 the liability under this insurance shall not exceed the proportion of such expenses that the amount insured hereunder bears to the value of the Vessel as stated herein, or to the sound value of the Vessel at the time of the occurrence giving rise to the expenditure if the sound value exceeds that value. Where the Underwriters have admitted a claim for total loss and property insured by this insurance is saved, the foregoing provisions shall not apply unless the expenses of suing and labouring exceed the value of such property saved and then shall apply only to the amount of the expenses which is in excess of such value.

11.5   When a claim for total loss of the Vessel is admitted under this insurance and expenses have been reasonably incurred in saving or attempting to save the Vessel and other property and there are no proceeds, or the expenses exceed the proceeds, then this insurance shall bear its pro rata share of such proportion of the expenses, or of the expenses in excess of the proceeds, as the case may be, as may reasonably be regarded as having been incurred in respect of the Vessel, excluding all special compensation and expenses as referred to in Clause 10.6; but if the Vessel be insured for less than its sound value at the time of the occurrence giving rise to the expenditure, the amount recoverable under this clause shall be reduced in proportion to the under-insurance.

11.6   The sum recoverable under this Clause 11 shall be in addition to the loss otherwise recoverable under this insurance but shall in no circumstances exceed the amount insured under this insurance in respect of the Vessel.

12 Deductible

12.1   No claim arising from a peril insured against shall be payable under this insurance unless the aggregate of all such claims arising out of each separate accident or occurrence (including claims under Clauses 8, 10 and 11) exceeds the deductible amount agreed in which case this sum shall be deducted. This Clause 12.1 shall not apply to a claim for total or constructive total loss of the Vessel or, in the event of such a claim, to any associated claim under Clause 11 arising from the same accident or occurrence.

12.2   Excluding any interest comprised therein, recoveries against any claim which is subject to the above deductible shall be credited to the Underwriters in full to the extent of the sum by which the aggregate of the claim unreduced by any recoveries exceeds the above deductible.

12.3   Interest comprised in recoveries shall be apportioned between the Assured and the Underwriters, taking into account the sums paid by the Underwriters and the dates when such payments were made, notwithstanding that by the addition of interest the Underwriters may receive a larger sum than they have paid.

13 Notice of Claim

In the event of accident whereby loss or damage may result in a claim under this insurance, notice must be given to the Underwriters promptly after the date on which the Assured, Owners or Managers become or should have become aware of the loss or damage and prior to survey so that a surveyor may be appointed if the Underwriters so desire.

If notice is not given to the Underwriters within twelve months of that date unless the Underwriters agree to the contrary in writing, the Underwriters will be automatically discharged from liability for any claim under this insurance in respect of or arising out of such accident or the loss or damage.

14 New for Old

General average payable without deduction new for old.

15 Agency Commission

In no case shall any sum be allowed under this insurance either by way of remuneration of the Assured for time and trouble taken to obtain and supply information or documents or in respect of the commission or charges of any manager, agent, managing or agency company or the like, appointed by or on behalf of the Assured to perform such services.

16 Constructive Total Loss

16.1   In ascertaining whether the Vessel is a constructive total loss, the insured value shall be taken as the repaired value and nothing in respect of the damaged or break-up value of the Vessel or wreck shall be taken into account.

16.2   No claim or constructive total loss based upon the cost of recovery and/or repair of the Vessel shall be recoverable hereunder unless such cost would exceed the insured value. In making this determination, only the cost relating to a single accident or sequence of damages arising from the same accident shall be taken into account.

234

17 Freight Waiver

In the event of total or constructive total loss no claim to be made by the Underwriters for freight whether notice of abandonment has been given or not.

18 Assignment

No assignment of or interest in this insurance or in any moneys which may be or become payable thereunder is to be binding on or recognised by the Underwriters unless a dated notice of such assignment or interest signed by the Assured, and by the assignor in the case of subsequent assignment, is endorsed on the Policy and the Policy with such endorsement is produced before payment of any claim or return of premium thereunder.

19 Disbursements Warranty

19.1   Additional insurances as follows are permitted:

19.1.1   *Disbursements, Managers' Commissions, Profits or Excess or Increased Value of Hull and Machinery.* A sum not exceeding 25% of the value stated herein.

19.1.2   *Freight, Chartered Freight or Anticipated Freight, insured for time.* A sum not exceeding 25% of the value as stated herein less any sum insured, however described, under 19.1.1.

19.1.3   *Freight or Hire, under contracts for voyage.* A sum not exceeding the gross freight or hire for the current cargo passage and next succeeding cargo passage (such insurance to include, if required, a preliminary and an intermediate ballast passage) plus the charges of insurance. In the case of a voyage charter where payment is made on a time basis, the sum permitted for insurance shall be calculated on the estimated duration of the voyage, subject to the limitation of two cargo passages as laid down herein. Any sum insured under 19.1.2 to be taken into account and only the excess thereof may be insured, which excess shall be reduced as the freight or hire is advanced or earned by the gross amount so advanced or earned.

19.1.4   *Anticipated Freight if the Vessel sails in ballast and not under Charter.* A sum not exceeding the anticipated gross freight on next cargo passage, such sum to be reasonably estimated on the basis of the current rate of freight at time of insurance plus the charges of insurance. Any sum insured under 19.1.2 to be taken into account and only the excess thereof may be insured.

19.1.5   *Time Charter Hire or Charter Hire for Series of Voyages.* A sum not exceeding 50% of the gross hire which is to be earned under the charter in a period not exceeding 18 months. Any sum insured under 19.1.2 to be taken into account and only the excess thereof may be insured, which excess shall be reduced as the hire is advanced or earned under the charter by 50% of the gross amount so advanced or earned but the sum insured need not be reduced while the total of the sums insured under 19.1.2 and 19.1.5 does not exceed 50% of the gross hire still to be earned under the charter. An insurance under this Section may begin on the signing of the charter.

19.1.6   *Premiums.* A sum not exceeding the actual premiums of all interests insured for a period not exceeding 12 months (excluding premiums insured under the foregoing sections but including, if required, the

premium or estimated calls on any Club or War etc. Risk insurance) reducing pro rata monthly.

19.1.7 *Returns of Premium.* A sum not exceeding the actual returns which are allowable under any insurance but which would not be recoverable thereunder in the event of a total loss of the Vessel whether by insured perils or otherwise.

19.1.8 *Insurance irrespective of amount against:*
Any risks excluded by Clauses 21, 22, 23 and 23 below.

19.2 Warranted that no insurance on any interests enumerated in the foregoing 19.1.1 to 19.1.7 in excess of the amounts permitted therein and no other insurance which includes total loss of the Vessel P.P.I., F.I.A., or subject to any other like term, is or shall be effected to operate during the currency of this insurance by or for account of the Assured, Owners, Managers or Mortgagees. Provided always that a breach of this warranty shall not afford the Underwriters any defence to a claim by a Mortgagee who has accepted this insurance without knowledge of such breach.

20 Returns for Lay-up and Cancellation

20.1 To return as follows:

20.1.1 pro rata monthly net for each uncommenced month if this insurance be cancelled by agreement,

20.1.2 for each period of 30 consecutive days the Vessel may be laid up in a port or in a lay-up area provided such port or lay-up area is approved by the Underwriters

(a) . . . . per cent net not under repair.

(b) . . . . per cent net under repair.

20.1.3 The Vessel shall not be considered to be under repair when work is undertaken in respect of ordinary wear and tear of the Vessel and/or following recommendations in the Vessel's Classification Society survey, but any repairs following loss of or damage to the Vessel or involving structural alterations, whether covered by this insurance or otherwise shall be considered as under repair.

20.1.4 If the Vessel is under repair during part only of a period for which a return is claimable, the return shall be calculated pro rata to the number of days under 20.1.2(a) and (b) respectively.

20.2 PROVIDED ALWAYS THAT

20.2.1 a total loss of the Vessel, whether by insured perils or otherwise, has not occurred during the period covered by this insurance or any extension thereof

20.2.2 in no case shall a return be allowed when the Vessel is lying in exposed or unprotected waters, or in a port or lay-up area not approved by the Underwriters

20.2.3 loading or discharging operations or the presence of cargo on board shall not debar returns but no return shall be allowed for any period during which the Vessel is being used for the storage of cargo or for lightering purposes

20.2.4 in the event of any amendment of the annual rate, the above rates of return shall be adjusted accordingly

20.2.5 in the event of any return recoverable under this Clause 20 being based on 30 consecutive days which fall on successive insurances effected for the same Assured, this insurance shall only be liable for an amount calculated at pro rata of the period rates 20.1.2(a) and/or (b) above for the number of days which come within the period of this insurance and to which a return is actually applicable. Such overlapping period shall run, at the option of the Assured, either from the first day on which the Vessel is laid up or the first day of a period of 30 consecutive days as provided under 20.1.2(a) or (b) above.

The following clauses shall be paramount and shall override anything contained in this insurance inconsistent therewith.

21 War Exclusion

In no case shall this insurance cover loss damage liability or expense caused by

21.1	war civil war revolution rebellion insurrection, or civil strife arising therefrom, or any hostile act by or against a belligerent power
21.2	capture seizure arrest restraint or detainment (barratry and piracy excepted), and the consequences thereof or any attempt thereat
21.3	derelict mines torpedoes bombs or other derelict weapons of war.

22 Strikes Exclusion

In no case shall this insurance cover loss damage liability or expense caused by

22.1	strikers, locked-out workmen, or persons taking part in labour disturbances, riots or civil commotions
22.2	any terrorist or any person acting from a political motive.

23 Malicious Acts Exclusion

In no case shall this insurance cover loss damage liability or expense arising from

23.1	the detonation of an explosive
23.2	any weapon of war

and caused by any person acting maliciously or from a political motive.

24 Radioactive Contamination Exclusion Clause

In no case shall this insurance cover loss damage liability or expense directly or indirectly caused by or contributed to by or arising from

24.1	ionising radiations from or contamination by radioactivity from any nuclear fuel or from any nuclear waste or from the combustion of nuclear fuel
24.2	the radioactive, toxic, explosive or other hazardous or contaminating properties of any nuclear installation, reactor or other nuclear assembly or nuclear component thereof
24.3	any weapon of war employing atomic or nuclear fission and/or fusion or other like reaction or radioactive force or matter.

Institute Time Clauses—Hulls—Total Loss Only (Including Salvage, Salvage Charges and Sue and Labour)

1/11/95—(FOR USE ONLY WITH THE CURRENT MAR POLICY FORM)

This insurance is subject to English law and practice

1 Navigation

1.1   The Vessel is covered subject to the provisions of this insurance at all times and has leave to sail or navigate with or without pilots, to go on trial trips and to assist and tow vessels or craft in distress, but it is warranted that the Vessel shall not be towed, except as is customary or to the first safe port or place when in need of assistance, or undertake towage or salvage services under a contract previously arranged by the Assured and/or Owners and/or Managers and/or Charterers. This Clause 1.1 shall not exclude customary towage in connection with loading and discharging.

1.2   This insurance shall not be prejudiced by reason of the Assured entering into any contract with pilots or for customary towage which limits or exempts the liability of the pilots and/or tugs and/or towboats and/or their owners when the Assured or their agents accept or are compelled to accept such contracts in accordance with established local law or practice.

1.3   The practice of engaging helicopters for the transportation of personnel, supplies and equipment to and/or from the Vessel shall not prejudice this insurance.

1.4   In the event of the Vessel being employed in trading operations which entail cargo loading or discharging at sea from or into another vessel (not being a harbour or inshore craft) no claim shall be recoverable under this insurance for loss of or damage to the Vessel from such loading or discharging operations, including whilst approaching, lying alongside and leaving, unless previous notice that the Vessel is to be employed in such operations has been given to the Underwriters and any amended terms of cover and any additional premium required by them have been agreed.

1.5   In the event of the Vessel sailing (with or without cargo) with an intention of being (a) broken up, or (b) sold for breaking up, any claim for loss of or damage to the Vessel occurring subsequent to such sailing shall be limited to the market value of the Vessel as scrap at the time when the loss or damage is sustained, unless previous notice has been given to the Underwriters and any amendments to the terms of cover, insured value and premium required by them have been agreed. Nothing in this Clause 1.5 shall affect claims under Clause 8.

2 Continuation

Should the Vessel at the expiration of this insurance be at sea and in distress or missing, she shall, provided notice be given to the Underwriters prior to the expiration of this insurance, be held covered until arrival at the next port in good safety, or if in port and in distress until the Vessel is made safe, at a pro rata monthly premium.

3 Breach of warranty

Held covered in case of any breach of warranty as to cargo, trade, locality, towage, salvage services or date of sailing, provided notice be given to the Underwriters immediately after receipt of advices and any amended terms of cover and any additional premium required by them be agreed.

4 Classification

4.1	It is the duty of the Assured, Owners and Managers at the inception of and throughout the period of this insurance to ensure that
4.1.1	the Vessel is classed with a Classification Society agreed by the Underwriters and that her class within that Society is maintained,
4.1.2	any recommendations requirements or restrictions imposed by the Vessel's Classification Society which relate to the Vessel's seaworthiness or to her maintenance in a seaworthy condition are complied with by the dates required by that Society.
4.2	In the event of any breach of the duties set out in Clause 4.1 above, unless the Underwriters agree to the contrary in writing, they will be discharged from liability under this insurance as from the date of the breach provided that if the Vessel is at sea at such date the Underwriters' discharge from liability is deferred until arrival at her next port.
4.3	Any incident condition or damage in respect of which the Vessel's Classification Society might make recommendations as to repairs or other action to be taken by the Assured, Owners or Managers must be promptly reported to the Classification Society.
4.4	Should the Underwriters wish to approach the Classification Society directly for information and/or documents, the Assured will provide the necessary authorization.

5 Termination

This Clause 5 shall prevail notwithstanding any provision whether written typed or printed in this insurance inconsistent therewith.

Unless the Underwriters agree to the contrary in writing, this insurance shall terminate automatically at the time of

5.1	change of the Classification Society of the Vessel, or change, suspension, discontinuance, withdrawal or expiry of her Class therein, or any of the Classification Society's periodic surveys becoming overdue unless an extension of time for such survey be agreed by the Classification Society, provided that if the Vessel is at sea such automatic termination shall be deferred until

arrival at her next port. However where such change, suspension, discontinuance or withdrawal of her Class or where a periodic survey becoming overdue has resulted from loss or damage covered by Clause 6 of this insurance or which would be covered by an insurance of the Vessel subject to current Institute Time Clauses Hulls or Institute War and Strikes Clauses Hulls —Time such automatic termination shall only operate should the Vessel sail from her next port without the prior approval of the Classification Society or in the case of a periodic survey becoming overdue without the Classification Society having agreed an extension of time for such survey,

5.2 any change, voluntary of otherwise, in the ownership or flag, transfer to new management, or charter on a bareboat basis, or requisition for title or use of the Vessel, provided that, if the Vessel has cargo on board and has already sailed from her loading port or is at sea in ballast, such automatic termination shall if required be deferred, whilst the Vessel continues her planned voyage, until arrival at final port of discharge if with cargo or at port of destination if in ballast. However, in the event of requisition for title or use without the prior execution of a written agreement by the Assured, such automatic termination shall occur fifteen days after such requisition whether the Vessel is at sea or in port.

A pro rata daily net return of premium shall be made provided that a total loss of the Vessel, whether by insured perils or otherwise, has not occurred during the period covered by this insurance or any extension thereof.

6 Perils

6.1 This insurance covers total loss (actual or constructive) of the subject-matter insured caused by

6.1.1 perils of the seas rivers lakes or other navigable waters

6.1.2 fire, explosion

6.1.3 violent theft by persons from outside the Vessel

6.1.4 jettison

6.1.5 piracy

6.1.6 contact with land conveyance, dock or harbour equipment or installation

6.1.7 earthquake volcanic eruption or lightning

6.1.8 accidents in loading discharging or shifting cargo or fuel.

6.2 This insurance covers total loss (actual or constructive) of the subject-matter insured caused by

6.2.1 bursting of boilers breakage of shafts or any latent defect in the machinery or hull

6.2.2 negligence of Master Officers Crew or Pilots

6.2.3 negligence of repairers or charterers provided such repairers or charterers are not an Assured hereunder

6.2.4 barratry of Master Officers or Crew,

6.2.5 contact with aircraft, helicopters or similar objects, or objects falling therefrom

provided that such loss has not resulted from want of due diligence by the Assured, Owners, Managers or Superintendents or any of their onshore management.

6.3 Masters Officers Crew or Pilots not to be considered Owners within the meaning of this Clause 6 should they hold shares in the Vessel.

7 Pollution hazard

This insurance covers total loss (actual or constructive) of the Vessel caused by any governmental authority acting under the powers vested in it to prevent or mitigate a pollution hazard or damage to the environment, or threat thereof, resulting directly from damage to the Vessel caused by a peril covered by this insurance, provided that such act of governmental authority has not resulted from want of due diligence by the Assured, Owners or Managers to prevent or mitigate such hazard or damage, or threat thereof. Master Officers Crew or Pilots not to be considered Owners within the meaning of this Clause 7 should they hold shares in the Vessel.

8 Salvage

8.1   This insurance covers the Vessel's proportion of salvage and salvage charges, reduced in respect of any under-insurance.

8.2   No claim under this Clause 8 shall in any case be allowed where the loss was not incurred to avoid or in connection with the avoidance of a peril insured against.

8.3   No claim under this Clause 8 shall in any case be allowed for or in respect of

8.3.1   special compensation payable to a salvor under Article 14 of the International Convention on Salvage, 1989 or under any other provision in any statute, rule, law or contract which is similar in substance

8.3.2   expenses or liabilities incurred in respect of damage to the environment, or the threat of such damage, or as a consequence of the escape or release of pollutant substances from the Vessel, or the threat of such escape or release.

8.4   Clause 8.3 shall not however exclude any sum which the Assured shall pay to salvors for or in respect of salvage remuneration in which the skill and efforts of the salvors in preventing or minimising damage to the environment as is referred to in Article 13 paragraph 1(b) of the International Convention on Salvage, 1989 have been taken into account.

9 Duty of assured (Sue and Labour)

9.1   In case of any loss or misfortune it is the duty of the Assured and their servants and agents to take such measures as may be reasonable for the purpose of averting or minimising a loss which would be recoverable under this insurance.

9.2   Subject to the provisions below the Underwriters will contribute to charges properly and reasonably incurred by the Assured their servants or agents for such measures. General average, salvage charges (except as provided for in Clause 9.5), special compensation and expenses as referred to in Clause 8.3 and collision defence or attack costs are not recoverable under this Clause 9.

9.3   Measures taken by the Assured or the Underwriters with the object of saving, protecting or recovering the subject-matter insured shall not be considered as a waiver or acceptance of abandonment or otherwise prejudice the rights of either party.

9.4   When expenses are incurred pursuant to this Clause 9 the liability under this insurance shall not exceed the proportion of such expenses that the amount insured hereunder bears to the value of the Vessel as stated herein, or to the sound value of the Vessel at the time of the occurrence giving rise to the expenditure if the sound value exceeds that value. Where the Underwriters have admitted a claim for total loss and property insured by this insurance is saved, the foregoing provisions shall not apply unless the expenses of suing and labouring exceed the value of such property saved and then shall apply only to the amount of the expenses which is in excess of such value.

9.5   When a claim for total loss of the Vessel is admitted under this insurance and expenses have been reasonably incurred in saving or attempting to save the Vessel and other property and there are no proceeds, or the expenses exceed the proceeds, then this insurance shall bear its pro rata share of such proportion of the expenses, or of the expenses in excess of the proceeds, as the case may be, as may reasonably be regarded as having been incurred in respect of the Vessel, excluding all special compensation and expenses as referred to in Clause 8.3; but if the Vessel be insured for less than its sound value at the time of the occurrence giving rise to the expenditure, the amount recoverable under this clause shall be reduced in proportion to the under-insurance.

9.6   The sum recoverable under this Clause 9 shall be in addition to the loss otherwise recoverable under this insurance but shall in no circumstances exceed the amount insured under this insurance in respect of the Vessel.

10 Sistership

Should the Vessel hereby insured receive salvage services from another vessel belonging wholly or in part to the same Owners or under the same management, the Assured shall have the same rights under this insurance as they would have were the other vessel entirely the property of Owners not interested in the Vessel hereby insured; but in such cases the amount payable for the services rendered shall be referred to a sole arbitrator to be agreed upon between the Underwriters and the Assured.

11 Notice of claim

In the event of accident whereby loss or damage may result in a claim under this insurance, notice must be given to the Underwriters promptly after the date on which the Assured, Owners or Managers becomes or should have become aware of the loss or damage and prior to survey so that a surveyor may be appointed if the Underwriters so desire.

If notice is not given to the Underwriters within twelve months of that date unless the Underwriters agree to the contrary in writing, the Underwriters will be automatically discharged from liability for any claim under this insurance in respect of or arising out of such accident or the loss or damage.

12 Constructive total loss

12.1   In ascertaining whether the Vessel is a constructive total loss, the insured value shall be taken as the repaired value and nothing in respect of the damaged or break-up value of the Vessel or wreck shall be taken into account.

12.2   No claim for constructive total loss based upon the cost of recovery and/or repair of the Vessel shall be recoverable hereunder unless such cost would exceed the insured value. In making this determination, only the cost relating to a single accident or sequence of damages arising from the same accident shall be taken into account.

13 Freight waiver

In the event of total or constructive total loss no claim to be made by the Underwriters for freight whether notice of abandonment has been given or not.

14 Assignment

No assignment of or interest in this insurance or in any moneys which may be or become payable thereunder is to be binding on or recognised by the Underwriters unless a dated notice of such assignment or interest signed by the Assured, and by the assignor in the case of subsequent assignment, is endorsed on the Policy and the Policy with such endorsement is produced before payment of any claim or return of premium thereunder.

15 Disbursement warranty

15.1 Additional insurances as follows are permitted:

15.1.1 *Disbursements, Managers' Commissions, Profits or Excess or Increased Value of Hull and Machinery.* A sum not exceeding 25% of the value stated herein.

15.1.2 *Freight, Chartered Freight or Anticipated Freight, insured for time.* A sum not exceeding 25% of the value as stated herein less any sum insured, however described, under 15.1.1.

15.1.3 *Freight or Hire, under contracts for voyage.* A sum not exceeding the gross freight or hire for the current cargo passage and next succeeding cargo passage (such insurance to include, if required, a preliminary and an intermediate ballast passage) plus the charges of insurance. In the case of a voyage charter where payment is made on a time basis, the sum permitted for insurance shall be calculated on the estimated duration of the voyage, subject to the limitation of two cargo passages as laid down herein. Any sum insured under 15.1.2 to be taken into account and only the excess thereof may be insured, which excess shall be reduced as the freight or hire is advanced or earned by the gross amount so advanced or earned.

15.1.4 *Anticipated Freight if the Vessel sails in ballast and not under Charter.* A sum not exceeding the anticipated gross freight on next cargo passage, such sum to be reasonably estimated on the basis of the current rate of freight at time of insurance plus the charges of insurance. Any sum insured under 15.1.2 to be taken into account and only the excess thereof may be insured.

15.1.5 *Time Charter Hire or Charter Hire for Series of Voyages.* A sum not exceeding 50% of the gross hire which is to be earned under the charter in a period not exceeding 18 months. Any sum insured under 15.1.2 to be taken into account and only the excess thereof may be insured, which excess shall be reduced as the hire is advanced or earned under the charter by 50% of the gross amount so advanced or earned but the sum insured need not be reduced while the total of the sums insured under 15.1.2 and 15.1.5 does not exceed 50% of the gross hire still to be earned under the charter. An insurance under this Section may begin on the signing of the charter.

15.1.6 *Premiums.* A sum not exceeding the actual premiums of all interests insured for a period not exceeding 12 months (excluding premiums insured under the foregoing sections but including, if required, the

premium or estimated calls on any Club or War etc. Risk insurance) reducing pro rata monthly.

15.1.7   *Returns of Premium.* A sum not exceeding the actual returns which are allowable under any insurance but which would not be recoverable thereunder in the event of a total loss of the Vessel whether by insured perils or otherwise.

15.1.8   *Insurance irrespective of amount against:*
Any risks excluded by Clauses 17, 18, 19 and 20 below.

15.2   Warranted that no insurance on any interests enumerated in the foregoing 15.1.1 to 15.1.7 in excess of the amounts permitted therein and no other insurance which includes total loss of the Vessel P.P.I., F.I.A., or subject to any other like term, is or shall be effected to operate during the currency of this insurance by or for account of the Assured, Owners, Managers or Mortgagees. Provided always that a breach of this warranty shall not afford the Underwriters any defence to a claim by a Mortgagee who has accepted this insurance without knowledge of such breach.

16   Returns for lay-up and cancellation

16.1   To return as follows:

16.1.1   pro rata monthly net for each uncommenced month if this insurance be cancelled by agreement,

16.1.2   for each period of 30 consecutive days the Vessel may be laid up in a port or in a lay-up area provided such port or lay-up area is approved by the Underwriters

       (a)   .... per cent net not under repair

       (b)   .... per cent net under repair.

16.1.3   The Vessel shall not be considered to be under repair when work is undertaken in respect of ordinary wear and tear of the Vessel and/or following recommendations in the Vessel's Classification Society survey, but any repairs following loss of or damage to the Vessel or involving structural alterations, whether covered by this insurance or otherwise shall be considered as under repair.

16.1.4   If the Vessel is under repair during part only of a period for which a return is claimable, the return shall be calculated pro rata to the number of days under 16.1.2(a) and (b) respectively.

16.2   PROVIDED ALWAYS THAT

16.2.1   a total loss of the Vessel, whether by insured perils or otherwise, has not occurred during the period covered by this insurance or any extension thereof

16.2.2   in no case shall a return be allowed when the Vessel is lying in exposed or unprotected waters, or in a port or lay-up area not approved by the Underwriters

16.2.3   loading or discharging operations or the presence of cargo on board shall not debar returns but no return shall be allowed for any period during which the Vessel is being used for the storage of cargo or for lightering purposes

16.2.4   in the event of any amendment of the annual rate, the above rates of return shall be adjusted accordingly

16.2.5   in the event of any return recoverable under this Clause 16 being based on 30 consecutive days which fall on successive insurances effected for the same Assured, this insurance shall only be liable for an amount calculated at pro rata of the period rates 16.1.2(a) and/or (b) above for the number of days which come within the period of this insurance and to which a return is actually applicable. Such overlapping period shall run, at the option of the Assured, either from the first day on which the Vessel is laid up or the first day of a period of 30 consecutive days as provided under 16.1.2(a) or (b) above.

The following clauses shall be paramount and shall override anything contained in this insurance inconsistent therewith.

17 War exclusion

In no case shall this insurance cover loss damage liability or expense caused by

17.1 war civil war revolution rebellion insurrection, or civil strife arising there-from, or any hostile act by or against a belligerent power

17.2 capture seizure arrest restraint or detainment (barratry and piracy excepted), and the consequences thereof or any attempt threat

17.3 derelict mines torpedoes bombs or other derelict weapons of war.

18 Strikes exclusion

In no case shall this insurance cover loss damage liability or expense caused by

18.1 strikers, locked-out workmen, or persons taking part in labour disturbances, riots or civil commotions

18.2 any terrorist or any person acting from a political motive.

19 Malicious acts exclusion

In no case shall this insurance cover loss damage liability or expense arising from

19.1 the detonation of an explosive

19.2 any weapon of war

and caused by any person acting maliciously or from a political motive.

20 Radioactive contamination exclusion clause

In no case shall this insurance cover loss damage liability or expense arising directly or indirectly caused by or contributed to by or arising from

20.1 ionising radiations from or contamination by radioactivity from any nuclear fuel or from any nuclear waste or from the combustion of nuclear fuel

20.2 the radioactive, toxic, explosive or other hazardous or contaminating properties of any nuclear installation, reactor or other nuclear assembly or nuclear component thereof

20.3 any weapon of war employing atomic or nuclear fission and/or fusion or other like reaction or radioactive force or matter.

Institute Voyage Clauses Freight

1/11/95—(FOR USE ONLY WITH THE CURRENT MAR POLICY FORM)

This insurance is subject to English law and practice

1 Navigation

1.1   The Vessel has leave to dock and undock, to go into graving dock, to sail or navigate with or without pilots, to go on trial trips and to assist and tow vessels or craft in distress, but it is warranted that the Vessel shall not be towed, except as is customary or to the first safe port or place when in need of assistance, or undertake towage or salvage services under a contract previously arranged by the Assured and/or Owners and/or Managers and/or Charterers. This Clause 1 shall not exclude customary towage in connection with loading and discharging.

1.2   This insurance shall not be prejudiced by reason of the Assured entering into any contract with pilots or for customary towage which limits or exempts the liability of the pilots and/or tugs and/or towboats and/or their owners when the Assured or their agents accept or are compelled to accept such contracts in accordance with established local law or practice.

1.3   The practice of engaging helicopters for the transportation of personnel, supplies and equipment to and/or from the Vessel shall not prejudice this insurance.

2 Craft risk

Including risk of craft and/or lighter to and from the Vessel.

3 Change of voyage

Held covered in case of deviation or change of voyage or any breach of warranty as to towage or salvage services, provided notice be given to the Underwriters immediately after receipt of advices and any amended terms of cover and any additional premium required by them be agreed.

4   Perils

4.1   This insurance covers loss of the subject-matter insured caused by
4.1.1   perils of the seas rivers lakes or other navigable waters
4.1.2   fire, explosion
4.1.3   violent theft by persons from outside the Vessel
4.1.4   jettison
4.1.5   piracy
4.1.6   contact with land conveyance, dock or harbour equipment or installation
4.1.7   earthquake volcanic eruption or lightning
4.1.8   accidents in loading discharging or shifting cargo or fuel.
4.2   This insurance covers loss of the subject-matter insured caused by
4.2.1   bursting of boilers breakage of shafts or any latent defect in the machinery or hull
4.2.2   negligence of Master Officers Crew or Pilots
4.2.3   negligence of repairers or charterers provided such repairers or charterers are not an Assured hereunder
4.2.4   barratry of Master Officers or Crew
4.2.5   contact with aircraft, helicopters or similar objects, or objects falling therefrom
         provided that such loss has not resulted from want of due diligence by the Assured, Owners, Managers or Superintendents or any of their onshore management.
4.3   Masters Officers Crew or Pilots not to be considered Owners within the meaning of this Clause 4 should they hold shares in the Vessel.

5   Pollution hazard

This insurance covers loss of the subject matter insured caused by any governmental authority acting under the powers vested in it to prevent or mitigate a pollution hazard or damage to the environment, or threat thereof, resulting directly from a peril covered by this insurance, provided that such act of governmental authority has not resulted from want of due diligence by the Assured, Owners and Managers to prevent or mitigate such hazard or damage, or threat thereof. Masters Officers Crew or Pilots not to be considered Owners within the meaning of this Clause 5 should they hold shares in the Vessel.

6   Freight collision

6.1   It is further agreed that if the Vessel shall come into collision with any other vessel and the Assured shall in consequence thereof become liable to pay and shall pay by way of damages to any other person or persons any sum or sums in respect of the amount of freight taken into account in calculating the measure of the liability of the Assured for
6.1.1   loss of or damage to any other vessel or property of any other vessel
6.1.2   delay to or loss of use of any such other vessel or property thereon
6.1.3   general average of, salvage of, or salvage under contract of, any such other vessel or property thereon,
         the Underwriters will pay the Assured such proportion of three-fourths of such sum or sums so paid applying to freight as their respective subscriptions hereto bear to the total amount insured on freight, or to the gross

freight earned on the voyage during which the collision occurred if this be greater.

6.2 Provided always that:

6.2.1 liability of the Underwriters in respect of any one such collision shall not exceed their proportionate part of three-fourths of the total amount insured hereon on freight, and in cases in which, with the prior consent in writing of the Underwriters, the liability of the Vessel has been contested or proceedings have been taken to limit liability, they will also pay a like proportion of three-fourths of the costs, appertaining proportionately to the freight portion of damages, which the Assured shall thereby incur or be compelled to pay:

6.2.2 no claim shall attach to this insurance:

6.2.2.1 which attaches to any other insurances covering collision liabilities

6.2.2.2 which is, or would be, recoverable in the terms of the Institute 3/4ths Collision Liability Clause if the Vessel were insured in the terms of such Institute 3/4ths Collision Liability Clause for a value not less than the equivalent in pounds sterling, at the time of commencement of this insurance, of the Vessel's limit of liability calculated in accordance with Article 6.1(b) of the 1976 Limitation Convention,

6.2.3 this Clause 6 shall in no case extend or be deemed to extend to any sum which the Assured may become liable to pay or shall pay for in respect of:

6.2.3.1 removal or disposal, under statutory powers or otherwise, of obstructions, wrecks, cargoes or any other thing whatsoever

6.2.3.2 any real or personal property or thing whatsoever except other vessels or property on other vessels

6.2.3.3 pollution or contamination, or threat thereof, of any real or personal property or thing whatsoever (except other vessels with which the insured Vessel is in collision or property on such other vessels) or damage to the environment, or threat thereof, save that this exclusion shall not extend to any sum which the Assured shall pay for or in respect of salvage remuneration in which the skill and efforts of the salvors in preventing or minimising damage to the environment as is referred to in Article 13 paragraph 1(b) of the International Convention on Salvage, 1989 have been taken into account

6.2.3.4 the cargo or other property on or the engagements of the Vessel

6.2.3.5 loss of life, personal injury or illness.

7 Sistership

Should the Vessel named herein come into collision with or receive salvage services from another vessel belonging wholly or in part to the same Owners or under the same management, the Assured shall have the same rights under this insurance as they would have were the other vessel entirely the property of Owners not interested in the Vessel named herein; but in such cases the liability for the collision or the amount payable for the services rendered shall be referred to a sole arbitrator to be agreed upon between the Underwriters and the Assured.

8   General average and salvage

8.1	This insurance covers the proportion of general average, salvage and/or salvage charges attaching to freight at risk of the Assured, reduced in respect of any under-insurance.
8.2	Adjustment to be according to the law and practice obtaining at the place where the adventure ends, as if the contract of affreightment contains no special terms upon the subject; but where the contract so provides the adjustment shall be according to the York-Antwerp Rules.
8.3	No claim under this Clause 8 shall in any case be allowed where the loss was not incurred to avoid or in connection with the avoidance of a peril insured against.
8.4	No claim under this Clause 8 shall be in any case allowed for or in respect of
8.4.1	special compensation payable to a salvor under Article 14 of the International Convention on Salvage, 1989 or under any other provision in any statute, rule, law or contract which is similar in substance;
8.4.2	expenses or liabilities incurred in respect of damage to the environment, or the threat of such damage, or as a consequence of the escape or release of pollutant substances from the Vessel, or the threat of such escape or release.
8.5	Clause 8.4 shall not however exclude any sum which the Assured shall pay to salvors for or in respect of salvage remuneration in which the skill and efforts of the salvors in preventing or minimising damage to the environment as is referred to in Article 13 paragraph 1(b) of the International Convention on Salvage, 1989 have been taken into account.

9   Franchise

This insurance does not cover partial loss, other than general average loss, under 3% unless caused by fire, sinking, stranding or collision with another vessel. Each craft and/or lighter to be deemed a separate insurance if required by the Assured.

10   Measure of indemnity

10.1	The amount recoverable under this insurance for any claim for loss of freight shall not exceed the gross freight actually lost.
10.2	Where insurances on freight other than this insurance are current at the time of the loss, all such insurances shall be taken into consideration in calculating the liability under this insurance and the amount recoverable hereunder shall not exceed the rateable proportion of the gross freight lost, notwithstanding any valuation in this or any other insurance.
10.3	In calculating the liability under Clause 8 all insurances on freight shall likewise be taken into consideration.
10.4	Nothing in this Clause 10 shall apply to any claim arising under Clause 12.

11   Loss of time

This insurance does not cover any claim consequent on loss of time whether arising from a peril of the sea or otherwise.

12   Total loss

12.1   In the event of the total loss (actual or constructive) of the Vessel named herein the amount insured shall be paid in full, whether the Vessel be fully or partly loaded or in ballast, chartered or unchartered.

12.2   In ascertaining whether the Vessel is a constructive total loss, the insured value in the insurances on hull and machinery shall be taken as the repaired value and nothing in respect of the damaged or break-up value of the Vessel or wreck shall be taken into account.

12.3   Should the Vessel be a constructive total loss but the claim on the insurances on hull and machinery be settled as a claim for partial loss, no payment shall be due under this Clause 12.

13   Assignment

No assignment of or interest in this insurance or in any moneys which may be or become payable thereunder is to be binding on or recognised by the Underwriters unless a dated notice of such assignment or interest signed by the Assured, and by the assignor in the case of subsequent assignment, is endorsed on the Policy and the Policy with such endorsement is produced before payment of any claim or return of premium thereunder.

The following clauses shall be paramount and shall override anything contained in this insurance inconsistent therewith.

14   War exclusion

In no case shall this insurance cover loss damage liability or expense caused by

14.1   war civil war revolution rebellion insurrection, or civil strife arising therefrom, or any hostile act by or against a belligerent power

14.2   capture seizure arrest restraint or detainment (barratry and piracy excepted), and the consequences thereof or any attempt thereat

14.3   derelict mines torpedoes bombs or other derelict weapons of war.

15   Strikes exclusion

In no case shall this insurance cover loss damage liability or expense caused by

15.1   strikers, locked-out workmen, or persons taking part in labour disturbances, riots or civil commotions

15.2   any terrorist or any person acting from a political motive.

16   Malicious acts exclusion

In no case shall this insurance cover loss damage liability or expense arising from

16.1   the detonation of an explosive

16.2   any weapon of war

and caused by any person acting maliciously or from a political motive.

17   Radioactive contamination exclusion clause

In no case shall this insurance cover loss damage liability or expense directly or indirectly caused by or contributed to by or arising from

17.1   ionising radiations from or contamination by radioactivity from any nuclear fuel or from any nuclear waste or from the combustion of nuclear fuel

17.2   the radioactive, toxic, explosive or other hazardous or contaminating properties of any nuclear installation, reactor or other nuclear assembly or nuclear
component thereof

17.3   any weapon of war employing atomic or nuclear fission and/or fusion or other
like reaction or radioactive force or matter.

Institute Voyage Clauses Hulls

1/11/95—(FOR USE ONLY WITH THE CURRENT MAR POLICY FORM)

This insurance is subject to English law and practice

1 Navigation

1.1 The Vessel is covered subject to the provisions of this insurance at all times and has leave to sail or navigate with or without pilots, to go on trial trips and to assist and tow vessels or craft in distress, but it is warranted that the Vessel shall not be towed, except as is customary or to the first safe port or place when in need of assistance, or undertake towage or salvage services under a contract previously arranged by the Assured and/or Owners and/or Managers and/or Charterers. This Clause 1.1 shall not exclude customary towage in connection with loading and discharging.

1.2 This insurance shall not be prejudiced by reason of the Assured entering into any contract with pilots or for customary towage which limits or exempts the liability of the pilots and/or tugs and/or towboats and/or their owners when the Assured or their agents accept or are compelled to accept such contracts in accordance with established local law or practice.

1.3 The practice of engaging helicopters for the transportation of personnel, supplies and equipment to and/or from the Vessel shall not prejudice this insurance.

1.4 In the event of the Vessel being employed in trading operations which entail cargo loading or discharging at sea from or into another vessel (not being a harbour or inshore craft) no claim shall be recoverable under this insurance for loss of or damage to the Vessel or liability to any other vessel arising from such loading or discharging operations, including whilst approaching, lying alongside and leaving, unless previous notice that the Vessel is to be employed in such operations has been given to the Underwriters and any amended terms of cover and any additional premium required by them have been agreed.

2 Change of Voyage

Held covered in case of deviation or change of voyage or any breach of warranty as to towage or salvage services, provided notice be given to the Underwriters immediately after receipt of

252

advices and any amended terms of cover and any additional premium required by them be agreed.

3 Classification

3.1 It is the duty of the Assured, Owners and Managers at the inception of and throughout the period of this insurance to ensure that

3.1.1 the Vessel is classed with a Classification Society agreed by the Underwriters and that her class within that Society is maintained,

3.1.2 any recommendations requirements or restrictions imposed by the Vessel's Classification Society which relate to the Vessel's seaworthiness or to her maintenance in a seaworthy condition are complied with by the dates required by that Society.

3.2 In the event of any breach of the duties set out in Clause 3.1 above, unless the Underwriters agree to the contrary in writing, they will be discharged from liability under this insurance as from the date of the breach provided that if the Vessel is at sea at such date the Underwriters' discharge from liability is deferred until arrival at her next port.

3.3 Any incident condition or damage in respect of which the Vessel's Classification Society might make recommendations as to repairs or other action to be taken by the Assured, Owners and Managers must be promptly reported to the Classification Society.

3.4 Should the Underwriters wish to approach the Classification Society directly for information and/or documents, the Assured will provide the necessary authorization.

4 Perils

4.1 This insurance covers loss of or damage to the subject-matter insured caused by

4.1.1 perils of the seas rivers lakes or other navigable waters

4.1.2 fire, explosion

4.1.3 violent theft by persons from outside the Vessel

4.1.4 jettison

4.1.5 piracy

4.1.6 contact with land conveyance, dock or harbour equipment or installation

4.1.7 earthquake volcanic eruption or lightning

4.1.8 accidents in loading discharging or shifting cargo or fuel.

4.2 This insurance covers loss of or damage to the subject-matter insured caused by

4.2.1 bursting of boilers breakage of shafts or any latent defect in the machinery or hull

4.2.2 negligence of Master Officers Crew or Pilots

4.2.3 negligence of repairers or charterers provided such repairers or charterers are not an Assured hereunder

4.2.4 barratry of Master Officers or Crew,

4.2.5 contact with aircraft, helicopters or similar objects, or objects falling therefrom provided such loss or damage has not resulted from want of due diligence by the Assured, Owners' Managers or Superintendents or any of their onshore management.

4.3   Master Officers Crew or Pilots not to be considered Owners within the meaning of this Clause 4 should they hold shares in the Vessel.

5   Pollution Hazard

This insurance covers loss of or damage to the Vessel caused by any governmental authority acting under the powers vested in it to prevent or mitigate a pollution hazard or damage to the environment, or threat thereof, resulting directly from damage to the Vessel for which the Underwriters are liable under this insurance, provided that such act of governmental authority has not resulted from want of due diligence by the Assured, Owners or Managers to prevent or mitigate such hazard or damage, or threat thereof. Master Officers Crew or Pilots not to be considered Owners within the meaning of this Clause 5 should they hold shares in the Vessel.

6   3/4ths Collision Liability

6.1   The Underwriters agree to indemnify the Assured for three-fourths of any sum or sums paid by the Assured to any other person or persons by reason of the Assured becoming legally liable by way of damages for

6.1.1   loss of or damage to any other vessel or property on any other vessel

6.1.2   delay to or loss of use of any such other vessel or property thereon

6.1.3   general average of, salvage of, or salvage under contract of, any such other vessel or property thereon,

where such payment by the Assured is in consequence of the Vessel hereby insured coming into collision with any other vessel.

6.2   The indemnity provided by this Clause 6 shall be in addition to the indemnity provided by the other terms and conditions of this insurance and shall be subject to the following provisions:

6.2.1   where the insured Vessel is in collision with another vessel and both vessels are to blame then, unless the liability of one or both vessels becomes limited by law, the indemnity under this Clause 6 shall be calculated on the principle of cross-liabilities as if the respective Owners had been compelled to pay to each other such proportion of each other's damages as may have been properly allowed in ascertaining the balance or sum payable by or to the Assured in consequence of the collision,

6.2.2   in no case shall the Underwriters' total liability under Clauses 6.1 and 6.2 exceed their proportionate part of three-fourths of the insured value of the Vessel hereby insured in respect of any one collision.

6.3   The Underwriters will also pay three-fourths of the legal costs incurred by the Assured or which the Assured may be compelled to pay in contesting liability or taking proceedings to limit liability, with the prior written consent of the Underwriters.

EXCLUSIONS

6.4   Provided always that this Clause 6 shall in no case extend to any sum which the Assured shall pay for or in respect of

6.4.1	removal or disposal of obstructions, wrecks, cargoes or any other thing whatsoever
6.4.2	any real or personal property or thing whatsoever except other vessels or property on other vessels
6.4.3	the cargo or other property on, or the engagements of, the insured Vessel
6.4.4	loss of life, personal injury or illness
6.4.5	pollution or contamination, or threat thereof, of any real or personal property or thing whatsoever (except other vessels with which the insured Vessel is in collision or property on such other vessels) or damage to the environment, or threat thereof, save that this exclusion shall not extend to any sum which the Assured shall pay for or in respect of salvage remuneration in which the skill and efforts of the salvors in preventing or minimising damage to the environment as is referred to in Article 13 paragraph 1(b) of the International Convention on Salvage, 1989 have been taken into account.

7 Sistership

Should the Vessel hereby insured come into collision with or receive salvage services from another vessel belonging wholly or in part to the same Owners or under the same management, the Assured shall have the same rights under this insurance as they would have were the other vessel entirely the property of Owners not interested in the Vessel hereby insured; but in such cases the liability for the collision or the amount payable for the services rendered shall be referred to a sole arbitrator to be agreed upon between the Underwriters and the Assured.

8 General Average and Salvage

8.1	This insurance covers the Vessel's proportion of salvage, salvage charges and/or general average, reduced in respect of any under-insurance, but in case of general average sacrifice of the Vessel the Assured may recover in respect of the whole loss without first enforcing their right of contribution from other parties.
8.2	Adjustment to be according to the law and practice obtaining at the place where the adventure ends, as if the contract of affreightment contained no special terms upon the subject; but where the contract of affreightment so provides the adjustment shall be according to the York-Antwerp Rules.
8.3	When the Vessel sails in ballast, not under charter, the provisions of the York-Antwerp Rules, 1994 (excluding Rules XI(d), XX and XXI) shall be applicable, and the voyage for this purpose shall be deemed to continue from the port or place of departure until the arrival of the Vessel at the first port or place thereafter other than a port or place of refuge or a port or place of call for bunkering only. If at any such intermediate port or place there is an abandonment of the adventure originally contemplated the voyage shall thereupon be deemed to be terminated.
8.4	No claim under this Clause 8 shall in any case be allowed where the loss was not incurred to avoid or in connection with the avoidance of a peril insured against.
8.5	No claim under this Clause 8 shall in any case be allowed for or in respect of

8.5.1	special compensation payable to a salvor under Article 14 of the International Convention on Salvage, 1989 or under any other provision in any statute, rule, law or contract which is similar in substance
8.5.2	expenses or liabilities incurred in respect of damage to the environment, or the threat of such damage, or as a consequence of the escape or release of pollutant substances from the Vessel, or the threat of such escape or release.
8.6	Clause 8.5 shall not however exclude any sum which the Assured shall pay to salvors for or in respect of salvage remuneration in which the skill and efforts of the salvors in preventing or minimising damage to the environment as is referred to in Article 13 paragraph 1(b) of the International Convention on Salvage, 1989 have been taken into account.

9 Duty of Assured (Sue and Labour)

9.1	In case of any loss or misfortune it is the duty of the Assured and their servants and agents to take such measures as may be reasonable for the purpose of averting or minimising a loss which would be recoverable under this insurance.
9.2	Subject to the provisions below and to Clause 10 the Underwriters will contribute to charges properly and reasonably incurred by the Assured their servants or agents for such measures. General average, salvage charges (except as provided for in Clause 9.5), special compensation and expenses as referred to in Clause 8.5, and collision defence or attack costs are not recoverable under this Clause 9.
9.3	Measures taken by the Assured or the Underwriters with the object of saving, protecting or recovering the subject-matter insured shall not be considered as a waiver or acceptance of abandonment or otherwise prejudice the rights of either party.
9.4	When expenses are incurred pursuant to this Clause 9 the liability under this insurance shall not exceed the proportion of such expenses that the amount insured hereunder bears to the value of the Vessel as stated herein, or to the sound value of the Vessel at the time of the occurrence giving rise to the expenditure if the sound value exceeds that value. Where the Underwriters have admitted a claim for total loss and property insured by this insurance is saved, the foregoing provisions shall not apply unless the expenses of suing and labouring exceed the value of such property saved and then shall apply only to the amount of the expenses which is in excess of such value.
9.5	When a claim for total loss of the Vessel is admitted under this insurance and expenses have been reasonably incurred in saving or attempting to save the Vessel and other property and there are no proceeds, or the expenses exceed the proceeds, then this insurance shall bear its pro rata share of such proportion of the expenses, or of the expenses in excess of the proceeds, as the case may be, as may reasonably be regarded as having been incurred in respect of the Vessel, excluding all special compensation and expenses as referred to in Clause 8.5; but if the Vessel be insured for less than its sound value at the time of the occurrence giving rise to the expenditure, the amount recoverable under this clause shall be reduced in proportion to the under-insurance.
9.6	The sum recoverable under this Clause 9 shall be in addition to the loss otherwise recoverable under this insurance but shall in no circumstances exceed the amount insured under this insurance in respect of the Vessel.

10   Deductible

10.1   No claim arising from a peril insured against shall be payable under this insurance unless the aggregate of all such claims arising out of each separate accident or occurrence (including claims under Clauses 6, 8 and 9) exceeds the deductible amount agreed in which case this sum shall be deducted. Nevertheless the expense of sighting the bottom after stranding, if reasonably incurred specially for that purpose shall be paid even if no damage be found. This clause 10.1 shall not apply to a claim for total or constructive total loss of the Vessel or, in the event of such a claim, to any associated claim under Clause 9 arising from the same accident or occurrence.

10.2   Claims for damage by heavy weather occurring during a single sea passage between two successive ports shall be treated as being due to one accident. In the case of such heavy weather extending over a period not wholly covered by this insurance the deductible to be applied to the claim recoverable hereunder shall be the proportion of the above deductible that the number of days of such heavy weather falling within the period of this insurance bears to the number of days of heavy weather during the single sea passage. The expression "heavy weather" in this Clause 10.2 shall be deemed to include contact with floating ice.

10.3   Excluding any interest comprised therein, recoveries against any claim which is subject to the above deductible shall be credited to the Underwriters in full to the extent of the sum by which the aggregate of the claim unreduced by any recoveries exceeds the above deductible.

10.4   Interest comprised in recoveries shall be apportioned between the Assured and the Underwriters, taking into account the sums paid by the Underwriters and the dates when such payments were made, notwithstanding that by the addition of interest the Underwriters may receive a larger sum than they have paid.

11   Notice of Claim and Tenders

11.1   In the event of accident whereby loss or damage may result in a claim under this insurance, notice must be given to the Underwriters promptly after the date on which the Assured, Owners or Managers become or should have become aware of the loss or damage and prior to survey and so that a surveyor may be appointed if the Underwriters so desire.

If notice is not given to the Underwriters within twelve months of that date, unless the Underwriters agree to the contrary in writing, the Underwriters will be automatically discharged from liability for any claim under this insurance in respect of or arising out of such accident or the loss or damage.

11.2   The Underwriters shall be entitled to decide the port to which the Vessel shall proceed for docking or repair (the actual additional expense of the voyage arising from compliance with the Underwriters' requirements being refunded to the Assured) and shall have a right of veto concerning a place of repair or a repairing firm.

11.3   The Underwriters may also take tenders or may require further tenders to be taken for the repair of the Vessel. Where such a tender has been taken and a tender is accepted with the approval of the Underwriters, an allowance shall be made at the rate of 30% per annum on the insured value for time lost between the despatch of the invitations to tender required by the Underwriters and the acceptance of a tender to the extent that such time is lost solely as the result of tenders having been taken and provided that the tender is accepted without delay after receipt of the Underwriters' approval.

Due credit shall be given against the allowance as above for any amounts recovered in respect of fuel and stores and wages and maintenance of the Master Officers and Crew or any member thereof, including amounts allowed in general average, and for any amounts recovered from third parties in respect of damages for detention and/or loss of profit and/or running expenses, for the period covered by the tender allowance or any part thereof.

Where a part of the cost of the repair of damage other than a fixed deductible is not recoverable from the Underwriters the allowance shall be reduced by a similar proportion.

11.4   In the event of failure by the Assured to comply with the conditions of Clauses 11.2 and/or 11.3 a deduction of 15% shall be made from the amount of the ascertained claim.

12 New for Old

Claims payable without deduction new for old.

13 Bottom Treatment

In no case shall a claim be allowed in respect of scraping gritblasting and/or other surface preparation or painting of the Vessel's bottom except that

13.1   gritblasting and/or other surface preparation of new bottom plates ashore and supplying and applying any "shop" primer thereto,

13.2   gritblasting and/or other surface preparation of:
the butts or area of plating immediately adjacent to any renewed or refitted plating damaged during the course of welding and/or repairs,
areas of plating damaged during the course of fairing, either in place or ashore,

13.3   supplying and applying the first coat of primer/anti-corrosive to those particular areas mentioned in 13.1 and 13.2 above,

shall be allowed as part of the reasonable cost of repairs in respect of bottom plating damaged by an insured peril.

14 Wages and Maintenance

No claim shall be allowed, other than in general average, for wages and maintenance of the Master, Officers and Crew, or any member thereof, except when incurred solely for the necessary removal of the Vessel from one port to another for the repair of damage covered by the Underwriters, or for trial trips for such repairs, and then only for such wages and maintenance as are incurred whilst the Vessel is under way.

15 Agency Commission

In no case shall any sum be allowed under this insurance either by way of remuneration of the Assured for time and trouble taken to obtain and supply information or documents or in respect of the commission or charges of any manager, agent, managing or agency company or the like, appointed by or on behalf of the Assured to perform such services.

16 Unrepaired Damage

16.1 The measure of indemnity in respect of claims for unrepaired damage shall be the reasonable depreciation in the market value of the Vessel at the time this insurance terminates arising from such unrepaired damage, but not exceeding the reasonable cost of repairs.

16.2 In no case shall the Underwriters be liable for unrepaired damage in the event of a subsequent total loss (whether or not covered under this insurance) sustained during the period covered by this insurance or any extension thereof.

16.3 The Underwriters shall not be liable in respect of unrepaired damage for more than the insured value at the time this insurance terminates.

17 Constructive Total Loss

17.1 In ascertaining whether the Vessel is a constructive total loss, the insured value shall be taken as the repaired value and nothing in respect of the damaged or break-up value of the Vessel or wreck shall be taken into account.

17.2 No claim for constructive total loss based upon the cost of recovery and/or repair of the Vessel shall be recoverable hereunder unless such cost would exceed the insured value. In making this determination, only the cost relating to a single accident or sequence of damages arising from the same accident shall be taken into account.

18 Freight Waiver

In the event of total or constructive total loss no claim to be made by the Underwriters for freight whether notice of abandonment has been given or not.

19 Assignment

No assignment of or interest in this insurance or in any moneys which may be or become payable thereunder is to be binding on or recognised by the Underwriters unless a dated notice of such assignment or interest signed by the Assured, and by the assignor in the case of subsequent assignment, is endorsed on the Policy and the Policy with such endorsement is produced before payment of any claim or return of premium thereunder.

20 Disbursements Warranty

20.1 Additional insurances as follows are permitted:

20.1.1 *Disbursements, Managers' Commissions, Profits or Excess or Increased Value of Hull and Machinery.* A sum not exceeding 25% of the value stated herein.

20.1.2 *Freight, Chartered Freight or Anticipated Freight, insured for time.* A sum not exceeding 25% of the value as stated herein less any sum insured, however described, under 20.1.1.

20.1.3 *Freight or Hire, under contracts for voyage.* A sum not exceeding the gross freight or hire for the current cargo passage and next succeeding cargo passage (such insurance to include, if required, a preliminary and an intermediate ballast passage) plus the charges of insurance. In the case of a voyage charter where payment is made on a time basis, the sum permitted for insurance shall be calculated on the estimated duration of the voyage, subject to the limitation of two cargo passages as laid down herein. Any sum insured under 20.1.2 to be taken into account and only the excess thereof may be insured, which excess shall be reduced as the freight or hire is advanced or earned by the gross amount so advanced or earned.

20.1.4   *Anticipated Freight if the Vessel sails in ballast and not under Charter.* A sum not exceeding the anticipated gross freight on next cargo passage, such sum to be reasonably estimated on the basis of the current rate of freight at time of insurance plus the charges of insurance. Any sum insured under 20.1.2 to be taken into account and only the excess thereof may be insured.

20.1.5   *Time Charter Hire or Charter Hire for Series of Voyages.* A sum not exceeding 50% of the gross hire which is to be earned under the charter in a period not exceeding 18 months. Any sum insured under 20.1.2 to be taken into account and only the excess thereof may be insured, which excess shall be reduced as the hire is advanced or earned under the charter by 50% of the gross amount so advanced or earned but the sum insured need not be reduced while the total of the sums insured under 20.1.2 and 20.1.5 does not exceed 50% of the gross hire still to be earned under the charter. An insurance under this Section may begin on the signing of the charter.

20.1.6   *Premiums.* A sum not exceeding the actual premiums of all interests insured for a period not exceeding 12 months (excluding premiums insured under the foregoing sections but including, if required, the premium or estimated calls on any Club or War etc. Risk insurance) reducing pro rata monthly.

20.1.7   *Returns of Premium.* A sum not exceeding the actual returns which are allowable under any insurance but which would not be recoverable thereunder in the event of a total loss of the Vessel whether by insured perils or otherwise.

20.1.8   *Insurance irrespective of amount against:*
Any risks excluded by Clauses 21, 22, 23 and 24 below.

20.2   Warranted that no insurance on any interests enumerated in the foregoing 20.1.1 to 20.1.7 in excess of the amounts permitted therein and no other insurance which includes total loss of the Vessel P.P.I., F.I.A., or subject to any other like term, is or shall be effected to operate during the currency of this insurance by or for account of the Assured, Owners, Managers or Mortgagees. Provided always that a breach of this warranty shall not afford the Underwriters any defence to a claim by a Mortgagee who has accepted this insurance without knowledge of such breach.

The following clauses shall be paramount and shall override anything contained in this insurance inconsistent therewith.

21 War Exclusion

In no case shall this insurance cover loss damage liability or expense caused by

21.1   war civil war revolution rebellion insurrection, or civil strife arising therefrom, or any hostile act by or against a belligerent power

21.2   capture seizure arrest restraint or detainment (barratry and piracy excepted), and the consequences thereof or any attempt thereat

21.3 derelict mines torpedoes bombs or other derelict weapons of war.

22 Strikes Exclusion

In no case shall this insurance cover loss damage liability or expense caused by

22.1 strikers, locked-out workmen, or persons taking part in labour disturbances, riots or civil commotions

22.2 any terrorist or any person acting from a political motive.

23 Malicious Acts Exclusion

In no case shall this insurance cover loss damage liability or expense arising from

23.1 the detonation of an explosive

23.2 any weapon of war

and caused by any person acting maliciously or from a political motive.

24 Radioactive Contamination Exclusion Clause

In no case shall this insurance cover loss damage liability or expense directly or indirectly caused by or contributed to by or arising from

24.1 ionising radiations from or contamination by radioactivity from any nuclear fuel or from any nuclear waste or from the combustion of nuclear fuel

24.2 the radioactive, toxic, explosive or other hazardous or contaminating properties of any nuclear installation, reactor or other nuclear assembly or nuclear component thereof

24.3 any weapon of war employing atomic or nuclear fission and/or fusion or other like reaction or radioactive force or matter.

Institute Voyage Clauses—Hulls—Total Loss, General Average and 3/4ths Collision Liability (Including Salvage, Salvage Charges and Sue and Labour)

1/11/95—(FOR USE ONLY WITH THE CURRENT MARINE POLICY FORM)

This insurance is subject to English law and practice

1   Navigation

1.1   The Vessel is covered subject to the provisions of this insurance at all times and has leave to sail or navigate with or without pilots, to go on trial trips and to assist and tow vessels or craft in distress, but it is warranted that the Vessels shall not be towed, except as is customary or to the first safe port or place when in need of assistance, or undertake towage or salvage services under a contract previously arranged by the Assured and/or Owners and/or Managers and/or Charterers. This Clause 1.1 shall not exclude customary towage in connection with loading and discharging.

1.2   This insurance shall not be prejudiced by reason of the Assured entering into any contract with pilots or for customary towage which limits or exempts the liability of the pilots and/or tugs and/or towboats and/or their owners when the Assured or their agents accept or are compelled to accept such contracts in accordance with established local law or practice.

1.3   The practice of engaging helicopters for the transportation of personnel, supplies and equipment to and/or from the Vessel shall not prejudice this insurance.

1.4   In the event of the Vessel being employed in trading operations which entail cargo loading or discharging at sea from or into another vessel (not being a harbour or inshore craft) no claim shall be recoverable under this insurance for loss of or damage to the Vessel or liability to any other vessel arising from such loading or discharging operations, including whilst approaching, lying alongside and leaving, unless previous notice that the Vessel is to be employed in such operations has been given to the Underwriters and any amended terms of cover and any additional premium required by them have been agreed.

2   Change of Voyage

Held covered in case of deviation or change of voyage or any breach of warranty as to towage or salvage services, provided notice be given to the Underwriters immediately after receipt of

262

advices and any amended terms of cover and any additional premium required by them be agreed.

3 Classification

3.1 It is the duty of the Assured Owners and Managers at the inception of and throughout the period of this insurance to ensure that

3.1.1 the Vessel is classed with a Classification Society agreed by the Underwriters and that her class within that Society is maintained,

3.1.2 any recommendations requirements or restrictions imposed by the Vessel's Classification Society which relate to the Vessel's seaworthiness or to her maintenance in a seaworthy condition are complied with by the dates required by that Society.

3.2 In the event of any breach of the duties set out in Clause 3.1 above, unless Underwriters agree to the contrary in writing, they will be discharged from liability under this insurance as from the date of the breach provided that if the Vessel is at sea at such date Underwriters' discharge from liability is deferred until arrival at her next port.

3.3 Any incident condition or damage in respect of which the Vessel's Classification Society might make recommendations as to repairs or other action to be taken by the Assured, Owners or Managers must be promptly reported to the Classification Society.

3.4 Should the Underwriters wish to approach the Classification Society directly for information and/or documents, the Assured will provide the necessary authorization.

4 Perils

4.1 This insurance covers total loss (actual or constructive) of the subject-matter insured caused by

4.1.1 perils of the seas rivers lakes or other navigable waters

4.1.2 fire, explosion

4.1.3 violent theft by persons from outside the Vessel

4.1.4 jettison

4.1.5 piracy

4.1.6 contact with land conveyance, dock or harbour equipment or installation

4.1.7 earthquake volcanic eruption or lightning

4.1.8 accidents in loading discharging or shifting cargo or fuel.

4.2 This insurance covers total loss (actual or constructive) of the subject-matter insured caused by

4.2.1 bursting of boilers breakage of shafts or any latent defect in the machinery or hull

4.2.2 negligence of Master Officers Crew or Pilots

4.2.3 negligence of repairers or charterers provided such repairers or charterers are not an Assured hereunder

4.2.4 barratry of Master Officers or Crew

4.2.5 contact with aircraft, helicopters or similar objects, or objects falling therefrom provided such loss or damage has not resulted from want of due diligence by the Assured, Owners, Managers or Superintendents or any of their onshore management.

4.3   Masters Officers Crew or Pilots not to be considered Owners within the meaning of this Clause 4 should they hold shares in the Vessel.

5   Pollution Hazard

This insurance covers total loss (actual or constructive) of the Vessel caused by any governmental authority acting under the powers vested in it to prevent or mitigate a pollution hazard or damage to the environment, or threat thereof, resulting directly from damage to the Vessel for which the Underwriters are liable under this insurance, provided that such act of governmental authority has not resulted from want of due diligence by the Assured. Owners or Managers to prevent or mitigate such hazard or damage, or threat thereof. Masters Officers Crew or Pilots not to be considered Owners within the meaning of this Clause 5 should they hold shares in the Vessel.

6   3/4ths Collision Liability

6.1   The Underwriters agree to indemnify the Assured for three-fourths of any sum or sums paid by the Assured to any other person or persons by reason of the Assured becoming legally liable by way of damages for

6.1.1   loss of or damage to any other vessel or property on any other vessel

6.1.2   delay to or loss of use of any such other vessel or property thereon

6.1.3   general average of salvage of, or salvage under contract of, any such other vessel or property thereon,

where such payment by the Assured is in consequence of the Vessel hereby insured coming into collision with any other vessel.

6.2   The indemnity provided by this Clause 6 shall be in addition to the indemnity provided by the other terms and conditions of this insurance and shall be subject to the following provisions:

6.2.1   where the insured Vessel is in collision with another vessel and both vessels are to blame then, unless the liability of one or both vessels becomes limited by law, the indemnity under this Clause 6 shall be calculated on the principle of cross-liabilities as if the respective Owners had been compelled to pay to each other such proportion of each other's damages as may have been properly allowed in ascertaining the balance or sum payable by or to the Assured in consequence of the collision,

6.2.2   in no case shall the Underwriters' total liability under Clauses 6.1 and 6.2 exceed their proportionate part of three-fourths of the insured value of the Vessel hereby insured in respect of any one collision.

6.3   The Underwriters will also pay three-fourths of the legal costs incurred by the Assured or which the Assured may be compelled to pay in contesting liability or taking proceedings to limit liability, with the prior written consent of the Underwriters.

EXCLUSIONS

6.4   Provided always that this Clause 6 shall in no case extend to any sum which the Assured shall pay for or in respect of

6.4.1	removal or disposal of obstructions, wrecks cargoes or any other thing whatsoever
6.4.2	any real or personal property or thing whatsoever except other vessels or property on other vessels
6.4.3	the cargo or other property on, or the engagements of, the insured Vessel
6.4.4	loss of life, personal injury or illness
6.4.5	pollution or contamination, or threat thereof, of any real or personal property or thing whatsoever (except other vessels with which the insured Vessel is in collision or property on such other vessels) or damage to the environment, or threat thereof, save that this exclusion shall not extend to any sum which the Assured shall pay for in respect of salvage remuneration in which the skill and efforts of the salvors in preventing or minimising damage to the environment as is referred to in Article 13 paragraph 1(b) of the International Convention on Salvage, 1989 have been taken into account.

7 Sistership

Should the Vessel hereby insured come into collision with or receive salvage services from another vessel belonging wholly or in part to the same Owners or under the same management, the Assured shall have the same rights under this insurance as they would have were the other vessel entirely the property of Owners not interested in the Vessel hereby insured; but in such cases the liability for the collision or the amount payable for the services rendered shall be referred to a sole arbitrator to be agreed upon between the Underwriters and the Assured.

8 General Average and Salvage

8.1	This insurance covers the Vessel's proportion of salvage, salvage charges and/ or general average, reduced in respect of any under-insurance.
8.2	**This insurance does not cover partial loss of and/or damage to the Vessel except for any proportion of general average loss or damage which may be recoverable under Clause 8.1 above.**
8.3	Adjustment to be according to the law and practice obtaining at the place where the adventure ends, as if the contract of affreightment contained no special terms upon the subject; but where the contract of affreightment so provides the adjustment shall be according to the York-Antwerp Rules.
8.4	When the Vessel sails in ballast, not under charter, the provisions of the York-Antwerp Rules, 1994 (excluding Rules XI(d), XX and XXI) shall be applicable, and the voyage for this purpose shall be deemed to continue from the port or place of departure until the arrival of the Vessel at the first port or place thereafter other than a port or place of refuge or a port or place of call for bunkering only. If at any such intermediate port or place there is an abandonment of the adventure originally contemplated the voyage shall thereupon be deemed to be terminated.
8.5	No claim under this Clause 8 shall in any case be allowed where the loss was not incurred to avoid or in connection with the avoidance of a peril insured against.
8.6	No claim under this Clause 8 shall in any case be allowed for or in respect of

8.6.1   special compensation payable to a salvor under Article 14 of the International Convention on Salvage, 1989 or under any other provision in any statute, rule, law or contract which is similar in substance

8.6.2   expenses or liabilities incurred in respect of damage to the environment, or the threat of such damage, or as a consequence of the escape or release of pollutant substances from the Vessel, or the threat of such escape or release.

8.7   Clause 8.6 shall not however exclude any sum which the Assured shall pay to salvors for or in respect of salvage remuneration in which the skill and efforts of the salvors in preventing or minimising damage to the environment as is referred to in Article 13 paragraph 1(b) of the International Convention on Salvage, 1989 have been taken into account.

9   Duty of Assured (Sue and Labour)

9.1   In case of any loss or misfortune it is the duty of the Assured and their servants and agents to take such measures as may be reasonable for the purpose of averting or minimising a loss which would be recoverable under this insurance.

9.2   Subject to the provisions below and to Clause 10 the Underwriters will contribute to charges properly and reasonably incurred by the Assured their servants or agents for such measures. General average salvage charges (except as provided for in Clause 9.5), special compensation and expenses as referred to in Clause 8.6 and collision defence or attack costs are not recoverable under this Clause 9.

9.3   Measures taken by the Assured or the Underwriters with the object of saving, protecting or recovering the subject-matter insured shall not be considered as a waiver or acceptance of abandonment or otherwise prejudice the rights of either party.

9.4   When expenses are incurred pursuant to this Clause 9 the liability under this insurance shall not exceed the proportion of such expenses that the amount insured hereunder bears to the value of the Vessel as stated herein, or to the sound value of the Vessel at the time of the occurrence giving rise to the expenditure if the sound value exceeds that value. Where the Underwriters have admitted a claim for total loss and property insured by this insurance is saved, the foregoing provisions shall not apply unless the expenses of suing and labouring exceed the value of such property saved and then shall apply only to the amount of the expenses which is in excess of such value.

9.5   When a claim for total loss of the Vessel is admitted under this insurance and expenses have been reasonably incurred in saving or attempting to save the Vessel and other property and there are no proceeds, or the expenses exceed the proceeds, then this insurance shall bear its pro rata share of such proportion of the expenses, or of the expenses in excess of the proceeds, as the case may be, as may reasonably be regarded as having been incurred in respect of the Vessel, excluding all special compensation and expenses as referred to in Clause 8.6; but if the Vessel be insured for less than its sound value at the time of the occurrence giving rise to the expenditure, the amount recoverable under this clause shall be reduced in proportion to the under-insurance.

9.6   The sum recoverable under this Clause 9 shall be in addition to the loss otherwise recoverable under this insurance but shall in no circumstances exceed the amount insured under this insurance in respect of the Vessel.

10 Deductible

10.1 No claim arising from a peril insured against shall be payable under this insurance unless the aggregate of all such claims arising out of each separate accident or occurrence (including claims under Clause 6, 8 and 9) exceeds the deductible amount agreed in which case this sum shall be deducted. This Clause 10.1 shall not apply to a claim for total or constructive total loss of the Vessel or, in the event of such a claim, to any associated claim under Clause 9 arising from the same accident or occurrence.

10.2 Excluding any interest comprised therein, recoveries against any claim which is subject to the above deductible shall be credited to the Underwriters in full to the extent of the sum by which the aggregate of the claim unreduced by any recoveries exceeds the above deductible.

10.3 Interest comprised in recoveries shall be apportioned between the Assured and the Underwriters, taking into account the sums paid by the Underwriters and the dates when such payments were made, notwithstanding that by the addition of interest the Underwriters may receive a large sum than they have paid.

11 Notice of Claim

In the event of accident whereby loss or damage may result in a claim under this insurance, notice must be given to the Underwriters promptly after the date on which the Assured Owners or Managers become or should have become aware of the loss or damage and prior to survey so that a surveyor may be appointed if the Underwriters so desire.

If notice is not given to the Underwriters within twelve months of that date unless the Underwriters agree to the contrary in writing, the Underwriters will be automatically discharged from liability for any claim under this insurance in respect of or arising out of such accident or the loss or damage.

12 New for Old

General average payable without deduction new for old.

13 Agency commission

In no case shall any sum be allowed under this insurance either by way of remuneration of the Assured for time and trouble taken to obtain and supply information or documents or in respect of the commission or charges of any manager, agent, managing or agency company or the like, appointed by or on behalf of the Assured to perform such services.

14 Constructive Total Loss

14.1 In ascertaining whether the Vessel is a constructive total loss, the insured value shall be taken as the repaired value and nothing in respect of the damaged or break-up value of the Vessel or wreck shall be taken into account.

14.2 No claim for constructive total loss based upon the cost of recovery and/or repair of the Vessel shall be recoverable hereunder unless such cost would exceed the insured value. In making this determination, only the cost relating to a single accident or sequence of damages arising from the same accident shall be taken into account.

267

15 Freight Waiver

In the event of total or constructive total loss no claim to be made by the Underwriters for freight whether notice of abandonment has been given or not.

16 Assignment

No assignment of or interest in this insurance or any moneys which may be or become payable thereunder is to be binding on or recognised by the Underwriters unless a dated notice of such assignment or interest signed by the Assured, and by the assignor in the case of subsequent assignment, is endorsed on the Policy and the Policy with such endorsement is produced before payment of any claim or return of premium thereunder.

17 Disbursements Warranty

17.1 Additional insurance as follows are permitted:

17.1.1 *Disbursements, Managers' Commissions, Profits or Excess or Increased Value of Hull and Machinery.* A sum not exceeding 25% of the value stated herein.

17.1.2 *Freight, Chartered Freight or Anticipated Freight, insured for time.* A sum not exceeding 25% of the value as stated herein less any sum insured, however described, under 17.1.1.

17.1.3 *Freight or Hire, under contracts for voyage.* A sum not exceeding the gross freight or hire for the current cargo passage and next succeeding cargo passage (such insurance to include, if required, a preliminary and an intermediate ballast passage) plus the charges of insurance. In the case of a voyage charter where payment is made on a time basis, the sum permitted for insurance shall be calculated on the estimated duration of the voyage, subject to the limitation of two cargo passages as laid down herein. Any sum insured under 17.1.2 to be taken into account and only the excess thereof may be insured, which excess shall be reduced as the freight or hire is advanced or earned by the gross amount so advanced or earned.

17.1.4 *Anticipated Freight if the Vessel sails in ballast and not under Charter.* A sum not exceeding the anticipated gross freight on next cargo passage, such sum to be reasonably estimated on the basis of the current rate of freight at time of insurance plus the charges of insurance. Any sum insured under 17.1.2 to be taken into account and only the excess thereof may be insured.

17.1.5 *Time Charter Hire or Charter Hire for Series of Voyages.* A sum not exceeding 50% of the gross hire which is to be earned under the charter in a period not exceeding 18 months. Any sum insured under 17.1.2 to be taken into account and only the excess thereof may be insured, which excess shall be reduced as the hire is advanced or earned under the charter by 50% of the gross amount so advanced or earned but the sum insured need not be reduced while the total of the sums insured under 17.1.2 and 17.1.5 does not exceed 50% of the gross hire still to be earned under the charter. An insurance under this Section may begin on the signing of the charter.

17.1.6 *Premiums.* A sum not exceeding the actual premiums of all interests insured for a period not exceeding 12 months (excluding premiums insured under the foregoing sections but including, if required, the

premium or estimated calls on any Club or War etc. Risk insurance) reducing pro rata monthly.

17.1.7   *Returns of Premium.* A sum not exceeding the actual returns which are allowable under any insurance but which would not be recoverable thereunder in the event of a total loss of the Vessel whether by insured perils or otherwise.

17.1.8   *Insurance irrespective of amount against:*
Any risks excluded by Clauses 18, 19, 20 and 21 below.

17.2   Warranted that no insurance on any interests enumerated in the foregoing 17.1.1 to 17.1.7 in excess of the amounts permitted therein and no other insurance which includes total loss of the Vessel P.P.I., F.I.A., or subject to any other like term, is or shall be effected to operate during the currency of this insurance by or for account of the Assured, Owners, Managers or Mortgagees. Provided always that a breach of this warranty shall not afford the Underwriters any defence to a claim by a Mortgagee who has accepted this insurance without knowledge of such breach.

The following clauses shall be paramount and shall override anything contained in this insurance inconsistent therewith.

18 War Exclusion

In no case shall this insurance cover loss damage liability or expense caused by

18.1   war civil war revolution rebellion insurrection, or civil strife therefrom, or any hostile act by or against a belligerent power

18.2   capture seizure arrest restraint or detainment (barratry and piracy excepted), and the consequences thereof or any attempt thereat

18.3   derelict mines torpedoes bombs or other derelict weapons of war.

19 Strikes Exclusion

In no case shall this insurance cover loss damage liability or expense caused by

19.1   strikers, locked-out workmen, or persons taking part in labour disturbances, riots or civil commotions

19.2   any terrorist or any person acting from a political motive.

20 Malicious Acts Exclusion

In no case shall this insurance cover loss damage liability or expense arising from

20.1   the detonation of an explosive

20.2   any weapon of war

and caused by any person acting maliciously or from a political motive.

21 Radioactive Contamination Exclusion Clause

In no case shall this insurance cover loss damage liability or expense directly or indirectly caused by or contributed to by or arising from

21.1   ionising radiations from or contamination by radioactivity from any nuclear fuel or from any nuclear waste or from the combustion of nuclear fuel

21.2   the radioactive, toxic, explosive or other hazardous or contaminating properties of any nuclear installation, reactor or other nuclear assembly or nuclear component thereof

21.3   any weapon of war employing atomic or nuclear fission and/or fusion or other like reaction or radioactive force or matter.

Institute War Clauses Builders' Risks

1/6/88—(FOR USE ONLY WITH THE NEW MARINE POLICY FORM)

This insurance is subject to English law and practice.

1 Attachment

This insurance shall not attach to the subject-matter insured until the Vessel is launched and then shall attach only to such part of the subject-matter as is built into or is in or on the Vessel at the time of the launch. The insurance against the said risks shall attach to the remainder of the subject-matter insured only as it is placed in or on the Vessel subsequent to the launch.

2 Perils

Subject always to the exclusions hereinafter referred to, this insurance covers loss of or damage to the subject-matter insured caused by

   2.1   war civil war revolution rebellion insurrection, or civil strife arising therefrom, or any hostile act by or against a belligerent power

   2.2   capture seizure arrest restraint or detainment, arising from perils covered under 2.1 above, and the consequences thereof or any attempt thereat

   2.3   derelict mines torpedoes bombs or other derelict weapons of war.

3 Protection and indemnity

This insurance also covers, subject to the limitation of liability provided for in Clauses 19.5 and 19.6 of the Institute Clauses for Builders' Risks 1/6/88, the liability under Clause 19 of the Institute Clauses for Builders' Risks 1/6/88 which is excluded by Clauses 21, 22.2 and 23.
Provided however that such cover shall not attach until the vessel is launched.

4 Incorporation

The Institute Clauses for Builders' Risks 1/6/88 except Clauses 4, 5.1 and 5.2, 7, 8, 21, 22, 23 and 24 are deemed to be incorporated in this insurance, in so far as they do not conflict with the provisions of these clauses.

5   Detainment

In the event that the Vessel shall have been the subject of capture seizure arrest restraint or detainment, and the Assured shall thereby have lost the free use and disposal of the Vessel for a continuous period of 12 months then for the purpose of ascertaining whether the Vessel is a constructive total loss the Assured shall be deemed to have been deprived of the possession of the Vessel without any likelihood of recovery.

6   Exclusions

This insurance excludes

6.1	loss damage liability or expense arising from
6.1.1	any detonation of any weapon of war employing atomic or nuclear fission and/or fusion or other link reaction or radioactive force or matter, hereinafter called a nuclear weapon of war
6.1.2	the outbreak of war (whether there be a declaration of war or not) between any of the following countries: United Kingdom, United States of America, France, the Union of Soviet Socialist Republics, the People's Republic of China
6.1.3	confiscation expropriation requisition or pre-emption
6.1.4	capture seizure arrest restraint or detainment by or under the order of the government or any public or local authority of the country in which the Vessel is owned or registered
6.1.5	arrest restraint or detainment under quarantine regulations or by reason of infringement of any customs or trading regulations
6.1.6	the operation of ordinary judicial process, failure to provide security or to pay any fine or penalty or any financial cause
6.1.7	any claims based upon loss of or frustration of any voyage or contract for sale or other adventure,
6.2	loss damage liability or expense covered by the Institute Clauses for Builders' Risks 1/6/88 or which would be recoverable thereunder but for Clause 10 thereof,
6.3	any claim for any sum recoverable under any other insurance on the property hereby insured or which would be recoverable under such insurance but for the existence of this insurance,
6.4	any claim for expenses arising from delay except such expenses as would be recoverable in principle in English law and practice under the York-Antwerp Rules 1974.

7   Termination

7.1	This insurance may be cancelled by either the Underwriters or the Assured giving 7 days notice (such cancellation becoming effective on the expiry of 7 days from midnight of the day on which notice of cancellation is issued by or to the Underwriters). The Underwriters agree however to reinstate this insurance subject to agreement between the Underwriters and the Assured prior to the expiry of such notice of cancellation as to new rate of premium and/or conditions and/or warranties.
7.2	Whether or not such notice of cancellation has been given this insurance shall TERMINATE AUTOMATICALLY

7.2.1	upon the occurrence of any hostile detonation of any nuclear weapon of war as defined in Clause 6.1.1 wheresoever or whensoever such detonation may occur and whether or not the Vessel may be involved
7.2.2	upon the outbreak of war (whether there be a declaration of war or not) between any of the following countries: United Kingdom, United States of America, France, the Union of Soviet Socialist Republics, the People's Republic of China
7.2.3	in the event of the Vessel being requisitioned, either for title or use.
7.3	In the event either of cancellation by notice or of automatic termination of this insurance by reason of the operation of this Clause 7 pro rata net return of premium shall be payable to the Assured.

This insurance shall not become effective if, subsequent to its acceptance by the Underwriters and prior to the intended time of its attachment, there has occurred any event which would have automatically terminated this insurance under the provisions of Clause 7 above.

Institute War Clauses (Cargo)

1/1/82—(FOR USE ONLY WITH THE NEW MARINE POLICY FORM)

Risks Clause

1   This insurance covers, except as provided in Clauses 3 and 4 below, loss of or damage to the subject-matter insured caused by

    1.1   war civil war revolution rebellion insurrection, or civil strife arising therefrom, or any hostile act by or against a belligerent power

    1.2   capture seizure arrest restraint or detainment, arising from risks covered under 1.1 above, and the consequences thereof or any attempt thereat

    1.3   derelict mines torpedoes bombs or other derelict weapons of war.

General Average Clause

2   This insurance covers general average and salvage charges, adjusted or determined according to the contract of affreightment and/or the governing law and practice, incurred to avoid or in connection with the avoidance of loss from a risk covered under these clauses.

Exclusions

General Exclusions Clause

3   In no case shall this insurance cover

    3.1   loss damage or expense attributable to wilful misconduct of the Assured

    3.2   ordinary leakage, ordinary loss in weight or volume, or ordinary wear and tear of the subject-matter insured

    3.3   loss damage or expense caused by insufficiency or unsuitability of packing or preparation of the subject-matter insured (for the purpose of this Clause 3.3 "packing" shall be deemed to include stowage in a container or liftvan but only when such stowage is carried out prior to attachment of this insurance or by the Assured or their servants)

    3.4   loss damage or expense caused by inherent vice or nature of the subject-matter insured

3.5   loss damage or expense proximately caused by delay, even though the delay be caused by a risk insured against (except expenses payable under Clause 2 above)

3.6   loss damage or expense arising from insolvency or financial default of the owners managers charterers or operators of the vessel

3.7   any claim based upon loss of or frustration of the voyage or adventure

3.8   loss damage or expense arising from the use of any weapon of war employing atomic or nuclear fission and/or fusion or other like reaction or radioactive force or matter.

Unseaworthiness and Unfitness Exclusion Clause

4   4.1   In no case shall this insurance cover loss damage or expense arising from unseaworthiness of vessel or craft,
unfitness of vessel craft conveyance container or liftvan for the safe carriage of the subject-matter insured,
where the Assured or their servants are privy to such unseaworthiness or unfitness, at the time the subject-matter insured is loaded therein.

4.2   The Underwriters waive any breach of the implied warranties of seaworthiness of the ship and fitness of the ship to carry the subject-matter insured to destination, unless the Assured or their servants are privy to such unseaworthiness or unfitness.

Duration

Transit Clause

5   5.1   This insurance

5.1.1   attaches only as the subject-matter insured and as to any part as that part is loaded on an oversea vessel
and

5.1.2   terminates, subject to 5.2 and 5.3 below, either as the subject-matter insured and as to any part as that part is discharged from an oversea vessel at the final port or place of discharge,
or
on expiry of 15 days counting from midnight of the day of arrival of the vessel at the final port or place of discharge,
whichever shall first occur;
nevertheless,
subject to prompt notice to the Underwriters and to an additional premium,
such insurance

5.1.3   reattaches when, without having discharged the subject-matter insured at the final port or place of discharge, the vessel sails therefrom,
and

5.1.4   terminates, subject to 5.2 and 5.3 below, either as the subject-matter insured and as to any part as that part is thereafter discharged from the vessel at the final (or substituted) port or place of discharge,
or
on expiry of 15 days counting from midnight of the day of re-arrival of the vessel at the final port or place of discharge or arrival of the vessel at a substituted port or place of discharge,

whichever shall first occur.

5.2   If during the insured voyage the oversea vessel arrives at an intermediate port or place to discharge the subject-matter insured for on-carriage by oversea vessel or by aircraft, or the goods are discharged from the vessel at a port or place of refuge, then, subject to 5.3 below and to an additional premium if required, this insurance continues until the expiry of 15 days counting from midnight of the day of arrival of the vessel at such port or place, but thereafter reattaches as the subject-matter insured and as to any part as that part is loaded on an on-carrying oversea vessel or aircraft. During the period of 15 days the insurance remains in force after discharge only whilst the subject-matter insured and as to any part as that part is at such port or place. If the goods are on-carried within the said period of 15 days or if the insurance reattaches as provided in this Clause 5.2

5.2.1   where the on-carriage is by oversea vessel this insurance continues subject to the terms of these clauses,

or

5.2.2   where the on-carriage is by aircraft, the current Institute War Clauses (Air Cargo) (excluding sendings by Post) shall be deemed to form part of this insurance and shall apply to the on-carriage by air.

5.3   If the voyage in the contract of carriage is terminated at a port or place other than the destination agreed therein, such port or place shall be deemed the final port of discharge and such insurance terminates in accordance with 5.1.2. If the subject-matter insured is subsequently reshipped to the original or any other destination, then *provided notice is given to the Underwriters before the commencement of such further transit and subject to an additional premium,* such insurance reattaches

5.3.1   in the case of the subject-matter insured having been discharged, as the subject-matter insured and as to any part as that part is loaded on the on-carrying vessel for the voyage;

5.3.2   in the case of the subject-matter not having been discharged, when the vessel sails from such deemed final port of discharge;

thereafter such insurance terminates in accordance with 5.1.4.

5.4   The insurance against the risk of mines and derelict torpedoes, floating or submerged, is extended whilst the subject-matter insured or any part thereof is on craft whilst in transit to or from the oversea vessel, but in no case beyond the expiry of 60 days after discharge from the oversea vessel unless otherwise specially agreed by the Underwriters.

5.5   *Subject to prompt notice to Underwriters, and to an additional premium if required,* this insurance shall remain in force within the provisions of these Clauses during any deviation, or any variation of the adventure arising from the exercise of a liberty granted to shipowners or charterers under the contract of affreightment.

(For the purpose of Clause 5

"arrival" shall be deemed to mean that the vessel is anchored, moored or otherwise secured at a berth or place within the Harbour Authority area. If such a berth or place is not available, arrival is deemed to have occurred when the vessel first anchors, moors or otherwise secures either at or off the intended port or place of discharge

"oversea vessel" shall be deemed to mean a vessel carrying the subject-matter from one port or place to another where such voyage involves a sea passage by that vessel.)

Change of Voyage Clause

6   Where, after attachment of this insurance, the destination is changed by the Assured, *held covered at a premium and on conditions to be arranged subject to prompt notice being given to the Underwriters.*

7   **Anything contained in this contract which is inconsistent with Clauses 3.7, 3.8 or 5 shall, to the extent of such inconsistency, be null and void.**

Claims

Insurable Interest Clause

8   8.1   In order to recover under this insurance the Assured must have an insurable interest in the subject-matter insured at the time of the loss.

8.2   Subject to 8.1 above, the Assured shall be entitled to recover for insured loss occurring during the period covered by this insurance, notwithstanding that the loss occurred before the contract of insurance was concluded, unless the Assured were aware of the loss and the Underwriters were not.

Increased Value Clause

9   9.1   If any Increased Value insurance is effected by the Assured on the cargo insured herein the agreed value of the cargo shall be deemed to be increased to the total amount insured under this insurance and all Increased Value insurances covering the loss, and liability under this insurance shall be in such proportion as the sum insured herein bears to such total amount insured.

In the event of claim the Assured shall provide the Underwriters with evidence of the amounts insured under all other insurances.

9.2   **Where this insurance is on Increased Value the following clause shall apply:**

The agreed value of the cargo shall be deemed to be equal to the total amount insured under the primary insurance and all Increased Value insurances covering the loss and effected on the cargo by the Assured, and liability under this insurance shall be in such proportion as the sum insured herein bears to such total amount insured.

In the event of claim the Assured shall provide the Underwriters with evidence of the amounts insured under all other insurances.

Benefit of Insurance

Not to Inure Clause

10   This insurance shall not inure to the benefit of the carrier or other bailee.

Minimising Losses

Duty to Assured Clause

11   It is the duty of the Assured and their servants and agents in respect of loss recoverable hereunder

11.1 to take such measures as may be reasonable for the purpose of averting or minimising such loss,
and

11.2 to ensure that all rights against carriers, bailees or other third parties are properly preserved and exercised

and the Underwriters will, in addition to any loss recoverable hereunder, reimburse the Assured for any charges properly and reasonably incurred in pursuance of these duties.

Waiver Clause

12 Measures taken by the Assured or the Underwriters with the object of saving, protecting or recovering the subject-matter insured shall not be considered as a waiver or acceptance of abandonment or otherwise prejudice the rights of either party.

Avoidance of Delay

Reasonable Despatch Clause

13 It is a condition of this insurance that the Assured shall act with reasonable despatch in all circumstances within their control.

Law and Practice

English Law and Practice Clause

14 This insurance is subject to English law and practice.

NOTE:

—It is necessary for the Assured when they become aware of an event which is "held covered" under this insurance to give prompt notice to the Underwriters and the right to such cover is dependent upon compliance with this obligation.

Institute War Cancellation Clause (Cargo)

1/12/82—(FOR USE ONLY WITH THE NEW MARINE POLICY FORM)

The cover against war risks (as defined in the relevant Institute War Clauses) may be cancelled by either the Underwriters or the Assured except in respect of any insurance which shall have attached in accordance with the conditions of the Institute War Clauses before the cancellation becomes effective. Such cancellation shall however only become effective on the expiry of 7 days from midnight of the day on which notice of the cancellation is issued by or to the Underwriters.

Institute War and Strikes
Clauses—Freight—Time

1/11/95—(FOR USE ONLY WITH THE CURRENT MAR POLICY FORM)

This insurance is subject to English law and practice.

1   Perils

Subject always to the exclusions hereinafter referred to, this insurance covers

1.1	loss (total or partial) of the subject-matter insured caused by
1.1.1	war civil war revolution rebellion insurrection, or civil strife arising therefrom, or any hostile act by or against a belligerent power
1.1.2	capture seizure arrest restraint or detainment, and the consequences thereof or any attempt thereat
1.1.3	derelict mines torpedoes bombs or other derelict weapons of war,
1.2	loss (total or partial) of the subject-matter insured arising from loss of or damage to the Vessel caused by
1.2.1	strikers, locked-out workmen, or persons taking part in labour disturbances, riots or civil commotions
1.2.2	any terrorist or any person acting maliciously or from a political motive
1.2.3	confiscation or expropriation.

2   Incorporation

The Institute Time Clauses—Freight 1/11/95 except Clauses 2, 3, 4, 5, 6, 7, 12, 17, 18, 19, 20 and 21 are deemed to be incorporated in this insurance in so far as they do not conflict with the provisions of these clauses.

Held covered in case of breach of warranty as to towage or salvage services provided notice be given to the Underwriters immediately after receipt of advices and any additional premium required by them be agreed.

3   Detainment

In the event that a claim for a constructive total loss of the Vessel is paid on the war risks insurance of the Vessel under Clause 3 (Detainment) of the Institute War and Strikes Clauses—Hulls—Time 1/11/95 or the Institute War and Strikes Clauses—Hulls—Voyage 1/11/95 as a result of the loss of the free use and disposal of the Vessel for a continuous period of 12 months due to capture, seizure, arrest, restraint, detainment, confiscation or expropriation whilst this insurance is in force, the amount insured hereunder shall be paid in full less any claims otherwise arising during the said period of 12 months which have been paid or are recoverable hereunder or under insurances subject to the Institute Time Clauses—Freight 1/11/95 and/or the Institute Voyage Clauses—Freight 1/11/95 and any recoveries made in respect of the said period.

4 Exclusions

This insurance excludes

4.1 loss (total or partial) or expense arising from

4.1.1 the outbreak of war (whether there be a declaration of war or not) between any of the following countries:

United Kingdom, United States of America, France, the Russian Federation, the People's Republic of China

4.1.2 requisition, either for title or use, or pre-emption

4.1.3 capture seizure arrest restraint detainment confiscation or expropriation by or under the order of the government or any public or local authority of the country in which the Vessel is owned or registered

4.1.4 arrest restraint detainment confiscation or expropriation under quarantine regulations or by reason of infringement of any customs or trading regulations

4.1.5 the operation of ordinary judicial process, failure to provide security or to pay any fine or penalty or any financial cause

4.1.6 piracy (but this exclusion shall not affect cover under Clause 1.2.1),

4.2 loss (total or partial) or expense directly or indirectly caused by or contributed to by or arising from

4.2.1 ionising radiations from or contamination by radioactivity from any nuclear fuel or from any nuclear waste or from the combustion of nuclear fuel

4.2.2 the radioactive, toxic, explosive or other hazardous or contaminating properties of any nuclear installation, reactor or other nuclear assembly or nuclear component thereof

4.2.3 any weapon of war employing atomic or nuclear fission and/or fusion or other like reaction or radioactive force or matter,

4.3 loss (total or partial) or expense covered by the Institute Time Clauses-—Freight 1/11/95 or which would be recoverable thereunder but for Clause 12 thereof,

4.4 any claim (not being a claim recoverable under the Institute War and Strikes Clauses Freight—Voyage 1/11/95) for any sum recoverable under any other insurance on the subject-matter insured or which would be recoverable under such insurance but for the existence of this insurance,

4.5 loss proximately caused by delay or any claim for expenses arising from delay except such expenses as would be recoverable in principle in English law and practice under the York-Antwerp Rules 1994,

4.6 any claim based upon loss of or frustration of any voyage or adventure.

5 Termination

5.1 This insurance may be cancelled by either the Underwriters or the Assured giving 7 days notice (such cancellation becoming effective on the expiry of 7

days from midnight of the day on which notice of cancellation is issued by or to the Underwriters). The Underwriters agree however to reinstate this insurance subject to agreement between the Underwriters and the Assured prior to the expiry of such notice of cancellation as to new rate of premium and/or conditions and/or warranties.

5.2   Whether or not such notice of cancellation has been given this insurance shall TERMINATE AUTOMATICALLY

5.2.1   upon the outbreak of war (whether there be a declaration of war or not) between any of the following countries:

United Kingdom, United States of America, France,

the Russian Federation, the People's Republic of China

5.2.2   in the event of the Vessel being requisitioned, either for title or use.

5.3   In the event either of cancellation by notice or of automatic termination of this insurance by reason of the operation of this Clause 5, or of the sale of the Vessel, pro rata net return of premium shall be payable to the Assured.

This insurance shall not become effective if, subsequent to its acceptance by the Underwriters and prior to the intended time of its attachment, there has occurred any event which would have automatically terminated this insurance under the provisions of Clause 5 above.

Institute War and Strikes Clauses—Freight—Voyage

1/11/95—(FOR USE ONLY WITH THE CURRENT MAR POLICY FORM)

This insurance is subject to English law and practice.

1   Perils

Subject always to the exclusions hereinafter referred to, this insurance covers

1.1	loss (total or partial) of the subject-matter insured caused by
1.1.1	war civil war revolution rebellion insurrection, or civil strife arising therefrom, or any hostile act by or against a belligerent power
1.1.2	capture seizure arrest restraint or detainment, and the consequences thereof or any attempt thereat
1.1.3	derelict mines torpedoes bombs or other derelict weapons of war,
1.2	loss (total or partial) of the subject-matter insured arising from loss of or damage to the Vessel caused by
1.2.1	strikers, locked-out workmen, or persons taking part in labour disturbances, riots or civil commotions
1.2.2	any terrorist or any person acting maliciously or from a political motive
1.2.3	confiscation or expropriation.

2   Incorporation

The Institute Voyage Clauses—Freight 1/11/95 except Clauses 2, 4, 9, 14, 15, 16 and 17 are deemed to be incorporated in this insurance in so far as they do not conflict with the provisions of these clauses.

Held covered in case of breach of warranty as to towage or salvage services provided notice be given to the Underwriters immediately after receipt of advices and any additional premium required by them be agreed.

3   Detainment

In the event that a claim for a constructive total loss of the Vessel is paid on the war risks insurance of the Vessel under Clause 3 (Detainment) of the Institute War and Strikes Clauses—Hulls—Time 1/11/95 or the Institute War and Strikes Clauses—Hulls—Voyage 1/11/95 as a result of the loss of the free use and disposal of the Vessel for a continuous period

283

of 12 months due to capture, seizure, arrest, restraint, detainment, confiscation or expropriation whilst this insurance is in force, the amount insured hereunder shall be paid in full less any claims otherwise arising during the said period of 12 months which have been paid or are recoverable hereunder or under insurances subject to the Institute Time Clauses—Freight 1/11/95 and/or the Institute Voyage Clauses—Freight 1/11/95 and any recoveries made in respect of the said period.

4 Exclusions

This insurance excludes

4.1	loss (total or partial) or expense arising from
4.1.1	the outbreak of war (whether there be a declaration of war or not) between any of the following countries:
	United Kingdom, United States of America, France,
	the Russian Federation, the People's Republic of China
4.1.2	requisition, either for title or use, or pre-emption
4.1.3	capture seizure arrest restraint detainment confiscation or expropriation by or under the order of the government or any public or local authority of the country in which the Vessel is owned or registered
4.1.4	arrest restraint detainment confiscation or expropriation under quarantine regulations or by reason of infringement of any customs or trading regulations
4.1.5	the operation of ordinary judicial process, failure to provide security or to pay any fine or penalty or any financial cause
4.1.6	piracy (but this exclusion shall not affect cover under Clause 1.2.1),
4.2	loss damage liability or expense directly or indirectly caused by or contributed to by or arising from
4.2.1	ionising radiations from or contamination by radioactivity from any nuclear fuel or from any nuclear waste or from the combustion of nuclear fuel
4.2.2	the radioactive, toxic, explosive or other hazardous or contaminating properties of any nuclear installation, reactor or other nuclear assembly or nuclear component thereof
4.2.3	any weapon of war employing atomic or nuclear fission and/or fusion or other like reaction or radioactive force or matter.
4.3	loss (total or partial) or expense covered by the Institute Voyage Clauses-—Freight 1/11/95 or which would be recoverable thereunder but for Clause 12 thereof,
4.4	any claim (not being a claim recoverable under the Institute War and Strikes Clauses Freight—Time 1/11/95) for any sum recoverable under any other insurance on the Vessel or which would be recoverable under such insurance but for the existence of this insurance,
4.5	loss proximately caused by delay or any claim for expenses arising from delay except such expenses as would be recoverable in principle in English law and practice under the York-Antwerp Rules 1994,
4.6	any claim based upon loss of or frustration of any voyage or adventure.

5 Termination

5.1	This insurance may be cancelled by either the Underwriters or the Assured giving 7 days notice (such cancellation becoming effective on the expiry of 7

days from midnight of the day on which notice of cancellation is issued by or to the Underwriters). The Underwriters agree however to reinstate this insurance subject to agreement between the Underwriters and the Assured prior to the expiry of such notice of cancellation as to new rate of premium and/or conditions and/or warranties.

5.2   Whether or not such notice of cancellation has been given this insurance shall TERMINATE AUTOMATICALLY

5.2.1   upon the outbreak of war (whether there be a declaration of war or not) between any of the following countries:

United Kingdom, United States of America, France, the Russian Federation, the People's Republic of China

5.2.2   in the event of the Vessel being requisitioned, either for title or use.

5.3   In the event either of cancellation by notice or of automatic termination of this insurance by reason of the operation of this Clause 5, or of the sale of the Vessel, a return of premium shall be payable to the Assured.

This insurance shall not become effective if, subsequent to its acceptance by the Underwriters and prior to the intended time of its attachment, there has occurred any event which would have automatically terminated this insurance under the provisions of Clause 5 above.

Institute War and Strikes Clauses
Hulls—Time

1/11/95—(FOR USE ONLY WITH THE CURRENT MAR POLICY FORM)

This insurance is subject to English law and practice.

1   Perils

Subject always to the exclusions hereinafter referred to, this insurance covers loss of or damage to the Vessel caused by

1.1	war civil war revolution rebellion insurrection, or civil strife arising therefrom, or any hostile act by or against a belligerent power
1.2	capture seizure arrest restraint or detainment, and the consequences thereof or any attempt thereat
1.3	derelict mines torpedoes bombs or other derelict weapons of war
1.4	strikers, locked-out workmen, or persons taking part in labour disturbances, riots or civil commotions
1.5	any terrorist or any person acting maliciously or from a political motive
1.6	confiscation or expropriation.

2   Incorporation

The Institute Time Clauses—Hulls 1/11/95 (including 3/4ths Collision Liability Clause amended to 4/4ths) except Clauses 1.4, 2, 3, 4, 5, 6, 12, 22.1.8, 23, 24, 25, 26 and 27 are deemed to be incorporated in this insurance in so far as they do not conflict with the provisions of these clauses.

Held covered in case of breach of warranty as to towage or salvage services provided notice be given to the Underwriters immediately after receipt of advices and any additional premium required by them be agreed.

3   Detainment

In the event that the Vessel shall have been the subject of capture seizure arrest restraint detainment confiscation or expropriation, and the Assured shall thereby have lost the free use and disposal of the Vessel for a continuous period of 12 months then for the purpose of ascertaining whether the Vessel is a constructive total loss the Assured shall be deemed to have been deprived of the possession of the Vessel without any likelihood of recovery.

4   Notice of claim and tenders

In the event of accident whereby loss or damage may result in a claim under this insurance, notice must be given to the Underwriters promptly after the date on which the Assured, Owners or Managers become or should have become aware of the loss of damage and prior to survey so that a surveyor may be appointed if the Underwriters so desire.

If notice is not given to Underwriters within twelve months of that date unless the Underwriters agree to the contrary in writing, the Underwriters will be automatically discharged from liability for any claim under this insurance in respect of or arising out of such accident or the loss or damage.

5   Exclusions

This insurance excludes

5.1	loss damage liability or expense arising from
5.1.1	the outbreak of war (whether there be a declaration of war or not) between any of the following countries:
	United Kingdom, United States of America, France, the Russian Federation, the People's Republic of China
5.1.2	requisition, either for title or use, or pre-emption
5.1.3	capture seizure arrest restraint detainment confiscation or expropriation by or under the order of the government or any public or local authority of the country in which the Vessel is owned or registered
5.1.4	arrest restraint detainment confiscation or expropriation under quarantine regulations or by reason of infringement of any customs or trading regulations
5.1.5	the operation of ordinary judicial process, failure to provide security or to pay any fine or penalty or any financial cause
5.1.6	piracy (but this exclusion shall not affect cover under Clause 1.4),
5.2	loss damage liability or expense directly or indirectly caused by or contributed to by or arising from
5.2.1	ionising radiations from or contamination by radioactivity from any nuclear fuel or from any nuclear waste or from the combustion of nuclear fuel
5.2.2	the radioactive, toxic, explosive or other hazardous or contaminating properties of any nuclear installation, reactor or other nuclear assembly or nuclear component thereof
5.2.3	any weapon of war employing atomic or nuclear fission and/or fusion or other like reaction or radioactive force or matter,
5.3	loss damage liability or expense covered by the Institute Time Clauses —Hulls 1/11/95 (including 3/4ths Collision Liability Clause amended to 4/4ths) or which would be recoverable thereunder but for Clause 12 thereof.
5.4	any claim for any sum recoverable under any other insurance on the Vessel or which would be recoverable under such insurance but for the existence of this insurance,
5.5	any claim for expenses arising from delay except such expenses as would be recoverable in principle in English law and practice under the York-Antwerp Rules 1994.

6   Termination

> **6.1**   This insurance may be cancelled by either the Underwriters or the Assured giving 7 days notice (such cancellation becoming effective on the expiry of 7 days from midnight of the day on which notice of cancellation is issued by or to the Underwriters). The Underwriters agree however to reinstate this insurance subject to agreement between the Underwriters and the Assured prior to the expiry of such notice of cancellation as to new rate of premium and/or conditions and/or warranties.
>
> **6.2**   Whether or not such notice of cancellation has been given this insurance shall TERMINATE AUTOMATICALLY
>
> **6.2.1**   upon the outbreak of war (whether there be a declaration of war or not) between any of the following countries:
>
> > United Kingdom, United States of America, France, the Russian Federation, the People's Republic of China
>
> **6.2.2**   in the event of the Vessel being requisitioned, either for title or use.
>
> **6.3**   In the event either of cancellation by notice or of automatic termination of this insurance by reason of the operation of this Clause 6, or of the sale of the Vessel, pro rata net return of premium shall be payable to the Assured.

This insurance shall not become effective if, subsequent to its acceptance by the Underwriters and prior to the intended time of its attachment, there has occurred any event which would have automatically terminated this insurance under the provisions of Clause 6 above.

Institute War and Strikes Clauses
Hulls—Time: Limited Conditions

1/11/95—(FOR USE ONLY WITH THE CURRENT MAR POLICY FORM)

This insurance is subject to English law and practice.

1 Perils

Subject always to the exclusions hereinafter referred to, this insurance covers loss of or damage to the Vessel caused by

1.1	war civil war revolution rebellion insurrection, or civil strife arising therefrom, or any hostile act by or against a belligerent power
1.2	capture seizure arrest restraint or detainment, arising from perils covered under 1.1 above, and the consequences thereof or any attempt thereat
1.3	derelict mines torpedoes bombs or other derelict weapons of war
1.4	strikers, locked-out workmen, or persons taking part in labour disturbances, riots or civil commotions
1.5	any terrorist or any person acting maliciously or from a political motive.

2 Incorporation

The Institute Time Clauses—Hulls 1/11/95 (including 3/4ths Collision Liability Clause amended to 4/4ths) except Clauses 1.4, 2, 3, 4, 5, 6, 12, 22.1.8, 23, 24, 25, 26 and 27 are deemed to be incorporated in this insurance in so far as they do not conflict with the provisions of these clauses.

Held covered in case of breach of warranty as to towage or salvage services provided notice be given to the Underwriters immediately after receipt of advices and any additional premium required by them be agreed.

3 Detainment

In the event that the Vessel shall have been subject of capture seizure arrest restraint or detainment, and the Assured shall thereby have lost the free use and disposal of the Vessel for a continuous period of 12 months then for the purpose of ascertaining whether the Vessel is a constructive total loss the Assured shall be deemed to have been deprived of the possession of the Vessel without any likelihood of recovery.

4   Notice of claim

In the event of accident whereby loss or damage may result in a claim under this insurance, notice must be given to the Underwriter promptly after the date on which the Assured, Owners or Managers become or should have become aware of the loss or damage and prior to survey so that a surveyor may be appointed if the Underwriters so desire.

If notice is not given to the Underwriters within twelve months of that date unless the Underwriters agree to the contrary in writing, the Underwriters will be automatically discharged from liability for any claim under this insurance in respect of or arising out of such accident or the loss or damage.

5   Exclusions

This insurance excludes

5.1	loss damage liability or expense arising from
5.1.1	the outbreak of war (whether there be a declaration of war or not) between any of the following countries:

> United Kingdom, United States of America, France, the Russian Federation, the People's Republic of China

5.1.2	confiscation expropriation requisition or pre-emption
5.1.3	capture seizure arrest restraint or detainment by or under the order of the government or any public or local authority of the country in which the Vessel is owned or registered
5.1.4	arrest restraint or detainment under quarantine regulations or by reason of infringement of any customs or trading regulations
5.1.5	the operation of ordinary judicial process, failure to provide security or to pay any fine or penalty or any financial cause
5.1.6	piracy (but this exclusion shall not affect cover under Clause 1.4),
5.2	loss damage liability or expense directly or indirectly caused by or contributed to by or arising from
5.2.1	ionising radiations from or contamination by radioactivity from any nuclear fuel or from any nuclear waste or from the combustion of nuclear fuel
5.2.2	the radioactive, toxic, explosive or other hazardous or contaminating properties of any nuclear installation, reactor or other nuclear assembly or nuclear component thereof
5.2.3	any weapon of war employing atomic or nuclear fission and/or fusion or other like reaction or radioactive force or matter
5.3	loss damage liability or expense covered by the Institute Time Clauses —Hulls 1/11/95 (including 3/4ths Collision Liability Clause amended to 4/4ths) or which would be recoverable thereunder but for Clause 12 thereof,
5.4	any claim for any sum recoverable under any other insurance on the Vessel or which would be recoverable under such insurance but for the existence of this insurance,
5.5	any claim for expenses arising from delay except such expenses as would be recoverable in principle in English law and practice under the York-Antwerp Rules 1994.

6   Termination

6.1   This insurance may be cancelled by either the Underwriters or the Assured giving 7 days notice (such cancellation becoming effective on the expiry of 7 days from midnight of the day on which notice of cancellation is issued by or to the Underwriters). The Underwriters agree however to reinstate this insurance subject to agreement between the Underwriters and the Assured prior to the expiry of such notice of cancellation as to new rate of premium and/or conditions and/or warranties.

6.2   Whether or not such notice of cancellation has been given this insurance shall TERMINATE AUTOMATICALLY

6.2.1   upon the outbreak of war (whether there be a declaration of war or not) between any of the following countries:

United Kingdom, United States of America, France, the Russian Federation, the People's Republic of China

6.2.2   in the event of the Vessel being requisitioned, either for title or use.

6.3   In the event either of cancellation by notice or of automatic termination of this insurance by reason of the operation of this Clause 6, or of the sale of the Vessel, a pro rata net return of premium shall be payable to the Assured.

This insurance shall not become effective if, subsequent to its acceptance by the Underwriters and prior to the intended time of its attachment, there has occurred any event which would have automatically terminated this insurance under the provisions of Clause 6 above.

Institute War and Strikes
Clauses—Hulls—Voyage

1/11/95—(FOR USE ONLY WITH THE CURRENT MAR POLICY FORM)

This insurance is subject to English law and practice.

1 Perils

Subject always to the exclusions hereinafter referred to, this insurance covers loss of or damage to the Vessel caused by

1.1	war civil war revolution rebellion insurrection, or civil strife arising therefrom, or any hostile act by or against a belligerent power
1.2	capture seizure arrest restraint or detainment, and the consequences thereof or any attempt threat
1.3	derelict mines torpedoes bombs or other derelict weapons of war
1.4	strikers, locked-out workmen, or persons taking part in labour disturbances, riots or civil commotions
1.5	any terrorist or any person acting maliciously or from a political motive
1.6	confiscation or expropriation.

2 Incorporation

The Institute Voyage Clauses—Hulls 1/11/95 (including 3/4ths Collision Liability Clause amended to 4/4ths) except Clauses 1.4, 3, 4, 10, 20.1.8, 21, 22, 23 and 24 are deemed to be incorporated in this insurance in so far as they do not conflict with the provisions of these clauses.

Held covered in case of breach of warranty as to towage or salvage services provided notice be given to the Underwriters immediately after receipt of advices and any additional premium required by them be agreed.

3 Detainment

In the event that the Vessel shall have been subject of capture seizure arrest restraint detainment confiscation or expropriation, and the Assured shall thereby have lost the free use and disposal of the Vessel for a continuous period of 12 months then for the purpose of ascertaining whether the Vessel is a constructive total loss the Assured shall be deemed to have been deprived of the possession of the Vessel without any likelihood of recovery.

4   Notice of claim

In the event of accident whereby loss or damage may result in a claim under this insurance, notice must be given to the Underwriters promptly after the date on which the Assured, Owners or Managers become or should have become aware of the loss or damage and prior to survey so that a surveyor may be appointed if the Underwriters so desire.

If notice is not given to the Underwriters within twelve months of that date unless the Underwriters agree to the contrary in writing, the Underwriters will be automatically discharged from liability for any claim under this insurance in respect of or arising out of such accident or the loss or damage.

5   Exclusions

This insurance excludes

5.1	loss damage liability or expense arising from
5.1.1	the outbreak of war (whether there be a declaration of war or not) between any of the following countries: United Kingdom, United States of America, France, the Russian Federation, the People's Republic of China
5.1.2	requisition, either for title or use, or pre-emption
5.1.3	capture seizure arrest restraint detainment confiscation or expropriation by or under the order of the government or any public or local authority of the country in which the Vessel is owned or registered
5.1.4	arrest restraint detainment or expropriation under quarantine regulations or by reason of infringement of any customs or trading regulations
5.1.5	the operation of ordinary judicial process, failure to provide security or to pay any fine or penalty or any financial cause
5.1.6	piracy (but this exclusion shall not affect cover under Clause 1.4),
5.2	loss damage liability or expense directly or indirectly caused by or contributed to by or arising from
5.2.1	ionising radiations from or contamination by radioactivity from any nuclear fuel or from any nuclear waste or from the combustion of nuclear fuel
5.2.2	the radioactive, toxic, explosive or other hazardous or contaminating properties of any nuclear installation, reactor or other nuclear assembly or nuclear component thereof
5.2.3	any weapon of war employing atomic or nuclear fission and/or fusion or other like reaction or radioactive force or matter,
5.3	loss damage liability or expense covered by the Institute Time Clauses —Hulls 1/11/95 (including 3/4ths Collision Liability Clause amended to 4/4ths) or which would be recoverable thereunder but for Clause 10 thereof,
5.4	any claim for any sum recoverable under any other insurance on the Vessel or which would be recoverable under such insurance but for the existence of this insurance,
5.5	any claim for expenses arising from delay except such expenses as would be recoverable in principle in English law and practice under the York-Antwerp Rules 1994.

6   Termination

6.1   This insurance may be cancelled by either the Underwriters or the Assured giving 7 days notice (such cancellation becoming effective on the expiry of 7 days from midnight of the day on which notice of cancellation is issued by or to the Underwriters). The Underwriters agree however to reinstate this insurance subject to agreement between the Underwriters and the Assured prior to the expiry of such notice of cancellation as to new rate of premium and/or conditions and/or warranties.

6.2   Whether or not such notice of cancellation has been given this insurance shall TERMINATE AUTOMATICALLY

6.2.1   upon the outbreak of war (whether there be a declaration of war or not) between any of the following countries:

United Kingdom, United States of America, France, the Russian Federation, the People's Republic of China

6.2.2   in the event of the Vessel being requisitioned, either for title or use.

6.3   In the event either of cancellation by notice or of automatic termination of this insurance by reason of the operation of this Clause 6, or of the sale of the Vessel, a return of premium shall be payable to the Assured.

This insurance shall not become effective if, subsequent to its acceptance by the Underwriters and prior to the intended time of its attachment, there has occurred any event which would have automatically terminated this insurance under the provisions of Clause 6 above.

INTERNATIONAL
UNDERWRITING ASSOCIATION

IUA Marine Policy

We, the Insurers, hereby severally agree, in consideration of the payment to us by or on behalf of the Insured of the premium specified in the Schedule, to insure against loss, damage, liability or expense in the proportions and manner hereinafter provided. Each Insurer shall be liable only for its own respective proportion.

In witness whereof the name of the Chief Executive of the **International Underwriting Association of London** ("IUA") is subscribed on behalf of each of the IUA members and such entities not being members of the IUA who are participating in a qualifying consortium arrangement with the IUA members in accordance with the Memorandum and Articles of Association of the IUA.

_____ Chief Executive

This policy is not valid unless it bears the embossment of the Policy Department of the International Underwriting Association of London.

SPECIMEN

Several Liability

The subscribing Insurers' obligations under this contract are several and not joint and are limited solely to the extent of their individual signed subscrpitions. The subscribing Insurers are not responsible for the subscription of any co-subscribing Insurer who for any reason does not satisfy all or part of its obligations.

Insurers Proportions

For use by the Policy Department of the
International Underwriting Association of London

The International Underwriting Association of London.
London Underwriting Centre
3 Minster Court, Mincing Lane, London EC3R 7DD

IUA 1

Index

*Pages in **bold** refer to where the actual text of the entry is set out*